Mickey Rooney

as

Archie Bunker

and Other TV Casting Almosts

by Eila Mell

Foreword by F. Murray Abraham

Published in the USA by:
BearManor Media
P O Box 71426
Albany, Georgia 31708
www.bearmanormedia.com

ISBN 1-59393-145-X

Printed in the United States of America.

Book & cover design by Darlene & Dan Swanson of Van-garde Imagery, Inc.

Contents:

Acknowledgements

THERE ARE SO MANY people I need to thank. I'll start with Mike Cesarano, without whose help this book would not be the same. I also need to give an extra special thank you to Iris Soricelli, F. Murray Abraham, Herbie J. Pilato, Ben Ohmart, David Black, Jerold Franks, Deborah Kohan, Mary Lee Laitsch, Ron Laitsch, Larry Mintz, Kelly Powers, Dayna Steele, Barbara Levy, Richard Levy, Evan Levy, Eric Burak, Rae Cesarano, Fred Cesarano, Alan Mell, Al Soricelli and Jack Cesarano.

I'm also extremely grateful for the help given to me by Caroline Aaron, Steven Adams, Pamela Adlon, Jane Alderman, Gloria Allred, Reynolds Anderson, Annette Andre, Dennis Aspland, Candice Azzara, Ian Baca, Jack Bannon, David Barnes, Orion Barnes, Allen Baron, Deborah Barylski, Fran Bascom, Frank Basile, Robert Berlinger, Bradley Bernstein, Sharon Bialy, William Bickley, John Billingsley, Bruce Bilson, Dyanne Bjorck, Chris Black, Mark Blake, Rosa Blasi, Jeff Bleckner, Paul Bogart, Gregory J. Bonann, Frank Bonner, Jay Bontatibus, David Braff, Marshall Brickman, Bill Brochtrup, Corbin Bronson, Eric Bross, Ellen Bry, Sheldon Bull, Michael J. Burg, Melanie Burgess, Leo Burmester, Allan Burns, Robyn Burt, Al Burton, Sarah Buxton, Coby Byerly, Karen Bystedt, Andy Cadiff, K Callan, Carmine Caridi, Robert Carradine, Crystal Carson, Thomas Carter, Max Casella, Christopher Cass, Michael Cerveris, Freddy Cesarano, Carly Chasen, Cy Chermak, Casey Childs, Andy Cohen, Stephanie Cohen, Cindy Collins, Gary Collins, Richard Compton, James L. Conway, Andrew Cooper, Judy Coppage, Ron Cowen, Missy Crider, Roark Critchlow, Jayson Crittenden, Ryan Cunningham, Emily Cutler, Brian Czako, Joe d'Angerio, Joan Darling, Kristin Dattilo, Matt Dearborn, Rob Decina, Zora De Horter-Majomi, Cristian de la Fuente, Claudia de Llano, Doug Denoff, Sam Denoff, Howard Deutch, Matthew Diamond, Vin Di Bona, Susan Diol, Micky Dolenz , Jim Drake, Keir Dullea, James Patrick Dunne, Leslie Easterbrook, Ahmet Elez, Berty Elkind, Vanessa Evigan, Stephen Fanning, Mike Fenton, Fern Field, Wayne Fitterman, John Fleck, Vivica A. Fox, James Frawley, Marlene Fuentes, Holly Fulger, John Gabriel, Laura Gallagher, David Garfield, Mary Garofalo, Dick Gautier, George Gaynes, Ann Geddes, Michael S. Gendler, Thea Gill, Robert Ginty, Judy Gold, Lee Goldberg, Leonard Goldberg, Michael Golden, Philip Goldfarb , Colleen Goodrich, Jodi Gottlieb, Joie Gould, David Graham, Gary Graham, Nick Granito, Brian Lane Green, Bruce Seth Green, Jeff Greenberg, Michael Greene, Renee Griffin, Charles Haid, Brian Haley, Jonathan Halyalkar, Matt Hankinson, Susan Harris, Gina Hecht, Grainger Hines, Marc Hirschfeld, Celeste Holm, Bader Howar, Kevyn Major Howard, Tim Hunter, Peter Ianucci, Salvatore Ianucci, Aloma Ichinose, Kimberly Ikeda, Jackie Ioachim, Sam Irvin, Ivy Isenberg, Bobby Iyer, David Jacobs, Ronald Jacobs, Conrad Janis, Maria Janis, Heidi Jarratt, Brigit Jensen Drake, Kenneth Johnson, Gemma Jones, Robert Joy, Todd Justice, Robert H. Justman, Steve Kanaly, Sean Kanan, Ellie Kanner, Darlene Kaplan, Marshall Karp, Barnet Kellman, Deveney Kelly, John S. Kelly, Larry Kennar, Darrell Kern, T'Keyah Crystal Keymah, Bruce Kimmel, Sally Kirkland, Peter Kluge, Adam Klugman, Jack Klugman, Gary Kroeger, Paul Kurta, Dino Ladki, Christine Lakin, Judy Landis, Karen Landry, Susan Lanier, Michael G. Larkin, Jack Larson, Linda Laundra, Ginger Lawrence, Lena Lees, Aine Leicht, Christopher Leitch, John Levey, Jerry Levine, Michael Lindsay-Hogg, Jon Lindstrom, William Link, Daniel Lipman, David Lipper, Jerry London, Scott Lowell, Tom Mankiewicz, Jeffrey Marcus, Ron

Mardigian, Kelli Maroney, James Marshall, Ron Masak, John Masius, Dakin Matthews, Gayle Max, Melanie Mayron, Rue McClanahan, Brian McConkey, McG, Virginia McKenna, Tom McLoughlin, Daniel McVicar, Eric Menyuk, Burt Metcalfe, Victoria Paige Meyerink, Judith A. Moose, Robert Moresco, Nathan Morris, Marianne Muellerleile, Shannon Mulholland, Chris Mulkey, Frederick Muller, David Mulligan, Rachel Neville-Fox, Wendy O'Brien, Al Onorato, Lori Openden, Sandy Oroumieh, Ion Overman, Peter Paige, Jennifer Paletz, Laura Pallas, Betsy Palmer, Frank Parker, Billy Parrott, John Pasquin, Michael Pavone, Thaao Penghlis, Diane Perez, John Philbin, Joe Pinto, Alisan Porter, John Posey, Stefanie Powers, Robert Prosky, Andrew Prowse, John Putch, Roxanna Raanan, Betsy Randle, Anna Liza Recto, Tracy Reiner, Gene Reynolds, John Rich, Thomas Richards, Lita Richardson, Meghan Ritchie, Fred Roos, Richard P. Rosetti, Ian Roumain, Joe Ruby, Victoria Leigh Russell, Bob Salvucci, Jay Sandrich, Linda Sandrich, Austin Sayles, Suzanne Schachter, Sekka Scher, Jesse Schiller, Linda Schuyler, Allen Schwartz, Ross Schwartz, Sherwood Schwartz, Kimberly Scott, Pamela Shae, Alys Shanti, Cari Shayne, Les Sheldon, Ed Sherin, Brent Jordan Sherman, Wil Shriner, Marcia Shulman, Meghan Schumacher, Charles Shyer, James B. Sikking, Tucker Smallwood, Paul Alan Smith, Cynthia Snyder, Marilyn Sokol, Jonathan Sommers, Frank South, Ken Spears, Steve Spiker, Sandor Stern, Stella Stevens, Judith A. Strow, George Sunga, Michael Swan, Hillary Swanson, Tony Thomas, Joel Thurm, Berlinda Tolbert, Jaime Toporovich, Erin Torpey, Marcelle Tosi, Lisa Troland, Ellen Travolta, Robert Tucker, Anthony Turk, Jud Tylor, Barry Van Dyke, Bonnie Ventis, Kristen Vigard, Karen Walker, Tonja Walker, Laura Warfield, Arthur Weingarten, Kim Weiskopf, Sam Weisman, Sharon Weisz, Michael J. Weithorn, Llewellyn Wells, Paul Wensley, Alice West, Kathleen Wilhoite, Dan Wilcox, John Will, JoBeth Williams, Jenny Wilson, Art Wolff, Ron Wolotzky, Michael York, Roger Young, John Zander, Bonnie Zane and Randy Zisk.

Foreword by F. Murray Abraham

THE BIGGEST IMPACT THAT turning down a role has is what you learn from it. The doubts that follow the decision to turn down a job are inevitable, but how you handle that decision is a pretty good indication of who you are. Are you going to whine eternally about the one that got away; do you really believe that there is only going to be one opportunity in your life? That's true only if you believe it. And more importantly, what ultimately do you expect from this whole process of auditioning, and studying and trying and making choices? What finally are you looking for; fame, fortune, what? You should clarify for yourself why you are doing this. "Because I love it" is a good beginning but not sufficient for the long haul. The thing that drives me is the continual search that this work demands of us. Since we change from moment to moment, how can we possibly incorporate these changes in a room full of strangers who have the power to make all our dreams come true--what pressure. But, in fact, this is the place to find out who you are--the real you is actually what these auditors want to see; if they knew who they wanted they wouldn't bother with auditions; they want to see someone they have never seen before, and why shouldn't that someone be you--not the phony egotist, but the valuable, talented, dedicated artist that you are, or are becoming. If you go in with this attitude it will help you with the biggest problem an actor faces in an audition, which is an overwhelming desire to please, rather than to center down into yourself enough to trust your talent and your instincts. The more confident you are with who you are, whatever that maybe, the more confidence you will inspire in whoever auditions you: directors, producers, and, most importantly, casting directors. Before you enter that room, or theater, or wherever, remind yourself that when casting directors call you in, you are representing them---They want you to be as good as you can be, because that is a reflection on them and their ability. In the sessions I have conducted, the toughest part of auditioning from the casting point of view is the need that I felt from some of the actors; some were so needy that they drained my energy, and we began to resent how uncomfortable it was in that room; whenever a true pro showed up I found myself relaxing in the knowledge that this was an actor who understood that if he didn't get this job, it wasn't his fault; and it wasn't because we didn't like him; it simply wasn't right THIS TIME; but you can bet that the next time I do a show I'm going to think of him. Your attitude should be positive no matter what. If the people you are facing are jerks, try to keep your temper, AND YOUR DIGNITY. Bear in mind that if they treat you like crap, it isn't the casting persons fault. This can be very hard sometimes; I myself have behaved very badly in the past, and have paid dearly for it; I would like to think that even without the Oscar I finally would have evolved to something more than a volatile maniac. (There is the story of Shelley Winters being asked what she had done lately, and she excused herself, went home, got her two Oscars, came back and said, "This is what I've done. What the fuck have *you* done?" But you shouldn't do this until you have at least one Oscar.) Maintain your equilibrium, then go home and work out; which by the way is my answer to many problems; honest.

It is an eye-opener to work on a casting session; as a go-fer, an assistant, a reader. Anything to see at first-hand the process, and to understand the difficulties of casting from the auditor's perspective. My last piece of advice is that you must never think of anything you go through as wasted time. Ever. The past is exactly that---past. If you can't think in the present, then you will never be any good as an actor.

As for the question "Does the system work?" I would be a fool if I said anything except yes. After all, as stinky as it is, it has been pretty good to me.

–F. Murray Abraham

Introduction By Michael Cesarano

THINK OF A SHOW—any show...

If there is a casting story to be told about the show it is likely contained in these pages.

In this volume, Eila Mell has uncovered some of the most interesting behind-the-scenes information that you will find, some of which might have otherwise been lost forever. Eila reports on the casting histories of hundreds of television shows, from the legendary to the obscure, from the cult to the wildly popular. For every *Hill Street Blues* listed in the book there are just about as many *Gong Shows*, so to speak.

The television shows listed in this book are arranged alphabetically by title. The actor who actually played the role is listed first along with the character's name. Immediately following in parenthesis, are the actors considered for the role followed by the story behind the casting decision.

Eila does not stand in judgment of the merits of these shows. While she is clearly a fan of television history, she functions as an objective (albeit enthusiastic) reporter. This journalistic style allows the reader to sit back and enjoy all of the casting permutations on which she reports without the persnickety editorial asides that too often accompany writing on the arts.

This book is the result of meticulous and extensive research. Eila interviewed over two hundred actors, producers, casting directors and writers, the names of whom are included in the bibliography. An index of names and titles is included for easy reference.

I don't think I'm going too far out on a limb to say that television is the most intimate medium. We watch it in our homes, in our beds, in our private spaces. Because it is so pervasive in our everyday lives, we often know television better than we think we do, or at least better than we are willing to admit. Have you ever told someone about a show you saw and followed up with the disclaimer: "I was just flipping channels and I happened to catch it." Sometimes it's true; sometimes it's a lie. We even become familiar with shows that we don't especially like because we just left the television on and got hooked in.

The commercial jingles and theme songs we can't get out of our heads; the catch-phrases we repeat, often to strangers, as if sharing an inside joke. "Where's the beef?" "Is that your final answer?" "Will the judges reveal their scores!" Some of us have come to know television more intimately than film or theatre simply because television has insinuated itself into our personal space throughout our lifetime. Well, I'm glad for that, because television history is important; television production and performance art is there to be studied. And you're holding a big chunk of it in your hands right now!

In his book, *Teleliteracy*, David Bianculli makes a case for television as a friend of literacy rather than an adversary. He quotes media studies professor Robert Thompson: "Because you're arguing in defense of television, [intellectuals] think you're therefore arguing for abolition of study of the classics. To them, it's like matter and antimatter. I don't think that intellectuals can understand that a person could in the morning read Shakespeare, and in the afternoon laugh at *Laverne & Shirley*."

Amen.

As she did in her first book, *Casting Might-Have-Beens*, Eila has once again put you—and me— in the director's chair, after the fact and with

the benefit of 20/20 hindsight.
    And ... action!

Michael Cesarano, Professor of Theatre and Media Studies
Queensborough Community College
Bayside, NY
May 2007

Also by Eila Mell:

Casting Might-Have-Beens: A Film by Film Directory (McFarland)

According to Jim (2001-)

Larry Joe Campbell as Andy (Sam Seder)

JIM BELUSHI WAS CAST in the title role of Jim in *According to Jim*. "When you have a strong male or female character driving the show, and it's a husband and wife, or partners, it's so important to get someone who can go toe to toe with them," said director Andy Cadiff. "Comedically, dramatically, in every way. You look at the success of *Roseanne*, and a lot of that is attributable to John Goodman, which was just such great casting for that show. With *According to Jim* we had a very strong personality in Jim. We really struggled a little bit to find the right person for him. I was always a huge fan of Courtney Thorne-Smith. I did receive a lot of resistance in the beginning from the network. I had a basic belief. The character Jim wanted to play was a little bit of a gorilla. He was loud, abrasive, he had his own opinions, he was sexist, just a big personality. You really wanted to make him likeable. My feeling was it was very important to cast a wife that would sort of say to the audience, "Hey, she loves him. If she loves him then we should love him.' What I knew about Courtney was that she had already been successful on two long running series. She had already proven her likeability. The TV watching audience already had given her the stamp of approval. So if you put her next to Jim, she softens Jim and gives Jim lovability. It was a perfect combination, even though in the beginning the network resisted. We finally did a chemistry read. That's when the network immediately said, " 'They work together.' I really think that the success of that show had a lot to do with their chemistry."

Sam Seder played Cheryl's brother Andy in the original pilot. The producers didn't think that Seder seemed like the brother of Kimberly Williams and Courtney Thorne-Smith. They decided they wanted to change types and go with a funny character actor instead. Larry Joe Campbell auditioned, and was great. According to casting director Jeff Greenberg, another thing going for Campbell was that, unlike Seder, he was physically bigger than Jim Belushi, and made Belushi seem more like a leading man. With Campbell on board the chemistry for the show was right.

The Addams Family (1964-1966)
Ted Cassidy as Lurch (John Astin)

CHARLES ADDAMS CREATED *The Addams Family* cartoon, which ran in The New Yorker magazine. One day Filmways Pictures executive David Levy passed a Doubleday bookstore window and saw Addams' work. He had the idea that the book should become a television series. He contacted Addams through the magazine. Addams was agreeable to the idea, and the series was born.

John Astin had a meeting with Filmways Pictures to discuss the possibility of playing the character that became Lurch, the butler. Astin later got a call from Levy, who instead thought he should play the lead role of Gomez. Astin was ideal for the role of the eccentric Mr. Addams and signed for the part. Ted Cassidy was later cast as Lurch.

Adventures of Superman (1952-1957)
George Reeves as Superman/Clark Kent (Kirk Alyn)

JERRY SIEGEL AND JOE SHUSTER created the character of Superman. The comic books debuted in 1938, and were enormously popular. In 1940 a radio show based on Superman was produced. It, too, was a hit, and ran until 1951. Cartoons followed, as well as live-action films. Eventually, a television series was planned.

Jack Larson

Jack Larson was offered the role of cub reporter Jimmy Olsen. "I didn't want to do it," said Larson. "I thought - Superman! Come on, I'd just been on the stage. What is this? I didn't want to do it, and the casting man, whose name was Harold Childes; he was a wonderful man. He talked to me very firmly. He said, "Look, you're a very mixed-up kid. I know that

you don't want to go to Fox. You don't want to have another stock contract, that you don't want to do this and that, and that you want to go to
New York.' Which is what I wanted to do. I wanted to go to New York
and try to get on the New York stage. And he said, "We understand you
don't have enough money to go to New York.' Which was true. My agent
had told him this. And he said, "Well, look. This is a season's work. We're
going to do 26 shows and probably no one will ever see it ...You should
really do it and take the money and go to New York.' I did it and I enjoyed
doing it enormously with the cast I worked with, and the crew. We had
a top crew. We had Orson Welles' sound crew. We had great cameramen
who later won Academy Awards. It was an amazing experience doing it so
quickly. I liked enormously working with, obviously, George Reeves, John
Hamilton, and Phyllis Coates, who was at that time our first Lois Lane in
'51. It was a wonderful experience.

"We shot at the old Selznick studio, which is now Sony, one of Sony's
enterprises, over on Washington Boulevard. It's just east of MGM. We
shot a lot of our street scenes (because Selznick didn't have a standing
New York street set) down at Hal Roach. And I had a wonderful time because I worshipped Laurel and Hardy and Carole Lombard, who'd been
in Hal Roach comedies, and Mabel Normand and everybody. It was a
craze with all of that. There used to be a little theater on Fairfax called
The Silent Movie Theater. You could see these things at that time. And so
I was thrilled working at Hal Roach. There are those hallowed streets. It
came to me that we were pioneers just like they were. That excited me
and I thought, I don't know if anyone will ever see this, but I'm going to
do the best possible job I can. And I never threw away any line of dialogue.
Every single thing I did through all those years was the best possible work
I could do under the circumstances."

Kirk Alyn starred as Superman in the 1948 film *Superman* as well as
the 1950 film, *Atom Man vs. Superman*. On the CBS morning show Alyn
said that he was offered the part of Superman on the television series. Ac-

cording to Larson, although Alyn thought he was considered, this is untrue. He said the producers didn't want anyone who had been in the Sam Katzman serial for the show, including Noel Neill who played Lois Lane.

Phyllis Coates was first cast as reporter Lois Lane. The pilot was shot in 1951, but didn't hit the air until about a year later. By that time Coates was offered the chance to play Jack Carson's wife in *The Jack Carson Show*, which she accepted. The producers of *Superman* had changed by then. The new producers had no problem with hiring actors from the Katzman serial, and hired Noel Neill as Coates' replacement. The show was an immediate hit and made the actors very famous instantly.

Airwolf (1984-1986)

Jan-Michael Vincent as Stringfellow Hawke (Barry Van Dyke)

BARRY VAN DYKE SAW THE PI-LOT script for the upcoming series *Airwolf*. He thought the show had great potential. Van Dyke ran into the series creator in an elevator and mentioned the show to him. He was told that Jan-Michael Vincent had already been hired. Van Dyke was a fan of Vincent's work, and knew he was perfectly cast.

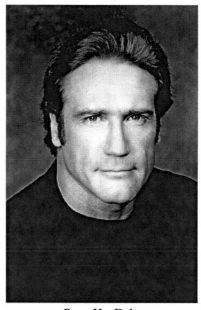

On a Friday during the first season Van Dyke received a call asking if he was available to start work in three days. The show had decided to replace Vincent. Van Dyke said yes, and a deal was made. The night

Barry Van Dyke

before he was to start work he got a call saying that Vincent was going to remain with the show after all. Van Dyke told them he was glad that things worked out. During the second season Van Dyke was contacted again to replace Jan-Michael Vincent. Van Dyke was willing to help them out, but once again the show decided to keep Vincent on. *Airwolf* was canceled in 1986, but Universal Studios brought it back in 1987. At that point Van Dyke was just offered the job. "Jan actually came up and did a transitional episode," said Van Dyke. "And I got along great with him. I like Jan a lot. That was one that took about three years for me to get the part!"

Alias (2001-2006)

Jennifer Garner as Sydney Bristow (Jacinda Barrett, Jenna Fischer)
Kevin Weisman as Marshall
    Flinkman (Michael J. Burg)

CASTING DIRECTORS JANET GILMORE and Megan McConnell saw several actresses for the starring role of spy Sydney Bristow. Jenna Fischer was a candidate. Fischer was told that, while her acting was great, she wasn't sexy enough for the part. One of the strongest contenders was Jacinda Barrett. Barrett, a former model, was one of the stars of MTV's *The Real World* in 1995. Series creator J.J. Abrams suggested Jennifer Garner. Abrams was a guest at Garner's wedding to Scott Foley, where he

Michael J. Burg
Photo: Douglas Gorenstein Studio

noticed she might have the charisma necessary for the role. Garner was brought in, and after five auditions landed the part.

Michael J. Burg auditioned for the supporting role of Marshall Flinkman. The character was described as a Beavis & Butthead-type intelligence agent. The normally clean-cut Burg went to the audition wearing a mullet hair extension and a Grateful Dead t-shirt. "J.J. really liked me, and loved that I dressed like the character," said Burg. "Anyway, the role of Marshall Flinkman went to the actor Kevin Weisman, who dresses and appears on the show like I do normally. Ironically, I think the fact that I showed him exactly what he thought he wanted made him decide he didn't want that at all. Bummer. I bet Marshall Flinkman wore a jacket and pressed shirt to the audition. You just never know."

Alien Nation (1989-1990)

Gary Graham as Matthew Sikes (Michael Beck, Colin Quinn, James Remar, Marc Singer, Michael Swan)

WHEN PRODUCER KENNETH JOHNSON was approached with the idea of developing the hit film *Alien Nation* into a television series he thought it would be no more than *Miami Vice* with Coneheads. Then he watched the film. He saw a scene where the alien, played by Mandy Patinkin, waved to his family. Johnson realized that the show was about being the world's newest minority.

Marc Singer was considered for the role of Matthew Sikes, the human detective. Singer had played Mike Donovan in *V* for Johnson. The actor's schedule was too busy for *Alien Nation*, and other candidates, including Michael Beck and James Remar, were contemplated. Another possibility was Michael Swan, who was put on tape. The choice was eventually narrowed down to Gary Graham and Colin Quinn. The role went to Graham. Graham said that the part of Matthew Sikes was a dream role. The scripts were great, as were the people working on the show.

All-American Girl (1994-1995)
Maddie Corman as Ruthie (Judy Gold)

ALL-AMERICAN GIRL STARRED stand-up comedian Margaret Cho as Margaret Kim. The series followed the modern Margaret and her traditional Korean family. Judy Gold originally auditioned for the part of Margaret's friend, Ruthie. Maddie Corman was cast instead, while Gold was given the part of Gloria, another friend of Margaret's.

All in the Family (1971-1979)
Carroll O'Connor as Archie Bunker (Mickey Rooney)
Rob Reiner as Michael Stivic (Harrison Ford, Tim McIntire, Chip Oliver)
Sally Struthers as Gloria Stivic (Candice Azzara, Penny Marshall, Kelly Jean
    Peters)
Mike Evans as Lionel Jefferson (Cleavon Little, D'Urville Martin)
Betty Garrett as Irene Lorenzo (Sada Thompson)

SERIES CREATOR NORMAN LEAR considered Mickey Rooney for the starring role of Archie Bunker. Lear told Rooney that the character was a bigot. Rooney stopped him and told him that if he went on the air with the show, he would be killed dead in the streets! Lear cast Carroll O'Connor instead.

A pilot, called *Justice For All*, was made in 1968. O'Connor and Jean Stapleton starred as Archie and Edith Justice. Kelly Jean Peters played their daughter Gloria, with Tim McIntire cast as her husband, Richard. Rounding out the cast was D'Urville Martin as their neighbor Lionel Jefferson. The pilot was unsuccessful, and was eventually scrapped. Another attempt was made in 1969, with Candice Azzara and Chip Oliver replacing Peters and McIntire. This second pilot fared as poorly as the first. Azzara didn't, and still doesn't, have any hard feelings. Said the actress, "I was grateful that Sally [Struthers] got the part. She was cuter; had better energy, she looked like Carroll O'Connor. She was better for the part. Norman Lear was right. If I'm not right, I don't want it."

Richard (called Dickie in the second pilot) was renamed Michael. Rob Reiner was eventually hired for the part, although Harrison Ford was also considered.

Penny Marshall tried out for Gloria, but lost the part to Sally Struthers.

Norman Lear wanted Cleavon Little to play Lionel Jefferson. Director John Rich thought that Little was too old for the part. Through a casting session Rich met Mike Evans. Evans was a student at Los Angeles City College, and had no acting experi-

Candice Azzara today

ence. Rich describes Evans' first audition as awful, but saw promise in him. Rich wondered how this inexperienced young man had managed to get the audition in the first place. Evans told him that he was hitch-hiking and was picked up by the actor who had auditioned right before him. Rich didn't think Evans could handle the job and took him out of the running. After ten more days of auditioning other actors Rich reconsidered, and called Evans back in. Although Evans needed a lot of work, Rich called Norman Lear to tell him he found a possible Lionel. Evans read for Lear, who questioned Rich's judgment. Rich told him that Evans had the right look. He felt that Evans would improve with a week of rehearsal. Rich told Lear if he was wrong, they would replace him with Cleavon Little as his brother. Lear reluctantly agreed. Rich worked with Evans, who blossomed. Evans was a hit as Lionel, a role he continued on the spin-off series, *The Jeffersons*.

The series' third pilot was successful. The show was picked up and premiered on January 12, 1971. *All in the Family* had a small audience at first, but the ratings improved steadily during the summer reruns. By that September the show was a number one hit.

In September of 1973 the characters of Frank and Irene Lorenzo were introduced. The Lorenzos were neighbors of the Bunkers. Vincent Gardenia was cast as Frank, while Sada Thompson was hired to play Irene. According to John Rich, although Thompson is a great actress, she was not a fit for the show. Betty Garrett soon replaced her.

Demond Wilson appeared as a burglar in the October 9, 1971 episode called "Edith Writes a Song." In the episode the family comes home to find burglars in the house. Wilson played Horace, and his partner Coke was played by Cleavon Little. Wilson was so good on that show it eventually led to his starring role of Lamont Sanford on the Norman Lear-produced *Sanford & Son*.

All My Children (1970–)

Susan Lucci as Erica Kane (Patricia Mauceri)
Michael E. Knight as Tad Martin (Christian J. LeBlanc)
Debbi Morgan as Angie Baxter (Tonya Pinkins)
Melissa Leo as Linda Warner (Julia Roberts)
Kari Gibson as Dixie Cooney (Crystal Carson)
Cady McClain as Dixie Cooney (Crystal Carson)
Trent Bushey as David Rampal (Michael Brainard)
Michael Nader as Dimitri Marick (Thaao Penghlis)
Matt Borlenghi as Brian Bodine (Scott Reeves)
Brian Lane Green as Brian Bodine (Chris Douglas, Dylan Neal, Austin Peck)
Sarah Michelle Gellar as Kendall Hart (Eva LaRue)
Eva LaRue as Maria Santos (Julianna Margulies)

PATRICIA MAUCERI AUDITIONED for the part of Erica Kane when *All My Children* was first produced. Mauceri had no idea that the part would become so popular. Susan Lucci got the job. Lucci has been on *All My Children* for 37 years, and is still with the show to date. She was nominated for the Daytime Emmy 18 times, before finally winning in 1999.

In 1973 the character of Tad Martin was introduced. The young boy had been abused by his father, Ray Gardner, and was taken in and adopted by the Martin family. Matthew Anton originated the role, which he played through 1977. In 1978 John E. Dunn was cast. He stayed with the show until 1981. After Dunn's departure Michael E. Knight and Christian J. LeBlanc were among the actors auditioning to replace him. The part went to Knight, who was enormously popular in the role. Knight, who has played Tad Martin on and off for the past 26 years (and counting) won three Daytime Emmys for the role.

Tonya Pinkins was considered for the part of Angie Baxter in the early 1980s. Debbi Morgan was cast instead. Casting director Joan D'Inecco remembered Pinkins ten years later when the part of lawyer Livia Frye was created. Pinkins was brought in to audition, and won the role.

A very young, unknown Julia Roberts auditioned to play Linda Warner. Joan D'Incecco saw a special, exotic quality in Roberts, but felt she wasn't right for the role. The part of Linda went to Melissa Leo.

Crystal Carson auditioned to play Dixie twice: first when the character was originated, and then when the role was recast. One of her audition call times was 5:00 a.m. Since Carson had just flown in from California, to her it was as if it were 2:00 a.m. She was extremely tired. "I was sitting in the makeup chair," said Carson. "They're trying to make you look awake." Kari Gibson originated the role of Dixie. When she left the show Cady McClain succeeded her.

Michael Brainard was up for the part of David Rampal. Brainard was put up at a hotel while he waited to hear if he got the job. Brainard's audition was on a Friday. He got a call the following Sunday night telling him that, although he didn't get the part of David, he was cast as Joey Martin instead.

Thaao Penghlis turned down the chance to play Dimitri Marick. "I liked Erica," he said. "I felt, at that time, she had had so many lovers, I'm

Brian Lane Green

going to be one more." The same day Penghlis said no he went to the gym He saw Michael Nader there. Nader was talking about moving to New York to play the part of Dimitri Marick on *All My Children*.

Gregory Gordon originated the role of Brian Bodine in 1990. He was gone by the next year. The decision was made to recast the role. Scott Reeves was up for the part. Reeves was torn because, although this was a good job, his wife Melissa Reeves was already working in California on *Days of Our Lives*. Reeves told *Soap Opera Digest* that he felt he had a good chance at getting the part. He realized that he didn't want to be so far away from his wife. Reeves called his agent and took himself out of the running. Soon after, Reeves got a steady job in California, on the soap *The Young and the Restless*.

Matt Borlenghi was hired to play Brian. When he eventually decided to leave the show the producers searched for a replacement. Austin Peck, Chris Douglas and Dylan Neal all auditioned. Brian Lane Green had just finished a 2-½-year-run playing Sam Fowler on *Another World*. Green read in a magazine that Borlenghi was leaving the show. Not long after, Green was brought in for an audition. "I went in for the casting director and then I screen tested," said Green. "I knew Matt. He was there when I tested. I was out of work for two weeks, and I screen tested and I got the part. It happened very quickly. I was shocked."

Eva LaRue auditioned to play Erica Kane's daughter, Kendall Hart. She lost out to Sarah Michelle Gellar. LaRue was cast as Maria Santos instead, a part she beat out Julianna Margulies for.

Former *Dallas* actor Steve Kanaly was offered the part of Dixie's father, Seabone Hunkle. Although he was made a handsome offer, Kanaly lived on a ranch with animals. Living in New York would be a challenge for him. He was persuaded to take the job by his wife. She and her mother had watched *All My Children* for 25 years.

Ally McBeal (1997-2002)
Calista Flockhart as Ally McBeal (Lara Flynn Boyle, Bridget Fonda, Cari Shayne)
Peter Roth as Network President (Les Moonves)

FILM ACTRESS BRIDGET FONDA was considered for the title role of lawyer Ally McBeal. At the time Fonda was not interested in working in television and turned the part down. Lara Flynn Boyle was considered, as were Cari Shayne and Calista Flockhart. Although Flockhart was unknown, her intelligence, wit, beauty and great sense of humor helped her nail the part. The show made Flockhart a star.

Fox Entertainment Group president Peter Roth played a network president on the December 15, 1997 episode. CBS's Les Moonves was originally approached for the cameo, but couldn't work out his schedule.

Almost Perfect (1995-1996)
Chip Zien as Gary Karp (Curtis Armstrong)

ALMOST PERFECT STARRED NANCY TRAVIS as TV executive producer Kim Cooper. The supporting role of writer Gary Karp was originally given to Curtis Armstrong. After the table read, the decision was made to replace him with Chip Zien.

American Dream (1981)
Stephen Macht as Danny Novak (Ned Beatty)

NED BEATTY WAS CONSIDERED for the part of former football player Danny Novak. However, producer Barney Rosenzweig liked an unknown actor named Stephen Macht. Macht was brought in for an interview. All involved thought he was a great choice. That is, until the next day. Executive Tom Werner worried that the series needed a star to play Danny Novak.

He thought the part should go to Beatty. Rosenzweig still wanted Macht. He didn't even think that Beatty was attainable. Beatty's representatives said that the actor would make the pilot only if he were guaranteed twelve episodes. Rosenzweig was surprised when ABC agreed to his terms. After four days of shooting ABC decided they had made a mistake, and that Beatty was not working out. He was let go and replaced by Stephen Macht.

Anatomy of a Hate Crime (2001)
Cy Carter as Matthew Shepard (Shane Meier)

ANATOMY OF A HATE CRIME told the true story of the murder of college student Matthew Shepard. Shepard was tied to a fence and left to die because he was gay. Finding an actor to play Shepard was a difficult task. "He had to look like Matthew Shepard," said director Tim Hunter. "He was gay, but we didn't want it to be a stereotype. We needed a certain type of vulnerability and a certain kind of innocence. It's just a very hard part to cast. Cy Carter showed up fairly late in the process, and it was a big relief to all of us." Had Carter not shown up the part would have gone to Shane Meier. The following year Meier played Matthew Shepard in CBS's *The Matthew Shepard Story*. The first airing of *Anatomy of a Hate Crime* was shown on MTV, without commercial interruption.

And the Band Played On (1993)
Alan Alda as Robert Gallo (Dakin Matthews)

THE 1993 HBO FILM *And the Band Played On* was based on Randy Shilts' book of the same name. It told the story of the discovery of the AIDS virus. The characters in the film were based on real people and their actual names were used. Matthew Modine was cast in the lead role of Dr. Don Francis, a retrovirologist with the Center for Disease Control.

Dakin Matthews
Photo: Keith Jochim

"It was a really important film at the time that it was made," said Dakin Matthews, who played Congressman Phillip Burton. Burton introduced the first legislation in Congress to fund AIDS research. "It was prestigious to be in that film to some extent," continued Matthews. "I actually auditioned originally for the role that Alan Alda played. Not only did I audition for it, I did the cast reading of it as well, because Alan was having difficulty clearing his schedule. If he said no, I was going to be playing that role. Even when the cast assembled to do their first reading I was still reading that because he was not in town. When he finally cleared his schedule, they asked me to take another role. My agent really aggressively wanted me to be in that show." The role Alda played was Dr. Robert Gallo, a retrovirologist with the National Cancer Institute.

The Andy Griffith Show (1960-1968)

Jim Nabors as Gomer Pyle (George Lindsey)

THE ANDY GRIFFITH SHOW starred Andy Griffith as Andy Taylor. Taylor was the sheriff of the small town of Mayberry, North Carolina, where he lived with his young son Opie and his Aunt Bee. Taylor's cousin Barney Fife was the deputy sheriff.

In 1962 the character of gas station attendant Gomer Pyle was introduced. George Lindsey auditioned, but lost out to Jim Nabors. Lindsey became a series regular in 1964 when he was awarded the role of Gomer's cousin, Goober Pyle.

Angie (1979-1980)

Donna Pescow as Angie Benson (Sandra Bernhard, Marilyn Sokol, Dee Wallace)
Robert Hays as Brad Benson (Mark Harmon, Jon Korkes)
Debralee Scott as Marie Falco (Rhea Perlman)

LARRY MINTZ AND ALAN EISENSTOCK created the ABC sitcom *Angie*. The title character was Angie Falco, a coffee shop waitress who married a rich doctor named Brad Benson. According to Mintz, Sandra Bernhard, Dee Wallace, Donna Pescow and Marilyn Sokol all auditioned to play Angie. Sokol said she was told she was too skinny for the part. Donna Pescow was chosen. Jon Korkes was cast as Brad, and a pilot was shot. Mintz was told that ABC agreed to pick up the series, contingent upon replacing

Larry Mintz

Korkes. Actors were brought in to try for the part, and the choice was eventually narrowed down to two: Mark Harmon and Robert Hays. Hays got the part and a new pilot was shot.

Rhea Perlman auditioned to play Angie sister, Marie Falco, but lost the part to Debralee Scott.

Another World (1956-)

Thomas Gibson as Sam Fowler (Brian Lane Green)
Danny Markel as Sam Fowler (Brian Lane Green)
Jensen Buchanan as Victoria Hudson/Marley Hudson (Ellen Wheeler)
Cynthia Watros as Victoria Hudson (Anne Heche)

ROBERT KELKER-KELLY originated the role of Sam Fowler in 1987. He stayed with the show for about three years. When he left, the producers had auditions to recast the role. Brian Lane Green was up for the part. He met with the executives in Los Angeles, and was then flown out to New York for a call back. He finally lost the part to Thomas Gibson. Gibson didn't stay on the show very long. Once again the producers wanted to recast. Green tested again, but lost out to Danny Markel. Markel left the show in 1991, at which point Green was finally awarded the role of Sam Fowler.

Ellen Wheeler originated the dual role of twins Marley and Vicky Hudson in 1984. She decided to leave in 1986, and was replaced by Anne Heche. Heche stayed with the show until 1991. The producers wanted to recast the role. Ellen Wheeler was brought in to audition. Despite the fact that she originated the role, and won an Emmy for her portrayal, she failed to win the part. Jensen Buchanan was cast instead.

In 1998 Jensen Buchanan fell ill and had to miss six episodes. Anne Heche was approached about reprising the role. Heche was open to the possibility, but the part eventually went to Cynthia Watros.

Any Day Now (1998-2002)
William Converse-Roberts as Matthew O'Brien (Michael Pavone, John Posey)

THE PILOT FOR *Any Day Now* was originally written about eight years before it was actually produced. The lead characters were two little girls: Mary Elizabeth and Rene. Executive producer Nancy Miller later redeveloped the show, and created the double time line. The grown-up versions of the characters were added, and the young girls only appeared in flashbacks. CBS was going to produce the series, but canceled it the day before shooting was about to start. Eight years later it was picked up by Lifetime. Pilot director Jeff Bleckner was in Atlanta on a casting search. On a Saturday morning two little girls came in: Mae Middleton and Shari Dyon Perry. The girls had come to know each other by auditioning for casting director Shay Griffin, who was very excited about them. Middleton was from Tennessee, and had come to Atlanta to read for the show. "We had been auditioning hundreds of girls in L.A., and had seen tapes of girls from Chicago, New York and all over the place," said Bleckner. "We were going on this last desperate trip to Atlanta. Shay said she found these two girls that might be what we were looking for. I remember Mae came in and read first. We flipped. She had this fabulous accent. She was real; she was this girl. We thought she was terrific. We asked her to wait outside. She said she wanted to stay and watch Shari's audition. I think we had her come back in and had them read together right after Shari read." Middleton and Perry won the parts of the young version of the show's lead characters Mary Elizabeth and Rene, played by Annie Potts and Lorraine Toussaint.

Lifetime originally didn't think Annie Potts should play Mary Elizabeth. Potts had just starred in *Dangerous Minds*, a television version of the hit film of the same name. The series didn't fare well, which was the reason Lifetime was unsure. They eventually decided she was the right actress and gave her the part.

Nancy Miller had trouble casting the role of Matthew O'Brien. The show was partly based on her real-life experiences, and the part was based on her father. She knew Michael Pavone, who worked for years in television as an executive producer. "I reminded her of her father," said Pavone. "I thought I would read just for the casting director and be put on tape. I was a nervous wreck. I hadn't auditioned in 19 years." Pavone went to audition. He walked into an office and was surprised to see about 30 of the most handsome men he had ever seen. He realized he was in the wrong place and had shown up at an audition for *Melrose Place*! Pavone finally arrived at the right room, where he ran into his friend, actor John Posey. Posey was also up for the role. Pavone felt like he didn't belong there. "My whole goal was to not embarrass Nancy Miller," he said. Miller soon came out and greeted Pavone with a hug and brought him in first. He expected it to just be Miller and the casting director in the room. Instead, there were about thirteen people there. They all knew Pavone as a producer, and were surprised to see him there to audition. They started firing questions at him. Pavone interrupted to ask to read the scene. After he was done he quickly left the room. He wished Posey good luck and left. That night he found out he got the part. Two days later, Miller called him to say

Michael Pavone

that Lifetime wanted him to read for them. He agreed and went to audition for the network. Eventually, he learned that Lifetime wanted him to screen test. The test was shot on the set of a TV movie on their last day of shooting. Pavone was put in a chair with one light on him. The people coming to work had no idea a screen test was going to be shot there. At the end of the day Nancy Miller told him that the film was unusable. Pavone told her to forget it. William Converse-Roberts was eventually cast in the role. Miller gave Pavone another part, the role of Jimmy O'Brien.

Anything But Love (1989-1992)

Ann Magnuson as Catherine Hughes (Holly Fulger)
Holly Fulger as Robin Dulitski (Talia Balsam)

ANYTHING BUT LOVE starred Jamie Lee
Curtis and Richard Lewis as co-workers
Hannah Miller and Marty Gold. Other
cast members included Louis Giam-
balvo, Richard Frank, Bruce Kirby and
Sandy Faison.

There were significant cast changes
for the series' second season. Giam-
balvo, Kirby and Faison were gone. New
characters were added, including Hannah's best friend Robin Dulitski and
Marty and Hannah's new boss Catherine
Hughes. Holly Fulger was brought in to
audition for Catherine. Fulger read, but

Holly Fulger

was then switched over to audition for the part of Hannah's best friend
Robin Dulitski. Her competition for the part of Robin was Talia Balsam.
"It was a fun audition," said Fulger. "We all came in to work with Jamie.
I was so nervous. She was so nice." Fulger got the part. "It was the most
wonderful cast," she said. Jamie's really fun to work with. So nice and re-
ally generous."

Archer (1975)

Brian Keith as Lew Archer (Leonard Nimoy, Burt Reynolds, Robert Vaughn)

BURT REYNOLDS, LEONARD NIMOY and Robert Vaughn were all considered to play the title role of detective Lew Archer. None of these actors
were available, and the role went to Brian Keith.

Archie: To Riverdale and Back (1990)

Christopher Rich as Archie Andrews (Gary Kroeger)

GARY KROEGER AUDITIONED for the lead role of comic book character Archie Andrews in the movie-of-the-week, *Archie: To Riverdale and Back*. He was cast as Reggie Mantle instead. Christopher Rich got the part of Archie.

Arrested Development (2003-2006)

Jason Bateman as Michael Bluth (Craig Bierko, Dan Futterman, Ron
    Livingston, Paul Rudd, Ben Shenkman)
Portia de Rossi as Lindsay Bluth Funke (Paula Cale, Jennifer Grey, Fay
    Masterson, Parker Posey, Sherie Rene Scott)
Will Arnett as GOB (Todd Robert Anderson, Jon Cryer, Wallace Langham,
    Ivan Martin, Alan Ruck, French Stewart, Nick Swardson, Rainn Wilson)

PAUL RUDD, CRAIG BIERKO, Ron Livingston and Dan Futterman were all pursued for the central role of Michael Bluth in the Fox comedy *Arrested Development*. Jason Bateman and Ben Shenkman were the final two choices of the creative team for the part. The team was split. Some were pushing for Shenkman, a wonderful New York actor who had just made a big splash being cast in *Angels in America*. He was interesting in an offbeat way, like the rest of the family. And he was a "find" and a new face to television, which the team found exciting. The rest of the team and the network (Fox) thought that Bateman was the right choice. Bateman, an actor who had grown up on television, had a familiar feel – too familiar, some thought. "However, Bateman represented a sane center in this group of crazies, someone, hopefully, the audience can identify with," said casting director Deborah Barylski. "With him, there's a 'way into' the family. Somebody's got to look and be a little normal. The network really pushed this idea and I think that really was the right choice. Once Bateman read at the network, all other fears about him disappeared. He was fabulous! It was really hard on Ben, though, because he never even got a chance to audition at the network."

In the pilot the part of the dad was not a series regular. Series creator Mitch Hurwitz worked with Jeffrey Tambor on the 1999 series *Everything's Relative*. He called Tambor and asked him to play George Bluth, Sr. Tambor read the script, loved it, and agreed. After the pilot was shot, it was shown to Fox. When they saw how great Tambor was, one of the conditions they made to the studio was that when the show was picked up, Tambor had to be made a series regular.

"I literally had about two weeks to cast *Arrested Development*," said Deborah Barylski. "It was a late pick-up and it was a single-camera show. Because its single camera it had to be shot early enough in pilot season to give the editors and the post-production team time to finish the film, at least 2-3 weeks (if it's a multiple-camera show, they're basically doing a rough cut as they shoot it).

"I literally had something like two weeks and three days before the table read. The cast was huge. I mean, there were ten people in the family alone, plus it seemed like dozens of these little parts — all those flashbacks and inserts. The small parts are sometimes really hard to find because really good actors are required but they only say one line, sometimes one word.

"It was happening so fast and, of course, I was casting a hot property. Absolutely everybody and their brother and their nephew and their great-aunt Tillie wanted to get a shot at this. The phones didn't stop ringing for two and a half weeks. I had to bring on extra help just to deal with the phones.

"Jessica [Walter] was actually in town for about a week of the audition process. Through some miscommunication in my office I never got the message. We had brought some people to the network for the role of Lucille Bluth, but none of the actresses booked it. The actresses were lovely, just not a perfect match for the character. I was going through my notes one night and all of a sudden I go, Jessica Walter! That's who should play this. I called her agent really early the next morning and said, 'I've got to get Jessica Walter in on this because I really think that she's perfect. This is her part. This is it.' And the agent said, 'Well, she was in Los Angeles for a week. I called you. She went back to New York and she's not coming back.' So I said, 'What do we do to get her on tape?' She said, 'Jessica Walter does not go on tape.' And I said, "Let's take it a step at a time. Send me some tape of hers. And she will have to go on tape.' Jessica called from the bathroom of Bloomingdale's in New York and said, 'Do I really have to go on tape?' And I said, 'Yeah, you do.' She said, 'I was there.' And I said, 'I know. I didn't get the message, and I actually fired the person who didn't give me the message. Had I known you were here I would have had you in last week.' So she went on tape. She didn't want to, but she did. I talked her through what they were wanting to do with the character." Walter felt that she knew who Lucille Bluth was.

Three other women were brought to the network to test for the part. None of them were right. Everyone was starting to get a little down. Barylski mentioned she had Jessica on tape. Walter later came out to test at the network and was the unanimous choice. "Ordinarily, somebody with Jessica's stature doesn't go on tape," added Barylski. "She shouldn't have to. She's got a career, a track record. But because she really felt a kinship with this character, and really, really felt like she should be doing it, she worked with me on it. It was to her own sense of knowing what was right for her that allowed her to do something she ordinarily wouldn't have done."

Parker Posey was pursued to play Lindsay Bluth Funke. Jennifer Grey and Paula Cale were among the actresses who auditioned for the role. Tests were made with Portia de Rossi, Fay Masterson and Broadway star Sherie Rene Scott. de Rossi gave an outstanding audition and won the part.

Barylski found that the hardest role to cast was GOB, because it was the strangest of all the parts. With GOB actors tended to fall into two categories: either they were from the sketch comedy world and, although they were funny, the choices were sometimes shallow, or they were really good actors who thought they had to play the part wacky. Jon Cryer, Alan Ruck and Wallace Langham all read for GOB, as did Rainn Wilson. Wilson gave a very good audition. He was a very close runner-up. However, he came off as too innocent, and not sleazy enough for the part.

French Stewart, Todd Robert Anderson, Nick Swardson and Ivan Martin tested, but the producers kept looking. "We had been to the network twice on this role," said Barylski. "We had to postpone the table read for a day or two because we couldn't find the right actor." On a Wednesday Barylski thought Will Arnett might be right. She called his manager in New York to see why he hadn't been submitted to her. She found out that Arnett was doing a play, and was unavailable. The next morning she received a call from Arnett's manager saying that Arnett had been fired from the play because American Equity wouldn't let him, a Canadian, be in the cast. He was suddenly available. Barylski told his manager that Arnett had to get on tape that very day. Barylski received the tape the following morning (Friday). When she showed the tape to the creative team, it was agreed he would fly to L.A. that weekend. He tested on Monday at the network and went to work later that day.

Hurwitz sent David Cross the script and told him he could do any part he wanted. Cross wasn't sure he wanted to be a regular on a series. Hurwitz assured him that they would use him as much or as little as he wanted. Like Jeffrey Tambor, the network also wanted Cross to be a regular. Once Cross fell in love with the character and the show, he didn't mind committing to the series.

The Art of Being Nick (1986)

Julia Louis-Dreyfus as Rachel (Sharon Stone)

THE CHARACTER OF NICK MOORE was created for the hit series *Family Ties*. Nick was such a popular character that he was spun off into his own series, *The Art of Being Nick*. In the series Nick goes to New York to become an artist. Sharon Stone auditioned for the supporting role of Rachel. She lost the part to Julia Louis-Dreyfus.

As Is (1986)

Robert Carradine as Rich (Jonathan Hogan)

DIRECTOR MICHAEL LINDSAY-HOGG had seen the Broadway production of *As Is,* and liked it. He signed on to direct the television version. "Showtime wanted someone with a bit of a name [to star]," he said. "I'd seen the play. At one point the author, William M. Hoffman, had wanted the two major actors from the theatre production to be in it [Jonathan

Hadary and Jonathan Hogan]. That wouldn't fly because neither of them was that well known. They were both very good, but of the two of them I was very struck by Jonathan Hadary. We were looking around for other actors who might be able to play the other guy, the one who gets sick. The producer, Michael Brandman, called me and said,

'We got a go from Showtime.' I said, 'Great. Who's going to play the part?' And he said, 'One of the Carradines. They

Robert Carradine

had a brand recognition name. And Bobby [Robert Carradine] did it and he was very good. He and Jonathan were very tight, and really worked together."

Robert Carradine was nominated for a CableACE award for his performance. "I think he was wonderful," said Lindsay-Hogg. "He was totally committed to it. A lot of the time in those days, some of the actors who were straight men were worried about playing gay men. But Bobby, once he decided to do it, really was very bold. I've never forgotten how wonderful he was, and how wonderful he was to work with, and just how much he gave of himself for that part."

As the World Turns (1956-)

Tom Wiggin as Kirk Anderson (Charles Grant)
Lucy Deakins as Lily Walsh (Martha Byrne)

CHARLES GRANT WAS UP for the part of Kirk Anderson on *As the World Turns*. Grant tested with Lisa Brown, who was already on the show as Iva Snyder. Although members of the cast told Grant he did very well, the part went to Tom Wiggin instead.

Martha Byrne auditioned to play Lily Walsh, but lost out to Lucy Deakins. Deakins stayed with the show less than a year, at which point Byrne replaced her. Byrne played the part until 1989. She decided to return to the role in 1993 and is still with the show to date.

Ask Harriet (1998)

Anthony Tyler Quinn as Jack Cody (Thomas Gibson)

THOMAS GIBSON TRIED FOR the starring role of the cross-dressing Jack Cody in the short-lived *Ask Harriet*. Gibson made it down to the final three, but lost the part to Anthony Tyler Quinn.

The Audrey Hepburn Story (2000)

Emmy Rossum as Young Audrey Hepburn (Eva Amurri)
Michael J. Burg as Truman Capote (Bill Dawes)

EVA AMURRI AUDITIONED to play the young Audrey Hepburn in the ABC TV movie *The Audrey Hepburn Story*. Jennifer Love Hewitt was already cast as the adult Hepburn. Amurri is about six inches taller than Hewitt, and lost the part to Emmy Rossum.

Michael J. Burg auditioned three times for the part of writer Truman Capote. Bill Dawes also auditioned, but Burg got the job. Burg later played Capote in the feature film *The Hoax* for director Lasse Hallstrom. Burg played playwright Tennessee Williams in the 2005 feature *Capote*, which starred Phillip Seymour Hoffman. Director Bennett Miller asked Burg not to tell Hoffman he played the part in a TV movie. Hoffman won the Oscar for his performance in the film.

Baby Bob (2002-2003)

Elliott Gould as Sam Spencer (Carl Reiner)

BABY BOB WAS ABOUT a six-month-old baby who could talk. Carl Reiner was hired for the part of Bob's grandfather, Sam Spencer. Reiner went to the first table reading. He then changed his mind and dropped out. Elliott Gould was brought in as his replacement.

Baby Boom (1988-1989)

Kate Jackson as J.C. Wiatt (Marilu
    Henner)

Charles Shyer

CHARLES SHYER DIRECTED the
1987 hit film *Baby Boom,* which he
wrote with his wife Nancy Meyers. Diane Keaton starred as successful New
York City businesswoman J.C. Wiatt
who leaves her job and moves to Vermont after inheriting a relative's baby.
In 1988 Shyer and Meyers adapted the
film for NBC. They were interested in
Marilu Henner for the role of J.C. Wiatt. However, Henner was in Italy, and
Meyers and Shyer didn't know that
she was interested. They gave the part
to Kate Jackson instead.

Baby Talk (1991-1992)

Julia Duffy as Maggie Campbell (Teri Hatcher, Connie Sellecca)
George Clooney as Joe (Ron Eldard)

BABY TALK WAS BASED ON the 1989 film *Look Who's Talking.* The film
starred Kirstie Alley as single mother Mollie. Bruce Willis provided the
voice of Mollie's infant son Mikey, who was heard only by the audience.

Teri Hatcher was considered for the starring role of Maggie for the
TV version. Connie Sellecca was also under consideration, and was even-
tually hired. Tony Danza was cast as the voice of Maggie's son Mickey.
Ron Eldard auditioned to play the supporting role of Joe, but lost out to
George Clooney.

Baby Talk went through many cast changes. Connie Sellecca was gone before the show ever hit the air, and was replaced by Julia Duffy. Duffy left after the first season. Mary Page Keller played Maggie in Season 2. George Clooney appeared in four episodes of *Baby Talk*. He was written out, and a new character, James Halbrook (played by Scott Baio), was brought in to fill the void.

The Ballad of Lucy Whipple (2001)

Meat Loaf Aday as Amos "Rattlesnake Jake" Frogge (Robert Carradine)

ROBERT CARRADINE AUDITIONED for the part of Amos "Rattlesnake Jake" Frogge in the 2001 CBS movie *The Ballad of Lucy Whipple*. Although the actor gave one of his more wild auditions, the role went to Meat Loaf Aday instead.

Barney Miller (1975-1982)

Max Gail as Stan "Wojo" Wojciehowicz (Charles Haid)

CHARLES HAID APPEARED in the pilot for the ABC sitcom *Barney Miller*, which was a made-for-TV movie called *The Life and Times of Captain Barney Miller*. He turned down the chance to do the series when it was picked up. "They thought I was crazy," said Haid. Max Gail took the part. Gail was nominated for an Emmy two times for his work on the series.

Batman (1966-1968)

Adam West as Bruce Wayne/Batman (Ty Hardin, Lyle Waggoner)
Burt Ward as Dick Grayson/Robin (Peter Deyell)
Cesar Romero as the Joker (Jose Ferrer)

Julie Newmar as the Catwoman (Suzanne Pleshette)
Myrna Fahey as Blaze (Angie Dickinson)

THE HIT COMIC BOOK *Batman* was adapted for television in 1966. Producer William Dozier's first choice for the title role of the caped crusader was Ty Hardin. Hardin was unavailable, and his agent suggested another client named Adam West. Dozier had West come in for a meeting and decided he was the guy. However, he also tested Lyle Waggoner because he felt he would have an easier time with the network if there was an alternate choice. All involved finally agreed that West was the right choice.

Burt Ward was cast as Batman's sidekick Robin, although Peter Deyell also tested.

Jose Ferrer was the first choice to play the villain the Joker. He turned it down, and Cesar Romero was cast instead.

Suzanne Pleshette was considered to play the evil Catwoman, eventually played by Julie Newmar.

Angie Dickinson's name was mentioned for the part of Blaze. The role was later given to Myrna Fahey.

Battlestar: Galactica (1978-1979)

Richard Hatch as Apollo (Kent McCord)
Dirk Benedict as Starbuck (Barry Van Dyke)

IT CAME DOWN TO FOUR actors for the two lead roles in the futuristic series *Battlestar: Galactica*: Dirk Benedict, Richard Hatch, Kent McCord and Barry Van Dyke. "We tested and we got fitted for the uniforms, I mean everything," said Van Dyke. "Before they decided, we tested over and over. Evidently, the network wanted one combination of guys and the studio wanted the other guys. They settled on Dirk Benedict and Richard Hatch and they got cast. After the first season the show was canceled." It was eventually decided that they would produce another season of the show, which was called *Galactica* 1980. The lead roles in the new version were given to Van Dyke and McCord.

Battlestar: Galactica (2004-)

Edward James Olmos as William Adama (Alan Alda, Alan Arkin, Bruce
    Greenwood, Ed Harris, William Hurt, Sam Neill, Roger Rees, Sam
    Shepard, David Strathairn, Donald Sutherland, Jon Voight)
Katee Sackhoff as Kara "Starbuck" Thrace (Abby Brammell, Lori Heuring,
    Sarah Shahi, Polly Walker, Kerry Washington)
Jamie Bamber as Lee "Apollo" Adama (Colin Egglesfield, Jay R. Ferguson, Jason
    London, Charlie O'Connell, Casper Van Dien, Christopher Wiehl)
James Callis as Gaius Baltar (Xander Berkeley, Jon Cryer, Robert Knepper)
Tricia Helfer as Number 6 (Madchen Amick, Melinda Clarke, Sarah Lancaster)

BATTLESTAR: GALACTICA was first produced for television in 1978 starring Dirk Benedict as Starbuck and Richard Hatch as Apollo. For the series revival the role of Starbuck was changed into a female. Kerry Washington, Polly Walker, Sarah Shahi, Katee Sackhoff, Abby Brammell and Lori Heuring all auditioned for the part. Katee Sackhoff was chosen but, although she was already in great shape, was not in the shape she needed to be for the part. "She committed to working with a trainer and got in amazing shape," said casting associate Corbin Bronson.

Alan Alda, Alan Arkin, David Strathairn, Sam Shepard and Sam Neill were all considered to play Cmdr. William Adama. Ed Harris, Jon Voight, William Hurt and Donald Sutherland were all approached, but none had interest in doing a series. Roger Rees auditioned, but the part went to Edward James Olmos instead.

Jamie Bamber's competition to play Apollo included Jason London, Casper Van Dien, Jay R. Ferguson, Christopher Wiehl, Colin Egglesfield and Charlie O'Connell.

Jon Cryer, Xander Berkeley and Robert Knepper all read for the part of Baltar. Bronson thought that Knepper's audition was fascinating. The actor ultimately lost the part to James Callis.

Melinda Clarke and Sarah Lancaster were up for Number 6, as well as Madchen Amick. Amick came close to getting the part, but Tricia Helfer was eventually chosen.

Baywatch (1989-2001)

David Hasselhoff as Mitch Buchannon (William Katt, Lorenzo Lamas, Adrian
    Paul, Jack Scalia, Jan-Michael Vincent, Tom Wopat)
Shawn Weatherly as Jill Riley (Pam Bowen)
Jeremy Jackson as Hobie Buchannon (Leonardo DiCaprio)
Pamela Anderson as C.J. Parker (Paula Abdul, Sandra Bullock, Tia Carrere,
    Alexandra Paul)
David Charvet as Matt Brody (Dean Cain)
Brooke Burns as Jessie Owens (Julia Schultz)

THE PRODUCERS OF *BAYWATCH* saw just about every leading man in Hollywood for the starring role of lifeguard Mitch Buchannon. Tom Wopat, Lorenzo Lamas, William Katt and Adrian Paul were among those who auditioned. Executive producer Gregory J. Bonann was interested in Jack Scalia. Scalia told him that he wasn't the right guy for the part; he wasn't a California guy. Jan-Michael Vincent met with the producers, but they decided to keep looking. NBC suggested David Hasselhoff. Going in, Bonann didn't think he would work out. After their meeting Bonann was won over, and Hasselhoff walked away with the part.

Pam Bowen was hired to play lifeguard Jill Riley. She won the role over Shawn Weatherly, who was Miss Universe 1980. A problem arose when it became clear that Bowen had a severe fear of the water. According to Bonann, Weatherly had always been a solid runner-up, and was, in many respects, his first choice. Since the character of Jill was a lifeguard and had to perform in the water, Bowen was replaced by Weatherly. After that, the show never hired anyone without a swimming test.

After the first year, the show went from NBC to first-run syndication. The producers wanted to carry over as many of the actors as possible. The buyers of the show wanted it to be as much like the network version as possible. The show couldn't afford the huge ensemble and their huge salaries. The ones that did come over were the ones who agreed to pay cuts.

Brandon Call played Mitch's son Hobie from 1989-1990. Call got a leading role on the show *Step by Step*, and was unable to continue with the show. When the part was being recast, a young actor named Leonardo DiCaprio was brought under consideration. Although DiCaprio was talented, he lost the part because he was about six years too old for the role. He also didn't seem like Hasselhoff's son. Jeremy Jackson was cast instead.

Richard Jaeckel's character in the pilot went over very big with audiences. The producers wanted to bring him back. NBC said no, since the character died. The producers didn't care, and when the show went into syndication Jaeckel was back. Bonann said that he did not receive a single letter about it.

"After the first year of syndication, and our second year overall Billy [Warlock] and Erika [Eleniak] wanted to leave," said Bonann. "We were worried because the show seemed to be going well. We just didn't want to rock the boat. As it turns out that was one of our best pieces of recasting. The lesson learned is nobody really gives a shit who you replace, just so long as you replace them well. If you don't replace them well then everybody cares. If you replace them well, nobody says a word. In fact, many times they forget who was there before. So we replaced Billy and Erika with Pam [Anderson] and David Charvet. The rest is history."

Erika Eleniak had been a Playboy Playmate, and the producers were looking for an actress who was similar to her physically. Alexandra Paul came in to audition. Coincidentally, David Hasselhoff stopped in. He read

with Paul, and the two had great chemistry. Everyone loved her, but she said that
the part wasn't really for her. Writer/ producer David Braff came up with an idea.
He told everyone, "There's Mitch's new
boss." The others in the room were initially surprised by the idea, but decided
to create the part of Stephanie Holden for
Paul.

David Braff

The producers wanted to cast Tia Carrere as C.J. The only require-
ment was that she had to come in to be seen in a bathing suit beforehand.
Carrere refused, and lost the part.

Sandra Bullock was another contender for C.J. She was rejected because she didn't have the right look. Paula Abdul was also up for the part.
At 5'2", Abdul was deemed way too short. Pamela Anderson came in to
audition. Anderson had been scheduled to come in four times already,
but kept missing her audition. When she finally came in, she was asked
if she minded playing 90% of her scenes in a red bathing suit. Anderson
answered that she would work in the nude if she could. She got the job.

Bonann wanted Dean Cain to play Matt Brody. Casting directors Susie Glicksman and Fern Orenstein thought that David Charvet was the
better choice. Bonann didn't think that Charvet had the right look. He
ultimately decided that Glicksman and Orenstein knew what they were
doing, and the part went to Charvet.

Brooke Burns and Julia Schultz competed for the part of Jessie Owens.
Almost everyone involved thought that Schultz should be hired. Bonann
was the only one who preferred Burns. "Julia Schultz was the Playmate of
the Month in a motorcycle leather outfit that everybody loved because we
didn't have a tough girl," said Bonann. "We had just had this girl named
Jennifer Campbell play in a motorcycle episode called 'Point Doom.' Everybody loved this tough girl in a helmet with leather. She could get off

a bike and all that stuff. I said, 'Great guys. All well and good, but look at Brooke Burns. She is perfect. Her father is Brad Burns, a swimmer in Texas. She was on Ally McBeal for just a heartbeat as a fantasy girl. That's all she had done. She came in to read for *Baywatch* and just was spectacular. So we had this motorcycle girl, Julia Schultz, Playmate of the Month who was about 5'4", another petite blonde against Brooke Burns who was 5'10", stud swimmer, father was a swimmer, just as good an actress, probably better, and who looked like a lifeguard. I could not believe that a room full of about five other guys wanted the motorcycle chick. I couldn't believe it. And I just went nuts. I rarely did go nuts, but I went nuts. I said, 'I cannot believe you guys don't see the difference in these two girls. I don't care what the role calls for.' Everybody wanted a motorcycle chick, so they'd written a motorcycle chick. I said, 'Take the motorcycle away. This is the lifeguard. We're looking for another lifeguard, a young new lifeguard. She's just the best one we've seen.' And I went on to reference things like Alexandra Paul when she walked into the room and nobody was looking for her, etc. Then I hit the petite factor. I said, 'This girl cannot pick up another man and carry him up the beach.' Pulled everything out that I could. Finally, we read the two over and over again. I did have Susie and Fern on my side. I can't remember them being wrong, even when they were against me, which they were frequently. It just so happened that in this case they were on my side. That was the only support I had." Bonann was so passionate that the other producers gave in, and Burns got the part.

Yasmine Bleeth was cast as a guest star in an episode that was directed by Bonann. He was so impressed with Bleeth's work he called the other producers over to see her. They agreed to make her a series regular.

Gena Lee Nolin was auditioned multiple times for the part of Neely Capshaw. "We knew were going to give her the part, but we didn't want her to know," said Bonann. "She thought she was reading one last time. David came in and held up a sign [which read] 'You Got the Part.' The cameras in the room were the *Entertainment Tonight* cameras. She thought they were the audition cameras. We had a big deal going on just for a new cast member. At the same time the Australian Emmys were looking for a hostess. They offered her $100,000 to go do it. There she was, not even on our show yet; she'd never been on the air. But the new *Baywatch* girl was hosting the Emmy awards in Australia for more money than she would make the whole year with us."

David Braff went to his niece's wedding in Chicago. While there he met a comedian, who told him that he always wanted to be on *Baywatch*. Soon after, the show was having trouble casting the character of Larry Loomin' Large. Braff said that he met this guy in Chicago who could do the part. The show contacted the comedian, named Jeff Garlin, who was on his honeymoon. He canceled the honeymoon and came in to do the show. *Baywatch* was Jeff Garlin's first job in television.

Actress Tai Collins started the Camp Baywatch/A Chance for Children Foundation for underprivileged children with the help of Bonann and lifeguard Richard Mark. The camp has made a difference in the lives of many children. Information about the foundation can be found at www.achanceforchildren.com.

Behind the Camera: The Unauthorized Story of Charlie's Angels (2004)

Tricia Helfer as Farrah Fawcett-Majors (Brooke Burns, Lisa Robin Kelly)
Christina Chambers as Jaclyn Smith (Brooke Burke)

BEHIND THE CAMERA: THE UNAUTHORIZED STORY OF CHARLIE'S ANGELS was the story of the show's first season. It was a very tongue-in-cheek look at Aaron Spelling's quest to find the actresses to star in *Charlie's Angels*. Lisa Robin Kelly (of *That '70s Show*) auditioned to play Farrah Fawcett-Majors as did Brooke Burns. Burns really wanted the part. She was brought to audition for NBC. "Her nose wasn't like Farrah's," said executive producer Michael G.

Larkin, "so we had her test with a prosthetic nose." Burns auditioned about six times, but eventually lost the part to Tricia Helfer.

Brooke Burke read for the part of Jaclyn Smith. Said Larkin, of her competition Christina Chambers, "Christina was so remarkably similar to Jaclyn Smith that she was hands down the winner."

Dan Castallaneta's audition so knocked out the producers Larkin and Matt Dorff that he was practically given the role of Aaron Spelling on the spot. Castallaneta is best known as the voice of Homer Simpson on *The Simpsons*.

Wallace Langham was cast to play Fawcett's manager Jay Bernstein. He played Bernstein a year earlier in the made-for-TV movie *Behind the Camera: The Unauthorized Story of Three's Company*, also for NBC.

Behind the Camera: The Unauthorized Story of Mork & Mindy (2005)
Robert Clarke as Conrad Janis (Conrad Janis)

CONRAD JANIS PLAYED Mindy's father Fred McConnell on *Mork & Mindy* for the show's entire run (1978-1982). Years later Janis visited writer David Misch with whom he had worked with on the show. The two worked on *Mork & Mindy* together. Misch was now working on a TV movie based on the series. Janis looked much the same in 2005 as he did in 1978, and was asked to play himself in the movie. He passed on the offer, and Robert Clarke played him instead.

Behind the Mask (1999)

Donald Sutherland as Bob
    Shushan (Marlon Brando)
Matthew Fox as James Jones
    (Vincent D'Onofrio, Chris
    Penn, Sean Penn, Gary
    Sinise)

Tom McLoughlin

DIRECTOR TOM McLOUGH-
LIN was offered the chance to
direct the CBS movie *Behind the
Mask.* "I wasn't doing TV movies
at that time," said McLoughlin.
"I had been doing them for nine
years and I needed to go back to
my feature career. Then I got a
phone call saying that, although
I don't do TV movies, would I like
to meet with Marlon Brando? I asked if he was really going to do the film. I was
assured that he really wanted to do this part, and that he liked my work. He just
needed to meet with me. I said, 'Okay, fine. I'd love to meet with Brando.' I had
a three-hour meeting with him, and he was aboard. We had an incredible cast.
The fact that Brando was doing it, there wasn't an actor in Hollywood - Sean
Penn, Chris Penn - the list of people that wanted to do this thing just went on
and on, until Marlon got cold feet (as he always does) and pulled out. So then
it became Donald Sutherland in the lead. We needed somebody to play this re-
tarded character that Gary Sinise and Vincent D'Onofrio were going to do. Les
Moonves put his foot down and said, 'Nope. I want Matthew Fox from *Party
of Five.* I said, 'But this kid has not done anything.' He was a model and then he
did *Party of Five.* 'I have incredible concerns about this very, very difficult part.

Plus, the character's written with no teeth. You're going to take a really good looking actor and make him unrecognizable.' He was insistent. So I said, 'Well, until I meet with Matthew I don't feel confident about saying yes and putting him onto the set.' As it turned out, he was really humble, really smart about how difficult this was going to be. He wanted as much guidance and help with the role because he also had to be doing *Party of Five* at the time we were shooting this in Vancouver. He had to fly back and forth, so it was really a lot on his plate. But he ended up being incredible."

Ben Casey (1961-1966)
Vince Edwards as Ben Casey (Russell Johnson)

RUSSELL JOHNSON CAME close to landing the title role of Doctor Ben Casey. He eventually lost the part to Vince Edwards.

Benson (1979-1986)
Missy Gold as Katie Gatling (Tracey Gold)

SISTERS TRACEY AND MISSY GOLD both auditioned to play Katie Gatling on *Benson*. Missy was chosen. In 1985 Tracey also got a regular role on a series when she was cast as Carol Seaver on *Growing Pains*.

The Beverly Hillbillies (1962-1971)
Irene Ryan as Granny Clampett (Bea Benaderet)

PAUL HENNING WAS A WRITER and producer of *The Bob Cummings Show*. He had always had a fascination with hillbillies. Producer Martin Ransohoff wanted to buy the rights to Ma and Pa Kettle for a television series. Filmways executive Al Simon told Ransohoff that Paul Henning was from the Ozarks, and suggested they meet. Ransohoff told Henning about his idea. But Henning said he didn't want to do a show about Ma and Pa Kettle; he would rather create his own characters. He came up with a show called *The Beverly Hillbillies*. Jim Aubrey, then the head of CBS, thought the show was great, and agreed to put it on the air.

Henning was interested in Bea Benaderet to play Granny. Irene Ryan was also under consideration, and gave a great audition. Benaderet herself thought that Ryan was a better choice for the part. The producers agreed, and Ryan was cast. Benaderet also joined the cast as cousin Pearl Bodine.

Max Baer, Jr. auditioned for the part of Jethro Bodine. Baer did not have the accent needed for the part, and pretended to be hoarse at his reading. He was asked to come back and read again in a few days. Baer got a Jonathan Winters album and an Andy Griffith album to listen to their voices. He did a combination of them at his audition. He was asked to test for the part. Before his test he went out to lunch with Irene Ryan, who bought Baer a couple of martinis. Baer went for his test. He read a scene with Buddy Ebsen, who was already signed for the starring role of Jed Clampett. The martinis affected Baer, who was not a big drinker. He bumped into a doorjamb and said excuse me to it. Nevertheless, Baer's test was impressive and he was signed for the part.

Beverly Hills 90210 (1990-2000)

Shannen Doherty as Brenda Walsh (Gabrielle Carteris, Kristin Dattilo)
Jason Priestley as Brandon Walsh (Bryan Dattilo)
James Eckhouse as Jim Walsh (Lyman Ward)
Jennie Garth as Kelly Taylor (Kellie Overbey, Tori Spelling)
Tina Lifford as Felicity Ashe (Angela Bassett)

BEVERLY HILLS 90210 followed teenagers Brandon and Brenda Walsh, who just moved from Minnesota to Beverly Hills. Real-life brother and sister Bryan and Kristin Dattilo were offered the roles of the Walsh twins as a package deal. Kristin was offered another show at the same time (*Hull High*), which she accepted instead.

Gabrielle Carteris came in to audition for the part of Brenda. She lost the role, but was cast as brainy Andrea Zuckerman instead.

The network was concerned that they might have to postpone the show because they couldn't find actors to play the twins. However, executive producer Aaron Spelling's daughter, Tori Spelling, had seen the movie *Heathers*. In the cast was Shannen Doherty. Tori suggested her for Brenda. Doherty came in and won the part. Bryan Dattilo screen tested with Doherty, but the role of Brandon was given to Jason Priestley instead.

Lyman Ward was originally cast as Brenda and Brandon's father, Jim Walsh. Ward was fired after the pilot was shot. His scenes were reshot with James Eckhouse.

Tori Spelling wanted to join the cast. Instead of asking her father for a part, she auditioned under a different name. She read for the part of Kelly Taylor. Also up for Kelly was Kellie Overbey. The part went to Jennie Garth instead. Tori Spelling was cast in the very small role of Donna, who was not a regular character. "Everyone knew who Tori Spelling was," said director Tim Hunter. "The plan was always to give her that small part." Spelling did well as Donna, and was soon made a permanent member of the cast.

The producers decided they needed another character, and wrote the James Dean-like role of Dylan McKay. Luke Perry auditioned to play Dylan. Aaron Spelling wanted to hire Perry, but Fox didn't think he was right. Spelling paid Perry's salary himself for two years in order to get the network to okay him.

Angela Bassett auditioned for a guest spot as Felicity Ashe. The role went to Tina Lifford instead.

Bewitched (1964-1972)

Elizabeth Montgomery as Samantha Stephens (Tammy Grimes)
Dick York as Darrin Stephens (Richard Crenna, Dick Sargent)
Sandra Gould as Alice Kravitz (Alice Ghostley)

TAMMY GRIMES WAS SOUGHT to play witch Samantha Stephens in the upcoming series *Bewitched*. She chose to do the play *Blithe Spirit* instead and turned down the part. At the same time producer/director William Asher and his wife Elizabeth Montgomery wanted to make another series. Their show was about a rich girl in love with a garage maintenance man. Executive producer Harry Ackerman wasn't interested in their show, but suggested they make *Bewitched*. "Bill and Elizabeth wanted to work together," said Herbie J. Pilato, author of *The Bewitched Book*. "Harry Ackerman presented the script. They loved it and history was made."

Dick Sargent told Pilato that he was approached before Dick York to play Darrin Stephens. He had to turn it down because he was committed to, ironically, *The Tammy Grimes Show*. However, William Sher said that York was always the first choice (although Richard Crenna was also considered).

Dick York sustained a back injury during the shooting of the 1959 film *They Came to Cordura*. He never recovered from it, and as a result was forced to leave the show in June of 1969. "He had missed, up to that point, about fourteen episodes of the show through the previous five years," said Pilato. "So what they did is they took those fourteen episodes and they played them out that summer without Darrin. When the fall of '69 approached Dick Sargent was just in place. ABC and everybody figured, 'Well, they weren't going to notice,' but we did!"

Alice Pearce was the original Alice Kravitz. Sadly, she died of cancer. Bill Asher asked Alice Ghostley to replace her as Mrs. Kravitz. Ghostley was good friends with Pearce, and felt uncomfortable with the idea. She turned the part down, but later came on the show as housekeeper Esmeralda.

Irene Vernon played Louise Tate in the first two seasons of the series,

Herbie J. Pilato
Photo: Sam Campanaro Photography

when Danny Arnold produced *Bewitched*. When he left the show to do *That Girl*, Irene Vernon was let go. According to Pilato, being replaced by Kasey Rogers devastated Vernon. She left her career in show business and went into real estate.

The Stephens children, Tabitha and Adam, were played by two sets of twins. David and Greg Lawrence played Adam, while Erin and Diane Murphy played Tabitha. "From what I understand, according to David and Greg Lawrence, allegedly they are the illegitimate sons of Tony Curtis," said Pilato.

Diane Murphy eventually left the show, leaving the role of Tabitha solely to Erin Murphy. Pilato said that Diane wasn't all that interested in continuing with the show, and that Erin started to look more like Elizabeth Montgomery.

Bewitched was a smash hit. The series is still in reruns to date. Its huge following led to the 2005 feature film version of the show, also called *Bewitched*. The movie follows the story of two actors starring in a remake of the classic show. Nicole Kidman plays the actress cast as Samantha. Kidman's character in the film is also a witch. Herbie J. Pilato was a consultant on the film.

Beyond the Break (2006-)

David Chokachi as Justin Healy (Greg Evigan, William Katt, Rick Springfield)

DAVID CHOKACHI'S COMPETITION for the part of surfing instructor Justin Healy included Rick Springfield, Greg Evigan and William Katt.

The Bionic Woman (1976-1978)

Lindsay Wagner as Jaime Sommers (Farrah Fawcett, Sally Field, Stefanie Powers)

LINDSAY WAGNER ORIGINATED the part of Jaime Sommers, the bionic woman, on the March 16, 1975 episode of *The Six Million Dollar Man*. Writer Kenneth Johnson named the character after a water skier at Sea

World. Johnson was told that the episode should end with Jaime dying, like the hit film *Love Story*. Audiences loved her so much that the facts were later changed; Jaime hadn't died. She suffered brain damage, and didn't remember that she had been in love with Steve Austin.

The character was extremely popular and Wagner was brought back to the show. It was eventually decided that Jaime should have her own series, *The Bionic Woman*. However, Wagner's contract had lapsed. Farrah Fawcett, Sally Field and Stefanie Powers were considered as possible replacements, but the actress the audience fell in love with was Wagner. Since she was so in demand, she was very highly paid for the series (about $25,000 an episode). Wagner won the Emmy for Outstanding Lead Actress in a Drama Series for her work on *The Bionic Woman* in 1977.

B.J. and the Bear (1978)

Claude Akins as Sheriff Lobo
    (Andy Griffith)

BRUCE BILSON DIRECTED THE 1978 made-for-television movie *B.J. and the Bear*. The 100-minute NBC movie served as the pilot for the series. Greg Evigan was already cast in the starring role of B.J. when Bilson was hired. Bilson had been an assistant director on *The Andy Griffith Show* in the 1960s. He tried to get Griffith to play Sheriff Lobo.

Bruce Bilson

Griffith wasn't interested, and the role eventually went to Claude Akins, who Bilson describes as "a wonderful guy."

Blossom (1991-1995)
Mayim Bialik as Blossom Russo (Jenna von Oy)

JENNA VON OY ORIGINALLY auditioned for the title role of teenager Blossom Russo. According to Executive Producer Tony Thomas, von Oy was much more right for the part of Blossom's best friend Six LeMeure. Von Oy was hired to play Six, while Mayim Bialik was cast as Blossom.

Bob Patterson (2001)
Jennifer Aspen as Janet (Susan Diol, Jennifer Grant, Elizabeth Perkins)

ELIZABETH PERKINS, JENNIFER GRANT and Susan Diol were all up for the role of Bob Patterson's ex-wife Janet. Diol won the role, but was later replaced by Jennifer Aspen.

Bodies of Evidence (1992-1993)
George Clooney as Ryan Walker (Lee Horsley)

BODIES OF EVIDENCE creator David Jacobs worked with Lee Horsley on the show Guns of Paradise. "When it went off, I wanted to do something else for him," said Jacobs. He wrote the part of Detective Ryan Walker in Bodies of Evidence for Horsley to play. At the time Lee Horsley wasn't sure if he wanted to do another series. David Jacobs got George Clooney to play Walker instead, although the network wasn't sure Clooney had enough authority for the part. Horsley later changed his mind, and Jacobs wrote another role for him to play - Lt. Ben Carroll.

The Bold and the Beautiful (1987-)

Ronn Moss as Ridge Forrester (Daniel McVicar)
Dylan Neal as Dylan Shaw (Eddie Cibrian)

DANIEL MCVICAR AUDITIONED for the original cast of *The Bold and the Beautiful* in 1986. He screen tested for the part of Ridge Forrester along with Ronn Moss. Moss was chosen instead. "He's the perfect Ridge," said McVicar. The role of Clarke Garrison was created for Daniel McVicar.

Eddie Cibrian lost out to Dylan Neal for the part of Dylan Shaw.

Sarah Buxton starred on *Sunset Beach* as Annie for the entire run of the show. *The Bold and the Beautiful* executive producer Brad Bell watched her on the show. One month after *Sunset Beach* went off the air the role of Morgan DeWitt on *The Bold and the Beautiful* was created for Buxton.

Boston Legal (2004-)

Monica Potter as Lori Colson (Sarah Buxton)
Jayne Taini as Maxine Berleth (Marianne Muellerleile)

SARAH BUXTON WAS CONSIDERED for the part of attorney Lori Colson on *Boston Legal*. She was called back a few times, but the part ultimately went to Monica Potter instead.

Marianne Muellerleile was offered the guest role of Principal Maxine Berleth on the November 1, 2005 episode called "Witches

Marianne Muellerleile

of Mass Destruction." Muellerleile was already committed to shooting a national commercial and had to turn it down. She loved the show, and was sorry to be unavailable for the episode.

The Bourne Identity (1988)
Jaclyn Smith as Marie St. Jacques (Lesley-Anne Down)

LESLEY-ANNE DOWN MET with director Roger Young to discuss the part of Marie St. Jacques in the 1988 ABC movie *The Bourne Identity*.

Roger Young

Young brought his wife along for the meeting at a restaurant in Malibu. "She was dressed very provocatively," said Young of Down. "It was sort of a strange lunch. I would say 'strained lunch,' after which I called the producer and said no. She called somebody at the network and said, 'All he did was look at my breasts.' That was reported to me by the producer. I said, 'You should have seen what she was wearing. I'm sure I did look at her breasts. But my wife was with me and so was her husband.'" Jaclyn Smith was eventually hired for the role.

The Boy in the Plastic Bubble (1976)

Diana Hyland as Mickey Lubitch
  (Ellen Travolta)

Ellen Travolta

JOHN TRAVOLTA WAS cast in the starring role of Tod Lubitch in the TV movie *The Boy in the Plastic Bubble*. He wanted his sister Ellen Travolta to play the part of Tod's mother Mickey Lubitch. "My agent was Diana Hyland's agent," said Ellen. "The network wanted Diana Hyland. John and I had just done *Bus Stop* on the road. He did not know Diana Hyland. He thought it would be a good idea if I was the mother. My agent called me and said, 'Bubby, this is a role that's important to her,' and at the time she was sick. 'The network wants her.' So I knew something was wrong. I called John and said, 'You know I think you'd better back off with this because they don't know me, John. Maybe this is the wrong thing.' So he didn't ask for me anymore, and then Diana Hyland came aboard, and he fell in love with Diana Hyland."

Sadly, Hyland was diagnosed with breast cancer. She died in Travolta's arms on March 27, 1977. Later that year Hyland won the Emmy for her work in the film. John Travolta accepted the award on her behalf.

Boy Meets World (1993-2000)
William Russ as Alan Matthews (Matt McCoy)

BEN SAVAGE STARRED as adolescent Cory Matthews in the ABC series *Boy Meets World*. Matt McCoy was originally cast as Cory's father, Alan Matthews, but was replaced by William Russ before the show hit the air.

The Boys (1991)
James Woods as Walter Farmer (Jack Lemmon, John Ritter)
John Lithgow as Artie Margulies (Walter Matthau, Henry Winkler)

RICHARD LEVINSON AND WILLIAM Link were writing partners for many years. Together, they created memorable television series, including *Columbo, Murder, She Wrote* and *Mannix*, as well as Broadway musicals and feature films. "Dick died tragically," said Link. "He couldn't give up smoking. We were together for 42 years. We saw each other more than we saw our wives. We met the first day of junior high school. It was devastating to me. Devastating. I'd never written with anybody else...The first script I wrote after his death was *The Boys*. ABC immediately said, 'We'll do it.' I produced it for my own company. Casting we knew was crucial; it always is. I don't care how good your series concept is, how good the other people are, and who the director is, when you cast it, that lead is it. We were thinking early, and my agent Bill Haber, who's now the big Broadway producer, he was really behind us because he felt Dick's loss too. We wanted Henry Winkler with his good friend John Ritter. Now I thought they were both terrific. I thought that would have been a very good combination. I met with both. I don't remember why it didn't work; I would have definitely gone with them. It was other commitments or something. Haber's client was Jimmy Woods. I was always a big fan. Sent him the script and he immediately said yes. Then I bumped into him. He said yes on a Friday. I was having lunch with some people in the Valley the following Sunday and he walks into the restaurant and said, 'It's an honor to do this.' So I felt very good. John Lithgow's name must have come up on a list 'cause I was a fan of him too. To me it was a dream cast, and I thought the picture turned out very well with them.

"Dick and I were friends with Walter Matthau. After Dick died Walter called and said, 'Let's get together for lunch.' He invited me to the Maple Drive Tennis Club. He'd gotten a script of *The Boys*. He said, 'I want to play this and I'll get Jack Lemmon to play the other writer. I said, 'Walter, that would be beyond the dream cast. But this is for TV. I can't pay you guys. I don't have the money.' So that was that. It would have been a small feature then. We had the commitment. I couldn't do anything."

The Brady Bunch (1969-1974)
Robert Reed as Mike Brady (Gene Hackman, Jeffrey Hunter)
Florence Henderson as Carol Brady (Joyce Bulifant)
Ann B. Davis as Alice Nelson (Kathleen Freeman, Monte Margetts)

THE BRADY BUNCH creator Sherwood Schwartz wanted Gene Hackman to play the starring role of architect Mike Brady, eventually played by Robert Reed. At the time Paramount had never heard of Hackman. "Later he did *The French Connection*, and then he never looked back at television," said Schwartz. "I liked him very much. He had a more rugged quality than Bob Reed. I didn't want just a handsome guy. I wanted somebody you could believe as an architect, not a clothes model." Film star Jeffrey Hunter was interested in the role. "He was too handsome," said Schwartz. "I wouldn't take him because he was too handsome. In the meeting I had with him, a casting meeting, it was really funny because he's trying to show me that he has little wrinkles around his eyes; he's not as handsome as he used to be. I was kidding; he had a great sense of humor too. I said, 'I know your problem about handsomeness. I suffer from the same problem!' I'm certainly not handsome. We joked about that. He was serious. He said, 'I'm getting older now and I think I could do it.' I said, 'To tell the truth, if this was a show in which this guy is a model for shirts or something in an advertising agency I'd give you the part. But I wanted a more rugged kind of quality. You're just too good looking and young.' So that was the end of that."

Robert Reed had a deal with Paramount. They considered him for two other pilots: a television version of the hit Neil Simon play *Barefoot in the Park*, in which he would play the lead, and *Houseboat*, in which he was to play the part Cary Grant played in the film. Neither pilot came to fruition. According to Schwartz, Reed felt he was stuck with *The Brady Bunch*.

Schwartz wanted Florence Henderson to read for the part of Carol Brady. Henderson was unavailable to test, and had to turn down the offer. The part went to Joyce Bulifant. Soon after, Henderson found a way to make it to the audition. Schwartz agreed to see her. Everyone involved thought that Henderson was better for the part, and Bulifant was replaced. "Just a little difference in the character of one person changes other people in the show. I had sort of a straight housekeeper [Monty Margetts] because Joyce Bulifant is funny. Florence Henderson is not automatic funny. She can do comedy lines and she's fine with that. But she doesn't walk in a room and everyone starts to laugh. But that happens with Joyce Bulifant. Now that I had Florence Henderson, and I was happy with her, I realized that I couldn't have a straight lady in the kitchen. In order to justify kitchen comedy I needed a comedienne. Ann B. Davis was in San Francisco doing comedy club stuff. Paramount says, 'She's got another 2-3 weeks to go. How important is she to the show?' And I said, 'Does the word crucial mean anything to you, because she's crucial.' There were only two people who could play that part, really. Kathleen Freeman could do it easily, but I preferred Ann B. Davis, and she was great.

"So I wound up with a very good cast. The problem there that I had was I had to get six kids. Casting kids is very different than casting grown-ups. If you're talking to a 5-6-year-old girl, you can't ask her, 'What have you done for the last 20 years?' So that's tough casting. And then I had the additional problem; at that point in the show's history I didn't know whether Mrs. Brady was going to be blonde or dark-haired. And I had to cast the kids first because there were so many of them. I was casting all that summer to find the six kids. And I had to get twelve kids. I cast three blonde girls and three dark-haired girls, and the same with the boys in reverse. So I had twelve kids. I spent the whole summer just looking at these kids. It's pretty quick. You're sitting with a 11-year-old boy or girl; you find out in about 60 seconds whether they're really bright and capable of being on a soundstage without getting involved in everything except the show, because they can't keep their minds on one thing at a time. I devised an idea, which worked very well with young kids. I put toys on the coffee table between us, and then I would ask them different questions. Before you know it, they were disregarding me and starting to play with the toys. You can't have that if you're trying to do a show. They have to be focused. So that was my adventure there."

The show ran for five years. "The show went off the air after five years because, first of all, Paramount had already decided to look for a different father," said Schwartz. "Bob Reed was such a problem. Every week he was up in the executives' office complaining about the script. The scripts had gotten us to be as good a family show as you can write and produce. And he kept complaining because there was no reality. He came from a lawyer show [The Defenders], which has to be accurate. Comedy can't be accurate. You have to exaggerate certain things and he could never stand that."

"If we were renewed, and if I wanted to continue, we would have to replace Bob Reed," said Schwartz. "That came after the final episode of the show. He made changes in the script. He wanted a whole new script the day of shooting. And he was impossible. Paramount said, 'We can't deal with him anymore.' I said, 'Neither can I, to tell you the truth.' I had to force his agent to admit that Bob Reed said he would not do this episode, because Paramount didn't want to pay him for that episode. They didn't want to pay him for reruns of that episode. I just simply wrote him out of the script. I took his lines in different scenes and gave them to Florence Henderson or Ann B. Davis. The show was intact except he wasn't in it. It happened to be a show in which he was very light in the show. I was shaving in the morning when his agent called me and said, 'No, he would not do the show.' I said, 'Okay, remember that now.' I finished shaving and on my way from my house to Paramount I'd already decided which scenes could go and which scenes could stay. By the time I got there I just had my secretary just take down the changes and within two hours everybody got new scripts and he was gone. Except he hung around there. It was very awkward, and it reached a point where I asked him please to stay out of the cast's eyeline. They're looking at you and realizing you didn't want to do this show. Finally, Paramount called me and said, 'Do you want us to physically take him off the set?' And I said, 'No. I'll deal with it. I don't want to see six kids watch as two guards lift him up and take him off the set. He just hung around and hung around. He finally gave up after 4-5 hours. He left and we just continued with the shooting.' The decision was eventually made to cancel the series. *Sanford & Son* was causing *The Brady Bunch's* ratings to dip, and the show was canceled."

The Brady Bunch Hour (1977)

Geri Reischl as Jan Brady (Eve Plumb)

EVE PLUMB CHOSE NOT to reprise her role of Jan Brady for the variety show *The Brady Bunch Hour*. At the time she wanted to do other things. The part was recast with Geri Reischl. *Brady* creator Sherwood Schwartz thought this show was a bad idea. Schwartz, who wasn't involved, said that it made no sense for Mike Brady, an architect, and his family to have a variety show on television. The show didn't make it to a second season.

The Bradys (1990)

Leah Ayres as Marcia Brady Logan (Maureen McCormick)

THE BRADYS FOLLOWED the Brady family in 1990 as they dealt with more serious issues than were addressed on *The Brady Bunch*. CBS insisted on airing the show at 8:00. Sherwood Schwartz wanted a later time slot, saying that this new show was a different type of *Brady* show. It had a serious theme, unlike the original, which was a comedy. He lost the battle and the show went on at 8:00 p.m. where, according to Schwartz, it died.

Maureen McCormick rose to fame playing Marcia Brady in *The Brady Bunch*. McCormick reprised her role in *The Brady Bunch Hour, The Brady Girls Get Married, The Brady Brides,* and *A Very Brady Christmas,* as well as in an episode of the series *Day By Day*. When she was asked to appear in the new dramatic series, *The Bradys,* McCormick declined. Leah Ayres replaced her.

Brian's Song (1971)

Billy Dee Williams as Gale Sayres (Lou Gossett, Jr.)

THE ROLE OF CHICAGO BEARS halfback Gale Sayres was initially cast with Lou Gossett, Jr. The future Oscar winner hurt himself training, and was replaced by Billy Dee Williams. Williams' work in the film was critically acclaimed. He was nominated for an Emmy for his performance.

Brideshead Revisited (1981)

Jeremy Irons as Charles Ryder (Tom Conti, Nigel Havers)
Anthony Andrews as Sebastian Flyte (Jeremy Irons)
Diana Quick as Julia Flyte (Kate Nelligan, Charlotte Rampling)
Nickolas Grace as Anthony Blanche (Simon Callow)
Stephen Moore as Jasper (Charles Dance)

PRODUCER DEREK GRANGER invited Michael Lindsay-Hogg to tea to discuss directing *Brideshead Revisited*. Lindsay-Hogg was thrilled and said yes. "The central issue was the casting," said Lindsay-Hogg. "I'd seen a play in the West End. It was written in the 1800s, early 1900s. It was a picaresque comedy. Playing in it was Jeremy Irons. He played a kind of foppish younger brother in the play. I thought he was a very funny actor. I said to Derek, 'I think I've got us our Sebastian.' Jeremy came in to meet us. He was dressed in a wonderful overcoat, and looked like an actor from the 1920s, very glamorous. We said, 'Here's the script we have at the moment. Have a look at it.' He knew the book. 'Do you want to play Sebastian?' After however long it was he came back and said, 'Yeah, it sounds great.' Then we were casting. Obviously we were looking for Julia, and obviously we were looking for Charles Ryder. The first person we thought of for Julia at the time was also someone who was doing very well in England. Some-one who was also a rising young woman star in the theatre, Kate Nelligan. Kate was interested for a while. She was sort of in place. Then we looked for Charles. Charles was a tricky one, especially early on. The early scripts didn't have any voice-over narration, and so he really didn't have much to do except go around and say dialogue. It wasn't his story yet, the way it had to become, because that's how the book is, which came in a bit later. We're going on and we don't really have a Charles. We're thinking who could it be? Then we saw a picture of Evelyn Waugh when he was a young man on a motorbike. He looked a bit like Malcolm McDowell. We made an approach to Malcolm. His movie career was doing fine. He was always getting interesting offers, and he didn't want to get involved in a television series. Not that he was against television, 'cause he did it. He didn't want a long-term commitment.

"Kate Nelligan was sort of interested, and Jeremy's playing Sebastian. I had seen a production of *The Taming of the Shrew* in the theatre, where Alan Bates played Petrucchio. Nickolas Grace played a comic character called Biandello. It's useful to see actors in the theatre because actors who work in the theatre have less protection than actors who work in television or movies, i.e., they're not as close up and they can't do it again. It's a different test for the actor. You get the measure of the actor a bit better. The part of Anthony Blanche, which is such a key part in the story about his being the person who sounds the warning notes to Charles Ryder, Simon Callow came in and met us. He's a wonderful actor and an entrancing human being. We thought maybe it would be good for Simon. I had got sort of hooked in my mind on a kind of quality that Nick Grace had. He was able to show a mean kind of wit. He's very, very funny. You needed to have a funny man play Anthony Blanche if you could get it. We saw other actors, of course, and it was very close in our minds between Simon and Nick. Then in the end Nick got it. It's just one of those funny things. Simon would have been wonderful also, but Nick got it.

"There was a moment when Tom Conti was maybe going to play Charles Ryder. He was in a play, and it didn't look like he could really do the dates.

"We're still looking for Charles Ryder, and time is going on. Kate Nelligan called up one day and said, and she's still not committed, but we're friends, she said she'd seen a television program the night before. She said Jeremy was in it, and was really good. She said, 'Maybe he could do your Charles Ryder.' Derek and I thought that was interesting. By that time we were starting to know we were going to have the voice-over to make it more attractive to the actor. We knew Jeremy was a good actor. We knew he was funny and he was quick. We also had a sense that in the serious moments he'd be good as well. We got him to come in. The clock is now ticking because we had a production start. On a production that size you have to hit the date running. We started out in Malta, which means you have to book hotels, you have to arrange airfares. There's a whole machinery going on underneath the top bit of the machinery. We had a start date of somewhere near the end of April of '79. We had to make that, and now we're probably talking at the end of February. We had, like, seven weeks to go. We had a lot of parts to cast. We had to rehearse them and costume them. We want to get things figured out. Kate's not sure. She's got, maybe, a movie offer. We say to Jeremy, 'Wouldn't it be great if you played Charles Ryder?' He said, 'I'm not sure. I don't think so, because I really love the part of Sebastian. I know what I can do with that.' We haven't made the switch yet; he's not sure he wants to do it. At that point Kate drops out. We don't have a Julia and we don't have a Charles. After thinking about it, and a great deal of persuasion on our part (because we genuinely thought he would make a great Charles), he said he would.

"We meet for Julia, Charlotte Rampling. She was very interested, and of course we were very interested in her. She's a wonderful actress. We had a really good meeting, and she's very bright and has a wonderful look. But she just married a young French musician, somewhat younger than her. We got the sense she didn't really want to be standing in a field in Yorkshire while he's over in Paris. She said no. We don't have a Julia, and we're looking for a Sebastian. It was a time, certainly with television and theatre to some degree, when most of the actors were playing what I call proletarian parts. Working man parts. There was a sort of movement which was not in favor of playing, what I would call aristo characters. Socially, at the time, there was just a lot of labor unrest in the country. There had been three-day work weeks. This is the beginning of Margaret Thatcher. A lot of actors didn't like these characters, and couldn't do the voice. A lot of them, no matter where they came from, were affecting working-class accents. That's the kind of drama that was being written. We met a lot of the few of them that might be able to do that. There was a good actor who we met who was quite close to getting it called Nigel Havers. Very bright and very nice actor. Derek and I were thinking. I then thought if Jeremy is playing Charles, and if Nigel is playing Sebastian -this isn't a question at all of talent. I thought their faces are very, very similar in construction. I thought if I'm cutting between Jeremy and Nigel it's sort of going to look like the same person. It wouldn't be the same person; they'd both have totally different qualities, but I was just worried that there was a physical similarity between the two men, which wouldn't serve us. It had nothing to do with Nigel's talent. Whilst this has been going on, an actor called Anthony Andrews had been to see us. He said, 'I'm the right person for Sebastian.' We'd had Jeremy in our minds for a long time for Sebastian, with those particular lean, sort of wolfish, foppish looks as it were. We weren't sure that Anthony was right. He had a rounder face - I mean a very good-looking man, but we weren't sure. So we don't have a Julia, we have a Charles and we don't have a Sebastian, and now the clock is really ticking. I'm not in England because I'm over here doing the American production of *Whose Life Is It Anyway?* I'm sort of commuting. Derek sends me a tape that Anthony Andrews had sent him. At that time Anthony hadn't done any theatre that we knew of. He was doing quite well in English television. He then had a hit in a series called *Danger UXB*, where he played a bomb disposal expert in World War II. He sent us this tape in which his character had a nervous breakdown. He was really wonderful. I'm in America, Derek's in England. We also discussed the fact that Anthony didn't have what I called the Nigel problem. He has a totally different facial construction than Jeremy. Very good looking; fuller face. It wasn't going to be the same look. We knew Jeremy had the chops for it from working in the theatre. We weren't as familiar with Anthony's work, but we thought he was really, really good on the tape. We thought, 'Let's roll with this one.'

"Jeremy had blondish hair at the time and Anthony had brownish hair. We thought it should actually be the other way around. We thought blond would probably make Anthony more dashing. Anthony Andrews went and had his hair dyed blond. The weekend before he was to fly to Malta he sat out in the garden of his home with his wife. He didn't wear a cap. Because of the reaction to his hair from the sun, his hair turned green. When he got to Malta, he had green hair. There are scenes that we shot early on, which eventually we dumped, with him wearing a cap until we could get his hair in shape.

"There was one day when we were meeting actors for some of the other parts like Kurt, Sebastian's lover, the doctor in Malta. These were some of the parts we would be needing pretty early on. We're meeting several actors over a period of days for these parts. On this particular day just before we start the casting session one of the ADs comes in and says we have a problem with British Airways, in that they had block booked twenty seats on the airplane going to Malta. To keep the seats they had to issue the tickets to the real names of the actors flying. That particular day every actor who came in got cast because we had to get them on the plane.

"Another actress who was doing very well was Diana Quick. Diana, at that time, was in a romance with Albert Finney. They had taken a trip down the Amazon, something like that. We want to offer the part to Diana, because it's now getting close. We couldn't get her because she's on the Amazon or somewhere. But eventually a script does get taken out to her by runners. She reads it and says yes."

Stephen Moore played the part of Jasper. "We cast an actor called Charles Dance to play the part," said Lindsay-Hogg. "He played it to start. Then there was a strike, which happened, and all the production was shut down for four months. Charles wasn't able to come back to it because he got another job, so then it was played by Stephen Moore."

The Bronx Zoo (1987-1988)
Kathleen Beller as Mary Caitlin Callahan (Kim Delaney)
Jerry Levine as Matthew Littman (Matthew Broderick)

MATTHEW BRODERICK WAS OFFERED the part of math teacher Matthew Littman on The Bronx Zoo, but turned it down. Jerry Levine auditioned for the same role. "My feeling was not to be denied," said Levine. "I went in and hit a home run. I knew it, it felt good to me." Levine got the job.

Kim Delaney was cast as Mary Caitlin Callahan, the art and drama teacher. A pilot was shot. "Kim Delaney was beautiful, great. I loved working with her," said Levine. When Levine came back to work after the pilot, he was surprised to learn that Kathleen Beller had replaced Delaney.

Brooklyn Bridge (1991-1993)

Marion Ross as Sophie Berger (Olympia Dukakis, Lee Grant, Joan Plowright)
Danny Gerard as Alan Silver (Leonardo DiCaprio)
Peter Friedman as George Silver (William H. Macy)

BROOKLYN BRIDGE WAS THE STORY of creator Gary David Goldberg's childhood in Brooklyn, New York. Paramount wanted a very funny actress to play the pivotal role of the grandmother Sophie Berger. Goldberg had just directed Olympia Dukakis in the movie *Dad*. She was the first choice for the role. Although Dukakis loved the script, she didn't want to commit to a weekly series. The next choice was Joan Plowright. After a lengthy period of negotiations it fell apart. "We were really scrambling," said executive producer Sam Weisman. "Around the same time I had been involved in some idea for a show that Henry Winker was trying to produce. He brought me in on it. We had a meeting with Marion Ross because she was interested in trying to do this show. So we met with Marion and I really just loved her. I went to Gary and said, 'I had this meeting with Marion Ross. You know Marion Ross could really play the part of your grandmother.' He first laughed. 'That's ridiculous. She's such a shiksa.' Then he started to think about it. I said, 'She's really strong, really funny. There's something about her that's very similar to Joan Plowright.' So we brought Marion in to read. She comes in and she looks like a Sherman Oaks housewife. She's got that Hollywood, Valley feel with all that white clothing and white shoes. Couldn't be more wrong. Plus, she's very strong and tall. She didn't feel Jewish at all. She comes in. There's something about her that's so warm. We sent her away. We said, 'Would you be willing to work with a dialect coach?' So we hired this fabulous woman named Jessica Drake. Marion had private sessions with Jessica Drake and she came back in dressed differently and she read again. She was a lot better. By that time we were already building the sets and we still didn't have anybody. We arranged to screen test two people. Like literally shoot filmed screen tests. The first was Lee Grant. Lee Grant comes in and she was this famous actress and it was like the anti-Sophie. She was very dramatic and very strong. She just didn't have the vulnerability. On another day we brought Marion in and put her in wardrobe and got a wig and everything. All of a sudden, as we were shooting she just began to play with the accent and with the character. Almost like a workshop. She really began to find it. I just felt that was it. It was always very elusive with her because she sometimes would approach a scene totally wrong. But ultimately I thought she was incredible."

The casting director pushed hard for a young actor to play the central role of Alan Silver. "He came in," said Weisman. "He was this great kid, really cute. But we just couldn't see him as part of a Jewish family. He was so enthusiastic about the script and so eager to do it we brought him in to read twice. Then, because we didn't have a pilot, when the network affiliates were meeting to announce their schedule, CBS needed something to show. We put together a multimedia presentation that included vintage footage from Brooklyn in the '50s, '50s music, photographs, all collaged together with dialogue from the pilot. We had to get some actors in to record the dialogue. So this kid who had come in – I said, 'Why don't we bring him in?' So we paid the actors $75. They came in for, like, half an hour or something and recorded the dialogue. And the kid who recorded the lead part, the teenage boy, this enthusiastic kid who had come in to read . . . Leonardo DiCaprio."

William H. Macy read for the part of Alan's dad, George Silver. Producer Brad Hall knew Macy from Chicago. Macy knew he wasn't right for the part. The role went to Peter Friedman instead.

The part of Alan's girlfriend Katie Monahan was based on Gary David Goldberg's wife. Jenny Lewis had been on the short-lived show *Shannon's Deal*, created by John Sayles. Casting director Judith Weiner told Sam Weisman that he had to see Jenny Lewis. Weiner brought in a tape of the pilot episode of *Shannon's Deal*. Weisman watched one scene. He thought Lewis was so great that he and Goldberg offered her the part without even having to audition.

The Brotherhood of Poland, New Hampshire (2003)
Chris Penn as Waylon Shaw (Brian Haley)

BRIAN HALEY WAS originally cast as Waylon Shaw in *The Brotherhood of Poland, New Hampshire*. The pilot was not working, and Haley was fired. "Waylon was brooding, troubled. He was the comedy equivalent of the wacky neighbor. He was the obvious fix," said Haley. "[Series creator] David E. Kelley said that I was

Brian Haley.
Photo: Laura Warfield

Emily Cutler

not the problem, and that he loved my work. It was the luck of the draw." Chris Penn was hired to replace Haley.

Brothers and Sisters (2006-)

Sally Field as Nora Walker (Betty Buckley)
Matthew Rhys as Kevin Walker (Jonathan LaPaglia)

THE ORIGINAL PILOT for *Brothers and Sisters* featured Betty Buckley as Nora Walker and Jonathan LaPaglia as Kevin Walker. When the series hit the air, they were replaced by Sally Field and Matthew Rhys.

Brother's Keeper (1998-1999)

Bess Meyer as Dena Draeger (Emily Cutler)

EMILY CUTLER AUDITIONED for the costarring role of sports agent Dena Draeger on *Brother's Keeper*. She lost the job to Bess Meyer. Cutler was brought on in Season 2 in a guest role of a pregnant woman. Not long after Cutler switched careers from actress to writer/producer. She has been very successful, with shows such as *Entourage* and *Less Than Perfect* under her belt.

Buddies (1996)

Christopher Gartin as John Butler (Jim Breuer)

DAVE CHAPPELLE AND JIM BREUER were both under contract to Disney Studios. Winddancer Productions was asked to create a series for them, which resulted in *Buddies*. Before the show hit the air, Breuer was replaced by Christopher Gartin.

Buffy the Vampire Slayer (1997-2003)

Sarah Michelle Gellar as Buffy Summers (Julie Benz, Katie Holmes)
Alyson Hannigan as Willow (Riff Regan)
Charisma Carpenter as Cordelia Chase (Sarah Michelle Gellar, Bianca Lawson)

JULIE BENZ AUDITIONED for the title role of vampire-slaying high-school student Buffy Summers. She failed to win the part, but was later cast as the vampire Darla. "I met Katie Holmes," said casting director Marcia Shulman. "A manager had found her in a model competition. He sent me Katie Homes. I said, 'I have found Buffy.' But Katie was, at that point, seventeen. Then I was told by the production people that Buffy had to be legally eighteen because there was going to be long hours and night shoots. I had to get off Katie Holmes. She just couldn't work the hours. However, the following year, when I got *Dawson's Creek* Katie Holmes was the first person I went to."

Marcia Shulman knew Sarah Michelle Gellar since the actress was four years old. She thought that Gellar was a very good actress. As a teenager Gellar won a Daytime Emmy for playing the role of nasty Kendall Hart on *All My Children*. According to Shulman it was a no-brainer to have Gellar come in for the role of the nasty Cordelia. "Sarah was just so terrific, and she had such star quality," said Shulman. The decision was made to move her to Buffy.

Bianca Lawson competed with Charisma Carpenter to play Cordelia. "The one thing that was really surprisingly good about Charisma is, I knew she could be bitchy, and I knew she could be beautiful but I didn't know how funny she was. And she just really made us laugh."

Riff Regan played Willow in an unaired pilot for the series. Marcia Shulman explained why Alyson Hannigan replaced Regan: "We just thought, after we saw the pilot, that everybody in the cast so embodied their roles. We just thought we didn't quite get Willow right."

The character of Angel was described as the hottest, sexiest, most mysterious guy on the planet. It was the day before the shoot, and Shulman hadn't found who she thought was the perfect actor for the part. A friend of Shulman's called her to tell her that a guy who walked his dog outside of his house was the right guy. The friend sent over David Boreanaz. As soon as Shulman saw him, she knew he was right. She took him to series creator Joss Whedon and the producers for a reading. They didn't see what Shulman saw in Boreanaz. Shulman offered to be fired if he was the wrong choice. Whedon agreed to give him a try. Shulman turned out to be right. Boreanaz was so good as Angel that the character was spun off into his own series, *Angel*.

Burke's Law (1994-1995)

Peter Barton as Peter Burke (Dan Cortese)

Burke's Law producer/director James L. Conway directing an episode of one of the *Star Trek* series.

THE 1994 SERIES *Burke's Law* was a continuation of the 1963 series *Amos Burke, Secret Agent*. Gene Barry reprised his role of cop Amos Burke. For the part of Burke's son Peter, the choice came down to two actors: Peter Barton and Dan Cortese. According to co-executive producer James L. Conway, the network liked Cortese, while executive producer Aaron Spelling wanted Barton. Out of respect to Spelling, CBS executive Jeff Sagansky yielded and gave the job to Peter Barton.

Tucker Smallwood

Café Americain (1993-1994)

Valerie Bertinelli as Holly Aldridge (Holly Fulger, Jessica Lundy, Jessica Tuck, Julie White)

HOLLY FULGER, JESSICA LUNDY, Jessica Tuck and Julie White all went to the network to audition for the starring role of waitress Holly Aldridge. Said Fulger, "It was a horrible experience. You went into this teeny little room. There were about 25 people in there. It was so creepy and spooky." The network rejected all of them and gave the part to Valerie Bertinelli instead.

Cagney & Lacey (1981-1988)

Carl Lumbly as Mark Petrie (Tucker Smallwood)

TUCKER SMALLWOOD WAS considered for the supporting part of Det. Mark Petrie on *Cagney & Lacey*. The role instead went to Carl Lumbly. Besides being an accomplished actor, Smallwood is also a former soldier and a writer. Smallwood served in the U.S. Army Infantry from 1967-1970, and commanded a Mobile Advisory Team during the Vietnam War. His book, *Return to Eden*, contains 33 essays about his tour of duty in Vietnam, his life afterwards and his return to Vietnam in 2004.

Campus Confidential (2005)

Katey Sagal as Naomi Jacobs (Melanie Mayron)

Campus Confidential starred Christy Carlson Romano as Violet Jacobs. Violet and her mother Naomi just moved from the city to the suburbs. Director (and actress) Melanie Mayron considered playing the part of Naomi Jacobs herself. The producers thought that would be too hectic for her, and the role went to Katey Sagal instead.

Carnivale (2003-2005)

Clancy Brown as Brother Justin Crowe
(Bruce Davison, Keir Dullea,
Edward Herrmann)

Tim DeKay as Clayton Jones
(Matthew Fox)

Clea DuVall as Sofie (Marguerite
Moreau)

Amy Madigan as Iris Crowe (Frances
Fisher)

Patrick Bauchau as Professor Lodz
(Michael Jeter)

Keir Dullea

CARNIVALE TOLD THE STORY of a traveling carnivale in the 1930s Dust Bowl. The final candidates for the part of Brother Justin Crowe were Bruce Davison, Keir Dullea, Edward Herrmann and Clancy Brown. The producers felt that Brown could play the power and badness the part required and gave him the job.

Matthew Fox tried for the part of Clayton Jones, but lost out to Tim DeKay.

Marguerite Moreau auditioned to play Clea DuVall's role of fortune teller Sofie.

Frances Fisher came close to landing the part of Justin Crowe's sister, Iris, eventually played by Amy Madigan.

Michael Jeter and Patrick Bauchau competed for the part of Professor Lodz. The two men were completely different types. The producers went with Bauchau, who gave the character a more upper-class feel.

The Carol Burnett Show (1967-1978)

Vicki Lawrence as Mama (Carol Burnett)

ONE OF THE MOST POPULAR recurring sketches on *The Carol Burnett Show* was the one in which Vicki Lawrence played Mama. Burnett played her daughter Eunice and Harvey Korman was Eunice's husband Ed. The part of Mama was originally intended for Burnett. She decided she would rather play Eunice, so Mama went to Vicki Lawrence. The sketches were so popular that Mama eventually (in 1983) got her own show, a sitcom called *Mama's Family*.

The Champions (1968)

Alexandra Bastedo as Sharon Macready (Annette Andre)

ANNETTE ANDRE WAS considered for the part of biologist Sharon Macready on the 1968 NBC series *The Champions*. The part eventually went not to Andre, but to Alexandra Bastedo.

Andre worked steadily as an actress throughout the 1960s, '70s and '80s. In 1989 she married writer/producer Arthur Weingarten. The two have both been active with the Born Free Foundation, an international wildlife charity working throughout the world to prevent wild animal suffering and to protect threatened species in the wild.

Annette Andre
Photo: Carole Latimer

Charles in Charge (1984-1990)

Scott Baio as Charles (Michael J. Fox)

MICHAEL J. FOX WAS BRIEFLY considered for the title role of Charles, eventually played by Scott Baio.

Baio wanted Ellen Travolta to play his mother. The producers wanted to see them together. They pulled footage from *Happy Days* and *Joannie Loves Chachi*. Travolta played Baio's mother in both of those series. The producers agreed to do one episode with her. Not long afterwards Travolta was made a series regular.

Charlie's Angels (1976-1981)

John Forsythe as Charlie Townsend (Gig Young)

Shelley Hack as Tiffany Welles (Barbara Bach, Shari Belafonte, Judith
    Chapman, Debbie Feuer, Claudia Jennings, Dian Parkinson, Michelle
    Pfeiffer, Suzanne Reed, Deborah Shelton)

Cesare Danova as Frank Bartone (Fernando Lamas)

CHARLIE'S ANGELS FOLLOWED three police-trained female detectives working for the mysterious Charlie Townsend, who they only communicated with on a speakerphone. Executive producers Leonard Goldberg and Aaron Spelling thought that Kate Jackson would be ideal for the part of angel Sabrina Duncan. They knew her already, and thought that her intelligence, along with her beauty worked well for the character.

When Leonard Goldberg ran Columbia Pictures Television they had a talent development program. One of the actresses in the program was Farrah Fawcett. Goldberg and Spelling later did a movie for television that she was in. "When you looked at Farrah you just went, 'Wow!'" said Goldberg. "She would be the wow factor in *Charlie's Angels.*"

Since they had already cast a brunette and a blonde, Goldberg and Spelling wanted a redhead to play the third angel. They later discarded the idea. "In both the series and the movie the first two parts came together very quickly, and the last part was hard," said Goldberg. "Finally, I think my wife may have mentioned to me that she saw this beautiful model on a commercial. As beautiful as she was, that's how likeable she was. And in television likeability is very, very important because unlike a movie theater, which is like a fantasy experience, you watch television in your own home. And you're going to watch them every week hopefully, and so they have to almost become like your friends. You're sitting there in your pajamas and there they are. Jackie [Jaclyn Smith] came in and read for us. She wasn't really an actress; she had just done a few parts. She was a model. But she was so gorgeous and likeable."

Goldberg and Spelling didn't realize how big a hit the show would be. The pilot episode got huge ratings. Farrah Fawcett was the breakout star of the show. Goldberg remembers that during shooting he noticed Fawcett looking tired and asked her about it. She told him that on the weekends she was doing a great deal of publicity. Goldberg suggested that from then on she only agree to do the interviews if she was on the cover and if she had semi-approval of the story. About a month later Goldberg saw her again, looking just as tired. He asked her what happened. She told him they all said yes.

After the first season, Fawcett decided to leave the show. "Although the show was a big hit," said Goldberg, "she was the hottest angel. We didn't know what

Leonard Goldberg

was going to happen. How would the public look at it? Would they look at it as if it was the network's fault, the producers' fault or her fault? Who was going to come out bad? I got a call that summer before we were going to go on the air for our second season from Michael Eisner, who was running Paramount at the time, Paramount movies. And he said, 'You're going to be interested in this. We did a test screening in Cincinnati of a movie we have called *Saturday Night Fever.*' I didn't know anything about the movie. He said, 'There's a scene where [John] Travolta's getting dressed to go out, and we cut to a shot. He's looking at a picture on a wall and it's Farrah's famous poster. The audience booed. So I think you're going to be all right.' That was encouraging news."

The producers decided to write Fawcett's character off and introduce a new character. Cheryl Ladd stepped right in. "Cheryl, who was previously known as Cheryl Stoppelmoor, did her first part for us in *The Rookies,*" said Goldberg. "We were somewhat familiar with her. She had then married David Ladd. She was gorgeous and a good actress."

After the third season Kate Jackson decided to leave the show. Jackson had been offered the role of Joanna Kramer in *Kramer vs. Kramer.* The show could not allow her the time off she needed to do the film. Meryl Streep was cast, and won an Oscar for her performance. Goldberg said that Jackson left the show in a gracious manner.

Many actresses auditioned to replace Jackson, including Judith Chapman, Debbie Feuer, Michelle Pfeiffer, Dian Parkinson, Deborah Shelton, Suzanne Reed and Claudia Jennings. Shari Belafonte and Barbara Bach were also considered, but the role eventually went to Shelley Hack. Coincidentally, at the time, Hack was appearing on a popular commercial for a perfume called Charlie.

Gig Young was hired to play the mysterious Charlie Townsend. Young had personal problems and was unable to do the job. He was quickly replaced by John Forsythe.

Fernando Lamas was offered a guest-starring role in the September 29,

1976 episode of the show called "The Mexican Connection." Lamas wasn't interested in the part of drug lord Frank Bartone and said no. Cesare Danova was cast in his place. "I loved Fernando," said Goldberg. "I thought he was a great guy. I always remember when he was directing The Rookies I came on the set one day. He said, 'Leonard, how are you?'" I said, 'I don't feel so good. I think I have the flu.' He said, 'It doesn't matter how you feel; it's how you look. You look marvelous.' He actually said that." In the 1980's Billy Crystal was a regular on *Saturday Night Live*. During his tenure on the show he appeared in many skits as Fernando Lamas, in which he repeatedly said the catch phrase 'You look marvelous.'

Sally Kirkland appeared in two episodes of the show. She was a student of the renowned acting teacher Lee Strasberg. Strasberg had discouraged his students from acting on television, saying that great actors only did theater and film. After her episode aired Kirkland went to The Actor's Studio, Strasberg's acting school. Said Kirkland, "He told the class, 'You can do our level of excellence and method acting on episodic television. She had me teary eyed watching her with Cheryl Ladd.'" Kirkland has continued to work in television as well as films. "You have to keep reinventing yourself," she said. "Television gives you a large canvas to do that."

Charmed (1998-2006)

Shannen Doherty as Prue Halliwell (Jamie Luner, Cari Shayne)
Alyssa Milano as Phoebe Halliwell (Shannen Doherty, Lori Rom)
Rose McGowan as Paige Matthews (Soleil Moon Frye, Jennifer Love Hewitt, Denise Richards, Tiffani Thiessen, Susan Ward)
Ted King as Andy Trudeau (Julian McMahon, Kerr Smith)

CONSTANCE M. BURGE created *Charmed*, which focused on three sisters who just happened to be witches. Jamie Luner and Cari Shayne were considered for the role of the oldest sister Prue Halliwell. Shannen Doherty was originally considered for the role of the youngest sister Phoebe. Doherty loved the script, but preferred to play Prue. *Charmed* was produced by Aaron Spelling. Spelling made Doherty a star when he cast her in the lead role of Brenda Walsh on his show *Beverly Hills 90210*. She was allegedly let go from that show because of questionable behavior. Spelling brought Doherty in for a meeting to discuss *Charmed*. She told the producers she would not be a problem to work with. Doherty also suggested her best friend, Holly Marie Combs, for the part of Piper Halliwell. Spelling cast Doherty and Combs, which surprised some of the series' producers who had no idea Doherty and Combs were even being considered. A 28-minute presentation was shot with Lori Rom as the third sister Phoebe. The series was picked up. At that point Rom spoke with producer/director Les Sheldon and told him that she didn't feel she could continue with the series. The WB wasn't happy, but they agreed to let Rom out of her contract. Alyssa Milano was asked to replace her. However, Milano was shooting *Fantasy Island* in Hawaii and was unavailable when *Charmed* would need her. In the nick of time the two productions were able to work it out and Milano joined the cast of *Charmed*.

In 2001 Doherty left the show. A new character named Paige Matthews was added to fill the void. Tiffani Thiessen, Jennifer Love Hewitt, Soleil Moon Frye, Susan Ward and Denise Richards were all considered for the part, but the only offer was made to Rose McGowan. Although McGowan had a big indie film following, she had never done a series before. She joined the cast, and the show ran for five more years.

Julian McMahon and Kerr Smith auditioned for the part of Andy Trudeau. Smith was too young for that role, but later joined the cast as Kyle Brody. McMahon was also cast in *Charmed*, as Phoebe's first husband Cole Turner. Andy Trudeau was played by Ted King.

Cheers (1982-1993)

Ted Danson as Sam Malone (William Devane, Fred Dryer)

Shelley Long as Diane Chambers (Julia Duffy, Lisa Eichhorn)

Nicholas Colasanto as Coach (Sid Caesar, Robert Prosky)

George Wendt as Norm Peterson (John Ratzenberger)

Woody Harrelson as Woody Boyd (John Philbin, Timothy Treadwell)

Kirstie Alley as Rebecca Howe (Colleen Camp, Kim Cattrall, Marg
   Helgenberger, Madolyn Smith, Sharon Stone)

Sharon Lawrence as Rachel (Peri Gilpin)

FORMER FOOTBALL PLAYER Fred Dryer was up for the starring role of baseball player-turned-bar owner Sam Malone in *Cheers*. However, Dryer was relatively new to acting. There was some concern that he wouldn't be able to carry the new series. Ted Danson and William Devane were the top two candidates. Devane, the better known of the two at the time, was the front-runner. An NBC executive thought that Danson was not a leading man. Devane auditioned for NBC reading a scene in which Sam is behind the bar. The actor wanted to play the scene barefoot. During his test Devane dropped and broke a glass. Without any shoes on Devane was distracted by the broken glass on the floor. His timing was off, which resulted in his losing the part to Danson.

About 150 actresses auditioned to play the uptight Diane Chambers. The choices were finally narrowed down to three: Lisa Eichhorn, Julia Duffy and Shelley Long. Although all three actresses were very good, the role went to Long.

John Ratzenberger read for the part of accountant Norm Peterson. It was the actor's first audition and he felt it didn't go well. He asked the producers if they had a bar know-it-all character. He spent about ten minutes improvising the character. A couple of days later Ratzenberger got a call saying they were going to incorporate his character in the show. The role of mail carrier (and know-it-all) Cliff Clavin was created for him, while George Wendt won the part of Norm.

Robert Prosky was asked to play the part of Coach Ernie Pantusso. "I accepted for two days," he said. "Then I realized that's all I would do with my career because I thought it was very good. The casting was good. The writing was good. I turned it down, which is a no-no out there. Indicative of their quality, they accepted that. Every other day I rethought the decision. But I would not have done all the feature films I did, or the Broadway that I've done or all the other things. It's been a very varied career." In the last season of the show Prosky was called in to play navy captain Franklin Howe, the father of Rebecca Howe.

Nicholas Colasanto was cast as Coach, although Sid Caesar was also considered. Sadly, Colasanto died on February 12, 1985 at the age of 61. Later that year a new bartender was added to the cast named Woody Boyd. John Philbin was called in to audition. Said Philbin, "I wasn't really interested in TV. My agent Steve Dontanville thought it would be good for me to meet them. I read five times. I loved the material. I was more surprised than anyone that it kept moving forward. Is this a job I want? I had a screen test with Ted. The screen test was new material. I didn't relate to the new material. I was told they were going with someone else, but I

John Philbin

knew that. I met Woody Harrelson at the audition. When he told me his real name was Woody, I said, 'Your name is Woody. This is your job!'"

Today, John Philbin is writing scripts, producing movies and looking for an acting job in television. He has an interesting website, which can be found at www. prosurfinstruction.com.

The 2005 documentary *Grizzly Man* told the story of Timothy Treadwell. For thirteen summers Treadwell lived among grizzly bears in Alaska. In the film Treadwell's father is interviewed. He said that

Robert Prosky
Photo: Stone Photography

Treadwell auditioned for Woody on *Cheers*, and that losing the role destroyed him. Five years after Woody Harrelson joined the cast of *Cheers*, Treadwell spent his first summer with the bears. He loved them, and dedicated his life to protecting them. Tragically, Treadwell and his girlfriend Amie Huguenard were attacked and killed by a grizzly bear on October 6, 2003.

In 1987 Shelley Long decided to leave *Cheers*. The producers wanted to wait until hiatus to cast a replacement character unless there was someone they wanted. Casting director Jeff Greenberg had seen Kirstie Alley play Maggie in Tennessee Williams' *Cat on a Hot Tin Roof* at the Mark Taper Forum. He suggested her for the role of Rebecca Howe. This new character was conceived as the exact opposite of Diane Chambers, both physically and emotionally. Greenberg contacted Alley's agent. At the time Alley had been offered a deal at every network and passed on all of them. But she was interested in joining the cast of *Cheers*. With Alley in mind as a prototype, audition scenes were written. Since she had already turned down an offer from NBC, they couldn't mention her to the network unless they were sure she was the one they wanted. On a Saturday she came to Paramount to read a scene with Ted Danson and a scene with Rhea Perlman. Her audition impressed the producers, and they wanted to move forward and offer her the part. By the time they brought her up to NBC, Alley was in Canada shooting a movie. Since she was unavailable to come back for a reading for the network, NBC vetoed Alley. Colleen Camp was considered. Other actresses were brought in to audition, including Sharon Stone, Marg Helgenberger, Kim Cattrall and Madolyn Smith. NBC thought that Smith was the best choice. Series creators Glen Charles, Les Charles and James Burrows still wanted Kirstie Alley. They were finally able to convince NBC. The network said yes, but would not approve the amount of money her agent was asking for. After more than a month the deal was finally made.

Peri Gilpin auditioned to play the guest role of sex addict Rachel on the May 13, 1993 episode called "The Guy Can't Help It." Gilpin lost the part to the better-known Sharon Lawrence. Not long after Gilpin was cast as Roz Doyle on the *Cheers* spin-off, *Frasier*.

Chiefs (1983)

Brad Davis as Sonny Butts
   (Robert Blake)

Jerry London

ROBERT BLAKE WAS CON-SIDERED for the supporting role of Sonny Butts in the 1983 miniseries *Chiefs*. Director Jerry London had another actor in mind - Brad Davis. "No one would consider him," said London. Davis had a wild reputation. London met with Brad Davis, and the two had a long talk. London kept interviewing other actors, but ultimately decided Davis was the right choice. London put his reputation on the line and hired him. He did not regret his choice. At the end of shooting the whole crew applauded Davis. Davis was so overcome he broke down. London was very glad he went out on a limb for Brad Davis.

China Beach (1988-1991)

Marg Helgenberger as K.C. (Meg Foster)
Concetta Tomei as Lila Garreau (Cristine Rose)
Chloe Webb as Laurette Barber (Chandra Wilson)

MEG FOSTER READ FOR the part of heroin-addicted hooker Karen Charlene 'K.C.' Koloski. According to casting director John Levcy, "We were very high on her." Ultimately, Foster was not approved by the network, and lost the part to Marg Helgenberger.

Chandra Wilson was originally cast as singer Laurette Barber. She was let go and a replacement was needed. Chloe Webb was considered for the part. Webb didn't know if she wanted to do a series. The network wanted to see film on her. They were shown Webb starring as The Sex Pistols' Sid Vicious' girlfriend Nancy Spungen in the film *Sid and Nancy*. They were alarmed, but ultimately agreed she was the right choice for the part.

Concetta Tomei was given the part of Maj. Lila Garreau, although Cristine Rose had also been considered.

The Chris Isaak Show (2001-2004)

Kristin Dattilo as Yola Gaylen
    (Sabrina Lloyd, Anne
    Ramsay, Katy Selverstone)
Jed Rees as Anson Drubner
    (Justin Louis)

Kristin Dattilo

SINGER CHRIS ISAAK PLAYED himself in *The Chris Isaak Show*. His real band members played all of his band members on the show. The only exception was the character of Anson Drubner. Justin Louis was considered for the part, which was eventually played by Jed Rees.

Sabrina Lloyd was offered the part of Yola Gaylen, but

turned it down. Kristin Dattilo was a strong contender for the role. Although she felt her studio audition was not great, she was still called back to test for the network. Her competition was Anne Ramsay and Katy Selverstone. "They said they knew I was the girl," said Dattilo, who landed the job.

A Christmas Visitor (2002)
William Devane as George Boyajian (Keith Carradine)

DIRECTOR CHRISTOPHER LEITCH was in Toronto during the Toronto Film Festival in 2002. He ran into Keith Carradine and approached him about the possibility of starring in A Christmas Visitor. "He was really up for doing it," said Leitch. "I had never really met him before. You find yourself standing next to someone with a drink in their hand and you say, 'Hey, I really love your work. I'm here prepping a movie for Hallmark. I think you'd be great for it.' The next thing you know he's going, 'Well, yeah. I'm available. That sounds great.' We took the negotiations pretty far with Keith. It just hit a sticking point with the network where they would not budge. It was over money. It wasn't a lot of money; but they wouldn't go for it. So then we found ourselves quickly approaching first day of principal photography without a lead actor." At that point casting director Reuben Cannon suggested William Devane, who took the job.

Cinderella (1997)
Brandy as Cinderella (Whitney Houston)

WHITNEY HOUSTON HAD the idea to make a television version of Cinderella. Houston planned to play the title role herself; however, her busy schedule became a problem. By the time the film was ready to go into production it was decided that she was better suited to play Cinderella's fairy godmother, and Brandy was hired for the title role of Cinderella.

Circus Boy (1956-1957)
Micky Dolenz as Corky (Paul Williams)

MICKY DOLENZ' FATHER, George Dolenz, was an actor. His agent would send Micky out on auditions occasionally. One of the auditions was for a show called *Circus Boy*. Dolenz, who was about eleven at the time, almost didn't go because he wanted to play baseball that day. He gave a good audition, and was asked to screen test. Dolenz got the job, but was asked to change his name and dye his hair. He went by the name Micky Braddock (the name of a great-uncle) for the series. Ten years later Dolenz went to the same building to audition for another series called *The Monkees*.

Many years after *Circus Boy*, Paul Williams told Micky Dolenz that he had also auditioned to play Corky. Williams jokingly told Dolenz that he never forgave him, because he also auditioned for *The Monkees*, which again Dolenz got and Williams didn't. The two worked together on the stage version of *Bugsy Malone* in England, which Dolenz wrote and directed. Williams wrote the music and lyrics for the stage version as well as for the 1976 film the musical was based on.

The Class (2006-2007)
Sam Harris as Perry Pearl (Bill Brochtrup)

BILL BROCHTRUP AUDITIONED for the part of Perry Pearl in *The Class*. The role was given to Sam Harris instead.

Cristian de la Fuente auditioned for the guest role of Aaron. "I went for the audition," he said. "I was a long shot. It wasn't supposed to be Latino. The name is not Latino at all - Aaron. When I was in the waiting room, everyone was so different. When you don't know what they're looking for the chances of getting it are less. So then I went in and I did my read. Jeffrey Klarik, one of the producers, was there. I felt like he liked what

I did because he responded. If you audition for a sitcom and they're laughing, that means you're on the right path. The casting director was having fun. We all had a lot of fun with the read, and I had the feeling that I could get it. I went home and then my manager called me and said that they really liked it, and that maybe I was going to get it. Then I got it.

"In the pilot I was in one scene to establish that my partner was gay. They decided to bring me back and then I was in almost all of the first eight episodes. A lot of people think I'm a regular, but I'm not."

Cristian de la Fuente

Clouds of Witness (1972)

Ian Carmichael as Peter Wimsey (John Neville)

IAN CARMICHAEL WANTED very much to play detective Peter Wimsey. The actor tried to get a program on the air in England, but was rejected numerous times. After five years the BBC finally decided to develop a show about Wimsey. However, the producer wasn't interested in Carmichael. John Neville was his choice. The producer eventually left the show. Richard Beynon was the new producer. Beynon thought that Carmichael was the ideal choice and gave him the part.

Coach (1989-1997)

Craig T. Nelson as Hayden Fox
   (Dabney Coleman, Ronny
   Cox, Ron Leibman, Gerald
   McRaney, Burt Reynolds,
   Tom Skerritt)
Shelley Fabares as Christine
   Armstrong (Shelley Smith)

DABNEY COLEMAN WAS
considered for the title role
of Minnesota State University football coach Hayden
Fox. The producers worried
that Coleman came off as a
little too hard edged. Executive Producer Sheldon Bull
explained that the film *9 to
5* (in which Coleman played

Sheldon Bull

the villainous boss) was still fresh in people's minds. They decided to
continue searching for an actor the audience might find more likeable.
Burt Reynolds was briefly considered. Tom Skerritt and Ronny Cox auditioned, as did Gerald McRaney and Ron Leibman. Leibman was so impressive that he was called back to audition for ABC. Craig T. Nelson's
name came up as another possibility. He had recently appeared in the series *Call to Glory*, and was not known for doing comedy. ABC dismissed
him as a dramatic actor at first, but eventually came around and gave him
a chance. He was so good that the choice finally came down to Nelson
and Gerald McRaney. Nelson was victorious. McRaney was soon cast in
the starring role of John MacGillis on the sitcom *Major Dad*.

Shelley Smith auditioned to play Hayden's girlfriend, TV newswoman

Christine Armstrong. According to Bull, "Shelley Smith was delightful. But she was more breakable. Shelley Fabares softened Craig. She could stand up to Craig." Fabares got the job.

Columbo (1971-1978)

Peter Falk as Columbo (Lee J. Cobb, Bing Crosby)

RICHARD LEVINSON AND William Link created *Columbo.* "When we got out of the Army, the peacetime Army in 1959, we were with the William Morris Agency," said Link. Their agent knew Peter Falk. "Peter was starting out and doing a lot of good television out of New York," he continued. "In those days some of the stuff was still live. Sometimes we used to have breakfast with Peter. We really respected his work. We thought he was a very interesting actor. Then we went out here [California]. We were under contract to Four Star, which was a small firm that Dick Powell ran (although they had thirteen series on the air, which was more than any other much bigger production company). There was a writer's strike I think in 1960 and we had to go on strike. It was going to be a very long one; we could see that coming so Dick and I went back to New York, 'cause we loved New York. We didn't like it out here. There was a loophole in the Writer's Guild contract. You could write for live television, not film. There was a mystery show called *The Chevy Mystery Show.* It was a replacement for Dinah Shore, which was a big variety show. And it was one of the first color shows, Dinah Shore. So we wrote a mystery called 'Enough Rope' and sent it to them. They bought it and it was on. We came out here, we watched it live - they did it in Burbank. Then we figured this would be a very easy adaptation as a stage play, because for live television you had very few sets and few characters. So we wrote a stage play. It was immediately produced by Paul Gregory. Thomas Mitchell, the old character actor, played Columbo. We had a hell of a cast: Joseph Cotten, who was

then a big movie star, played the murdering psychiatrist. Agnes Moore-
head played the wife that he kills. It was a very successful play. It played
a year and a half. It didn't go to Broadway because we wouldn't allow the
producer to bring it in, because he didn't let us make rewrites. We didn't
care at that point. We sold it to Universal a couple of years later. We were
not producers then. We sold it, we adapted our stage play. And then the
question was - Who's going to play Columbo? We wanted Bing Crosby.
He had a terrific sense of humor, which the cop had. Instead of the cigar,
the pipe, because he was famous for that pipe. He was a very good actor.
He won the Academy Award for *Going My Way*. We sent him a script.
He was very nice. He sent us a letter back saying it was very good, but
he heard television was a rat race and that wasn't for him. He was playing golf. He really left the business. He was doing like, one special a year
I think for CBS. Now we were stuck. Who could play him? We thought
maybe Lee J. Cobb. He was under contract to Fox. He was very bulky and
New York and gruff. Didn't see the humor in him. Luckily, we didn't cast
him because he died not that long after. Bing Crosby died eight years later.
It was good Crosby didn't want to do it either. We were in our office at
Universal and the phone rang and it was Falk. He was with William Morris; he was still there. We weren't with Morris anymore. He said, 'I got
hold of this script of yours, and I got to tell you, Bill, I'll kill to play that
cop.' So, we thought, you know, he's very intelligent, 'cause obviously the
character has a mind like a computer. Peter's smart as a person, and he's
definitely got the humor, even though he had played mostly heavies up to
that point. But we knew he had the humor. He was very New York; he had
the accent even though he grew up in Ossining and they don't have New
York accents there, so figure that one out! We said, you know he could be
very, very interesting, and that was it. He didn't read. He'd just done his
first feature and he was immediately nominated for the Oscar. That's how
that happened."

Complete Savages (2004 2005)
Vincent Ventresca as Jimmy Savage (Robert Carradine)

COMPLETE SAVAGES starred Keith Carradine as Nick Savage. Carradine's real-life brother, actor Robert Carradine, was turned down for the part of Nick's brother Jimmy. Both Robert and Keith were baffled, since Robert gave a very good audition. It's also hard to imagine that someone else would be more believable playing the brother of Keith Carradine than his real brother! The role was eventually given to Vincent Ventresca.

The Confession (1999)
Ben Kingsley as Harry Fertig (Patrick Stewart)

WRITER DAVID BLACK wanted Ben Kingsley to play the starring role of Harry Fertig in The Confession. At the time Kingsley was doing the play Waiting for Godot in London. His representatives were contacted, but Black was told that Kingsley wouldn't do the film. David Hugh Jones was hired to direct. Jones had previously run England's Royal Shakespeare Company, and was good friends with Kingsley. He sent the script directly to Kingsley, and the actor said yes. Later on Black met with Patrick Stewart. Stewart told him that Jones had wanted him to play Harry. Although Stewart was considered, the only actor Black wanted for the part of Harry was Ben Kingsley.

Cosby (1996-2000)
Phylicia Rashad as Ruth Lucas (Telma Hopkins)
Doug E. Doug as Griffin Vesey (Glenn Plummer)
T'Keyah Crystal Keymah as Erica Lucas (Audra McDonald)

BILL COSBY FOLLOWED UP his immensely popular series, The Cosby Show,

with a show called *Cosby*. Phylicia Rashad played his wife in both
shows. However, Rashad wasn't the
first actress cast as Ruth Lucas in
Cosby. Telma Hopkins had the part
first. In fact, there was a whole other
pilot, which never got on the air.
Audra McDonald was cast as Erica
Lucas, the daughter of Cosby's character, while Glenn Plummer had the
role of Erica's friend, Griffin Vesey.
The decision was made to recast the
show. T'Keyah Crystal Keymah was
doing a play out of town with Lorraine Toussaint and CCH Pounder.
When she got home her agent told
her they were revamping Cosby's new

T'Keyah Crystal Keymah

show, and that they wanted her to come in and read for the daughter. Keymah won the part. Doug E. Doug replaced Plummer as Griffin.

The Cosby Mysteries (1994)

Alice Playten as Oona Dowd (Rita Moreno)

THE COSBY MYSTERIES premiered as a two-hour TV movie, which served as
the series pilot. Writer/producer David Black suggested Alice Playten for the
part of the housekeeper Oona Dowd. Bill Cosby told Black that the part was
perfect for Rita Moreno. Cosby and Moreno had worked together previously
on *The Cosby Show* and *The Electric Company*. However, Cosby deferred to
Black and the pilot was shot with Playten. Black realized that Cosby was right,
and that, although Playten is a wonderful actress, her scenes just didn't work.
After the pilot the character of Oona was written out and replaced with a new

character, Angie Corea, played by
Rita Moreno. "The scenes came
alive," said Black. "Their chemistry
was undeniable."

The Cosby Show (1984-1992)

Phylicia Rashad as Clair Huxtable
    (Mary Wilson)
Lisa Bonet as Denise Huxtable
    (Whitney Houston)
Malcolm-Jamal Warner as Theo
    Huxtable (Carl Payne)
Keshia Knight Pulliam as Rudy
    Huxtable (Jaleel White)
Earle Hyman as Russell Huxtable (Dizzy Gillespie)

David Black

THE COSBY SHOW starred Bill Cosby as obstetrician Cliff Huxtable. Cliff
lived in Brooklyn, New York with his wife Clair, and their children.

Mary Wilson (of The Supremes) auditioned for the part of Cliff's
wife, attorney Clair Huxtable. Phylicia Rashad also came in to read. Director Jay Sandrich thought Rashad was wonderful. The part was hers.

"We found a beautiful young lady to play the part that Lisa Bonet
eventually played," said Sandrich. "When we all met in California this
young girl said, 'I can't be in every show 'cause I want to be a singer and
be able to go out on the road.' And I explained to her that if the show got
on the air and was successful her career would certainly be enhanced. She
said, 'No. I can't do it. I have to be able to tour.' I asked her if she had a
record contract. She said no. I said, 'Who told you you could sing?'" She
said, 'My mother and my cousin.' Her name was Whitney Houston."

Carl Payne was originally up for the role of Theo. He didn't get the job, but was brought on in the middle of the second season in the recurring role of Theo's friend Cockroach.

The youngest Huxtable child was named Rudy. The character was originally written as a little boy. Jaleel White auditioned, but failed to land the job. Keshia Knight Pullliam came in. Sandrich and the producers loved her and gave her the job.

Bill Cosby wanted jazz legend Dizzy Gillespie to play his father Russell Huxtable. Sandrich said that although Gillespie was very funny, he wasn't an actor. He asked Gillespie if he could remember lines. Gillespie responded, "No. Why do you think they call me Dizzy?" Earle Hyman was later cast in the part.

Couples (1994)
Jonathan Silverman as Jamie (David Schwimmer)

DAVID SCHWIMMER AUDITIONED for the part of Jamie in Couples. He made it all the way to the final auditions, but lost out to his friend Jonathan Silverman.

Coupling (2003)
Christopher Moynihan as Jeff Clancy (Breckin Meyer)
Rena Sofer as Susan Freeman (Melissa George)
Sonya Walger as Sally Harper (Emily Rutherford)

THE PILOT FOR THE AMERICAN version of Coupling starred Breckin Meyer, Melissa George and Emily Rutherford. Meyer's wife Deborah Kaplan was the show runner. A decision was made that the pilot was going to be reshot, and that some cast members (including Meyer) were going to be replaced. Kaplan felt very strongly that Meyer was the right actor to play Jeff Clancy. After he was replaced, she left the show. Christopher Moynihan was hired for the part, while Melissa George and Emily Rutherford were recast with Rena Sofer and Sonya Walger.

C.S.I.: *Crime Scene Investigation* (2000-)
Gary Dourdan as Warrick Brown (Morris Chestnut, Allen Payne)

THE FINAL THREE CANDIDATES for the part of audio/video analyst Warrick Brown were Morris Chestnut, Allen Payne and Gary Dourdan. Dourdan's look and style helped him get the job.

Sarah Buxton appeared on C.S.I. as a stripper on jury duty in January of 2004. About ten months later Buxton was called back to play another part. This time around she was cast as a transsexual named Wendy Garner. However, the role she really wanted to play went to Kate Walsh. Said Buxton, "Boy, did I want that. It was a smaller role, but a better role. It was meaty." Walsh played Mimosa, another transsexual.

Cutter to Houston (1983)
Alec Baldwin as Hal Wexler (Ron Silver)

CUTTER TO HOUSTON creator Sandor Stern wrote the part of Dr. Hal Wexler with Ron Silver in mind. Silver was approached, but was unavailable. Actors were brought in to read for the role. A young actor, who had been on a soap opera, Alec Baldwin, came in to audition. By looking at him Stern knew he wasn't right for the part. The casting director urged him to let him read. Stern agreed. Afterwards, Stern was won over. He brought Baldwin to audition at the network level. CBS executive Harvey Shepard told Stern that Baldwin didn't fit the part as written. Stern rewrote the part for Baldwin.

Cybill (1995-1998)

Christine Baranski as Maryann Thorpe (Sally Kellerman, Paula Poundstone)

CYBILL STARRED Cybill Shepherd as struggling actress Cybill Sheridan. Sheridan's best friend was Maryann Thorpe. "It was a buddy comedy," said director Robert Berlinger. "It gave one of the first looks at women at that age." Cybill and Maryann dealt with issues such as menopause, divorce, etc.

Cybill Shepherd's first choice for the role of Maryann Thorpe was Paula Poundstone. When Poundstone proved unavailable Sally Kellerman and Christine Baranski were considered. "It was clear she was the best right away," said Berlinger of Baranski. "She just knew the part." Baranski won an Emmy for her work on the show.

Daktari (1966-1969)

Erin Moran as Jenny Jones (Victoria Paige Meyerink)

VICTORIA PAIGE MEYERINK auditioned for the role of the seven-year-old orphan Jenny Jones on *Daktari*. "I wanted that because it was with all the animals," said Meyerink. "I was just, and still, so into animals. I wanted to work with the lion. But Erin got it."

Dallas (1978-1991)

Larry Hagman as J.R. Ewing (Robert Foxworth)
Linda Gray as Sue Ellen Ewing (Mary Frann)
Patrick Duffy as Bobby Ewing (Steve Kanaly)
Victoria Principal as Pam Ewing (Judith Chapman, Linda Evans)
Steve Kanaly as Ray Krebbs (Ken Kercheval, Martin Kove)

CBS HAD ACTRESS LINDA EVANS under contract. They suggested to *Dallas* creator David Jacobs that the series might be a good fit for her. Jacobs liked the idea of a Romeo and Juliet type of story with newlyweds

Pam and Bobby Ewing at the center of the story. Once the script was completed, the show turned out to be more of an ensemble piece, and Evans was never offered the part. Jacobs later said that Evans' inherent elegance would have been wrong for the character of Pam; that it would have been hard to believe she came from a blue-collar background. Judith Chapman auditioned to play Pam. Victoria Principal also wanted the role. She went after it, and was cast.

Steve Kanaly

Robert Foxworth was offered the part of J.R. Ewing, but turned it down. Larry Hagman's name was brought up. Jacobs thought it was the dumbest idea yet. He only knew of Hagman playing soft characters. He did arrange a meeting with Hagman, who showed up wearing a light gray suit, boots and a Stetson hat. As soon as he saw him, Jacobs knew Hagman was J.R.

Mary Frann was a possibility for the part of J.R.'s wife Sue Ellen Ewing. Linda Gray was eventually chosen.

Steve Kanaly got a call from his agent saying that they would like to see him for *Dallas*. He described three characters that Kanaly could play: J.R., Bobby and Ray Krebbs. Kanaly had to go that day, and had about an hour to get himself together. He decided that the role he would try for was Bobby Ewing. At the audition he saw a girl he knew who was reading for the part of Lucy. He took a look at the scene she was about to do between Lucy and Ray. As soon as he saw the scene Kanaly wanted to play Ray

Krebbs. He went in and told the producers that he would be terrific as Ray; he knew what he was all about. He made a good impression and was called back. He had two days to get ready. Kanaly had the dialect down, and felt he was right for the part. He gave a final audition. That night they offered him the job. Kanaly left for Dallas a week later.

Ken Kercheval had been considered to play Ray Krebbs. He was switched over to the part of Cliff Barnes instead. Besides Kercheval, Steve Kanaly's competition for the part of Ray Krebbs included Martin Kove. Kove came to fame a few years later when he won the part of Detective Victor Isbecki on *Cagney & Lacey*, a role he played for six years.

Dante's Cove (2005)

Clint Johnson as Derick (Jon Fleming)

WHEN JON FLEMING auditioned for *Dante's Cove*, he read for the role of Derick, a character who would appear in a couple of episodes. At the same time Stephen Amell, who played Adam in the first season, got the part of Teddy Gordon in the Richard Attenborough film *Closing the Ring*. Amell was no longer available to work on *Dante's Cove*. Fleming got bumped up to the larger role of Adam, while Clint Johnson was hired to play Derick.

Dark Angel (2000-2002)

Jessica Alba as Max Guevera (Ion Overman)

JAMES CAMERON AND Charles H. Eglee created *Dark Angel* for Fox. The futuristic series followed the main character of Max. Max was short for Maximum. She was genetically created to be the nth degree of human potential. Ion Overman auditioned to play Max, but the part went to Jessica Alba instead.

Actor Richard Gunn's uncle was a financial advisor to Charles H. Eglee. He recommended his nephew to Eglee. Gunn was brought in to audition for the series, and wound up with the part of Sketchy.

Dark Mansions (1986)

Joan Fontaine as Margaret Drake (Loretta
    Young)
Michael York as Jason Drake (Liam
    Neeson)

Michael York
Photo: Douglas Kirkland

LORETTA YOUNG WAS ORIGINALLY signed for the starring role of Margaret Drake. "Aaron Spelling got p.o.ed at her because of her demands and her attitude, etc. and he fired her," said producer Robert H. Justman. "It was really a great surprise, but he did what he had to do when he fired her and hired Joan Fontaine to play the role."

Director/producer Jerry London suggested Liam Neeson for the part of Jason Drake. Spelling wanted a recognizable name and hired Michael York instead.

The Daughters of Joshua Cabe (1972)

Buddy Ebsen as Joshua Cabe (Walter Brennan)

WALTER BRENNAN was considered for Buddy Ebsen's role of Joshua Cabe.

The David Cassidy Story (2000)

Katie Wright as Susan Dey (Kathy Wagner)

KATHY WAGNER WAS SOUGHT TO PLAY Susan Dey in the 2000 NBC film, *The David Cassidy Story*. Wagner already played Dey for ABC in *C'mon On Get Happy: The Partridge Family Story*. ABC refused to allow Wagner to play the part for NBC, and Katie Wright was cast instead.

Dawson's Creek (1998-2003)

Katie Holmes as Joey Potter (Selma Blair)
Mary Beth Peil as Evelyn Ryan (Rosemary Forsyth)
John Wesley Shipp as Mitch Leery (William Katt)

SELMA BLAIR WAS THE leading candidate for the part of Joey Potter on *Dawson's Creek*, until Katie Holmes' audition tape was viewed. Holmes was working on a high-school production of *Damn Yankees* at the time. She was asked to fly out the same day the play opened. Holmes did not want to miss the show and asked if she could come in later. Her request was granted, and she soon walked away with the part of Joey.

Rosemary Forsyth was considered to play Evelyn "Grams" Ryan. The role was later taken by Mary Beth Peil.

William Katt competed with John Wesley Shipp for the part of Dawson's father, Mitch Leery.

Days of Our Lives (1965-)

Paul Carr as Bill Horton (Edward Mallory, Frank Parker)
Bill Hayes as Doug Williams (John Aniston)
Elaine Princi as Linda Patterson Anderson (Lynn Benesch)
Jack Coleman as Jake Kositchek (Kevin Costner)

Crystal Chappell as Carly Manning (Susan Diol)
Michael Sabatino as Lawrence Alamain (Robert Mailhouse)

FRANK PARKER READ FOR the part of Bill Horton. The producers liked him, but felt he was too young for the part. Parker then suggested his friend Edward Mallory. Mallory was cast on creator Ted Corday's other show, *Morning Star*, and Paul Carr was hired to play Bill Horton. *Morning Star* was canceled shortly after its premiere. By then the part of Bill Horton was being recast. Mallory became the second actor to play the part.

John Aniston auditioned to play Doug Williams. He was asked to shave his moustache for his screen test. Aniston lost the part to Bill Hayes. A few weeks later the show called Aniston back and asked him to grow his moustache back to play Dr. Eric Richards. Aniston stayed with the show for about a year. About fifteen years later Aniston joined the cast again. This time around he was cast as Victor Kiriakis, a role he has played for over twenty years.

Scott Reeves initially auditioned for the part of Harris Michaels. Instead, he was cast as Jake Hogansen. While he was on *Days of Our Lives*, he met Melissa Brennan, who played Jennifer Horton. The two fell in love and were married about two years later. Brennan now goes by the name Melissa Reeves.

Lynn Benesch was brought in to audition to play Linda Patterson Anderson. Although Benesch thought her audition was good, she failed to nab the part. Elaine Princi was cast instead.

Casting director Fran Bascom brought an unknown Kevin Costner in for an audition. According to Bascom, Costner was the most wonderful person with a lot of humor. "He wasn't handsome enough for the producers," she said. "You become better looking the more famous you get." The role eventually went to Jack Coleman.

Susan Diol auditioned for the part of Carly Manning. She lost the role to Crystal Chappell. Diol was hired to play Emmy Borden a month later.

Robert Mailhouse was considered for the role of Lawrence Alamain. According to executive producer Al Rabin, Mailhouse took a dramatic scene and made it extremely funny. They considered making the character of Lawrence Alamain a funny villain, but eventually decided to give the part to Michael Sabatino. The part of Brian Scofield was created for Mailhouse.

Fran Bascom wanted her old friend, Academy Award nominee Sally Kirkland, to join the cast. Said Kirkland, "I turned her down for about six months." Bascom and Kirkland ran into each other at a friend's birthday party. Bascom told Kirkland they would write a part for her. "David O. Selznick trained me early to act anywhere," said Kirkland. "He said, 'There is no place that you shouldn't act. Just keep acting. Don't be too big for anything. There's no platform you can't act on.'" Kirkland agreed to join the show, but wanted a guaranteed amount of shows. "I was delighted when she consented to do it," said Bascom. "She's so creative and brings so many dimensions to her work. She's just the greatest." Kirkland had a very positive experience working on *Days of Our Lives*. "I shot 52 shows," she said. "I was disappointed when the storyline was over. It was very touching how complete strangers from all over the place would just know you. It was an amazing experience. I really had fun that year."

Canadian-born actor Roark Critchlow was relatively new to Los Angeles when he went to audition for the part of Mike Horton. "I was down from Canada," he said. "When you first get in L.A., it takes a while to learn the ins and outs of the business. It's a tough one. I'd had less than an audition per month for the first year that I was here. I was bartending and feeling like I was going nowhere. I got a cattle call for *Days of Our Lives*, which basically, I believe, means me and every other 6' tall relatively attractive male in the city. I can't imagine the numbers they went through. I read with Fran Bascom who was a doll." Critchlow got a call back to do the same scene again. He did well, and Bascom called him back four more times. "I asked my agent how many callbacks there would be. He kind of got mad and threw a little fit

Isenberg, Ivy

at me. He said, 'Well, if you want me to call up Fran, and push her to tell us things then that's fine. You can toss this away right now. I'll do it; I'll call her and impose on her.' I said, 'Hey, sorry!'" On a Friday Critchlow learned that he was one of the actors selected to screen test for the part. "Monday comes, no call from the agency. Tuesday, still no call. The last time I asked I'd gotten my head bitten off. I'm not going to call. I guessed they knew what they were doing." On Wednesday Critchlow did call to see what was going on. He was told that his agent quit over the weekend. "He left the agency and hadn't told anybody that I was screen testing. It was a life-changing audition and he hadn't mentioned it to anybody. Fortunately, it was the next day. On a soap you negotiate your contract terms before the screen test. There's five other guys, which is a good thing for them because if your agent tries to jack things too much, they've got a guy over here who's roughly similar. It's an interesting situation. We went in. They do the screen test after the days' shoots, right on the set; right in the soundstage. The director comes out and gives you your blocking. On soaps it's all one scene. They don't cut; the film they tape it as it goes. One guy was roaming around shadowboxing in the corner while the director was talking, being all cool and Hollywood. A half hour before the day's over they get you into makeup. Of course, the scene involved taking a shirt off. They brought in a couple of extra makeup artists to do body makeup. There was so much action in the makeup room. I was the last guy to get done. Due to circumstances I was in makeup until about two minutes before they called me to do my test. The scene was with Lisa Rinna, who I'd never met. Three or four of the other guys had gone before me. I get out there and they've got the camera going, it's all real. We finish the scene and she [Rinna] stands back and gave me an ovation. I'm like, 'Thank you. I think you just got me a job.' They asked me a couple of questions. One of them was, 'Who is your biggest hero?' I said my wife. 'Thank you very much' came over the loudspeaker and that was it." Critchlow learned he got the job while he was in the pre-labor room during the birth of his second daughter.

Dead Like Me (2003-2004)

Ellen Muth as George (Nicki Aycox, Rachel Blanchard, Erika Christensen,
    Emilie de Ravin, Anna Faris, Kelli Garner, Alexandra Holden, Scarlett
    Johansson, Susan May Pratt, Amber Tamblyn, Hillary Tuck)
Rebecca Gayheart as Betty Rhomer (Tammy Anderson, Jessica Collins, Idalis
    DeLeon, Laura Leighton, Missi Pyle, Lisa Thornhill)
Callum Blue as Mason (Ethan Embry, Adam Kaufman, Chad Willett)
Mandy Patinkin as Rube Sofer (David Alan Grier)

"Most pilots take a month to cast. This one took almost a year," said
casting director Ivy Isenberg. Many actresses were considered for the starring role of George, including future A-list star Scarlett Johansson. Amber
Tamblyn, Anna Faris, Emilie de Ravin, Kelli Garner, Nicki Aycox, Rachel
Blanchard, Susan May Pratt, Erika Christensen, Alexandra Holden and
Hillary Tuck all tested. The role was given to Ellen Muth. "She was so
amazing, and raw," said casting director Zora DeHorter-Majomi. "At 19
she was also the perfect age."

Rebecca Gayheart beat out Lisa Thornhill, Laura Leighton, Idalis De-
Leon, Jessica Collins, Missi Pyle and Tammy Anderson for the part of
grim reaper Betty Rhomer.

Adam Kaufman, Ethan Embry and Chad Willett were all considered
to play Mason. The role was given to Callum Blue instead.

David Alan Grier was a possible choice for the part of Rube Sofer.
Grier booked another job before a deal could be made. The producers had
been interested in Mandy Patinkin all along. Patinkin was offered the part,
which he accepted.

The Dead Zone (2002-)
David Ogden Stiers as Gene Purdy (Michael Moriarty)

SERIES CREATOR MICHAEL PILLER'S prototype for the starring role of Johnny Smith was Anthony Michael Hall. Piller was very impressed by Hall's work as Bill Gates in the TV movie *Pirates of Silicon Valley*. At one point Hall's agent passed, saying Hall wasn't interested. After seeing some other actors Piller got in touch with Hall's manager. Piller's passion for Anthony Michael Hall was key in getting him signed for the show.

Michael Moriarty was originally cast as Rev. Gene Purdy. He was later replaced by David Ogden Stiers.

Deadly Skies (2005)
Rae Dawn Chong as Madison Kelsey (Thea Gill)

THEA GILL WAS CONSIDERED for the starring role of astronomer Madison Kelsey in *Deadly Skies*. The part was eventually played by Rae Dawn Chong.

Degrassi Junior High (1987-1991)
Pat Mastroianni as Joey Jeremiah (Billy Parrott)

FROM 1982-1986 THE Canadian network the CBC aired *The Kids of Degrassi Street*, which was a 26-part series of half hours featuring adolescents. Issues such as hospitals and superstitions were dealt with. At the time it was one of the only live-action shows for kids. It was very well received, and won numerous awards, including an International Emmy.

When the show went off the air producer Linda Schuyler realized that she wanted to keep working with some of the actors. She asked them if they wanted to keep their old characters or not, and left it up to a vote.

The kids wanted to play new roles. The new series was called *Degrassi Junior High*. This non-union Canadian show focused on a large group of junior high school kids. "In those days there were not a lot of professional kids," said Schuyler. It was the early 1980s, and there were only three major networks in Canada. The show cast directly from the neighborhood. Kids had the opportunity to audition for the show, as audition forms were posted in schools and community centers. Anyone who came to audi-

Linda Schuyler
Photo: Stephen Scott

tion first met with the producers. After that callbacks were held, where people were asked to read. Out of the hundreds of kids who showed up, a fraction were invited to participate in a three-week-long series of workshops. The workshops consisted of scene work, acting and movement exercises, improvs, etc. Most of the people who did the workshops were asked to join the series. "We couldn't do it again like that," said Schuyler. The show dealt with serious issues such as teenage pregnancy, abortion and drugs. It was important to the producers to not bring in day players to deal with a serious issue. They wanted the continuity. For example, a char acter named Spike became pregnant. She kept her baby, and dealt with the consequences for the rest of the run of the series.

The two actors competing for the part of Joey Jeremiah were Pat Mastroianni and Billy Parrott. "Through a series of workshops we both kept auditioning," said Parrott. "Ultimately they gave it to Pat because they saw him as a more mischievous, jokey sort of guy. They thought he could morph very nicely into that, and he did. He did an incredible job. They created the Shane character for me."

Degrassi: The Next Generation (2001-)

Melissa McIntyre as Ashley Kerwin (Deanna Casaluce, Lauren Collins)
Jonathan Torrens as Shane
McKay (Billy Parrott)

DEGRASSI: THE NEXT GENERATION was a continuation of the Canadian hit *Degrassi Junior High*, later titled *Degrassi High*. Although the series was last produced in 1992, it never went off the air. Executive producer Linda Schuyler missed working with kids and decided to do a new school show. It was pointed out to Schuyler that if they followed the chronology of the original series Spike's baby Emma would be en-

Billy Parrott

tering junior high school. They wrote the first show as a reunion of the old gang. They never realized that some of the characters would stay on the series. However, the old characters of Spike and Snake (played by Amanda Stepto and Stefan Brogren) became regular cast members, and were later joined by Pat Mastroianni and Stacie Mistysyn as Joey Jeremiah and Caitlin Ryan. When Mastroianni was contacted about the reunion show, he didn't know if he wanted to do it, although he soon signed on. Said Schuyler, "He came back and said, 'What actor gets this opportunity to revive a role at this age? I would be crazy not to do it.'"

Unlike the original series, *Degrassi: The Next Generation* was a union show. Long casting sessions were conducted. Miriam McDonald auditioned about five times for the pivotal role of Emma Nelson. After she landed the part a reporter asked McDonald if she was familiar with the old show. She responded by saying, "I wasn't born yet." Lauren Collins, Melissa McIntyre and Deanna Casaluce were all considered for the part of Ashley Kerwin. McIntyre was chosen, and Collins was cast as Paige Michalchuk. Casaluce joined the cast in 2003 as bad girl Alex Nunez. "We loved Lauren and Deanna," said Linda Schuyler. "We created roles for them." Another actress whose role was created for her was Sarah Barrable-Tishauer, who played Liberty Van Zandt.

Billy Parrott played Shane McKay on *Degrassi Junior High*. The character of Shane was to appear in the Season 3-episode of *Degrassi: The Next Generation*, called "Father Figure." Parrott got a call from the show asking him if he'd be interested in reprising the role. He said he might be, depending on how the character was written in the script. After reading the script Parrott decided against appearing on the show. Schuyler's husband suggested Jonathan Torrens. Torrens was the host of a Canadian variety-talk show called *Jonovision*. One episode of *Jonovision* featured a *Degrassi Junior High* reunion, for which it got its highest ratings ever. According to Schuyler, when Torrens was contacted he said, "You mean I get to be an actor on *Degrassi*?" "He was in L.A.," said Schuyler. "He changed his schedule to do it." With just days before shooting was to begin Jonathan Torrens got the part. "I thought he did a great job playing Shane," said Parrott.

Delvecchio (1976-1977)
Charles Haid as Paul Shonski (Ron Masak)

DELVECCHIO STARRED JUDD HIRSCH as Los Angeles police detective and law student Dominick Delvecchio. Ron Masak auditioned for the part of Delvecchio's partner Sgt. Paul Shonski. Masak came close to landing the role, but Charles Haid was chosen instead.

Desperate Housewives (2004-)
Teri Hatcher as Susan Mayer (Mary-Louise Parker)
Felicity Huffman as Lynette Scavo (Teri Hatcher)
Marcia Cross as Bree Van De Kamp (Nicollette Sheridan)
Brenda Strong as Mary Alice Young (Marcia Cross, Sheryl Lee)
Jesse Metcalfe as John Rowland (Kyle Searles)
Steven Culp as Rex Van De Kamp (Michael Reilly Burke, Brian Haley)
Christine Estabrook as Martha Huber (Harriet Sansom Harris)
Shirley Knight as Phyllis Van De Kamp (Sally Kirkland)

DESPERATE HOUSEWIVES creator Marc Cherry wrote the role of Susan Mayer for Mary-Louise Parker. After Parker turned the part down auditions were held. When Teri Hatcher had her first meeting for *Desperate Housewives*, it was unclear as to which part she would play. Although she wanted the part of Susan, there was some question as to whether or not she might play Lynette Scavo. However, she was not a sure bet by any means. Hatcher's career had cooled since her huge success with the series *Lois & Clark: The New Adventures of Superman*. Hatcher herself said that she was on a B list for *Desperate Housewives*, and she wasn't anyone's first choice initially. All that changed soon after, and she won the role of Susan. Hatcher won a Golden Globe for Outstanding Lead Actress in a Comedy Series in 2005.

Marcia Cross initially read for the part of Mary Alice Young. At her audition Cross was switched over to read for the part of Bree Van De Kamp, which she got.

Marc Cherry's first choice for the part of nosy Martha Huber was Christine Estabrook, with Harriet Sansom Harris as his second choice. Estabrook was cast, but Cherry knew that the character was going to die. He also knew that he needed an actress to play her sister, Felicia Tillman. Harris got the job.

Nicollette Sheridan was asked to audition to play the uptight Bree Van DeKamp. At the end of the reading, the director told her that he saw her as Edie Britt instead. Sheridan read for Edie, and won the role.

Sheryl Lee was cast as Mary Alice Young. Lee shot the original pilot, but a decision was made to replace her. Brenda Strong was hired as the new Mary Alice.

Like Sheryl Lee, both Kyle Searles and Michael Reilly Burke appeared in the unaired pilot. Searles played teenage gardener John Rowland, while Burke was cast as Bree's husband Rex. Brian Haley was asked to audition for the part of Rex, but decided against it. When the show hit the air Jesse Metcalfe was cast as John Rowland, while Steven Culp played Rex Van De Kamp

Sally Kirkland and Shirley Knight were both up for the part of Bree's mother-in-law, Phyllis Van De Kamp. The part went to Knight, who appeared on five episodes of the show.

Diagnosis Murder (1993-2001)

Charlie Schlatter as Jesse Travis (David Lipper)

DICK VAN DYKE PLAYED Dr. Mark Sloan on an episode of *Jake and the Fat-man*. He was told that if he liked doing the character CBS would do a bunch of TV movies, which eventually led to the weekly series *Diagnosis Murder*.

Mark Sloan's son was a cop. The part went to Van Dyke's real-life son Barry Van Dyke.

In 1995 the character of Dr. Jesse Travis was added to the cast. David Lipper was considered, but the part went to Charlie Schlatter instead.

The Dick Van Dyke Show (1961-1966)

Dick Van Dyke as Rob Petrie (Johnny Carson)
Mary Tyler Moore as Laura Petrie (Eileen Brennan)
Len Weinrib as Jackie Brewster (Shecky Greene)

IN THE 1950S CARL REINER worked with Sid Caesar as a writer/performer on two successful series: *Your Show of Shows* and *Caesar's Hour*. After both series were over Reiner was offered roles in sitcoms. His wife Estelle suggested to him that he should write a sitcom in which to star. Reiner realized that no one had done a show about television writers before. That week he wrote the pilot based on his real-life experiences working on Sid Caesar's *Your Show of Shows*. Reiner didn't stop writing when he finished the first episode. He wrote the first thirteen episodes before he brought it to the William Morris Agency. Actor Peter Lawford thought Reiner was on to something and put up money for the show. The pilot was shot starring Reiner in the lead role of television writer Rob Petrie. The supporting cast included Barbara Britton as Rob's wife Laura and Gary Morgan as their son Ritchie. Morty Gunty and Sylvia Miles played Rob's coworkers Buddy and Sally, while Jack Wakefield played his boss Alan Sturdy. The show, titled *Head of the Family*, aired on CBS on July 19,

1960. The network decided against picking it up. Reiner felt that that was his best shot, and had no plans to pursue the show further. Actor/producer/director Sheldon Leonard told Reiner that the problem with the pilot was that Reiner was wrong for the part of Rob. He advised him to recast the role, and to produce the show instead. Reiner had never been a producer before, but Leonard assured him that he would be fine.

Johnny Carson was considered to play Rob Petrie, but the role went to Dick Van Dyke instead.

Finding an actress to play Laura Petrie was very difficult. Eileen Brennan was a strong contender for the part. Danny Thomas, one of the show's producers, suggested they look for a girl with three names who had auditioned for him for *Make Room for Daddy*. She had been too mature for that particular part. Thomas remembered that she had been on a show where only her legs were shown (*Richard Diamond: Private Detective*). The girl turned out to be Mary Tyler Moore. She auditioned for, and won the part of Laura Petrie.

Rose Marie was hired to play Sally Rogers. At her suggestion the role of Buddy Sorrell went to Morey Amsterdam.

Carl Reiner took the part of Rob's boss, now renamed Alan Brady. "It started out he was only going to be the back of a head," explained producer Ronald Jacobs. "Alan Brady was never going to be a character. He was going to be the boss yelling in the other room. He was going to be the back of the head. And, of course, you've got a Carl Reiner, how are you not going to put him in front of a camera."

Shecky Greene was hired to play the guest role of nightclub comedian Jackie Brewster. Greene rehearsed, and then quit right in the middle of the show. "He had to fly to Vegas for a personal problem," said Ronald Jacobs. Len Weinrib was hired as a last-minute replacement.

The Dick Van Dyke Show ran for five years, and is still on in reruns to this day. It remains one of television's classic series.

A Different World (1987-1993)

Marisa Tomei as Maggie Lauten (Meg Ryan)

AN UNKNOWN MEG RYAN AUDITIONED for the part of Maggie Lauten on the *Cosby Show* spin-off *A Different World*. Ryan won the role, but her agents decided that she should have a movie career instead. Marisa Tomei was later hired to play Maggie. Meg Ryan had supporting roles in films such as *Top Gun* and *Innerspace*. However, it was her starring role of Sally Albright in the 1989 film *When Harry Met Sally...* that made Ryan a star.

Marisa Tomei has had a successful film career as well. In 1992 the mostly unknown Tomei co-starred with Joe Pesci in the film *My Cousin Vinny*. Tomei won an Academy Award for her standout performance as Mona Lisa Vito.

Diff'rent Strokes (1978-1986)

Dana Plato as Kimberly Drummond (Felice Schachter)
Janet Jackson as Charlene DuPrey (Rae Dawn Chong)

AL BURTON DEVELOPED and was the creative supervisor for *Diff'rent Strokes*. Conrad Bain was signed to star as the wealthy Philip Drummond, who takes in two young orphans, Arnold and Willis Jackson. Burton was aware of the young actor Gary Coleman, and cast him as the younger brother Arnold. Todd Bridges was brought on to play Willis. Bain made a deal in his contract that no one could make more money than he did. It turned out to be a very shrewd deal. Coleman was the show's breakout star, and was making a huge salary. No matter how high Coleman was paid, Bain was still paid more.

Felice Schachter auditioned for the part of Drummond's daughter Kimberly. She lost the role to Dana Plato. However, when the character of Mrs. Garrett, the housekeeper, got her own series (*The Facts of Life*), Schachter was chosen for a role on that show.

Rae Dawn Chong was hired and then fired from *Diff'rent Strokes*. Chong was told she wasn't ethnic enough to play Willis' girlfriend Charlene DuPrey, and was replaced at the last minute by Janet Jackson.

Do You Remember Love (1985)
Richard Kiley as George Hollis (Jason Robards)

JOANNE WOODWARD STARRED as Alzheimer's victim Barbara Wyatt-Hollis in the CBS movie *Do You Remember Love*. Director Jeff Bleckner was interested in having Jason Robards play Barbara's husband George Hollis. Unbelievably, a young CBS executive didn't know who the very famous Robards was and asked to see tape of his work. "As it turned out Jason Robards was not available," said Bleckner. "We ended up casting Richard Kiley, who got an Emmy nomination.

"We made that film when Alzheimer's was not a household word," continued Bleckner. "I think when I started making that film I had never even heard of Alzheimer's . . . Joanne was extraordinary; she won an Emmy.

"I remember one morning the phone rang at about 6:30 in the morning. You always get nervous when the phone rings that early at your house. I answered the phone. My wife said, 'Who is it?' I whispered, 'It's Paul Newman.' He was calling to tell me that she was sick. He was just being a husband He never showed up at the set. Everybody was hoping he would Joanne said he never would. He was out racing cars."

Doogie Howser, M.D. (1989-1993)
Neil Patrick Harris as Doogie Howser (Anthony Rapp)

THE IDEA FOR *DOOGIE HOWSER, M.D.* occurred to producer Steven Bochco after reading an article in *New York Magazine* by Tony Schwartz about child prodigies. The concept was not foreign to Bochco, whose own father had been a violin prodigy. Bochco decided to make the teenage Doogie Howser a doctor.

Anthony Rapp auditioned for the title role of teenage doctor Doogie Howser. "It was really down to the wire," said producer Philip M. Goldfarb. "We were building sets and were ready to go, and really didn't find Neil [Patrick Harris] until literally almost the last minute. Almost every kid in Hollywood either came in for a meeting or was tested. Neil had done one movie, *Clara's Heart*. He came in and met. Steven really sparked to him."

ABC wasn't sure if Harris was the right choice. Bochco was so determined to keep Harris that he threatened to shut down production until the network backed off.

James Sikking was in Vancouver shooting a film with Gene Hackman when he was offered the part of Doogie's dad, Dr. David Howser. "The dates conflicted," said Sikking. "Steven Bochco is a good friend. Steven said, 'I will make sure you're written light in those first few shows. We'll shoot you on Mondays.'" The director of the film let Sikking off on Mondays to work on the show.

Doogie Howser, M.D. ran for four years. Bochco had no idea that ABC was going to cancel the show, and so he was unable to write a final episode. He has stated publicly that he planned to end the series with Doogie giving up medicine to become a writer.

The Drew Carey Show (1995-2004)
Diedrich Bader as Oswald Lee Harvey (John Fleck)

THE DREW CAREY SHOW starred Drew Carey as a personnel director for a Cleveland department store. Like the actor, the character's name was also Drew Carey. Drew's friends included Oswald Lee Harvey, Kate O'Brien and Lewis Kiniski.

John Fleck and Diedrich Bader auditioned to play Oswald. Bader's reading was so funny the part was his.

Whoever played Kate had to be attractive and sexy, yet believable as a buddy of the guys. Christa Miller auditioned. "I definitely saw something in her," said casting director Ellie Kanner. "She was really good. She was just a little green. I brought her back and [series creator] Bruce Helford felt the same way. He really liked her. We kept bringing her back, and she kept getting better and better, and nailing it. I don't know if it was the studio or the network that was unsure if they wanted us to bring her in. I asked for tape on her to try and help push it forward; push it through. She did an episode of *Seinfeld* that was literally one or two lines, but it was funny. We got the tape. I remember Christa rushing it over, delivering it herself. I rushed it to whoever needed to see it, and they said, 'Great.' And then it ended up working out and we hired her. She was just terrific."

The character of Drew's nemesis Mimi Bobeck was originally supposed to be a guest spot. Kathy Kinney made the part her own, and was so successful with it that she became a regular cast member.

The Duchess of Duke Street (1976)
Gemma Jones as Louisa Trotter (Hayley Mills)

HAYLEY MILLS WAS PRODUCER John Hawkesworth's first choice for the starring part of Louisa Trotter on *Masterpiece Theatre's The Duchess of Duke Street.* Mills did a reading for Hawkesworth, which he thought was wonderful. Mills had to turn the part down, though, since after meeting with Hawkesworth she learned she was pregnant. Gemma Jones auditioned. "I had a two-year-old child," she said. "I took him to the audition in his push chair; I couldn't find a sitter." Jones won the role, which she said was completely against type.

Dynasty (1981-1989)
John Forsythe as Blake Carrington (George Peppard)
Joan Collins as Alexis (Sophia Loren)
George Hamilton as Joel Abrigore (John Gabriel)

JOHN FORSYTHE WAS CONSIDERED to play wealthy businessman Blake Carrington in *Dynasty*. Forsythe was already providing the voice of Charlie on the hit show *Charlie's Angels*. *Dynasty* co-creator Esther Shapiro worried that the two shows might run on the same night and cast George Peppard instead. Shapiro has publicly said that Peppard was difficult, and that he and some of the directors on the show saw the character of Blake differently. Shapiro didn't want to work things out with the actor, and offered to remove herself from the show. However, Peppard was removed instead. John Forsythe was reconsidered. He was sent a copy of the script. Forsythe read it and agreed to sign on. Since Forsythe and Peppard wore the same size clothes a new wardrobe was not needed.

Sophia Loren turned down the chance to play Blake's ex-wife Alexis. The role was given to Joan Collins, who was wildly popular in the part.

John Gabriel tested with Linda Evans for the part of Joel Abrigore. George Hamilton, who did not have to audition, later took the role.

Dynasty: The Reunion (1991)
Robin Sachs as Adam Carrington (Gordon Thomson)

GORDON THOMSON STARRED as Adam Carrington on *Dynasty* from 1982-1989. A reunion movie was scheduled for 1991. At the time Thomson was playing Mason Capwell on the daytime soap *Santa Barbara*, and was unavailable. Robin Sachs was suggested as a replacement. The British Sachs was auditioned over the phone to see if he could do an American accent. He could, and won the part.

An Early Frost (1985)

Sylvia Sidney as Beatrice McKenna (Eva Le Galliene, Jimmy Stewart)

AIDAN QUINN CALLED NBC to say he was very interested in playing the starring role of Michael Pierson in the groundbreaking TV movie *An Early Frost*. The film was the first made for TV movie to deal with the subject of AIDS. Quinn had been in Chicago, where he worked for some AIDS projects. "Back then in the early '80s it didn't have the network that it has now, the outreach that it has now," said writer/producer Daniel Lipman. "He went after the role. He wanted to play it, and he didn't care at the time that it was a gay character. I guess he had read the script and he really wanted to do it. I know that he was an emerging film star. He was just in a movie with Robert De Niro that had just been released. So he was kind of a hot young actor at the time. I think that [director] John Erman seized the opportunity to bring him to television and do this role." Quinn met with Lipman and co-writer/producer Ron Cowen. The three sat around the kitchen table and talked. "We thought he was terrific," said Cowen. "When you see somebody and he feels so right it's hard to move beyond that."

An offer was made to Eva Le Galliene to play Michael's grandmother Beatrice McKenna, which was accepted. Sometime after, director John Erman got a call from Sylvia Sidney, who lived in Connecticut, next door to Eva Le Galliene. Sidney told Erman that she was aware that an offer was make to Le Galliene, but that she didn't think she would be playing the part. When Erman asked why, she responded, "Because she's dead." Le Galliene was not dead, although she was very ill at the time. She was so ill that she was unable to do the role. Erman then asked Sidney, "So what are you doing?" Sidney got the part. Le Galliene died soon after. Cowen and Lipman later found out that Jimmy Stewart called to say that if they wanted to change the part to a grandfather he would do it.

Ed (2000-2004)

Tom Cavanagh as Ed Stevens (Elon Gold, Jon Henson, Dan Jenkins)
Julie Bowen as Carol Vessey (Megan Ward)
Michael Ian Black as Phil Stubbs (Donal Logue)

WHEN HIGH-PROFILE NEW YORK lawyer Ed Stevens gets fired, he goes back to his hometown of Stuckeyville. Stevens buys the town's bowling alley, where he sets up his law practice.

Tom Cavanagh was the third actor to audition for the title role of *Ed*. Although his audition was outstanding the producers continued to search. They saw about 300 actors for the part. Eventually, five actors were brought in to test for the network, including Jon Henson, Elon Gold, Dan Jenkins and Cavanagh. The day before the test each actor came in to rehearse with casting director Bonnie Zane. She told Jon Beckerman and Rob Burnett, the show's creators, that if CBS wanted to get the pilot made they would choose Cavanagh.

The next day Zane read with all the actors. During the scene the character she was reading cries. Tom Cavanaugh asked her to indicate when she was crying. During the test Zane actually started to cry. Cavanagh later said to her, "I can't believe I made you cry!" Zane was right about Cavanagh. His audition was so good he got the job.

Julie Bowen and Megan Ward were both considered to play Ed's high-school crush Carol Vessey. Bowen had a deal somewhere else and was unavailable. Megan Ward was cast. Although, she was fantastic in the role, Les Moonves only wanted Julie Bowen for the part. He bought out her other contract and cast her on *Ed*.

Donal Logue was offered the supporting role of Phil Stubbs. He turned it down, and accepted the starring role on the series *Grounded for Life*. Michael Ian Black was later cast as Phil.

Ed was initially supposed to air on CBS. They passed on the show. NBC asked for a rewrite, but agreed to make the show.

Edward & Mrs. Simpson (1978)

Cynthia Harris as Wallis Warfield Simpson (Joan Hackett)

JOAN HACKETT WAS OFFERED the starring role of American social-ite Wallis Simpson in the 1978 miniseries *Edward & Mrs. Simpson*. She turned it down and Cynthia Harris was cast in her place.

8 Simple Rules . . . for Dating My Teenage Daughter (2002-2005)

John Ritter as Paul Hennessy (John Goodman, Richard Jenkins, John Larroquette, Ed O'Neill)

Katey Sagal as Cate Hennessy (Judith Hoag, Wendy Makkena, Amy Yasbeck)

JOHN GOODMAN WAS MADE an offer to play the starring role of Paul Hen-nessy in *8 Simple Rules...for Dating My Teenage Daughter*. A deal was never finalized and other actors were considered, including John Larroquette, Ed O'Neill, Richard Jenkins and John Ritter. The part was given to John Ritter.

Ritter's wife Amy Yasbeck was briefly considered to play Paul's wife Cate. Tested for ABC were Katey Sagal, Wendy Makkena and Judith Hoag. Ritter loved Sagal, and felt he had the best connection with her. At first ABC was concerned that viewers might still perceive her as Peg Bundy, the role she played on *Married . . . with Children* for eleven years. They eventually agreed that she was the best choice, and gave her the part.

On September 11, 2003, during a rehearsal for the show, Ritter became ill. He was brought to the hospital where, tragically, he died several hours later. The cause of Ritter's death was an aortic dissection, which was caused by a pre-viously undiagnosed heart defect. The producers decided to deal with Ritter's death by having the character die as well. James Garner and David Spade were added to the cast to try and fill the void. The series ran for two more seasons.

John Ritter was nominated for an Emmy for his portrayal of Paul Hen-nessy.

The Electric Company (1971-1977)
Skip Hinnant as Fargo North, Decoder (Morgan Freeman)

THE CHILDREN'S TELEVISION WORKSHOP was created to produce the children's educational program *Sesame Street*. The show was so success-ful that they created another educational program for children called *The Electric Company*.

The show's original cast members were Jim Boyd, Morgan Freeman, Judy Graubart, Skip Hinnant, Rita Moreno, June Angela, Lee Chamberlin and Bill Cosby. The character of detective Fargo North, Decoder was writ-ten for cast member Morgan Freeman. That plan fell through, and Skip Hinnant played him instead.

Ellen (1994-1998)
Arye Gross as Adam Green (Greg Germann)

GREG GERMANN AUDITIONED FOR the supporting role of Adam Green on *Ellen*. At the time the show was called *These Friends of Mine*. Germann lost the part to Arye Gross, but gave such a good audition that he was cast in the recurring role of Rick.

The show premiered in 1994. The cast included Ellen DeGeneres as Ellen Morgan, Gross, Maggie Wheeler as Anita and Holly Fulger as Holly. The first year of production was tumultuous, and the show went through a huge retooling. Wheeler left, and Fulger followed. Joely Fisher was brought in to fill the gap they left, as Ellen's friend Paige. The ratings improved, and the show ran for five seasons.

Elvis (1990)

Michael St. Gerard as Elvis
   Presley (Sean Kanan)

Sean Kanan

SEAN KANAN WAS ASKED TO audition for the title role of Elvis Presley. "I saw Bob Denver as Gilligan," said Kanan. Not wanting to be typecast, Kanan turned down the audition. The part went to Michael St. Gerard. St. Gerard had played Elvis before in the film *Great Balls of Fire.*

Encore! Encore! (1998-1999)

Glenne Headly as Francesca
   Pinoni (Molly Price)

MOLLY PRICE WAS HIRED TO play the part of Francesca Pinoni in the Nathan Lane series *Encore! Encore!* According to Jeff Greenberg, the casting director, one of the producers' wives didn't like Price. She was replaced by Glenne Headly.

Equal Justice (1990-1991)

Joe Morton as Michael James (Cotter Smith)
Cotter Smith as Eugene Rogan (Joe Morton)

DIRECTOR AND SERIES CO-CREATOR Thomas Carter had dinner with his friend Sarah Jessica Parker. He was in the middle of casting his upcoming series *Equal Justice*. Carter realized Parker would be right for the part of lawyer Jo Ann Harris. Her agents (also his agents) at CAA weren't overly enthusiastic for her to do a series. It was very tough to make a deal. "They were driving a hard bargain," said Carter, "but I really wanted Sarah to be in the show, and she was very interested in doing it. So eventually we did work it out, and I was really happy that she came to be a part of the show. It was a great role for her."

The character of prosecutor Michael James was originally written as an Italian named Corelli. Joe Morton came to audition for the part of an African-American minister. He asked to read for Corelli. Thomas Carter agreed. "He read for Corelli, who was a guy who used to sing opera while he would make pasta for the other lawyers in the offices," said Carter. "He was terrific. He read and he was wonderful. He was the best guy who read the role. I have always been an advocate of being much more open - I mean I'm African American myself - but I'd been an advocate of Hollywood being much more open in casting ethnically. I thought there was no reason that role couldn't be African American. We brought Joe and some other people to the network. He was clearly the choice of the studio and the producer, and we cast him as Corelli. There was some discussion about it, because the network was looking at who's in the show, the balance of the actors. They were trying not to look at the ethnicity, but they were looking at it. So after some discussion we cast him. He was clearly the best actor. But even after I cast him, I got a call from the network. I was prepping the pilot, which was shot in Pittsburgh. I was in preproduction, about to shoot. I cast Joe and we changed the name after we cast Joe. We cast Joe in that role. We had cast Cotter Smith in the other role [of Eugene Rogan]. They said, 'Look, would you consider switching the roles?' Giving Joe Cotter's role and Cotter Joe's role. They were asking it because Joe's role, as I began to look at the script more carefully, was the more focal role in the piece because he was leading the big dramatic case in the movie. I think they were afraid to trust that to an African-American lead. Even in an ensemble show. They struggled with how to say this. They did it with many kinds of analyses, trying not to talk about what was obvious, and yet it was. I said, 'Well, no. I don't want to change it because I've cast these two actors in the roles that they're most right for. Cotter will be great in the role we've cast him in, and he was. And Joe will be terrific in this role. It's where I think their gifts would lead us. I'm very happy about it.' The studio was on the fence about it. I was sort of standing there, for a brief moment, alone, but I stuck to my guns about it and said, 'No, this is what I want to do.' Literally, I think this was a day or two before I was going to start shooting. We kept the roles as I had cast them, shot the pilot, cut it, showed it to the network. They said, 'Listen, it's terrific. We're sorry. We'll never do that again. Joe is fantastic in this role and Cotter's wonderful in his role. We're glad that you stuck to your guns about it.'"

The Equalizer (1985-1989)
Edward Woodward as Robert McCall (James Coburn)

ALTHOUGH JAMES COBURN WAS considered to star as secret agent Robert McCall (The Equalizer), the part went to Edward Woodward. A pilot was made. "The concept was off," said director Richard Compton. "It was never shown, but the network had looked at it. They were going to recast (not Edward), and bring some other people in. Then they decided, 'We don't need to do another pilot. We know we love the show, so why don't we just go to episode #1, and we'll call that the pilot.' I did episode #1.

But then they discovered, 'We shouldn't call this a pilot because if we do we'll have to pay Richard a royalty.' If you do a pilot and it sells you're supposed to be rewarded. It was already sold." Compton understood. He had a wonderful time working on *The Equalizer*. Compton worked on the first episode and stayed for the run of the series.

ER (1994-)

Sherry Stringfield as Susan Lewis (Lisa Zane)
Eriq La Salle as Peter Benton (Michael Beach)
Lisa Zane as Diane Leeds (Laura Innes)
Michael Michele as Cleo Finch (Nia Long)
Erik Palladino as Dave Malucci (Peter Sarsgaard, John Stamos)
Linda Cardellini as Samantha Taggart (Busy Phillips)
Christine Harnos as Jennifer Greene (Julianna Margulies)
Judy Parfitt as Isabelle Corday (Jeanne Moreau)
Wendy Phillips as Mrs. Lambright (Karen Landry)

MICHAEL CRICHTON WROTE *ER* as a screenplay in the early-mid-'70s. The original title was *EW*. Crichton was trained as a doctor, and worked in an emergency room during medical school. He wanted to show real life in a hospital emergency room. The script floated around for about twenty years. Steven Spielberg was interested in directing it. One day he casually asked Crichton what he was presently working on. Crichton told him that he was writing a book about dinosaurs and DNA. Spielberg put *ER* aside and directed Crichton's other book. The film was called *Jurassic Park*, and was an enormous hit.

The head of Amblin Entertainment's television department (Spielberg's company) suggested making *ER* as a series. Crichton and Spielberg agreed. Producer John Wells' agent Tony Krantz brought the script to his attention. Wells was drawn to the characters, and shortly after agreed to come on board.

ER was picked up for the fall schedule very late. As a result NBC had only 3½ weeks to cast the whole show.

John Wells went to casting director John Levey's office one day. Levey happened to have Anthony Edwards' picture out, as he was putting together the actors he wanted to audition for the part of Dr. Mark Greene. Wells was struck by Edwards' picture. Edwards gave an excellent audition for the part. However, he was going to direct a feature film, and was unavailable. At the last minute Edwards' schedule was cleared when his film got pushed back a few weeks. He was the only actor brought to test for NBC. Soon after Edwards was hired for the show.

George Clooney had just done the show *Sisters* for NBC. He had a development deal with the network. Another series, a buddy cop show, wanted him. John Levey snuck Clooney a copy of the *ER* script. Clooney liked it and met with John Wells, director Rod Holcomb, Levey and fellow casting director Barbara Miller in Miller's office. He told a story about an earthquake that occurred at 4:00 a.m. He and his roommate grabbed his pet pig and ran outside naked. Clooney concluded the story by saying, "Just another Friday night at my house." Rod Holcomb asked him to read a scene. Everyone was won over by Clooney. They asked Les Moonves (then the president of Warner Bros. Television) to

John Levey

approve his casting. Moonves agreed, and the other pilot Clooney was considering was never made.

Sherry Stringfield had done a year on *NYPD Blue* playing attorney Laura Kelly. According to Levey, her agent called him to say she wasn't happy doing the show. Stringfield was brought in to try for the role of Dr. Susan Lewis. She and Lisa Zane tested against each other for NBC. Stringfield won the part.

Agent Ilene Feldman represented Noah Wyle. She kept calling John Levey urging him to see her client. Said Levey, "I kept saying, 'I don't know him.' One day I got beaten down and said, 'Fuck it. Send him in.'" Wyle impressed Levey. The only day that series creator Michael Crichton came in was a day that Wyle was there. He watched as Wyle did a scene from the pilot. "Wyle was very funny. Crichton laughed his head off," said Levey. Noah Wyle won the part of Dr. John Carter. He was on *ER* for eleven years, the longest of any of the original cast members.

Michael Beach was tested for the part of Dr. Peter Benton. "Beach was the person we all wanted," said Levey. "[NBC executive] Don Ohlmeyer said, 'You can cast Michael, but I think there's someone righter.'" Eriq La Salle had already been cast in another series called *Medicine Ball*. Barbara Miller told Levey to stay away from La Salle because he was already committed to that show. However, his part had been changed from a regular to a recurring character for budgetary reasons. "Eriq brought a winning arrogance to the part. It was clear as a bell," said Levey. After some cajoling, Levey got permission from Miller to cast Eriq La Salle as Dr. Peter Benton.

Julianna Margulies read for the part of Mark Greene's wife Jennifer. The role went to Christine Harnos instead. Margulies was then given the part of nurse Carol Hathaway. At first, Margulies didn't want the part. She changed her mind after her agent reminded her it was a chance to work with Steven Spielberg and Michael Crichton. Hathaway was originally going to die in the pilot. Margulies was so good the character not only survived, but became a regular.

Laura Innes auditioned for the part of Diane Leeds. Luckily for Innes, she lost the part to Lisa Zane. Not long after Innes auditioned for, and won the part of Dr. Kerry Weaver. While the Diane Leeds character lasted just one season, Kerry Weaver was on the show for twelve years.

Maria Bello played Dr. Anna Del Amico from 1997-1998. Said John Levey, "Maria was among the people John Wells and I identified as people we wanted on the show. The role was created for her. If I have any regrets about *ER*, it's that Maria's trip with us was shorter than it should have been."

Alex Kingston was someone else whose role was created for her. French screen legend Jeanne Moreau was cast to play her character's mother Isabelle Corday. As a young boy John Levey loved Moreau. It took a lot of effort to get her to agree to do the show. Moreau had problems right away. The first thing that went wrong was her transportation. "Someone sent a teamster in a van to pick her up," said Levey. Later in the day she was smoking a cigarette and was told to put it out. Moreau told Levey and the producers that she needed to go back to Paris, and she was taken to the airport. John Levey was devastated. Judy Parfitt was brought in as Moreau's replacement.

George Clooney left *ER* in 1999. From the start, Clooney was the show's biggest star. While still on *ER*, Clooney began to have a very successful movie career. Since leaving the show he has emerged as one of the biggest stars in the world. In 2006 he was nominated for three Academy Awards. He was nominated as best director and best original screenplay for the film *Good Night, and Good Luck.* That same year he won the Oscar for Best Supporting Actor for the film *Syriana.*

Producer Kristin Harms saw Goran Visnjic in the 1997 film *Welcome to Sarajevo.* She brought him to John Wells' attention in a "post-Clooney panic." The part of Dr. Luka Kovac was created for him.

The character of Dr. Cleo Finch was intended to be a love interest for Peter Benton. Michael Michele was cast, although Nia Long was also considered.

John Stamos read for the part of Dave Malucci. "Everyone felt it was too soon after George," said Levey. "He was somewhat similar to George, and it felt like we were replacing him." Erik Palladino read, as did Peter Sarsgaard. The role went to Erik Palladino. Palladino was on the series from 1999-2001. In 2005 Stamos joined the cast as Dr. Tony Gates.

Busy Phillips read for the part of nurse Samantha Taggart. John Wells was very close to offering it to her, but instead gave the part to Linda Cardellini. Cardellini and Phillips worked together on the series *Freaks and Geeks*.

Scott Grimes and Paul McCrane were originally brought on the show as guest stars. Both actors excelled, and were asked to join the cast as regulars.

Other actors whose roles were created for them include Kellie Martin (Lucy Knight), Maura Tierney (Abby Lockhart), Sharif Atkins (Michael Gallant), Parminder Nagra (Neela Rasgotra) and Shane West (Ray Barnett).

Karen Landry auditioned for the guest-starring role of Mrs. Lambright in the December 4, 2003 episode entitled "Missing." Wendy Phillips played the role instead. Landry had no hard feelings, and said that Phillips was a very good actress.

E-Ring (2005-2006)

Benjamin Bratt as Jim Tisnewski (Billy Crudup, Thomas Jane, Dermot
    Mulroney, Jason Patric, Barry Pepper, Donnie Wahlberg)
Dennis Hopper as Eli McNulty (Ted Danson, Ed Harris, Harvey Keitel, Gary
    Oldman, James Woods)

BENJAMIN BRATT WAS OFFERED the starring role of Maj. Jim Tisnewski in the NBC drama *E-Ring*. Bratt wasn't interested in the part, and turned it down. Billy Crudup was also made an offer, which he declined. Barry Pepper, Dermot Mulroney, Jason Patric, Donnie Wahlberg and Thomas Jane were all considered. However, Bratt changed his mind and the part was his.

Casting director Marc Hirschfeld really wanted Ted Danson to play Col. Eli McNulty. He was unable to convince anyone else that Danson was the right choice, and considered other actors including Ed Harris. James Woods was offered the part, but was busy doing a feature. After rejections from Gary Oldman and Harvey Keitel, Dennis Hopper signed on for the role.

Even Stevens (2000-2003)

Shia LeBeouf as Louis Stevens (Brandon Baker, Joey Zimmerman)
Donna Pescow as Eileen Stevens (Annabelle Gurwitch)

SHIA LEBEOUF, BRANDON BAKER and Joey Zimmerman were among the young actors who auditioned for the part of Louis Stevens. According to Matt Dearborn, who created the series, LeBeouf was a wild card. He was funny, but Dearborn wasn't sure if he would stay focused. But while other kids were serviceable and hit the beats, LeBeouf was something different. The candidates were eventually narrowed down to three, including Shia LeBeouf. LeBeouf aced the final audition. "Shia was funny the minute he came in," said Dearborn. "Other kids got laughs in the scene. Shia was funny saying hello. Eventually you just couldn't say no. He's too funny to not give him the part."

Christy Carlson Romano was the best, most clear-cut case of an actor being right for the show, said Dearborn. He added that she was so perfect she had the part of Ren Stevens the second she walked in the door.

The role of the mother, Eileen Stevens, was given to Annabelle Gurwitch. After shooting the pilot Gurwitch decided she didn't want to do the series. Donna Pescow was brought in as her replacement.

Everybody Hates Chris (2005-)

Tyler James Williams as Chris (Tequan Richmond)

TEQUAN RICHMOND AUDITIONED for the starring role of Chris. Series co-creator Ali LeRoi said that Richmond was too cool for the part. He was cast as Chris' younger brother Drew instead, while Tyler James Williams was hired to play Chris.

Everybody Loves Raymond (1996-2005)

Patricia Heaton as Debra Barone (Amy Brenneman, Lisa Edelstein, Jane
    Sibbett, Maggie Wheeler)

Suzie Plakson as Joanne Glotz (Edie Falco)

Sherri Shepherd as Judy (Judy Gold)

EVERYBODY LOVES RAY-MOND starred Ray Romano as sports writer Ray Barone. Ray and his wife Debra lived in Lynbrook, New York with their three children. Living across the street were Ray's parents and (occasionally) his older brother Robert. Amy Brenneman, Maggie Wheeler and Lisa Edelstein were all considered for the part of Debra Barone. Series creator Phil Rosenthal liked Wheeler very much, but CBS was not sold. They felt that Wheeler was too ethnic. The network suggested Jane Sibbett. The blonde Sibbett

Judy Gold

was ultimately deemed not ethnic enough. Casting director Lisa Miller Katz brought in Patricia Heaton. Heaton proved to be the right choice and won the part.

"The part of Judy was basically written for me," said Judy Gold. "I was working on *The Rosie O'Donnell Show*. I had to fly out to read for the producers. I was told it was between me and another person. I flew in for the day, and I walk into this room full of black women. They lied! I knew the producers and the writers." Gold was turned down and the role of Robert's partner Judy went to Sherri Shepherd instead.

Phil Rosenthal saw Edie Falco at the Golden Globe Awards. He told Falco that he would like for her to play the guest-starring role of Robert's ex-wife Joanne. Falco was interested, but was ultimately unable to commit. The part was played by Suzie Plakson instead.

Everything's Relative (1987)
Gina Hecht as Emily Cabot (Leslie Easterbrook)

CBS TOLD WRITER MARSHALL KARP that they wanted to do a show about brothers. They asked Karp if he had any ideas. He came up with the sitcom *Everything's Relative,* which focused on brothers Julian and Scott Beeby.

"We did the casting in New York," said Karp. "I was involved. I still had a major day job as a creative director of an advertising agency. I remember as it got down toward the end, I don't remember who the finalists were, but I remember that we would pair the neurotic brother, Julian, with the cool construction guy, Scott. In the end we had three sets of brothers. Jason Alexander was somebody nobody knew. He was clearly the front-runner. He was just so good. He was just such a natural at being this neurotic, high-strung, needy guy. I remember being in the room and the first two guys come in and then the second two guys come in and then the third two guys come in. There was no question that it was going to be Jason and John [Bolger]. It was that simple.

"The show had a lot of potential. When the show got picked up for series, this was my second show. The first one was called *Melba,* with Melba Moore. I left my advertising job and I was the guy who was running the television show in a studio in New York on East 76th Street. We had an executive from Columbia come out, but he wasn't a creative executive.

So now here you have me, this guy who has never been in the television business, except that I'd written pilots. I get to the studio on the first day. There's about 100 people there. I said, 'What do all these people do?' They said, 'Hey, whatever you ask them.'

"A woman named Fran McConnell was now running Columbia Pictures Television. She had worked with Norman Lear. Fran was just an absolutely wonderful woman. She was probably one of the nicest people I ever met and worked with in the television business. She was incredibly, incredibly supportive. She knew she had a guy who knew how to write, but didn't know much about running a television show. I found out later on how little I knew. I eventually went to Hollywood and worked on television shows. It was a struggle. I quit my day job and all of a sudden I'm working on this television show.

"The president of Columbia Pictures hired Anne Jackson without telling me anything. I thought, 'Wow! The Anne Jackson. She's a pretty big deal.' The pilot is certainly about the two guys. The mother comes in, I guess in the same way that Doris Roberts would come in on *Everybody Loves Raymond*. She had a nice part, but she was the meddling mother. After about the third or fourth episode Anne Jackson asked me to have lunch with her. She said, 'I don't understand. I seem to just walk in the door and say a few things that are funny. I was told I was the star of the show.' I said, 'Well, Anne, do you remember when we did the pilot? Do you remember you saw what it said on the script?' When we did the pilot, it wasn't called *Everything's Relative*. The show was called *The Brothers Beeby*. I really like Anne. I think television was not easy for her because she was a stage actress. You have to memorize a script in a heartbeat. The script changes every day for five days and then you're shooting. Anne was having a lot of trouble just with lines. I loved Anne Jackson. Whoever gave her the job steered her wrong. She was great. As soon as we had lunch I said, 'You got it.' I wrote a show where she gets mugged. It was really her episode. The young kid who played her mugger was Rob Morrow."

Gina Hecht was flown to New York to audition to play Emily Cabot in *Everything's Relative*. She saw Leslie Easterbrook there, and thought that Easterbrook would get the job. Hecht was chosen instead. Hecht became friends with fellow cast member Jason Alexander, and the two remain close friends to this day.

Tony Deacon Nittoli played the local kid Mickey Murphy. Mickey idolized Scott. "He just nailed the performance," said Karp. "He just got it. He had no real training. He was just perfect, but he had no formal training. He was just a kind of street kid who would come in to the house. He's the kind of character when you put in a sitcom, you don't have him do any of the real work. You don't have him set up anything. You just give him punch lines. I figured out early on that Tony had no acting experience. He would come in to the room, he would say a line, he would get a big laugh and he'd keep talking. They director would cut. He'd say, 'Hey, Tony. That was very funny but you've got to wait for the laugh.' Tony said okay. The audience laughed again, and he keeps talking! You can't hear his next line. The director said, 'Tony, you've got to wait for the laugh.' He goes back, comes through the door and does the line. He's so full of energy that every time he does it he still gets laughs, and he screws it up again. I finally say to the director, 'Can I just make a suggestion to Tony?' He said, 'Go ahead, anything.' I said, 'Hey, Tony, you've got to wait for the silence.' He comes in and he does the line, he gets the laugh, he waits, he waits. The crowd shuts up and he does the next line! It was so amazing. He had no training and to him wait for the laugh meant start talking as soon as they start laughing. He didn't even have a concept of the fact that the crowd was stepping on his line. He was just adorable. He was really good at what he did."

When CBS announced their upcoming fall schedule in May, *Everything's Relative* was set to air on Mondays at 8:30 following *Kate & Allie*. During the summer those plans changed and *Frank's Place* got the time slot. *Everything's Relative* was relegated to 8:00 on Saturday. Karp was told by CBS that they needed cannon fodder.

Marshall Karp wrote the 1999 feature film *Just Looking*. Karp suggested that Jason Alexander direct. Producer Jean Doumanian sent the script to Alexander. The script didn't have Karp's name on it. When Alexander came to New York to have an interview with the writer, he learned it was his old friend. "I remember having dinner with him," said Karp. "We just talked for hours. He's such a nice man; he's a real mensch. He's easy to work with. I knew he didn't have much directing experience, but I really wanted to give it a shot. We wound up giving John Bolger a part in the movie."

Marshall Karp's first novel was called *The Rabbit Factory*. The book takes place in Hollywood. The two protagonists are cops Mike Lomax and Terry Biggs. His follow-up novel, called *Blood Thirsty*, continues to follow Lomax and Biggs. In *Blood Thirsty* an actor is kidnapped. The paparazzi not only witnessed the kidnapping, but also made a video of

(From left) Marshall Karp, Jason Alexander and John Bolger on the set of *Just Looking* in 1999

it. The cops go to interview the two brothers who shot the video. The cops get to this dumpy area of Los Angeles. They go into a building and go to the green metal door of the brothers' duplex loft. The sign on the door said *The Brothers Beeby*, and then in Italian said tutto a possibile. "That is what the set decorator painted on the green metal door meaning everything is possible," said Karp. "When the show ended I took a picture of that door and at the wrap party I gave away about 50 pictures of that door. I framed it and gave it everyone in the cast and crew." Lomax and Biggs are greeted by Julian Beeby, who is described in the book as looking like the guy who played Seinfeld's neurotic friend George. Scott Beeby joins them. The cops question the two brothers about why they sold their footage of the crime. Julian responds, 'Hey, man, everything's relative.'"

The Evidence (2006)
Rob Estes as Sean Cole (Nicky Katt)

NICKY KATT WAS INITIALLY CAST in the role of Sean Cole in *The Evidence*. "Nicky was brilliant, but had a dark presence," said casting director John Levey. He was replaced by Rob Estes, who Levey said had a brighter quality.

The Execution of Private Slovik (1974)
Martin Sheen as Eddie Slovik (Dustin Hoffman)

NBC WANTED DUSTIN HOFFMAN to star in the title role of Private Eddie Slovik. Writers Richard Levinson and William Link wanted Martin Sheen instead. They had already worked with Sheen on *My Sweet Charlie* and *That Certain Summer*. Hoffman came to Universal to spend a day with Levinson and Link. Although they thought that Hoffman was a great actor, they persisted and eventually got their choice, Martin Sheen.

Eyes of a Stranger (1993)
Linda Fiorentino as Susan Gittes (Sean Young)

DIRECTOR SAM IRVIN met with Sean Young to discuss her playing the starring role of Susan Gittes in *Eyes of a Stranger*. "She was doing a lot of nutty things. The producers were concerned she would be trouble on a very tight schedule," said Irvin. He envisioned the character exactly like the offbeat character of Kiki in Martin Scorsese's *After Hours*. He went to the mat and pleaded to get Linda Fiorentino, who had played Kiki, for the part of Susan. Irvin was happy when she was signed for the role.

The Facts of Life (1979-1988)
Nancy McKeon as Jo Polniaczek (Tracy Reiner)

THE FACTS OF LIFE WAS a spin-off of the hit series *Diff'rent Strokes*. Series creator Al Burton did a wide search for the girls to star in the show, even looking in different dancing schools. The first season of *The Facts of Life* centered on Charlotte Rae as Mrs. Edna Garrett (the character she played on *Diff'rent Strokes*). Mrs. Garrett was the new housemother at Eastland, a boarding school for girls. The principal cast was large; there were seven girls in her charge. Kim Fields was cast as the youngest girl Tootie. Fields was about ten years old at the time, and was so small that Burton had her wear roller skates so she would be tall enough to be in the camera shots. Although Burton liked the large cast, it was decided that there were too many girls for the audience to keep track of. Actresses Felice Schachter, Julie Piekarski, Julie Anne Haddock and Molly Ringwald were let go as regulars, while Lisa Whelchel, Mindy Cohn and Kim Fields remained. A new character was added named Joanna "Jo" Marie Polniaczek, a tough girl from the Bronx. Tracy Reiner was offered the part. At the time, Reiner had no interest in doing a series (although she feels differently now) and turned the part down. After an extensive search, the part went to Nancy McKeon.

In 1983 Pamela Adlon (then known as Pamela Segall) joined the cast as the streetwise teenager Kelly Affinado. "When they told me I was going to be on *The Facts of Life*," said Adlon, "I was in San Francisco. I was understudying *Brighton Beach Memoirs*. I was with the original company of *Brighton Beach Memoirs*. I watched Matthew Broderick become a star. It was an amazing thing. And then I found out that I was going to be doing

The Facts of Life and I just couldn't believe it. Their whole intention was to try to feminize Nancy McKeon's character, and have me take over being the tough one.

"At Universal Studios there was an area that was all the NBC shows: *Silver Spoons, Diff'rent Strokes, Facts of Life, The Jeffersons* and *Charles In Charge.* Everybody was in all of these soundstages and going to school in the trailers and hanging out together. It was crazy! I even did an episode of *The Jeffersons* a few years later. I robbed George's dry cleaners. I robbed Edna's Edibles *and* George Jefferson's dry cleaners!"

Fame (1982-1987)

Erica Gimpel as Coco Hernandez (Irene Cara)
Janet Jackson as Cleo Hewitt (Melissa Etheridge)

THE 1980 FILM *Fame* followed a group of students through their high-school years at the High School for the Performing Arts, a real school, in New York City. The movie was hugely popular, and was turned into a television series in 1982. Irene Cara starred as Coco in the film. She was offered the chance to reprise the role for the series but decided against it. Erica Gimpel was cast instead.

An unknown Melissa Etheridge went to an open call for the show. She received a call back and was eventually one of the final two actresses being considered to play student Cleo Hewitt. After reading with Debbie Allen, the star of the show, Etheridge saw that the other contender was Janet Jackson. Allen took Etheridge aside and told her that the part was obviously going to Jackson, but that she was very talented and should keep pursuing her singing.

Michael Cerveris was living in New York when he auditioned for the Adam Ant-like character of Ian Ware. At the time Cerveris had minimal television experience. He first auditioned in New York, and was put on

tape by the casting director. "I had to sing a song," he said. "I played guitar and sang 'Young Americans,' which was my choice - the David Bowie
song. I had to read a couple of scenes with an English accent. The one
funny thing I remember about the audition was that someone (the casting assistant or the person behind the desk), as I was sitting out there said
something about - I think I asked to be sure that I should be doing an English accent - and she said, 'You should do it the whole time. You should
just go in talking in the accent so it's easier for them to believe you as that.'
So I went in with what I'm sure was not a terribly good English accent and
did that the whole time. The fact that they're asking me questions about
where I was from and I was saying, 'West Virginia,' but with an English
accent, nobody batted an eye. I think I went in once, probably for a pre-
screening thing, and then I came back again later when the actual casting
director was in. They put me on tape and sent it out to California." The
next thing Cerveris knew, the part was his. He joined the show in 1986,
and stayed through the end of the series in 1987.

Family (1976-1980)

Meredith Baxter as Nancy Lawrence Maitland (Cheryl Ladd)
Brooke Adams as Lizzie (Blair Brown, Glynnis O'Connor)

FAMILY FOLLOWED THE TRIALS and tribulations of the Lawrence family.
"We were fortunate in that Mike Nichols was our co-executive producer,
and owned the show with Aaron [Spelling] and I," said executive producer Leonard Goldberg. "We had a great script by Jay Presson Allen. She
was a writer who did not come to television easily. We had Mike Nichols
and we had Mark Rydell, who had agreed to direct the pilot. So we could
get every actor in Hollywood to come in and audition because they really
wanted to meet Mike Nichols."

James Broderick was cast as patriarch Doug Lawrence, while Sada

Thompson played his wife Kate. Gary Frank played their son Willie, and Kristy McNichol was cast as their youngest daughter Letitia, who went by the name Buddy. Two serious contenders for the part of the older daughter Nancy were Cheryl Ladd and Meredith Baxter. Baxter eventually got the job. Leonard Goldberg said that Ladd was probably too gorgeous for the part.

In 1977 the feature film *The Goodbye Girl* was released. The 10-year-old Quinn Cummings' gave such a great performance that she was nominated for an Oscar for the film. She also caught the attention of the producers of *Family*. Leonard Goldberg remembers a lunch meeting with Cummings and her mother. "During lunch she said, 'It's so hard to break a hard roll gracefully," said Goldberg. "And I thought, 'How old is she!' But she was great. We thought we needed another character and she would be very fun." Quinn Cummings joined the cast as Annie Cooper, a young girl the Lawrence family took in.

Blair Brown and Glynnis O'Connor read for the guest-starring role of Lizzie. O'Connor was dismissed as too vulnerable. Brooke Adams auditioned and won the part.

Family Album (1993)
Pamela Reed as Denise Lerner (Gina Hecht)
Nancy Cassaro as Sheila DeMattis (Gina Hecht)

GINA HECHT AUDITIONED for the supporting part of Sheila DeMattis on *Family Album* She was good friends with Marta Kauffman, who created the series with David Crane. Kauffman thought Hecht would be better cast in the lead role of Denise Lerner. Said Hecht, "This was not my part. I knew my casting. Reluctantly, I read it at her house. I knew she was looking for a Pam Dawber type." Kauffman liked Hecht's reading, and brought her to audition for CBS. The network didn't want to cast Hecht, but deferred to Kauffman's judgment. During the table read, Hecht could see that the first scene wasn't working as written. CBS fired her and replaced her with Pamela Reed.

Family Business (1983)

Jeffrey Marcus as Jeffrey Stern (Joel Polis)

FAMILY BUSINESS was a play written by Dick Goldberg. The first off-Broadway production was at the Astor Place Theatre in 1978, where it ran for a year. The show was then produced by the Roundabout Theatre Company and moved to a theater on 23rd Street between 8th and 9th Avenue. The PBS series American Playhouse decided to do a version of the play for television. The cast would mostly remain the same; however, Harold Gary, who played the role of the father Isaiah Stern, was replaced by Milton Berle. Joel Polis was also replaced. On stage Polis looked fine to play his character of the youngest Stern brother. However, on television, he just read too old. Jeffrey Marcus was brought in as his replacement.

David Garfield played Norman Stein in the TV version, as well as both New York productions. He was very glad to have had the opportunity to work with Milton Berle. "Milton didn't think twice about giving other actors notes!" he said. He enjoyed working with Berle, and thought that he was very good in the film.

Family Ties (1982-1989)

Michael J. Fox as Alex P. Keaton (Matthew Broderick)
Meredith Baxter as Elyse Keaton (Donna McKechnie)
Michael Gross as Steven Keaton (Chris Sarandon)
Justine Bateman as Mallory Keaton (Pamela Adlon, Laura Dern)
Tracy Pollan as Ellen Reed (Deborah Goodrich, Meg Ryan, Marisa Tomei)
Cindy Fisher as Kimberly Blanton (Justine Bateman)

JUDITH WEINER CAST THE PILOT episode of *Family Ties*. Weiner loved actor Michael J. Fox, and brought him in to read for the part of Alex P. Keaton. Fox was the very first person to read for the role. After his reading producer Lloyd Garver said that he was fine. Producer Michael J.

Weithorn and Judith Weiner both agreed. However, series creator Gary David Goldberg talked for about ten minutes about how Fox was all wrong to play Alex. The casting process continued for another couple of months unsuccessfully. A tape of Matthew Broderick was sent from New York. Goldberg loved him. He said, "This is Alex. We've got to get him." "Matthew absolutely wasn't going to leave New York at that time 'cause his father [James Broderick] was dying, and just couldn't do the series," said Weithorn. "I remember Gary was very disappointed and crushed and saw the whole thing slipping away. Judith said, 'Can I bring back Michael Fox?' Gary said, 'What the hell. The thing is dead.' She brought back Michael. I remember it very well. Gary talked to him for a long time when he first came in and said, 'This is what was wrong the first time ' He gave him this whole speech and Michael said, 'So, what you're saying is either I get the part or I don't.' He read and he gave the identical reading. It was really the same thing. Timing being everything, he left and Gary said, 'I love him!' Brought him to the network. It was not by any means an easy sale. The famous quote that was said, [Brandon] Tartikoff did say, I was sitting right there, 'Is this the kind of kid who's going to wind up on lunchboxes?' He wasn't really sold on him even after we shot the pilot. Gary really did stick with him at that point. He said it was this kid or nobody."

When *Family Ties* debuted the main focus of the show was the parents, Steven and Elyse Keaton. Fox was so popular with audiences that the show went in another direction, and he became the breakout character. The show was an enormous hit, and Fox's face was indeed on lunchboxes.

Meredith Baxter and Broadway star Donna McKechnie were both strongly considered for the part of Elyse Keaton. Baxter was chosen, and runner-up McKechnie was later hired to play a guest role in the show's second season.

Laura Dern and Pamela Adlon read for the part of the Keatons' oldest daughter, Mallory. Adlon came very close to getting the part, but was ultimately unable to take the job. Justine Bateman initially came in to read for the guest role of Kimberly Blanton. At the time Bateman had very little acting experience. Michael J. Weithorn was struck by Bateman's beauty, and suggested her for Mallory. She came back another day and read for the part. "She had no technique at all," said Weithorn. "She was all over the place but she had something. She had a very infectious smile and a look, and just the quality. There was another girl who was, at that point, the preemptive favorite, who had basically been told by Gary she had the part. Then the day she shows up to read at the network there's this other girl, Justine. The network agreed that Justine was a very appealing new face."

The role of Steven Keaton was the last to be cast. "We went to the network, I think the day before the table read with Michael Gross and Chris Sarandon," said Weithorn. "Both excellent actors. They both read and they both read well. I remember that it wasn't even decided in the room. We drove back from Burbank to Hollywood. We were sitting in the office and Gary was on the phone back and forth with [Brandon] Tartikoff, and he didn't know, and nobody seemed to know. Gary asked me, 'Which one do you like better?' I said, 'Well, they're both really good. I think Michael Gross is funnier.' He said, 'He is! You're right! He's funnier!' He called Tartikoff back, 'Gross is funnier!' I don't think I was the one who made the decision so much as maybe just tipped it, gave it a tiny poke and pushed it in that direction."

Weithorn wrote the episode that introduced the character of Alex's love interest Ellen Reed. Marisa Tomei came very close to getting the part. However, her thick New York accent was wrong and she was passed over. Meg Ryan also read. The character was written as an intellectual arty type. Ryan came off as adorable, and had a different energy. Deborah Goodrich was seriously considered, and was actually the second choice, but the part went to Tracy Pollan instead. Pollan and Fox met on the set of *Family Ties*. They fell in love and were married in 1988.

The Famous Teddy Z (1989-1990)
Alex Rocco as Al Floss (Hector Elizondo)

JON CRYER PLAYED the title role of agent Ted Zakalokis (Teddy Z). Hector Elizondo gave a very impressive reading for the part of Ted's fellow agent Al Floss. However, Alex Rocco was the first choice of show creator and executive producer Hugh Wilson as he was writing the script. Rocco won the part, and was so good in the role that he won an Emmy for it.

Fantasy Island (1978-1984)
Ricardo Montalban as Mr. Roarke (Orson Welles)

EXECUTIVE PRODUCERS LEONARD Goldberg and Aaron Spelling wanted to cast Fantasy Island nontraditionally. ABC wanted Orson Welles for the starring role of Mr. Roarke. "We thought we should go in a different direction, and I think it was Aaron who suggested Ricardo [Montalban]," said Goldberg. "Of course we all knew Ricardo. He was a great movie star and a matinee idol. But he wasn't the typical Middle American star. But we thought he would be great. He also brought great dignity to it. He had that command. The way he walked and the way he stood. We went after Ricardo first. We were fortunate to get him. Aaron knew him fairly well.

"Then, we thought, 'Who's going to play Tattoo?' We had seen Herve Villechaize in the James Bond movie The Man with the Golden Gun, and we thought why not go all the way and take a shot. We brought Herve in. It was hard to understand what he was saying. The two of them together, it was either going to be great or a disaster."

The pilot episode of Fantasy Island was somewhat dark. The network ordered the show, but asked that it be lightened up. Fantasy Island was a very big hit, which ran for six years.

Farscape (1999-2003)

Anthony Simcoe as D'Argo (Lani Tupu)
Rebecca Riggs as Grayza (Raelee Hill)

LANI KUPU CAME IN to read for the part of D'Argo on *Farscape*. The role went to Anthony Simcoe instead. The producers felt that Tupu was such a good actor they had to use him somewhere in a substantial role. He was cast as the suave and dangerous Captain Crais.

Raelee Hill auditioned to play the part of Grayza. Executive producer David Kemper took one look at her audition tape and was completely smitten. The role of Sikozu was created for her, while Rebecca Riggs was cast as Grayza.

Fast Track (1997)

Keith Carradine as Richard Beckett (Kevin Anderson, Richard Dean
    Anderson, Armand Assante, Adam Baldwin, Gil Bellows, Jim Belushi,
    Tom Berenger, Peter Berg, Patrick Bergin, Corbin Bernsen, Michael Biehn,
    Powers Boothe, Bryan Brown, Robert John Burke, Gabriel Byrne, John
    Corbett, Peter Coyote, Willem Dafoe, Tony Danza, Bruce Davison, Matt
    Dillon, Patrick Duffy, Emilio Estevez, Jeff Fahey, Thomas Gibson, Richard
    E. Grant, Harry Hamlin, C. Thomas Howell, William Hurt, Chris Isaak,
    Kris Kristofferson, Anthony LaPaglia, Kyle MacLachlan, Tim Matheson,
    Dylan McDermott, Christopher McDonald, John C. McGinley, Matthew
    Modine, Viggo Mortensen, George Newbern, Michael O'Keefe, Ken
    Olin, Ryan O'Neal, Peter Onorati, Michael Ontkean, Joe Penny, William
    Petersen, Lou Diamond Phillips, Aidan Quinn, Campbell Scott, Kyle
    Secor, Ted Shackleford, John Shea, Craig Sheffer, James Spader, Vincent
    Spano, David Strathairn, Treat Williams, Michael Wincott)

THERE WERE MANY ACTORS considered for the starring role of Dr. Richard Beckett (listed above). The producers met with Keith Carradine and loved him. Soon after, Carradine was signed for the part.

Fastlane (2002-2003)

Tiffani Thiessen as Billie Chambers (Melinda Clarke, Rebecca DeMornay)

REBECCA DEMORNAY WAS considered for the part of police lieutenant Billie Chambers in the action series *Fastlane*. Eventually, the contenders for the role were narrowed down to two: Tiffani Thiessen and Melinda Clarke. Tiffani Thiessen got the part. Clarke was given the role of Julie Cooper on *Fastlane* creator McG's subsequent show *The O.C.*

Felicity (1998-2002)

Keri Russell as Felicity Porter (Kate Hudson, Tara Reid)
Scott Speedman as Ben Covington (Scott Foley)
Tangi Miller as Elena Tyler (Ion Overman)

KATE HUDSON AND TARA REID both auditioned for the title role of Felicity Porter. Keri Russell was also brought in to read. She surprised everyone with her vulnerability, sense of humor and self-effasiveness, and won the part.

Casting director Marcia Shulman knew Scott Foley from an episode of *Buffy the Vampire Slayer*. She brought him in for the part of Noel Crane. Later on, Shulman had the idea to switch Foley to the part of Ben Covington. Foley agreed to the switch. Shulman eventually remembered a tape she had seen three years earlier of Scott Speedman. She tracked Speedman down by calling his mother. Speedman put himself on tape for Shulman, who took the tape to the series creators J.J. Abrams and Matt Reeves. "They were literally dancing a jig," said Shulman. They took the tape to the WB. All involved agreed that Speedman was the right choice to play Ben Covington. Shulman had to go to Foley once again and ask him to switch back to the part of Noel. Foley thought the project was so good that he graciously agreed. The pilot started shooting three days later.

Ion Overman tested for the part of Elena Tyler. The role went to Tangi Miller instead.

Firefly (2002-2004)

Morena Baccarin as Inara Serra (Rebecca Gayheart)

REBECCA GAYHEART WAS cast as Inara Serra in the Joss Whedon series *Firefly*. Gayheart ultimately left the show, and a replacement was sought. Morena Baccarin auditioned. She did well and was brought in the next day to test for the network. Baccarin won the role that day, and started work the following day.

The Flintstones (1960-1966)

Alan Reed as Fred Flintstones (Daws Butler)
Bea Benaderet as Betty Rubble (June Foray)

DAWS BUTLER WAS ORIGINALLY cast as Fred Flagstone in the unaired pilot for *The Flintstones*, then called *The Flagstones*. The series was a cartoon version of the hit show *The Honeymooners*. Fred was the cartoon version of Jackie Gleason's character of Brooklyn bus driver Ralph Kramden. Butler played the part of Fred as an exact takeoff of Gleason. The producers thought it was too dead-on and replaced him with Alan Reed. June Foray played Betty Rubble in the original pilot. When the show finally hit the air, Foray was replaced by Bea Benaderet.

For Richer, for Poorer (1992)

Jonathan Silverman as Michael Katourian (Patrick Dempsey)

JACK LEMMON WAS CAST in the starring role of millionaire Aram Katourian in the HBO movie *For Richer, for Poorer*. Director Jay Sandrich wanted Patrick Dempsey to play his son Michael Katourian. Dempsey turned the part down, and it was given to Jonathan Silverman instead.

Four Kings (2006)

Seth Green as Barry (Dan Fogler)

CASTING DIRECTOR JEFF Greenberg spent about 15 weeks casting *Four Kings*. Dan Fogler auditioned on tape for the part of Barry. "He gave one of the best auditions I've ever seen," said Greenberg. At the time Fogler was in the off-Broadway production of *The 25th Annual Putnam County Spelling Bee*. Greenberg wanted to bring him to L.A. to test. Said Greenberg, "Within the two days that it took to get the tape, to watch the tape, to call him up, the production got a pickup to go to Broadway. He decided he didn't want to be in the TV show now. So of course when you say, 'I don't want it,' everyone now had to have him. They were throwing money at him. They said, 'You don't have to audition, it's an offer.' Anything they could do to make him say yes. But he held his ground, which was very smart. He ended up winning the Tony, and he's now starring in movies. He made the right decision."

Frankie & Hazel (2000)

Mischa Barton as Frankie Humphries (Lindsay Lohan)

DIRECTOR JOBETH WILLIAMS wanted Joan Plowright to star as Phoebe Harkness in the Showtime movie *Frankie & Hazel*. Williams didn't think that Plowright would accept, but made an offer anyway. To her surprise (and delight) Plowright signed on for the film. She told Williams that one of the reasons she did was to support women directors.

Lindsay Lohan was offered the chance to play Frankie. "We had her up until about a week and a half before we started shooting," said Williams. "I remember we were already up in Vancouver and her mother decided that the timing wasn't right. They pulled out. So we were left a week and a half before we were supposed to start shooting with no leading lady. And I needed a leading lady who you could believe as a ballerina and as an athlete. It was a frantic search. I believe I came down to L.A. and auditioned again. I saw Mischa [Barton] in something. I didn't audition her. She was just on the cusp of being a young teenager, but she still could play a tomboy. She couldn't do it now! She did very well. She had never had a dance lesson in her life. So we had to get her quickly working with someone, and we happened to find a fabulous ballet double for her. She looked a lot like her. So, it worked out. But it was tough."

JoBeth Williams

Frasier (1993-2004)

Jane Leeves as Daphne Moon (Lisa Maxwell, Cynthia Nixon)
David Hyde-Pierce as Niles Crane (Peter MacNichol)
John Mahoney as Martin Crane (Robert Prosky)
Peri Gilpin as Roz Doyle (Caroline Aaron, Patricia Clarkson, Hope Davis,
    Lisa Edelstein, Holly Fulger, Janeane Garofalo, Salma Hayek, Laura Innes,
    Allison Janney, Lisa Kudrow, Rita Wilson)

THE CHARACTER OF PSYCHIATRIST Frasier Crane came from the hit show *Cheers*. When *Cheers* ended it was decided that Kelsey Grammer, who played Frasier, would get his own show. The character moved from Boston to Seattle, where he took a job as a radio psychiatrist. The producers of *Frasier* did not originally intend to have Frasier's brother as a character on the show. Casting director Sheila Guthrie remarked that an actor named David Hyde-Pierce looked like he could be Kelsey Grammer's brother. The producers already had the show *Wings* on the air, which revolved around two brothers. They didn't want a repeat of that show. They eventually warmed up to the idea of adding Frasier's brother Niles Crane. "They realized that what was so great with Frasier on *Cheers* was that he had a co-Frasier in the form of Lilith," said casting director Jeff Greenberg. "While there were differences, they were very similar. They thought, 'Well, maybe we could have someone be Frasier's brother who is more Frasier than Frasier. So we met with David Hyde-Pierce, who they thought would be perfect. No script yet. David was very much an actor looking for his next job. It just felt right. He took a leap of faith because he said yes when he found out that we really wanted him. And it was a leap of faith for us too, because it wasn't written. No one had any idea that would be the breakout character from the show. He's just a good actor. That came together because he looked like Kelsey."

The last season of *Cheers* was still in production during the casting process for *Frasier*. Around the time the role of Frasier's father Martin Crane was being created, Greenberg had recently hired John Mahoney for a guest spot on *Cheers*. "While he was there, he was loving it," said Greenberg. "I asked him, would he ever consider doing another show of this style. He said, 'Well, if it's as good as *Cheers*, I sure would.' I ran to tell Grubb Street. They said, 'We love him.' I said, 'Then you'd better make this as good as *Cheers*.' When the script was finished and John was back in Chicago, where he lived, my producers flew there with the script in

Jeff Greenberg

hand and a bottle of Jameson's, and wined and dined him. By the time they got back to L.A. he read the script and said, 'I'd love to do it.'"

In the event things hadn't worked out with either Pierce or Mahoney the producers had Peter MacNichol and Robert Prosky as their second choices for Niles and Martin. Prosky had no idea he had ever been considered.

When the show was pitched to NBC, Warren Littlefield wanted to see if there was a role for Jane Leeves. Greenberg showed the producers film on her from episodes of *Seinfeld* and *Murphy Brown* she had done. They liked her, and especially liked the fact that she was English. They felt it could help define the character of Daphne Moon. Leeves was brought in to read. "We had to do it very fast because she had a couple of other offers from other shows," said Greenberg. "I put together a quick session with three other actors, one of whom was Cynthia Nixon, pre-*Sex and the City*, of course. Jane was the best. We loved her. We had Kelsey come over from the *Cheers* stage to read with her. He loved her, and just said, 'Be careful it doesn't become *Nanny and the Professor*.' Years later I asked Jane her memories of that audition. She said, 'All I thought was that I was too tall for Kelsey!' Kelsey's 6'2". Jane, with heels, is about that. That wasn't a concern. NBC didn't need to audition her because they loved her already. So we had our Daphne."

Holly Fulger auditioned to play Frasier's producer Roz Doyle. At the same time she was offered a role on *These Friends of Mine*. Although she was advised to go for *Frasier*, Fulger accepted the part of Holly on *These Friends of Mine*. The show was later renamed *Ellen*.

The producers weren't sure of what they wanted Roz to be like. They were looking for the funniest actress they could find. Over 100 actresses ranging from their early 20s to their 60s (and every ethnicity) read for the part. Among the actresses who came in were Patricia Clarkson, Janeane Garofalo, Salma Hayek, Rita Wilson, Lisa Edelstein, Laura Innes, Allison Janney, and Hope Davis. It was eventually narrowed down to about seven actresses, including Caroline Aaron. Grammer read with all of them. It was then narrowed down to the top two: Peri Gilpin and Lisa Kudrow. "We took the two of them over to NBC to test for the role," said Greenberg. "I read with them. They gave the role to Lisa. The network really liked her. She earned the part. She was our Roz." A few days before the show was to be shot in front of a studio audience, director James Burrows brought a test audience in. "Lisa did the show that night," Greenberg said. "The show wasn't working as a whole. The scenes at the radio station were not balancing the scenes at home. And it became obvious only that night that Frasier needed somehow a more worthy opponent at the office. Lisa's version of Roz was sort of intersecting a little bit with Daphne. It wasn't working. Jim Burrows did not know that Peri had tested for the role. He said, 'You know who you need for the part? Peri Gilpin.' He had worked with her a couple of times. We said that was our second choice. He said, 'Get her here for tomorrow. I'll talk to the network.' I had to, unfortunately, fire Lisa, who we loved. She didn't do anything wrong. We just hired the wrong actress. It was our fault. We had to let her go. We tracked down Peri that night at Orso in L.A. I had to bring her to the phone and say, 'What are you doing tomorrow?' She said, 'Nothing.' I said, 'Well, you're going to work on *Frasier*.' She screamed, and left the restaurant. By the time I got to rehearsal the next day she was wearing Lisa Kudrow's costume. I don't even think they'd had time to dry clean it. We had the right Roz. It was happy endings all around, obviously because the following season *Friends* happened and it was a better role for Lisa. She became a megastar."

Freddie (2005-2006)
Madchen Amick as Allison (Megyn Price)

THE ABC SITCOM *Freddie* starred Freddie Prinze, Jr., and was inspired by his life growing up among a house full of women. In the series Prinze played Freddie Moreno, a chef living with his grandmother, niece and sister-in-law.

Finding an actress to play the role of his sister-in-law Allison proved to be a difficult task. As shooting was drawing near Megyn Price was asked to just do the pilot in order to get something on the air. After the pilot was sold, Price was given the chance to remain with the show. She decided against it. After another search the part went to Madchen Amick.

The Fresh Prince of Bel-Air (1990-1996)

Vivica A. Fox as Janet (Halle Berry, Lela Rochon)

VIVICA A. FOX, HALLE Berry and Lela Rochon all auditioned for the guest-starring role of Janet on the February 4, 1991 episode of *The Fresh Prince of Bel-Air* called "It Had to Be You." Janet was the sister of Jazz, played by DJ Jazzy Jeff, also known as Jeffrey A. Townes. Fox won the part.

Friends (1994-2004)

Jennifer Aniston as Rachel Green (Elizabeth Berkley, Courteney Cox, Jami Gertz, Jane Krakowski, Tea Leoni, Parker Posey, Denise Richards, Melissa Rivers, Nicollette Sheridan)

Courteney Cox as Monica Geller (Mariska Hargitay, Jessica Hecht, Tammy Lauren, Julianna Margulies, Nancy McKeon, Leah Remini)

Lisa Kudrow as Phoebe Buffay (Christine Cavanaugh, Kathleen Wilhoite)

David Schwimmer as Ross Geller (Craig Bierko, Eric McCormack, Mitchell Whitfield)

Matthew Perry as Chandler Bing (Craig Bierko, Jon Cryer, Jon Favreau, Terrence Howard, Alex Nevil, Harland Williams)

Matt LeBlanc as Joey Tribbiani (Hank Azaria, Vince Vaughn)

THE ROLE OF MONICA GELLER was originally envisioned as a Jeaneane Garofalo type. Garofalo was made an offer, but passed. Leah Remini auditioned for the part. She gave a good audition and was called back. At her call back she saw Courteney Cox there. At that point Remini knew she was not going to get the role.

Casting director Ellie Kanner had Courteney Cox in mind for the role of Rachel Green. Cox auditioned for the part, and did very well. Kanner thought that Cox was good enough to be seen by the executives at NBC. The actress had anther idea; she wanted to play Monica Geller instead. She asked, and was allowed to read for Moncia. Cox was called back to test for the network, but as Rachel. She insisted that the part she was right for was Monica. "We all agreed to let her read for Monica," said Kanner, "but then we were going to just offer her Rachel. And in the room she nailed Monica so perfectly that we gave her the role."

Other possible Monica contenders were Tammy Lauren, Mariska Hargitay, Julianna Margulies and Nancy McKeon, who was the runner-up for the role. Jessica Hecht also auditioned. "They loved her, but she wasn't quite right," said Kanner. Hecht was instead cast as Susan Bunch, the girlfriend of Ross Geller's ex-wife Carol.

Tea Leoni was offered the part of Rachel. She wasn't interested and said no. Jami Gertz passed as well. Nicollette Sheridan and Parker Posey turned down the chance to audition. Denise Richards, Jane Krakowski, Elizabeth Berkley and Melissa Rivers read, but lost the part to Jennifer Aniston.

Kathleen Wilhoite, Christine Cavanaugh and Lisa Kudrow auditioned to play the quirky Phoebe Buffay. There was about a month between Kudrow's initial audition and her test. She had a lot of time to think about the character. The day before her test she called Kanner to ask if she could try her reading a different way in front of Kanner and *Friends* co-creator Marta Kauffman. Afterwards, Kauffman and Kanner advised her to do it the way she originally planned the following day for the network. Kudrow heeded their advice. She did a great job reading the character's monologue in the pilot and won the part.

Craig Bierko was offered the choice of playing either Ross Geller or

Chandler Bing. The actor had a deal with NBC at the time. Bierko passed on *Friends* to make another pilot, entitled *Best Friends,* in which he was the star. Unfortunately for Bierko *Best Friends* wasn't picked up.

Mitchell Whitfield read for the part of Ross, as did Eric McCormack. David Schwimmer was pursued for the part. The actor was in Chicago doing theatre and wasn't interested in doing a series at the time. He changed his mind when he learned that the show featured an ensemble cast.

The producers thought Matthew Perry might be right to play Chandler. At the time Perry was already committed to another series about baggage handlers in the future called *LAX 2194.* Other actors were also considered, including Terrence Howard, Jon Favreau, Alex Nevil and Harland Williams. Jon Cryer was in London when he was asked to audition for the part of Chandler Bing. He auditioned in England and a tape was sent to Los Angeles. Cryer was definitely a backup choice if Matthew Perry didn't nail it at the network. However, Perry did so well that the producers decided to take a chance that *LAX 2194* wouldn't be picked up and gave him the part. They turned out to be right.

Matt LeBlanc, Hank Azaria and Vince Vaughn all auditioned to play actor Joey Tribbiani. LeBlanc made the character sweet, which won him the part.

The Fugitive (1963-1967)
David Janssen as Richard Kimble (Dennis Weaver)

DENNIS WEAVER WAS offered the starring role of fugitive Dr. Richard Kimble. He turned it down, and David Janssen was cast instead.

Full House (1987-1995)

Bob Saget as Danny Tanner (John
   Posey, Paul Reiser)
David Lipper as Viper (Danny
   Comden)

PAUL REISER, BOB SAGET and
John Posey were all seriously considered for the starring role of
Danny Tanner on *Full House*. Bob
Saget was chosen, but was unavailable. Paul Reiser was also made
an offer, but he chose the series
My Two Dads instead. John Posey
got the part. A pilot was made,
but soon afterwards Saget became
available. Creator Jeff Franklin was

John Posey

still interested in him. He made his feelings known to ABC. The network
allowed the switch. Posey was fired, and the pilot was reshot with Bob
Saget. It cost about $500,000 to reshoot the pilot. ABC's investment paid
off. *Full House* was a smash hit, and ran for eight years.

For the role of the infant daughter Michelle, the producers looked at
many sets of twins. "The reason the Olsen twins have a career is because
of all the twins, they cried the least," said writer/producer Kim Weiskopf.

In 1994 the character of Viper was added to the cast. Danny Comden
auditioned, but lost the role to David Lipper.

Crystal Carson

General Hospital (1963-)

Cheryl Richardson as Jenny Eckert (Cari Shayne)
John J. York as Mac Scorpio (Paul Satterfield)
Crystal Carson as Julia Barrett (Lisa Rinna)
Robert Fontaine as Frankie Greco (Antonio Sabato, Jr.)
Gerald Hopkins as A.J. Quartermaine (Sean Kanan)
Jon Lindstrom as Ryan Chamberlain (Michael O'Leary)
Jennifer Hammon as Karen Wexler (Cari Shayne)

CRYSTAL CARSON AND LISA RINNA both auditioned for the part of Julia Barrett. Said Carson of her screen test, "I got on the set and they called my name to go next. I forgot to bring my shoes; I only had Birkenstock sandals! I called my friend. He had to break into my house through a window to bring my shoes to me.

"They gave us new lines that day. I did those. They asked us to come back down to the set, where they had us do an improv with Tony Geary. I remember just watching my hand knock on the door; the stage manager took my hand and made it knock." Carson didn't know what to do, and figured she had nothing to lose. "I just clicked in and went for it. All the cameramen started clapping. Tony Geary said, 'It doesn't get any better than that.'" Carson won the part. A very gracious Lisa Rinna sent Carson a very sweet card to congratulate her. Rinna wrote that she was glad when good people work. Soon after, Rinna landed the role of Billie on *Days of Our Lives*. Carson sent her a card to congratulate her.

Antonio Sabato, Jr. auditioned for the part of Frankie Greco. He lost out to Robert Fontaine, although Sabato was eventually hired by *General Hospital*. In 1992, he was cast in the breakout role of Jagger Cates.

Paul Satterfield auditioned to play the Australian Mac Scorpio. John J. York won the part instead. Satterfield was hired for the show as well. He played Paul Hornsby from 1991-1994. Satterfield, an American, was relieved he didn't have to play a character with an Australian accent.

Mark Teschner brought Jon Lindstrom in to read for a role when Gloria Monty was running the show. Monty soon left, and the part was never developed. About six months later the role of Ryan Chamberlain came up. Teschner tracked Lindstrom down. "I went through a series of auditions for that," said Lindstrom. "The final one was between me and Michael O'Leary. That was supposed to be a three-month non-contract role. It eventually did turn into a contract, and five years and another show [*Port Charles*]. Three months turned into eleven years."

Cari Shayne
Photo: Lesley Bohm Photography

Sean Kanan and Gerald Hopkins were both up for the part of A.J. Quartermaine. Hopkins was chosen. In 1992 Hopkins was let go, and a replacement was sought. Kanan got the job.

Cari Shayne auditioned for the part of Jenny Eckert. The role was given to Cheryl Richardson instead. Shayne later originated the role of Karen Wexler, a part she played from 1992-1995. In 1997 the show decided to bring the character back. Shayne was contacted to see if she wanted to reprise the role. "I was doing a lot of TV movies," said Shayne. "I was doing some other show. At that point I had no interest in daytime. It's such a grueling schedule." Jennifer Hammon was later cast as Karen.

Generations (1989-1991)

Joan Pringle as Ruth Marshall (Jonelle Allen)
Vivica A. Fox as Maia (Nia Long)

JONELLE ALLEN WAS CALLED to audition for the part of Ruth Marshall. Allen went to read, although she wanted a different part instead. If she had it her way, she would be auditioning to play Doreen Jackson, the showier role. Allen read for Ruth, but read with Doreen in mind. She was able to convey that she was right for Doreen, and the producers asked her to audition for the part. She was told to play it sexy. She came to her audition in a black-lace teddy. Allen nailed the audition, and the part was hers.

Vivica A. Fox and Nia Long were the final two contenders for the part of Maia on *Generations*. Whoever was chosen would work opposite Kristoff St. John, who played Adam Marshall. "I was a little taller to go with Kristoff," said Fox, who got the job. "I worked with a lot of very experienced actors on that show. I learned so much. I used to always look at myself in the monitor, until they said, 'You can't do that!' I really learned to act on that show."

George Lopez (2002-2007)

Constance Marie as Angie Lopez (Alex Meneses)

GEORGE LOPEZ was a semi-autobiographical show about George Lopez's life. Lopez wanted real Latinos to play his onscreen family.

Constance Marie and Alex Meneses vied for the part of George's wife Angie. Meneses seemed too young to be the mother of the Lopez' two children and the role went to Constance Marie.

Get Smart (1965-1970)

Dick Gautier as Hymie (King
  Moody)

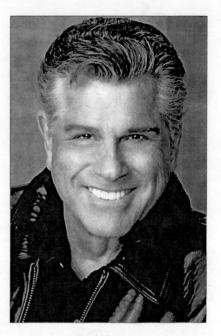

Dick Gautier

DON ADAMS APPEARED on *The Bill Dana Show*. On the show he played a character named Detective Byron Glick. Glick was very similar to Maxwell Smart, the role he played on *Get Smart*.

Barbara Feldon auditioned for the part of 99. Everyone loved her, and she won the role. After *Get Smart* was sold, a problem arose. Feldon had made a commercial for a company who was a competitor for *Get Smart's* advertiser. They wanted Feldon removed from the cast. She had to go to New York for a meeting in which she convinced the company not to run her other commercials.

Get Smart co-creator Buck Henry invited Paul Bogart to direct the show's second episode. "I had never done comedy before," said Bogart. "I thought it would be fun. It was lovely to meet Don Adams, Barbara Feldon and Edward Platt. I enjoyed it. It was way out of my usual routine."

Dick Gautier was called in to interview for the series. "I had no idea what it was, they just wanted to see me," said Gautier. "I went in and talked to them and they said, 'It's the part of a white-collar robot. You're not in any costume or anything; you're you. How would you play it?' And I said, 'Well, I don't really know, but I remember when I was a kid in Canada I remember seeing a guy, like a mannequin in a department store window. He was moving stiffly and moving his head strangely, blinking one eye.

The deal was, if you broke him up, if he cracked, you made $100. I was a kid, like nine or ten years old, and all my friends were there trying to make him laugh. Finally, I started imitating him, and I did it fairly well I guess, because he started to smile. But he didn't really crack so I didn't get the money." So I harked back to that moment and that's how I got the role of Hymie the Robot."

King Moody was also up for the part of Hymie. He was eventually cast as different KAOS agents, before getting the recurring role of Shtarker.

The Ghost and Mrs. Muir (1968-1970)
Hope Lange as Carolyn Muir (Gene Tierney)

GENE TIERNEY STARRED as Mrs. Muir in the 1947 film *The Ghost and Mrs. Muir.* She offered to play the part for the television version. The decision was made to go with a younger actress. Hope Lange was a star at 20th Century-Fox, where the show was produced. She was offered the part, which she accepted.

Producer Gene Reynolds had a hard time finding the right actor to play Captain Gregg. The part called for an attractive leading man who was stalwart, large and a very good actor who could play both romantic and comedic. Edward Mulhare fit the bill.

"When I was in New York, I saw a bunch of people for the character of the real estate agent," said Reynolds. "I met Charles Nelson Reilly. I had seen his work before and I thought this would be a very good character because he's outrageous; he's wild. I remember Doug Cramer, who was the studio producer of the show, looked over my shoulder. He saw Charles Nelson Reilly; he thought I was thinking of him for the captain. He said, 'That's interesting.' I said, 'No, no! Not for the captain!' That would have been crazy." Reilly won the part of Claymore Gregg. He was so good in the role that he was nominated for a Best Supporting Actor Emmy.

Gideon's Crossing (2000-2001)

John Carroll Lynch as Sonny Green (John Billingsley)

JOHN BILLINGSLEY WAS CAST to play the guest role of the mayor of Boston in the November 1, 2000 episode of *Gideon's Crossing*. After the episode was shot ABC saw it and decided to recast the role with John Carroll Lynch. Billingsley was told he wasn't mayoral enough.

John Billingsley

Gilligan's Island (1964-1967)

Bob Denver as Gilligan (Jerry Van Dyke)

Alan Hale, Jr. as Skipper Jonas Grumby (Carroll O'Connor)

Tina Louise as Ginger Grant (Kit Smythe)

Russell Johnson as Roy Hinkley (The Professor) (Dabney Coleman, John
    Gabriel)

Dawn Wells as Mary Ann Summers (Nancy McCarthy, Pat Priest, Raquel
    Welch)

GILLIGAN'S ISLAND creator Sherwood Schwartz's first choice for the title role of Gilligan was Jerry Van Dyke. He brought Van Dyke out from Texas. At the time Van Dyke did not have an agent. "I told him my agent's name," said Schwartz. Schwartz's agent had no faith in *Gilligan's Island*. "I didn't know that," he continued. "Meanwhile, I went to a different agent who had said to me that anytime I am unhappy with my agent to call him. So I did. It's tough enough for an agent to try and sell something to the network. If he has any doubts about the show, or about the potential of it, I don't want him going near it. So when I knew George Rosenberg's feeling about this project of mine, I said, 'No. You don't have to do it. Somebody else wants to do it and goodbye. Meanwhile, Jerry signed up with him, my then agent George Rosenberg. When he did, George told him to take this other deal because he thought it had great possibility. He wound up not becoming Gilligan, and that was the biggest favor anyone ever did for him. He was not on *Gilligan's Island*, which would have pulled him off the shelf. By the time he got *Coach* the salaries had been increased by like, eight or ten times. He was better off not getting *Gilligan's Island*."

Bob Denver's agent at William Morris called Schwartz to arrange a lunch meeting. "It just took that one lunch and I knew he was the perfect guy," said Schwartz.

Schwartz felt that the Skipper was the hardest role in the series to cast. Carroll O'Connor flew in from New York to test for the role. "You have a great big guy bellowing at this poor little schnook," he said. "I wrote a test scene, which is about 2 ½ pages long, where Gilligan had done something wrong and the Skipper was just berating him for two pages. Anybody who could survive that would be the Skipper. And Carroll O'Connor couldn't survive that. He sounded mean. Not personally mean. But he couldn't overcome his size and demeanor really; to get sympathy from the audience Alan Hale was so important to that show. I knew at the beginning that he would be the most difficult guy to cast, and it proved to be right. Everybody else was set and we were all ready to depart for Hawaii to do the pilot and I had no Skipper. Luck and coincidence plays a big part in our business. Who you ask for, the best casting director in the world can't give you somebody who's already set in another situation. I was really bemoaning my problem at that point. I was with my wife and we were out to dinner. Behind was the old Fox studio lot. We're at dinner and who do you confide in? Your wife. So we're sitting there having dinner and I looked across the room and there's Alan Hale in a Civil War uniform. I couldn't go up to him; I didn't know him. So I said, "Well, I'll call in the morning; I'll call his agent.' I found his agent and I called. This is the next morning after I saw him. I said, 'Does he have a continuing role in whatever he's doing, and is he available to be one of the stars of a new TV series?' And he said, 'Well, it's hard to talk to him right this minute 'cause he's in St. George, Utah. And that's at the bottom of a canyon and you can't even go there.' I said, 'Well, I have to get him interviewed at CBS, and I don't know how to go about that.' I had heard that that particular place, you have to get there on horseback. You can't even get there with a car. I explained the circumstance and he explained his circumstance. I said, 'We've got this pilot coming up in about five weeks, and I have to cast it now and I have to get new film, because CBS would not take any old film on anybody. That was a rule in those years because they found out a guy they cast who weighed 280 lbs. was on a diet and weighed 110! I said, 'I have to get him here now.' I had to get CBS to keep its facilities open on a Sunday because we shoot six days a week on location. So he's on location on this Civil War story. He arranged with another guy on a horse on the same shoot. They went up on a horse to the main highway, which is not too far from Las Vegas. He got a ride on a truck from where he left the guy with his horse and he went to Las Vegas and he got on a plane and came to L.A. I had the facilities open. He went straight there. He read just 2 ½ pages, but the relationship had to be there. And so we tested him. He got back on a plane, went back to Las Vegas and went back to his friend who was waiting with his horse." Schwartz knew as soon as Hale and Denver were in a shot together that Hale was the right guy. "He had such a teddy bear quality, and you knew no matter how he yelled he loved him anyway," said Schwartz. "He was just doing things for his own good to yell at him."

Schwartz and Jim Backus were old friends from the days of radio. Backus was already involved with another pilot. The pilot didn't sell and Backus was free to take the role of millionaire Thurston Howell III.

Kit Smythe and Nancy McCarthy played the two young women in the original unaired pilot, Ginger and Bunny. Both women were secretaries. Schwartz felt that it was a mistake; that they were indistinguishable from one another. When the show went on the air, Bunny was renamed Mary Ann. Schwartz made Ginger a movie star and Mary Ann a farm girl - complete opposites of one another.

John Gabriel appeared in the unaired pilot as the Professor, who was a high-school teacher. Schwartz felt that Gabriel was too young for the part. He was let go from the show. Dabney Coleman was tested for the Professor, but the actor who ended up with the part was Russell Johnson.

Dawn Wells beat out Raquel Welch and Pat Priest to play farm girl Mary Ann Summers. Series creator Sherwood Schwartz said that there was no way you could get rid of Welch's sophistication.

Gilmore Girls (2000-)
Edward Herrmann as Richard Gilmore (Dakin Matthews)

GILMORE GIRLS told the story of Lorelai Gilmore, age 32, and her teenage daughter Rory.

Dakin Matthews originally auditioned for the part of Lorelai's father, Richard Gilmore. Edward Herrmann was cast instead. "When they created the role of the headmaster (Hanlin Charleston) they asked me back for it based on the audition I had done for the other role," said Matthews. Matthews recurred on the show from 2000-2004.

The Girl from U.N.C.L.E. (1966-1967)
Stefanie Powers as April Dancer (Mary Ann Mobley)

THE MAN FROM U.N.C.L.E. premiered in 1964. The series was a big hit, and a spin-off was planned. The starring role of April Dancer was introduced on the February 25, 1966 episode of The Man from U.N.C.L.E. Mary Ann Mobley played April.

Stefanie Powers was under contract to Columbia Pictures. "In my contract I was not allowed to do television," said Powers, "in spite of the fact that Columbia had Screen Gems, the television station. I had done fifteen movies in five years on a straight seven-year contract. They owned some properties that had been plays, Under the Yum Yum Tree, and things like that. I wanted to do Under the Yum Yum Tree, so I went to San Francisco and I opened the play Under the Yum Yum Tree. It eventually ran for six years. Nobody from the studio would even come up and have a look. They obviously were not interested in my career. It was a sequence of other incidents like that. There were parts that I, as a contract player, should have been championed for. Then they'd offer me some terrible thing, which they hoped I'd turn down, which I did. Then I'd go on suspension, and not be allowed to work. In the meantime, what I didn't know was that MGM

Stefanie Powers divides her time between homes in Hollywood and Kenya,
where she is active in animal conservation efforts.

had discussed *The Girl from U.N.C.L.E.* with Columbia and they refused to loan me out for it. They went ahead and did a spin-off show introducing the character of the girl from U.N.C.L.E. with another actress. That was Mary Ann Mobley, who is my neighbor. Her sidekick was Norman Fell." The network agreed to buy thirteen episodes of the show. A decision was made that Mobley would not return. "They went back to Columbia and made an offer to buy me out of my contract," said Powers. "That's how I was the girl from U.N.C.L.E."

Gleason (2002)

Brad Garrett as Jackie Gleason (Mark Addy)

BRAD GARRETT VERY MUCH wanted to make a film in which he played Jackie Gleason. He went to CBS with the idea, but the network wasn't interested. About five years later CBS indeed decided to make a film about Gleason. Garrett contacted Leslie Moonves, the network's president, and asked for an audition. Moonves couldn't imagine the 6'8 ½", thin Garrett as the overweight, average height Gleason. Moonves hired Mark Addy, an actor whose physical stature resembled Gleason more closely. Addy later dropped out of the film. Moonves then suggested Garrett to director Howard Deutch. Some time earlier, Deutch was making a movie. His agent suggested that he consider Ray Romano in the film. Deutch watched episodes of Romano and Garrett's sitcom, *Everybody Loves Raymond*. He liked Garrett's performance as Robert Barone. After Moonves mentioned Garrett to Deutch he looked at a tape of his work. He recognized him as the actor he had liked so much and Garrett was signed to play Gleason. Since Garrett was much taller than Jackie Gleason actually was, everybody else needed custom-made heels to lessen the difference in height. Garrett was nominated for an Emmy for his performance as Jackie Gleason.

Goddess of Love (1988)

David Naughton as Ted
   Beckman (Harry Anderson,
   Peter Scolari)

GODDESS OF LOVE was a re-
make of the film *One Touch
of Venus*. *Wheel of Fortune's*
Vanna White was set for the
starring role of Venus. Finding
a leading man proved difficult.
Harry Anderson and Peter
Scolari were considered, but
turned the part of Ted Beckman down. David Naughton
finally signed on for the role.

Betsy Palmer

   Betsy Palmer was the first
choice for the small role of
Hera. Director Jim Drake was very glad when she agreed to do the part.
Palmer was able to complete her role in one day of shooting.

The Goldbergs (1949-1956)

Harold J. Stone as Jake Goldberg (Robert H. Harris, George Tobias)
Eli Mintz as Uncle David (Irving Jacobson, Zvee Scooler)

PHILIP LOEB ORIGINATED the role of Jake Goldberg on the 1949 series
The Goldbergs. Loeb was accused of being a communist sympathizer. Although the actor testified under oath that he was not a communist, it did
no good. He was being replaced as Jake Goldberg. Gertrude Berg, the star
of *The Goldbergs*, contacted Robert H. Harris and Harold J. Stone about

playing the part. Harris' schedule was booked, and was unavailable. Stone wasn't interested, and told Berg to get her friend George Tobias for the part. Berg took his advice and had Tobias in to read. She told him that he had to go into rehearsal the next day. Tobias needed three days, so he was out of the running. Harold J. Stone received a call the next day that the part was his. A couple of months later Berg wanted Stone to replace George Tobias on her radio program *The House of Glass*. Since Stone wasn't too keen on the part of Jake Goldberg in the first place, he agreed. Robert H. Harris was contacted again, and this time accepted the part of Jake.

Gertrude Berg told Eli Mintz that he was going to replace Menasha Skulnik as Uncle David. Skulnik himself had recommended Mintz. Mintz still had to screen test. Among his competition were Zvee Scooler and Irving Jacobson. Berg stayed true to her word and gave the part to Mintz.

The Golden Girls (1985-1992)

Beatrice Arthur as Dorothy Zbornak (Lee Grant, Elaine Stritch)
Betty White as Rose Nylund (Celeste Holm, Rue McClanahan)
Rue McClanahan as Blanche Devereaux (Betty White)

LEE GRANT WAS CONSIDERED for the role of Dorothy Zbornak in *The Golden Girls*. Another possible choice was Broadway legend Elaine Stritch. She auditioned, but failed to win the part. Creator Susan Harris wanted Bea Arthur all along. In fact, the character was described as a Bea Arthur type. Arthur was reluctant at first, but finally agreed to sign for the show.

Legendary actress Celeste Holm was offered the chance to play Rose Nylund. Holm turned it down, not wanting to play such a ditsy character.

Betty White was the first choice for the role of Blanche Devereaux. The part was similar to Sue Anne Nivens, the role she played on *The Mary Tyler Moore Show*. White came in for an interview. After reading about four lines she was stopped and told the job was hers.

Finding an actress to play Rose Nylund proved more difficult. Many actresses were seen, including Rue McClanahan. McClanahan played a character very much like Rose on the series *Maude*. After McClanahan read for Rose, director Jay Sandrich asked her to also read Blanche. McClanahan knew that Betty White was already cast. Sandrich told her that he just wanted to hear how she would do the part. McClanahan asked if she could try the character with a southern accent. She went out to look at the script. Fifteen minutes later McClanahan returned and read

Jay Sandrich

the part. Sandrich called the executive producers Susan Harris, Tony Thomas and Paul Junger Witt to tell them they needed to hear Rue McClanahan read Blanche. "Of course we all knew how brilliant she was," said Sandrich. "Now I go back to New York because I'm doing *The Cosby Show*," he continued. "I don't talk to Betty. I just assumed that somebody had called Betty up and said, 'You're not playing Blanche, you're doing Rose.' Somehow it didn't happen. So we show up for the first reading and Betty pulls me aside and said, 'How could you do this to me? Nobody told me. I don't know what to do.' And I just said, 'Well, basically, I think she's not dumb. She just believes everything she hears. She takes things very innocently.' And so, she did the reading and she was brilliant."

Estelle Getty was the first actress to read for the role of Dorothy's mother Sophia Petrillo. Executive producer Tony Thomas said that she killed every line. After her outstanding audition, Susan Harris said there was no question the role would be hers.

The Gong Show (1976-1980)
Chuck Barris as Host (John Barbour)

IN 1975 TELEVISION PRODUCER Chuck Barris came up with the idea for a new show. It was an amateur talent show called *The Gong Show*. If an act was very bad one of the three celebrity judges would hit the gong, and they would be finished.

Gary Owens was hired to host the pilot, which was well received, and picked up for the air.

A daytime version of the show was also produced. John Barbour was chosen to emcee. Soon after, it was decided that Barbour was too sensitive for the job. Barris took him aside and tried to explain to Barbour that it wasn't a real talent show. He eventually made the decision to host the show himself. Barris was a big hit with audiences, and not long after also took over the hosting job of the nighttime version as well.

Good Advice (1993-1994)
George Wyner as Artie Cohen (Morey Amsterdam, Buddy Hackett, Mort Sahl)

BUDDY HACKETT, Morey Amsterdam and Mort Sahl all auditioned for the part of dentist Artie Cohen in the 1993 sitcom *Good Advice*. George Wyner was hired instead.

Good Morning, Miami (2002-2004)
Tiffani Thiessen as Victoria Hill (Heather Locklear)

HEATHER LOCKLEAR WAS considered for the role of Victoria Hill in *Good Morning, Miami*. The part was eventually given to Tiffani Thiessen.

Good Morning World (1967-1968)

Julie Parrish as Linda Lewis (Goldie Hawn)

GOOD MORNING WORLD was based on Sam Denoff and Bill Persky's experience working at the New York radio station WNEW. The two men went on to produce *The Dick Van Dyke Show*, and later created *That Girl* and *Good Morning World*. *Good Morning World* starred Joby Baker and Ronnie Schell as disc jockeys David Lewis and Larry Clarke. An unknown Goldie Hawn came in to audition for the part of David Lewis' wife Linda. Said Denoff, "She read for the wife, but we made her the next door neighbor instead." Hawn played Sandy Kramer, while Julie Parrish won the part of Linda Lewis. The show was canceled in 1968. Hawn wasn't out of work very long; she soon joined the cast of *Rowan & Martin's Laugh-In*.

Grass Roots (1992)

James Wilder as Jerry Lomax (Dean Cain)

DEAN CAIN AUDITIONED for the part of Jerry Lomax in the made-for-TV movie *Grass Roots*. He lost the job to James Wilder.

Green Acres (1965-1971)

Eddie Albert as Oliver Douglas (Don Ameche)

DON AMECHE WAS CONSIDERED to play Oliver Douglas. Ameche had dinner with producer Paul Henning, series creator Jay Sommers and Al Simon, the president of Filmways, at Chasen's. According to Henning, Ameche sent back all the food he ordered complaining that it was not done correctly. At the end of the night Henning told Sommers that he thought that Ameche's behavior at dinner suggested he might be a nitpicker on the set. He was concerned that with the time limitations they would have, Ameche might not be the right choice. The part later went to Eddie Albert.

Grey's Anatomy (2005-)

Patrick Dempsey as Derek Shepherd (Isaiah Washington)

PATRICK DEMPSEY and Isaiah Washington competed for the role of brain surgeon Dr. Derek Shepherd on *Grey's Anatomy*. Dempsey won the part, while Washington was cast as cardiothoracic surgeon Dr. Preston Burke instead.

Growing Pains (1985-1992)

Tracey Gold as Carol Seaver (Elizabeth Ward)
Leonardo DiCaprio as Luke Brower (Justin Whalin)

GROWING PAINS centered on the Seaver family. Mom Maggie was just going back to work as a journalist, while dad Jason moved his psychology practice from an office to his home. Joanna Kerns was cast to play Maggie. After an exhaustive search, Alan Thicke was chosen for the part of Jason. Kirk Cameron won the role of the Seaver's oldest child, Mike. Jeremy Miller played Ben, their youngest child.

Tracey Gold was rushed in to audition for the part of the Seaver's middle child, bookworm Carol Seaver, at the last minute. She hadn't had a chance to work with anyone prior to this network audition, and ended up rushing through her lines. Gold's stepfather and manager Harry Gold was told that Tracey didn't look the way the writers envisioned the character. Elizabeth Ward was cast instead. A pilot was shot. Before ABC committed to picking up the series, they tested the pilot. The show tested higher than any other show that season. ABC went ahead with the show, on the condition that the character of Carol be recast. One problem was that Ward didn't look like the rest of the family. Her chemistry with Kirk Cameron also wasn't quite right. Tracey Gold was the only actress under serious consideration to replace Ward. She came in to read and won the part. Carol's scenes in the pilot were reshot with Gold.

The character of Luke Brower was added to *Growing Pains* at the end of the series' sixth season. The final two candidates for the part were Leonardo DiCaprio and Justin Whalin. "From the first 2-3 times we saw each of them," said executive producer Dan Wilcox, "the entire writing team was convinced Whalin was it. Leo got stronger and stronger. By the time we went to the network Leo had done the better audition." Wilcox felt terrible for Justin Whalin. He called him at home that night. Within a short time Whalin was cast as Jimmy Olsen in *Lois & Clark: The New Adventures of Superman*.

In the series seventh and final season DiCaprio was offered the starring role opposite Robert De Niro in the film *This Boy's Life*. DiCaprio's agent asked that he be released from *Growing Pains* before the season was over. Casting director John Levey went to the young actor's defense by saying that, since the chances of the show coming back for another season were almost nil, they shouldn't deprive him of this opportunity. DiCaprio was finally allowed to go make the movie, but only because it was for Warner Bros. *Growing Pains* was produced by Warner Bros. Television.

The Guiding Light (1952-)

Kristen Vigard as Morgan Richards (Lisa Brown)
Kassie DePaiva as Chelsea Reardon (Mary Ellen Stuart)
Nicolette Goulet as Meredith Reade (Mary Ellen Stuart)
Carl T. Evans as Alan-Michael Spaulding (Brad Pitt)
Oliver Macready as Romeo Jones (Matthew Bomer)
Tom Pelphrey as Jonathan Randall (John Driscoll)

LISA BROWN TRIED for the part of Morgan Richards. Head writer Doug Marland thought that Brown was more of a vamp than an ingénue. The part of Nola Reardon was created specifically for her.

Brad Pitt lost out to Carl T. Evans for the part of Alan-Michael Spaulding.

Mary Ellen Stuart auditioned for the roles of Chelsea Reardon and Meredith Reade. Although she lost both parts, she was hired to play another role, Jenny Lewis.

Ricky Paull Goldin had already worked on *Another World* and *The Young and the Restless* by the time the role of Gus Aitoro came up. The character was described as a blond, blue-eyed graduate of Yale Law School. "They wanted a preppie Yale guy," said casting director Rob Decina. "Ricky Paull Goldin wanted to come in for the role. I said, 'I love Ricky Paull, but he's not right for the role. He's not what we're looking for.' Ricky Paull Goldin's manager at the time called me and said, 'Ricky will come in and read for you. And he'll read for you. I mean, he'll pre-read. He's not even saying he has to go to producers. He'll read for you.' So I said, 'Okay, let Ricky come in and read for me. Out of respect to Ricky let him come in and read for me.' I had actually never met Ricky so I thought that would be a good way to meet him. I was in Los Angeles and Ricky came in and read with a bunch of blond-haired, blue-eyed guys. He was great. I put him on videotape for my callbacks, and I came back to New York. I said, 'This is what you're looking for,' to the executive producer at the time, 'and here's Ricky Paull.' And the executive producer had known his work too, and he said, 'You know what, what the hell. Let's test him.' Sure enough we threw him in the screen test with a bunch of blond-haired blue-eyed guys, and some other similar types. At the screen test he was the best actor. The head writer then said, 'You know, I was thinking the role was going to be this way, but now that I'm seeing what Ricky does, he could be so and so's brother or son or whatever they were pitching at the time. They made it work, and they hired Ricky Paull Goldin. There was an actor who had done other shows. He put his ego aside and he was willing to pre-read for me to prove he was the guy. It turned out he was the guy."

Joan Collins' agent called Decina to say that she was available to appear on the show. Decina thought for five minutes and then went to his executive producer with the news. Although they did not have a role open,

Decina suggested that Collins would make a great Alexandra Spaulding. The executive producer agreed, and Collins was cast.

Matthew Bomer initially read for the part of Romeo Jones. He was asked to test, but he was unavailable to do the part. Some time later the role of Ben Reade came up. Decina knew that Bomer was the right actor for the part. He called him and found he was now available. Although he tested along with about six other people, Bomer got the job.

Tom Pelphrey tested for the part of Jonathan Randall along with John Driscoll. The part went to Pelphrey. Driscoll went over so big though, that they found another part for him to play - Henry Cooper "Coop" Bradshaw.

Gun Shy (1983)
Barry Van Dyke as Russell Donovan (Don Johnson)

THE FINAL TWO CANDIDATES for the part of Russell Donovan in the 1983 CBS series *Gun Shy* were Don Johnson and Barry Van Dyke. "I thought, 'Well, I'm done, forget it,'" said Van Dyke. To Van Dyke's surprise he won the part. "We went on opposite *The A-Team*," he said. "It premiered right after the *Superbowl* and went through the roof. They stuck us on opposite them right when that show took off. So that was the end of us."

Happy Days (1974-1984)
Henry Winkler as Arthur "Fonzie" Fonzarelli (Micky Dolenz)
Tom Bosley as Howard Cunningham (Harold Gould)
Billy Warlock as Flip (Jeffrey Marcus)
Dick Gautier as Dr. Ludlow (Vincent Price)

HAPPY DAYS began as an episode on the anthology series *Love, American Style*. The episode was called "Love and the Happy Days" and focused on the 1950s Milwaukee, WI family, the Cunninghams. Garry Marshall produced the episode and hoped to make it into a series. A year and a half after the episode aired the film *American Graffiti* was released. The film was a big hit and suddenly '50s nostalgia was popular. Coincidently, Ron Howard, the star of *American Graffiti*, was also in "Love and the Happy Days." ABC asked producer Garry Marshall to make another pilot, which sold. Tom Bosley replaced Harold Gould, who'd played patriarch Howard Cunningham on *Love, American Style*.

Micky Dolenz, one of the stars of The Monkees, was up for the part of Fonzie. According to Dolenz, fellow auditionee Henry Winkler thought he had no chance of beating Dolenz out for the part. According to producer William Bickley, Winkler was new on the scene. "He was one of the least likely actors to be thought of for the part," said Bickley. "He was gentle, soft spoken, so mild he was not a likely candidate. But once he read, he became the character in a way you never dreamed." Winkler won the role, which made him a huge star. "He made a much, much better Fonzie than I would have," said a gracious Dolenz. "I'm thrilled that he got it."

The original concept for Fonzie was that he would not speak until the end of every show. He was written as a real mystery man. The role was very low on the cast list both salary-wise and storyline-wise. That changed when the producers saw the powerful chemistry between Winkler and Ron Howard. Fonzie was the show's breakout character, and was heavily featured in all the episodes.

Jeffrey Marcus auditioned to play the brother of Ted McGinley's character Roger Phillips. Marcus auditioned with Henry Winkler. "He was incredibly unkind," said Marcus. "During the audition he threw me up against the wall and gave me lines that weren't in the script." The role of Leopold "Flip" Phillips went to Billy Warlock instead.

The February 28, 1978 episode of *Happy Days* was called "My Favorite Orkan." In the episode Richie Cunningham (Ron Howard) has a dream in which he encounters an alien named Mork. Robin Williams walked off the street into casting director Bobby Hoffman's office. "It was so clear that he was a star from the moment he opened his mouth," said producer James Patrick Dunne. Williams won the role. Dunne said that the entire cast of the show knew Williams was a star. Even people from other shows on the Paramount lot came over to see Williams as Mork. The episode was such a hit that less than a year later Williams and the character were spun-off into the series *Mork & Mindy*.

Dick Gautier guest starred in an episode called "Welcome to My Nightmare" in the series' eighth season. Said Gautier, "Jerry Paris called me. He had directed the pilot of *When Things Were Rotten* [in which Gautier starred as Robin Hood]. They called me and they said, 'Vincent Price was supposed to do this role and he got ill. Could you come in and do it on two days' notice?' Everyone else had five or six days. I had to go in and do it on two days' notice. It was actually two roles. It was the part of a doctor who treats Fonzie, and then Fonzie has a dream, and in it the doctor is very Bela Lugosi-ish. And it was a real wild and silly sketch. I went in and did it and just had a ball."

The producers considered doing a spin-off featuring the characters of Ralph Malph and Potsie Weber. "They wanted to call the show *Ralph, Potsie and Maxine*," said Melanie Mayron. "It would have been Ralph and Potsie, Anson Williams and Donny Most. But they knew they needed a strong somebody to go with them. So Fred Silverman wanted me to play Maxine. I just was afraid I was going to get typed and never work again if I did this show. They were offering me a lot of money at the time. I said no to it. It was a real fork in the road. Everybody and their mother was saying, 'Why didn't you do the show?' I stood my ground. I didn't want to do it. I didn't want to make that choice to star in a series at that point."

Hardcastle and McCormick (1983-1986)

Daniel Hugh Kelly as Mark "Skid" McCormick (Robert Carradine)

ROBERT CARRADINE was hired to costar with Brian Keith in *Hardcastle and McCormick*. According to Carradine he and director Roger Young got along great. However, the same could not be said for his relationship with his costar. Said Carradine, "Brian Keith didn't cotton to me. He would do his off-camera for me, and when he did it was flat." Carradine was soon fired with no reason given. Daniel Hugh Kelly replaced him.

The Harlem Globetrotters on Gilligan's Island (1981)

Constance Forslund as Ginger Grant (Judith Baldwin, Cassandra Peterson)
The Harlem Globetrotters as themselves (The Dallas Cowboys Cheerleaders)

NBC's FRED SILVERMAN wanted the Dallas Cowboys Cheerleaders to appear on the 1981 *Gilligan's Island* reunion movie. They were unable to get out of their contract with CBS, and creator Sherwood Schwartz changed it to the Harlem Globetrotters.

Judith Baldwin replaced Tina Louise, the original Ginger Grant, in the first reunion movie *Rescue from Gilligan's Island*. This time around Baldwin was unavailable. Cassandra Peterson auditioned to play Ginger. Schwartz said that she was pretty good, and very attractive. Most people know Peterson as Elvira. The part of Ginger went to Constance Forslund.

Harry-O (1974-1976)

Henry Darrow as Manny Quinlan (Clu Gulager)

CLU GULAGER WAS CAST as police lieutenant Milt Bosworth in *Harry-O*. Gulager later decided to drop out of the series, and was replaced by Henry Darrow. The character's name was changed to Manny Quinlan.

Hart to Hart (1979-1984)

Robert Wagner as Jonathan Hart (George Hamilton)
Stefanie Powers as Jennifer Hart (Kate Jackson, Suzanne Pleshette, Natalie Wood)
Lionel Stander as Max (Sugar Ray Robinson)

AARON SPELLING AND LEONARD Goldberg brought the idea for *Hart to Hart* to writer Tom Mankiewicz. "I had not yet directed," said Mankiewicz. "Aaron Spelling and Leonard Goldberg said, 'We have this old script of Sidney Sheldon's, which is basically *The Thin Man*. We can't sell it. If you'll rewrite it so we can sell it you can direct the two-hour movie.' I looked at it and it was a very effete couple living in a penthouse with a butler, and they were cat burglars. I said, 'You've got to make them real. They've got to be very wealthy, yes, but give them the kind of wonderful home that everybody would like to have. Let them be the kind of people that you'd love to have to dinner. Give her a job - she's a writer. Don't have an effete butler, have an ex-prize-fighter who turns out to be Lionel Stander. Make them accessible. R.J. [Robert] Wagner was a big television star at the time and he was available. For Jonathan Hart you needed somebody you would like to have all that money. ABC was talking about George Hamilton at the time. Now, George is a friend of mine, but I said, 'No. They'll resent him for having the money. They won't like George with all that money. They don't resent R.J. having a zillion dollars at all.'"

Tom Mankiewicz at work

For a time Wagner's real-life wife Natalie Wood was considered for Jennifer. "I knew Natalie very well," said Mankiewicz. "R.J. and Natalie were both friends. I'd worked with him once before. I'd never worked with her although we were very good friends. In the beginning, at the time on television, 90-minute shows were a big deal like *Columbo* and *McCloud*. They were very popular. I was flying over to Hawaii to give the script to R.J. He was doing a miniseries there called *Pearl* with Angie Dickinson. ABC said, 'Here's what we'd like. Maybe Natalie and R.J. would play the Harts, and we would do half a dozen 90-minute shows a year.' I didn't say anything to R.J. before I went over. R.J., Natalie and I had dinner in Hawaii, and she went to the ladies' room and I said, 'You know, R.J., they're talking about maybe six 90-minute shows with you and Natalie.' And he said the smartest thing I've ever heard an actor say. He said, 'You know what Mank, I sell soap. My wife sells tickets.' She's a movie star. There aren't two people who'd walk around the corner to see me starring in a picture, but let me tell you something. If you put Natalie in a series opposite me I'll kill her.' And that was true. He said, 'Let's do a regular hour show and let's find a co-star.'

"Kate Jackson wanted to leave *Charlie's Angels* at the time. She was maybe going to be Jennifer Hart. I said, 'Too complicated.' R.J. had worked with Stefanie [Powers] on a series he'd done called *Switch*. He said, 'I've done two episodes with her. She'd be perfect.' In those days her TV Q was very low. She had been in a series called *Feather and Father* that only lasted six episodes. She once was the girl from U.N.C.L.E., but it didn't last a year. But R.J. had co-star approval and he insisted, we all insisted. When the show became a hit, everywhere we went people thought they were married. The casting was absolutely crucial. If you get the wrong Jonathan Hart, you've got no series."

Suzanne Pleshette was also considered for the part of Jennifer; however, Wagner's choice was Powers. "I was doing *Cyrano de Bergerac* when I got a phone call from Robert Wagner and Tom Mankiewicz," said Stefanie Powers. "They asked me to come to a meeting about doing a pilot for a television series called *Hart to Hart*. I was just finishing rehearsals; it was just before we were opening in *Cyrano de Bergerac* with Stacy Keach, and we were intending or hoping to go to Broadway. There was an impending writers' strike as we opened out of town. It was as a result of the writers' strike that we didn't go into New York, and I did the pilot for *Hart to Hart*."

Robert Wagner wanted Sugar Ray Robinson to play Max, the Hart's butler. "Sugar Ray Robinson, at the time, was the most famous fighter in the world, even though he was retired," said Mankiewicz. "Many people still will tell you pound for pound the greatest fighter that ever lived. R.J. knew Sugar Ray. He said, 'This will be great. The people love Sugar Ray.' ABC said, and probably quite rightly, 'You are not going to have a black man cleaning the house and driving the car.' And R.J. said, 'But he's not a black man. He's Sugar Ray.' I remember the original draft. I thought Sugar Ray Robinson was going to be Max. The original draft ended with the Harts in Africa. They were on safari and you heard drums in the distance. R.J. said to Sugar Ray, 'What do the drums say?' And Sugar Ray answered, 'I won't know till I hear the piano.'

"I was having lunch in the Fox commissary and Lionel Stander was on line. I looked up. He had on one of those silly hats he always wore and a cigar sticking out of his mouth (in those days you could smoke in the commissary). I said, 'Who the hell is that?' The person with me said, 'That's Lionel Stander.' I went up to him in line and I said, 'Excuse me, Mr. Stander. My name is Tom Mankiewicz.' He said, 'Yeah, I heard of you,' with that voice Lionel had. I said, 'We're doing a two-hour film here. It's going to be a series with Robert Wagner and Stefanie Powers, kind of like *The Thin Man*. Are you available to discuss a part?' He said, 'Where's your office? Do I have time to have lunch?' I said, 'Yes, you can have lunch. It's right around the corner.' So he came in and he looked at me and he said, 'Here's the deal. I want to do the least amount of work for the most amount of money.' I said, 'Lionel, I think you've come to the right spot.' I called Leonard Goldberg and I said, 'I'm sending Max over.' He said. 'Who is it?' I said, 'I'm not going to tell you. I'm just sending him over.' And he went over to Leonard's office. Leonard called me back and said, 'You're right. That's him. It's done.'"

Hawaii (2004)
Michael Biehn as Sean Harrison (Michael Madsen)

MICHAEL MADSEN WAS CAST in the role of Sean Harrison on the NBC series *Hawaii*. According to an insider from the show, Madsen's behavior at the table read was unusual. Soon after he left the show and was replaced by Michael Biehn.

Hello, Larry (1968-1980)
Krista Errickson as Diane Alder (Lisa Whelchel)
Kim Richards as Ruthie Alder (Felice Schachter)

HELLO, LARRY starred McLean Stevenson as radio talk show host Larry Alder. Larry lived in Portland, Oregon with his two teenage daughters, Diane and Ruthie. Felice Schachter auditioned to play Ruthie. She made it down to the final auditions, but eventually lost the part to Kim Richards. Producer Al Burton liked Schachter so much that he assured her that he would find something for her to do. Not long after he created *The Facts of Life*, in which Schachter was cast as Nancy Olson.

Donna Wilkes was cast as the older sister Diane. The actress had personal problems and Burton looked for a replacement. Lisa Whelchel auditioned and was offered the part. She turned it down in order to star as Blair Warner on *The Facts of Life*. The role of Diane was eventually given to Krista Errickson.

Help Me Help You (2006-2007)

Jim Rash as Jonathan (Peter Paige, Christopher Shea)

THE FINAL THREE CONTENDERS for the part of Jonathan on the Ted Danson sitcom *Help Me Help You* were Peter Paige, Jim Rash and Christopher Shea. The role was won by Rash.

Her Deadly Rival (1995)

Lisa Zane as Lynne (Susan Diol)

SUSAN DIOL AUDITIONED for the role of Lynne in the 1995 TV movie *Her Deadly Rival*. The part went to Lisa Zane instead, while Diol was given the smaller role of Jean.

Hercules and the Amazon Women (1994)

Roma Downey as Hippolyta (Lucy Lawless)

LUCY LAWLESS AUDITIONED for the part of Hippolyta in the 1994 TV movie *Hercules and the Amazon Women*. According to producer Eric Gruendemann, Lawless lit up the room. He was struck by her power, presence and maturity. Despite her impressive audition Lawless lost the role to Roma Downey. She was given the smaller part of Lysia instead.

Hercules: The Legendary Journeys (1995-1999)

Lucy Lawless as Xena (Vanessa Angel)

THE CHARACTER OF XENA started out as a three-episode arc on *Hercules: The Legendary Journeys*. Vanessa Angel won the part. Director Bruce Seth Green met Angel, who was studying martial arts. Green later heard that Angel was unable to do the part, and had dropped out. They looked for actresses in New Zealand to replace her. Lucy Lawless had previously appeared as Lysia in the TV movie, *Hercules and the Amazon Women*. Green saw her and thought she was great. "Basically she got the part because she was available, she was in New Zealand and we thought she could do it," said Green. Lawless was so impressive in the role the producers realized that she should have her own show. *Xena: Warrior Princess* premiered in 1995, and ran until 2001. The series was on the air longer than *Hercules: The Legendary Journeys*.

Bruce Seth Green

Hidden Hills (2002-2003)

Justin Louis as Doug Barber (Gary Kroeger)

GARY KROEGER AUDITIONED for the lead role of family man Doug Barber in *Hidden Hills*. He lost the part to Justin Louis, but was cast as the effeminate neighbor Brad instead.

Highway to Heaven (1984-1989)

Brian Lane Green as Gary Duncan (Leif Garrett)

HIGHWAY TO HEAVEN opened its second season with a two-part episode entitled "A Song for Jason." Former teen idol Leif Garrett auditioned to play the guest role of Gary Duncan, but lost out to relative newcomer Brian Lane Green.

Hill Street Blues (1981-1987)

Daniel J. Travanti as Frank Furillo (Charles Haid)

STEVEN BOCHCO AND CHARLES Haid ran into each other at a birthday party for actor Rene Auberjoinois' wife, Judith. Bochco told Haid that he had a part for him in a show he was developing called *Hill Street Blues*. The part was an Italian police captain named Frank Furillo. He told Haid they could make him Irish and change the name to Flannery. When Bochco went to NBC with the idea, they vetoed it. Daniel J. Travanti was cast as Furillo, while Haid was cast as police officer Andy Renko.

Michael Conrad played Sgt. Phil Esterhaus. Sadly, he died of cancer during the third season of the show. A new character was written in named Sgt. Stan Jablonski. Robert Prosky was cast in the role. "Conrad was greatly appreciated by the actors and by the audience," said Prosky. "I was coming in as a character who had quite a reputation within the police department, but he was sort of on the spot here. By that time, at least I was known very much among actors because of all the experience on Broadway and other places. Both the character and Prosky were on the line. That parallel was useful to me as an actor."

Charles Haid

Home Improvement (1991-1999)

Patricia Richardson as Jill Taylor (Debra Engle, Frances Fisher, Bonnie Hunt,
    Betsy Randle)

Earl Hindman as Wilson (John Bedford Lloyd)

Pamela Anderson as Lisa (Ashley Judd)

Home Improvement was developed with comedian Tim Allen in mind. The producers hooked up Allen, a beginning actor, with an acting teacher at Wayne State University. John Pasquin was asked to direct the pilot. At the time there was no script. However, Pasquin saw the potential in Allen, and agreed to take the job.

Pasquin was from the theatre, and had a great reputation for knowing how to work with actors. He closed the set during rehearsals, so that Allen wouldn't become self-conscious. "To his credit, he came in, he admitted he didn't know much about acting, and, like any comic, was suspicious of acting," said Pasquin. "Sometimes it involves emotion and most comics bury their emotion, and that's what their comedy is about. But he listened. As a comic too, you're up there, hopefully you're in the moment, you're responding to what's going on, and what you're thinking, how the crowd is. He had already a fairly highly developed sense of being able to be in the moment, and that's what actors end up having to learn. To his credit he listened, and he was patient, he tried new stuff, he was brave. He was a pretty credible actor by the time he was done."

For the part of Jill Taylor the producers wanted an actress who would ground Tim Allen. One of the first people that casting director Deborah Barylski thought of was Patricia Richardson. Richardson was already attached to another series and was unavailable. Bonnie Hunt met with series creators Carmen Finestra, Matt Williams and David McFadzean as well as Tim Allen. The meeting was very cordial, but all involved thought that Hunt should star in her own show, rather than play a supporting role. Betsy Randle and Debra Engle auditioned, as did Frances Fisher. Fisher and Allen had great chemistry together, and after everyone tested at the network, the part went to Frances. As much as everyone loved her, it was clear that she wasn't accessible or Midwestern enough for the part. "Right around the third or fourth day it just wasn't working," said Pasquin. "It wasn't clicking; it wasn't funny. All the great sitcoms have this sort of ground person, the person the audience knows, 'You're not going to be able to fool this person.' It's Judd Hirsch in *Taxi*. We needed someone who was more grounded. We decided - and this was the fourth day, the fifth day of rehearsing. We're going to shoot the pilot in about three days. Pat had done a series [which was called off by then] and she had just had twins. Someone at ABC said, 'Did we look at her?' We took a chance. We just offered her the role and she came in. She was slightly overweight and she was

worried about that. But she was able to handle him and was equally as funny. Her being so solid and so grounded allowed him to be much more extreme. That's the kind of winning combination that you need in some half hours. You need someone the audience can really connect to, and then it allows the extreme people to be as extreme as they can be."

Although Betsy Randle lost the part of Jill, she was cast in the recurring role of Jill's best friend

John Pasquin

Karen Kelly, and then subsequently was cast as the mom on *Boy Meets World*.

John Bedford Lloyd originally auditioned to play Tim's assistant Glen. He was also asked to look at the part of Tim's neighbor Wilson. He did well, and was offered to test for the part of Wilson. The concept for the character was that Wilson would always be behind a fence, and his face would always be partially obscured. A week before shooting, Lloyd's agent called to say he would not play a part that required him to be behind a fence. Earl Hindman was brought in for the part. Hindman loved that aspect of the character. "Earl was a New York actor," said Pasquin. "It's one of the better jobs on television. Laurie Metcalf in *Roseanne*, Earl Hindman in *Home Improvement*. You have two scenes maybe a week. You come in for a couple of days and then you're done. He was so thankful to be working on a show that had some notoriety, and looked like it was going to run, and he embraced it and loved the idea of it. He was the spiritual center of the show. Because he's an actor, and been to New York, and been around a long time he insisted in his contract - and literally had put in his contract - that he would always make $1

Betsy Randle

more than Taran Noah Smith [who played the youngest Taylor child], so that he would know he would not be the least paid actor! He loved the idea of it. He suggested he take his curtain call holding something in front of his face."

The role of Lisa the Tool Time girl was originally offered to Ashley Judd. Judd didn't want to be tied up with a series and turned the show down. After auditioning many women the role was given to Pamela Anderson.

Stephen Tobolowsky was selected to play Tim's Tool Time sidekick Glen. However, Tobolowsky was already set for a movie, and unavailable to shoot the pilot. The producers decided that, just for the pilot, a different, but similar character would assist Tim. This character was called Al. If the show was picked up then Tobolowsky would come on board. Richard Karn was chosen to play Al. He was told that he would work on the pilot, but not the series. Once the show was picked up, Tobolowsky was still unavailable. So Al was brought back, but just for a few episodes. Karn's time with the show kept getting extended until it was finally decided that he would become a permanent member of the cast.

Homeroom (1981)

Michael Spound as Craig Chase (Tom Cruise)
Ally Sheedy as Karen Chase (Heather Locklear, Janine Turner)

HOMEROOM WAS A SHOW set in a high school, which centered on twins, much like Beverly Hills 90210. Tom Cruise auditioned to play the male twin Craig, but lost out to Michael Spound. Heather Locklear and Janine Turner auditioned to play Craig's sister Karen. Both actresses were very young and inexperienced. The part went to Ally Sheedy instead.

Hot Properties (2005)
Christina Moore as Emerson (Audra Blaser)

AUDRA BLASER WAS ORIGINALLY cast as Emerson in the series *Hot Properties*. She was replaced by Christina Moore before the show hit the air.

Hothouse (1988)
Susan Diol as Claudia (Annette Bening)

ANNETTE BENING AND SUSAN Diol were both up for the role of Claudia in the drama *Hothouse*. Diol won the part. *Hothouse* debuted in 1988 and lasted seven episodes. That same year Bening appeared in her first feature film, *The Great Outdoors*, in which she played the wife of Dan Aykroyd's character. Her career took off, and three years later she was nominated for an Oscar for her performance in the film *The Grifters*.

Hour Magazine (1980-1988)
Pat Mitchell as Co-Host (Mary Ann Mobley)

IN 1980 GARY COLLINS told his wife, Mary Ann Mobley, that he wanted to get a real job. "I was tired of screwing around," he said. He told his agency he would like to do a reality show. "Mary Ann and I had done so many live shows. I thought I could compete. Westinghouse had a show called *Hour Magazine*. I auditioned and got it." Mobley's name was brought up as a possible co-host, but it was eventually decided that it was "too close to the grain" to have the real-life couple on the air together. Pat Mitchell, who went on to run NPR, was hired as Collins' co-host.

House (2004-)

Hugh Laurie as Gregory House (Patrick Dempsey, Denis Leary)

DENIS LEARY AND PATRICK Dempsey were briefly considered to play the title role of Doctor Gregory House. Fox casting executive Marcia Shulman told her boss Gail Berman that Hugh Laurie was the right actor to play the part. Berman was surprised, since she primarily knew Laurie from the *Stuart Little* films. "When Hugh came in and read I cried," said Shulman. "When you see an actor come in and breathe the kind of life into a role that's written that way it's thrilling. And it's emotional. I had really put myself on the line by saying it was Hugh Laurie. I was so relieved because if it didn't happen I really didn't know where to go. And we all loved the script, and we wanted to make it. If you don't have that guy, you don't have a show."

I Dream of Jeannie: 15 Years Later (1985)

Wayne Rogers as Tony Nelson (Larry Hagman)

LARRY HAGMAN RECEIVED a call asking him to come for a costume fitting for the 1985 *I Dream of Jeannie* reunion movie. Hagman was quite surprised, since no one had asked him to appear in the film. He called producer William Asher, who was under the impression that Hagman was on board to reprise the role of Major Tony Nelson in a cameo appearance. After a day of phone calls, Hagman was made an official offer, which he declined. Hagman said he would rather be paid whatever Barbara Eden (Jeannie) was getting. His counteroffer was not accepted. Hagman, who was already working on *Dallas* at the time, chose to not appear in the film. The role was recast with Wayne Rogers.

I Love Lucy (1951-1957)

Vivian Vance as Ethel Mertz (Bea Benaderet)
William Frawley as Fred Mertz (Gale Gordon)

LUCILLE BALL AND HER REAL-LIFE husband Desi Arnaz produced and starred in the 1951 CBS series *I Love Lucy*. Arnaz played bandleader Ricky Ricardo, while Ball played Ricky's wife Lucy. The couple lived in an apartment building in New York City. Their landlords and best friends were Fred and Ethel Mertz.

Bea Benaderet and Gale Gordon were the first choices for the costarring roles of Fred and Ethel. Bea Benaderet was already playing Blanche Morton on *The George Burns and Gracie Allen Show*. Gale Gordon was busy with *Our Miss Brooks*. Although neither actor was available for the regular roles, they both later made guest appearances on the show.

I'm With Her (2003-2004)

Teri Polo as Alex Young (Maggie Lawson, Brooke Shields, Jennifer Westfeldt)
David Sutcliffe as Patrick Owen (Dan Futterman)

I'M WITH HER was loosely based on series co-creator Chris Henchy's real-life relationship with Brooke Shields. Shields and Henchy had just had a baby and she didn't want to play the part of actress Alex Young, which was based on her. Casting director Jeff Greenberg's first choice to play Alex was Teri Polo. He brought Polo in immediately. She won the producers over. Also tested were Maggie Lawson, who was too young, and Jennifer Westfeldt.

Dan Futterman and David Sutcliffe tested for the Chris Henchy-inspired role of Patrick Owen. "Dan was the leading contender going in by far," said Greenberg. "In front of the network over at ABC, Teri and David Sutcliffe - the chemistry was so strong. Where they do the test at ABC is a screening room. Someone in the booth, that wasn't supposed to be there, inadvertently turned on a film of something. It was going on while they were auditioning. It was like they were into each other, they were falling in love. It was a great romantic scene. Even with this enormous distraction they didn't break, and our concentration didn't break. It was so palpable that we knew we had our two leads. While Dan Futterman was initially a little funnier, the chemistry wasn't there. The sexuality wasn't there."

Rhea Seehorn auditioned on tape from New York. She was brought to L.A. to read. "She was so fresh and so interesting," said Greenberg. "She'd never tested for a show. She said, 'What am I doing here? This is happening so fast. What's going on?' She was wearing the de rigueur all black and pigtails. She was sort of rough around the edges, but in a really sexy way. She came in and took that part, not even realizing she was doing it."

Greenberg was a huge fan of Danny Comden's. Greenberg helped him with his audition. He told Comden to take every word as an opportunity to do something interesting. Comden nailed his audition and won the part of Stevie Hanson.

In Living Color (1951-1957)
Carla Garrido as Fly Girl (Jennifer Lopez)

IN LIVING COLOR was a sketch comedy show created by Keenen Ivory Wayans. The cast included a group of female dancers called the Fly Girls. At one point in the show's run, a slot was open for a new Fly Girl. Auditions were held. One of the dancers vying for the spot was an unknown Jennifer Lopez. Lopez was flown out to California to audition for Wayans, only to lose the job to Carla Garrido. Lopez went home to New York. Not long after she received a call saying there was another slot open, and the job was hers.

Shortly after In Living Color went off the air Lopez landed a costarring role in director Gregory Nava's film, My Family. Lopez was singled out by the critics for her strong performance in the film, and has since gone on to become one of the most popular actresses working today.

In Pursuit of Honor (1995)

Rod Steiger as Owen Stuart
    (James Sikking)

James Sikking
Photo: TNT Photo

JAMES SIKKING WAS CALLED in to read for the part of Col. Owen Stuart in the HBO film *In Pursuit of Honor*. Sikking was told he gave a terrific reading, but the next day found out that Rod Steiger came with the role. Sikking took the news in stride. Later on Sikking was contacted and told that he looked a lot like General Douglas MacArthur. He was offered the chance to play MacArthur. Sikking always wanted to play the famous general, and accepted the role.

The Incredible Hulk (1978-1982)

Lou Ferrigno as The Incredible Hulk (Richard Kiel, Arnold Schwarzenegger)

SERIES CREATOR KENNETH JOHNSON considered only one actor for the starring role of Dr. David Bruce Banner - Bill Bixby. In the original comic by Stan Lee the character's name was Bruce Banner. Johnson thought the alliteration was too "comic booky," and changed his first name to David, while keeping Bruce as his middle name. Stan Lee flipped out, but Johnson was finally able to convince him that the world of the television show had to be the real world, not a comic book world. Lee was also appeased by the fact that the full name (including Bruce) appeared on a tombstone in the opening sequence on every episode.

Arnold Schwarzenegger was considered to play Banner's alter-ego The Incredible Hulk. Schwarzenegger suggested Lou Ferrigno might be right for the part. "Ferrigno was a sheet metal worker. He had no acting experience," said Johnson. Johnson gave the part to Richard Kiel. Johnson had seen Kiel on the

Kenneth Johnson

TV series *The Wild Wild West*. He was impressed by him, and thought he could carry the weight of the performance. "He was wonderful," said Johnson. "He shot for a week. Although he was 7'2" he didn't have the physical presence that was needed. It was a tough choice." Johnson called Kiel himself. Kiel was very understanding. Ferrigno was brought back in. Since there were no lines to read Johnson had him improvise a scene. "He was pretty 'green,' and a bit stiff," said Johnson. "But he understood the creature. He was able to get the pathos across."

The Inheritance (1997)
Cari Shayne as Edith Adelon (Carla Gugino, Marisa Tomei)

CBS WANTED EITHER MARISA TOMEI or Carla Gugino to star as Edith Adelon in the 1997 movie *The Inheritance*. The director, Bobby Roth, felt strongly that they were the wrong choices for the role, and gave the part to Cari Shayne instead.

It's All Relative (2003-2004)
Paige Moss as Maddy O'Neil (Christine Lakin)

CHRISTINE LAKIN TESTED for the part of Maddy O'Neil in the ABC comedy, *It's All Relative*. The role went to Paige Moss instead.

It's Always Sunny in Philadelphia (2005-)
Kaitlin Olson as Dee Reynolds (Kristen Wiig)

KRISTEN WIIG AND KAITLIN Olson were the final two contenders for the part of Dee Reynolds in *It's Always Sunny in Philadelphia*. Olson got the job, while Wiig went on to join the cast of *Saturday Night Live*.

It's Garry Shandling's Show (1986-1990)
Molly Cheek as Nancy Bancroft (Gina Hecht)

GINA HECHT WAS CALLED in to audition for the part of Nancy Bancroft in *It's Garry Shandling's Show* at the twelfth hour of the audition process. She read with series star Garry Shandling. The two had fabulous chemistry. Hecht was called back to audition for the network. Shandling called her the night before to tell her how great she was. Hecht arrived at the network the following day where she saw a beautiful girl waiting to audition.

Hecht thought she couldn't compete with this girl, and gave a poor audition. While she was still there, she found out that the girl was not there to audition for her part, and that she was their number one choice. She went back in and did the scene again. "I was so flustered and off track I couldn't get it together," said Hecht. She lost the part to Molly Cheek.

Gina Hecht

Jane Doe (1983)

David Huffman as David (Mark Harmon)

CASTING DIRECTOR DAVID GRAHAM brought Mark Harmon in to read for the supporting role of David in the 1983 CBS movie *Jane Doe*. Graham felt so strongly about Harmon that he kept pushing him for the part. So much in fact, that he almost lost his job over it. In the end Harmon lost the part to David Huffman.

The Jeffersons (1975-1985)

Roxie Roker as Helen Willis (Madge Sinclair)

BERLINDA TOLBERT had been living in California a very short time when she got a job doing a guest role on the ABC drama *The Streets of San Francisco*. She went to San Francisco to shoot the episode, in which an actor named Mike Evans played opposite her. A few days later Tolbert returned to Pasadena. She didn't have a phone at the time. She checked in with her answering service and found out that Norman Lear's office had called. They wanted her to report to CBS Television Center right away. She got a ride and ran in. She walked down a long hallway, which was full of people. Tolbert finally arrived in Norman Lear's office. She did not read that day; they just talked. She was asked questions about her family, and growing up in North Carolina. Tolbert was later asked to

David Graham

come back in to read for the part of Jenny Willis. She eventually won the part. Her on-screen husband was played by Mike Evans.

Madge Sinclair was originally cast as Jenny's mother Helen Willis. She was later replaced by Roxie Roker. The company was called in on a Saturday for an emergency rehearsal with Roker. When the first episode aired there was an error, and Sinclair's name appeared in the show's closing credits. The mistake was eventually fixed for reruns.

Berlinda Tolbert

Jeremiah (2002-2004)

Luke Perry as Jeremiah (Misha Collins, Roger Floyd, Brody Hutzler, Eric Mabius)

Malcolm-Jamal Warner as Kurdy (Jake Busey, Harley Cross, Keith Robinson)

ERIC MABIUS, BRODY Hutzler, Misha Collins and Roger Floyd were all brought in for the final round of auditions for the title role of Jeremiah. The network didn't think any of them were right, and then offered the part to Luke Perry, who agreed to take the role.

Malcolm-Jamal Warner tested for the co-starring role of Kurdy along with Jake Busey, Keith Robinson and Harley Cross. The candidates were eventually narrowed down to two: Warner and Busey. According to casting director Zora DeHorter-Majomi, Warner's brilliant audition helped him win the part.

Jesus (1999)

Jeremy Sisto as Jesus (Anthony LaPaglia)

Jeroen Krabbe as Satan (Gary Oldman)

JEREMY SISTO WAS THE FIRST CHOICE to play Jesus. CBS wanted to see more actors, at which point director Roger Young considered Anthony LaPaglia. LaPaglia said to Young, "Why the hell would you think of me for Jesus?" Sisto was eventually cast.

When Gary Oldman was approached to star in Jesus, the producers wanted him for the part of Satan. Oldman was interested in the project, just not that part. He chose to play Pontius Pilate instead.

The Job (2001-2002)
Diane Farr as Jan Fendrich (Callie Thorne)

DENIS LEARY AND PETER TOLAN created *The Job*. Leary also starred in the series as New York detective Mike McNeil. Everyone who tested for the show read with Leary in New York, while ABC watched the feed in California.

The role of cop Frank Harrigan went to Lenny Clarke. Leary wanted him to play it, and the role was always his.

Diane Farr and Callie Thorne were the final two actresses to test for the part of Jan Fendrich. The role went to Farr, who had just come off of the MTV show *Loveline*.

John and Yoko: A Love Story (1985)
Mark McGann as John Lennon (Mark Lindsay Chapman)

JOHN AND YOKO: A LOVE STORY was shot in London. The role of Yoko One was cast in the United States, while John Lennon was cast out of London. Director Sandor Stern had a lot of trouble finding the right actor to play John Lennon. He finally found an actor named Mark Lindsay. Lindsay didn't have much acting experience at the time, but Stern thought he was great to play Lennon. Stern and Lindsay flew to New York so that Lindsay could read with Kim Miyori, who was already cast as Yoko Ono. NBC loved Lindsay and hired him. He revealed to Stern that his real name was Mark Lindsay Chapman; almost exactly the same name as Lennon's assassin Mark David Chapman. He asked Stern if that was going to be a problem. Stern replied by telling him it was NBC's call. Word got to Yoko Ono, who told Stern that she thought the fans would be very upset by the situation. NBC decided that Mark Lindsay Chapman would have to be replaced. Stern told the actor personally. NBC paid Lindsay in full and promised him a starring role in another television movie. Not long after Chapman starred in *Annihilator* for the network.

Production on the film had to be postponed so that a new actor to play John Lennon could be found. An actor named Mark McGann was brought in to see Stern for the second time. McGann had been the first actor to read for the role in the original casting sessions. At the time Stern had just come off a long flight and was completely drained. He dismissed McGann then, but this time he realized that he was perfect for the part and hired him.

Sandor Stern

About eight or nine years after the film aired Stern's sister called him. She asked him if he was proud of Mike Myers' success. She reminded him that he had hired Myers for the small role of a delivery boy in *John and Yoko: A Love Story*. A few years after that conversation Stern and Myers ran into each other at a wedding. Myers introduced Stern to everyone at his table saying that Stern had saved his life in London. He went on to say that, although Myers' small part only required him to work for one day, Stern knew that Myers needed money. He brought him back for two extra days of work in order to help him out. Myers told the same story to Johnny Carson on *The Tonight Show*.

Jump (2006)

Scott Caan as Dick Davis (David Lipper)

DAVID LIPPER AUDITIONED for the part of Dick Davis on *Jump*. The star of the show, Danny Comden, and Lipper had known each other years earlier when they both auditioned against each other for various roles. Said Lipper, "He told me, 'God, you keep taking all these parts away from me, man. I'm really tired of it.' Now I'm auditioning for his show! The part went to Scott Caan, who's been doing big movies. He has a big name value."

Just Shoot Me! (1997-2003)

Laura San Giacomo as Maya Gallo (Justine Bateman, Connie Britton, Jane Krakowski, Leah Remini, Sarah Silverman)

George Segal as Jack Gallo (Barry Bostwick, Ken Howard, Chris Sarandon)

Wendie Malick as Nina Van Horn (Loni Anderson, Mariette Hartley, Kate Jackson, Allison Janney, Sally Kellerman, Donna McKechnie, Susan Sullivan, Joan Van Ark, Raquel Welch)

Enrico Colantoni as Elliot DiMauro (Tim Hopper, Joel Murray, Jeremy Ratchford, Saul Rubinek)

Journalist Maya Gallo was *Just Shoot Me's* central character. Maya is forced to work at her father's fashion magazine after being fired from her previous job. Justine Bateman, Leah Remini, Jane Krakowski, Sarah Silverman and Connie Britton all auditioned for the role, which ended up going to Laura San Giacomo.

Ken Howard was strongly considered for the role of Maya's father Jack Gallo. Barry Bostwick and Chris Sarandon both gave notable auditions. George Segal was another candidate. He came in for a meeting and charmed everyone. By the time the meeting was over the role was Segal's.

Raquel Welch, Loni Anderson, Sally Kellerman, Kate Jackson, Allison

Janney, Joan Van Ark, Mariette Hartley, Susan Sullivan and Donna McKe-chnie were all considered to play former model Nina Van Horn. However, the original idea for the character was an older Wendie Malick. Malick received a call from creator Steven Levitan asking her if she might be in-terested in playing the part herself. She wasn't sure at first, but eventually became interested. At the time Malick was working on another series and doing a film. She was put on tape, which was shown to the network. The producers asked NBC to take her in 2nd position, which means that she would only be available for the series if her other show wasn't picked up. The network did their homework, and decided they didn't think her other show would go. They were right, and Malick was signed to play Nina.

Saul Rubinek, Jeremy Ratchford, Joel Murray and Tim Hopper audi-tioned to play photographer Elliot DiMauro. Enrico Colantoni eventually won the role.

David Spade's character of Dennis Finch was not in the show's original pilot. There was a different character instead. The role was much smaller; in fact, the character had only three lines. The role didn't test well with men aged 18-35 and was pulled from the show. Bernie Brillstein and Brad Grey were executive producers on the show. They were also David Spade's managers. The role was made bigger for Spade, who was cast without hav-ing to audition.

Kate Columbo (1979)
Kate Mulgrew as Kate Columbo (Brenda Vaccaro)

NBC's FRED SILVERMAN had the idea to make a follow-up series to the immensely popular *Columbo*. *Columbo* creators Richard Levinson and Wil-liam Link thought it was a bad idea and had no involvement. "We washed our hands of it," said Link. "And [Peter] Falk was livid because we had a pact, Peter, Dick and I, that the audience would never see Mrs. Columbo."

Levinson and Link were asked for suggestions as to who should play Mrs. Columbo. They brought up Brenda Vaccaro. "We did the studio a favor," said Link. "We went to her home, the house Michael Douglas had given her after they split up. We spent about two hours with her. We said, 'Look, if you're going to do it, you're going to have to do it right. We're not going to be involved.' But we could see Brenda. She's got that New York-y, down to earth quality. She's got the humor. We thought she would be a good choice. They went with a woman who was a good enough actress [Kate Mulgrew], but I just felt was wrong casting for it. Dead wrong in appearance, in her style. Just not right, but Freddy Silverman called the shots. It was not successful and we were very happy."

Kate McShane (1975)

Anne Meara as Kate McShane (Brenda Vaccaro)

THE ORIGINAL CONCEPT for Kate McShane was to feature a John F. Kennedy type as a private lawyer. The script was submitted to CBS. The network was interested in the series, but preferred the main character to be a female. They suggested Brenda Vaccaro for the lead, but the part of Kate McShane went to Anne Meara instead.

The King of Queens (1998-2007)

Leah Remini as Carrie Heffernan (Joely Fisher, Leila Kenzle, Dawn Maxey, Megan Mullally, Kirsten Nelson)
Jerry Stiller as Arthur Spooner (John Astin, Red Buttons, Jack Carter, Howard Hesseman, Al Lewis, Dick Martin, Abe Vigoda)

THE KING OF QUEENS was originally developed for Kevin James at NBC, where he had a holding deal. The network later decided against doing the series, and it moved to CBS. The show starred James as Doug Heffernan. Heffernan lived in Queens, New York with his wife Carrie and father-in-law Arthur Spooner.

When series creators Michael J. Weithorn and David Litt wrote the pilot, they pictured Leah Remini as Carrie. At the time Remini was on the show *Fired Up*. When *The King of Queens* was ordered, they sent a script to Remini's agent. Her agent sent a message back saying that Remini was still in production on *Fired Up* and was not interested. Many actresses auditioned to play Carrie, including Megan Mullally, Joely Fisher, Leila Kenzle, Kirsten Nelson and Dawn Maxcy. "The problem was Kevin is such a powerful force as a performer that all these good, very professional comedic actresses were just blown off the stage," said Weithorn. "It just wasn't working. About the second or third time we went to CBS with an actress to read and it didn't work, Les Moonves started getting very impatient with the whole process. Everyone had the list in front of us and he said, 'What about Leah Remini?' I said, 'We went to her right at the beginning. She said no.' He said, 'Let's make her an offer. Let's put money on the table. Offer her the part right now.' Timing is everything. When we first went to Leah she wasn't ready to consider something like this, and then it was two months later or whatever and now things had changed. *Fired Up* was dead. We went back to her and she came in and met with Kevin. They started talking, and they knew someone in common. They got into an animated discussion about this person. I was looking at them having this conversation and I said, 'Oh my God, I hope she's going to want to do this cause this is going to work.' I could see it. I could see that she was a personality that could stand up to him. And of course, she did agree. She sort of felt the same thing."

Jerry Stiller was offered the part of Arthur Spooner. He was in negotiations, but then backed out at the last minute. Red Buttons, Al Lewis and John Astin read for the part. Abe Vigoda was interested, but refused to read for the network. Series creator Michael J. Weithorn spent an hour on the phone with Vigoda, trying to convince him to read, to no avail. The network suggested aging a younger actor. They tried it with Howard Hesseman, who Weithorn said did a wonderful job. However, as great as he was, it just didn't work. Dick Martin's name came up, but the part eventually went to Jack Carter, who shot the pilot. The network was not enthusiastic about the show; they felt that something was wrong with the pilot. Michael J. Weithorn realized that Carter had to be replaced. He went back to Stiller, and gave him a copy of the shot pilot to watch. "I thought my chances of that succeeding were about one in twenty, but it was worth a try," said Weithorn. A couple of days later Weithorn got a call saying that Stiller loved the pilot, and would be happy to join the cast. They reshot Carter's scenes in the pilot with Stiller.

The King of Queens premiered on September 21, 1998. The show was a hit, and ran through 2007.

King of the Hill (1997-)
Johnny Hardwick as Dale Gribble (Stephen Root)
  Brittany Murphy as Luanne Platter (Pamela Adlon, Ashley Gardner)

THE FOX NETWORK and writer/producer Mike Judge discussed creating an animated series to follow *The Simpsons* on Sunday nights. Judge had the original concept for the show, and brought Greg Daniels on as his co-creator.

They did a 2-3-minute pencil test for Fox in which Judge voiced the main character of Hank Hill. In the test Hill spoke directly to John Matoian, who was then the president of the network, and pitched the series. The show was picked up based on that test as well as the script.

When actors were brought in to audition for the show, the producers didn't want to see them as they were reading. They made sure that they would only hear their voices, since it was an animated series.

Judge remained in the cast as Hank Hill, while Kathy Najimy played his wife Peggy. Stephen Root auditioned for the part of Hank's friend Dale Gribble. He read the part, but it didn't seem right to him. He then read the part of Bill Dauterive. He was more comfortable with that role. Mike Judge was unable to be at Root's audition, so he read for him over the phone. Judge gave the okay to hire him as Bill. *King of the Hill* writer/ producer Johnny Hardwick was cast as Dale.

Pamela Adlon

Pamela Adlon and Ashley Gardner both auditioned for the part of Hank's niece Luanne Platter. Adlon was cast in the larger role of the Hill's son Bobby instead, and it came down to a choice between Gardner and Brittany Murphy. Murphy won the part of Luanne, and Gardner was cast as Nancy Gribble and Didi Hill. "You have to be fearless," said Adlon of performing in the show, "because you're sitting there, and you're in a fishbowl. Thirty people are watching you contort your body and your face. You have to just strip that away and just say, 'Fuck it.' You just don't care how you look and how you're perceived because it's not going to sound good if you're trying to look good."

In 2002 Adlon won an Emmy for her performance as Bobby Hill. A few years later she went to an audition. The casting director hadn't seen her face on TV for a while, and assumed Adlon hadn't been working. "When I went up for pilot season I went in to an audition," she said. "The casting director said, 'I was so glad to hear you were back acting again.' I said, 'Yeah, I took a few years off to win an Emmy, but now I'm back.'"

Kingpin (2003)

Yancey Arias as Miguel Cadena (Andy Garcia)
Bobby Cannavale as Chato Cadena (Steven Bauer)

ANDY GARCIA WAS OFFERED the part of drug kingpin Miguel Cadena in the 2003 NBC mini-series *Kingpin*. Garcia declined, and Yancey Arias was eventually hired. Steven Bauer was initially cast as Chato Cadena. "Steven was terrific, but we needed to make a change," said casting executive Pamela Shae. The part was given to Bobby Cannavale.

Knight Rider (1982-1986)

David Hasselhoff as Michael Knight (Don Johnson)

DON JOHNSON LOST out to David Hasselhoff for the starring role in *Knight Rider*.

The Knights of Prosperity (2007)

Mick Jagger as Himself (Jeff Goldblum, Regis Philbin, Donald Trump)

THE KNIGHTS OF PROSPERITY was pitched with the working title *I Want to Rob Jeff Goldblum*. Goldblum's name was used as a place holder, although he was approached for the series. Goldblum signed to play the title role in *Raines* instead. Donald Trump and Regis Philbin were also considered in place of Goldblum. The president of ABC, Steve McPherson, suggested Mick Jagger, who agreed to play himself.

Knots Landing (1979-1993)

Constance McCashin as Laura Avery (Patty Duke)
Ava Gardner as Ruth Galveston (Olivia de Havilland)

KNOTS LANDING was based on the 1957 movie No Down Payment. The film was about four couples living in a California housing development.

Creator David Jacobs wanted Constance McCashin to play the part of Laura Avery. Patty Duke was also considered, but was unavailable. John Pleshette was already cast as Laura's husband Richard. CBS balked at the idea of McCashin and Pleshette together, thinking they made such an odd couple. However, that was what Jacobs had intended. CBS wanted McCashin to audition. McCashin's husband Sam Weisman advised her not to audition. "I said to her (this is our first year of marriage), 'Honey, your not going to get the part,'" said Weisman. "You should just say that you're refusing. He wrote the part for you. You're going to read for the part that was based on you and you're not going to get it.' And I remember our agent saying, 'Oh my God, you're destroying her life. You're destroying her career.' And I said, 'Listen to me, you're not getting the part.' So she stood firm and then they said, 'Okay, will you at least come in and meet the director?' And I said, 'That's all horseshit. They're going to try to get you to read. They're looking for an excuse not to cast you. The director's going to ask you to read, and if he does don't do it.' She goes in and meets the director and ten minutes into the meeting he says, 'Would you mind reading a little?' She says, 'No.' So he gets all frustrated and then she goes home. I remember we get into this huge fight, she's crying. And while she's crying the phone rings and it's our agent saying, 'They want to make a deal for you.'"

David Jacobs went to Europe and met Olivia de Havilland to discuss a role on the show, as William Devane's character's mother. Jacobs and his wife had dinner with the legendary de Havilland, who got applause in the restaurant. "I just rattled off a story about the mother character," said Jacobs. "It was great!" However, de Havilland didn't want the part. It was later offered to Ava Gardner, who accepted.

Kojak (1973-1978)

F. Murray Abraham as Solly Nurse (Carmine Caridi, Hank Garrett)

THE SEPTEMBER 14, 1975 episode of Kojak was titled "A Question of Answers." The final candidates for the role of tough guy Solly Nurse were F. Murray Abraham, Carmine Caridi and Hank Garrett. Abraham knew who the competition was. Caridi was 6'4" and tough looking. Garrett was smaller, but built like a tank. Abraham's first inclination was to play the part like a leg breaker. He then reconsidered. He knew he couldn't play tough the same way as the other two could. Instead, he played the character quiet, and a little crazy. Abraham's audition was impressive and he won the role.

Kung Fu (1972-1975)

David Carradine as Kwai Chang Caine (Bruce Lee)

BRUCE LEE AUDITIONED for the starring role of Kwai Chang Caine. During his audition he did an air kick to one of the Warner Bros. executives. Lee was viewed as too tough for the role, and lost out to David Carradine. Because of this rejection Bruce Lee went back to China and became a martial arts icon.

The L Word (2004-)

Jennifer Beals as Bette Porter (Erin Daniels)
Katherine Moenning as Shane McCutcheon (Leisha Hailey)
Eric Mabius as Tim Haspel (Scott Bairstow)
Ion Overman as Candace Jewell (Lisa Canning)

THE SHOWTIME SERIES The L Word followed the lives and loves of a group of lesbian friends in Los Angeles. Erin Daniels originally auditioned for the role of Bette Porter. Jennifer Beals was also being pursued for the part. Once

Beals signed on Daniels was moved over to the part of tennis player Dana Fairbanks.

Leisha Hailey auditioned to play Shane McCutcheon. Her reading was good, but she wasn't the best choice for the part. It went to Katherine Moenning instead. Hailey was asked to join the cast as writer Alice Pieszecki.

Scott Bairstow was given the part of Tim Haspel. In December of 2003 Bairstow pleaded guilty to second-degree assault, and was sentenced to four months in jail. Bairstow was accused of having sex with a twelve-year-old relative of his ex-wife's. Eric Mabius was brought in to replace him on *The L Word*. "It's very sad it didn't work out with Scott," said executive producer Larry Kennar.

Ion Overman auditioned for the part of Candace Jewell on *The L Word* on a Wednesday. She read some scenes on tape, which went to Canada for the producers to see. The next day Overman found out she was one of three actresses still in the running for the part. Later in the day it was narrowed down to just two. Overman tested against Lisa Canning. By Friday Ion Overman was on a plane to Canada to start work on The L Word.

Ion Overman.
Photo: Karen Bystedt www.karenbphotography.com

L.A. Dragnet (2003-2004)
Ed O'Neill as Joe Friday (Danny Huston)

DANNY HUSTON WAS ORIGINALLY cast as Sgt. Joe Friday in the 2003 version of the 1951 series *Dragnet*. Huston was later dropped from the show and replaced by Ed O'Neill.

L.A. Law (1986-1994)
Steve Buscemi as David Lee (Joe d'Angerio)

JOE D'ANGERIO was considered for the guest role of David Lee in the November 7, 1991 episode of *L.A. Law* called "Spleen It to Me, Lucy." The part was cast with Steve Buscemi instead.

Lackawanna Blues (2005)
S. Epatha Merkerson as Rachel "Nanny" Crosby (L. Scott Caldwell, Loretta
    Devine, April Grace, Jenifer Lewis)
Macy Gray as Pauline (Davenia McFadden)
Terrence Howard as Bill Crosby (Hill Harper, Chi McBride)

ESTEEMED DIRECTOR GEORGE C. WOLFE was signed to direct the 2005 HBO movie *Lackawanna Blues*. The movie was based on the true story of actor Ruben Santiago-Hudson and his relationship with his guardian Rachel "Nanny" Crosby. Santiago-Hudson first developed *Lackawanna Blues* as a one-man show, in which he portrayed over twenty characters. He also wrote the teleplay for the HBO film, in which he played the role of Freddie Cobbs. Marcus Franklin was hired to play Santiago-Hudson as a young man. Loretta Devine, Jenifer Lewis, L. Scott Caldwelll and April Grace were among the actresses up for the role of guardian Rachel "Nanny" Crosby. The role was given to S. Epatha Merkerson, who won an Emmy for her performance.

Davenia McFadden came close to getting the part of Pauline. Macy Gray was also under consideration. She came in to meet for the part. Gray auditioned, and got the job.

Chi McBride gave a very good audition for the part of Bill Crosby. Hill Harper was also up for it, but the part went to Terrence Howard instead. Hill Harper was still cast in the film; he was given the role of the adult Ruben Santiago-Hudson.

The Larry Sanders Show (1992-1998)

Rip Torn as Artie (John Glover)

Megan Gallagher as Jeannie Sanders (Rosanna Arquette, Kim Cattrall, Courteney Cox, Patricia Heaton, Felicity Huffman, Cherry Jones, Jane Kaczmarek)

THE LARRY SANDERS SHOW starred Garry Shandling as the late-night talk show host Larry Sanders. The two candidates for the part of Larry's producer Artie were Rip Torn and John Glover. John Glover was, "a very different way to go," said casting director Marc Hirschfeld. "Garry [Shandling] had a vision of what the show would be. It was really up to him. Rip did not want to audition. He decided to read with just Garry in the room. We spent an hour waiting. It was very nerve wracking." Shandling finally chose Rip Torn. Torn was nominated for an Emmy six times for his work on the show, winning once in 1996.

Courteney Cox, Patricia Heaton, Felicity Huffman, Kim Cattrall, Jane Kaczmarek, Rosanna Arquette and Cherry Jones all read for the part of Larry's wife, Jeannie. Megan Gallagher won the role instead.

Las Vegas (2003-)

James Caan as Ed Deline (Don Johnson)

Josh Duhamel as Danny McCoy (Matthew Davis)

Marsha Thomason as Nessa Holt (Vanessa Marcil)

Dave Foley as Mertens (Roark Critchlow)

JAMES CAAN WAS THE FIRST choice to play Ed Deline, the head of the surveillance team for the Montecito Resort & Casino. Caan passed on the part a number of times. Don Johnson was considered, but after a lot of going back and forth with Caan's representatives the actor finally decided to take the role.

The casting of Ed Deline's protégé, Danny McCoy, came down to a choice between Josh Duhamel and Matthew Davis. According to casting director Marc Hirschfeld, "It was a split room. A lot of people wanted to go with Matt Davis. It took a lot of convincing to go with Josh. Matt was a little rougher around the edges."

Vanessa Marcil competed with Marsha Thomason for the part of pit boss Nessa Holt. Thomason won the role. Marcil was loved so much that the part of Sam Marquez was created for her.

Roark Critchlow was brought in to audition for a guest spot on *Las Vegas*. The character was a comic relief role. Critchlow read, and got laughs from everyone in the room. He then asked if he could try the character with a British accent, which they allowed. Again, Critchlow got laughs. He was told that Dave Foley had already been offered the part. If Foley didn't accept the job, it was Critchlow's. He was also told that the job started the next day, and there had been no word from Foley yet. However, at 4:30 that afternoon, Foley's people called to accept the part.

Lassie (1954-1974)

June Lockhart as Ruth Martin (Jeanne Baird)

CLORIS LEACHMAN STARRED as Ruth Martin in *Lassie* when it debuted in 1957. After one season she left the show and a replacement was needed. Jeanne Baird was offered the part, which her agent accepted on her behalf. A few days later Baird's agent told her that June Lockhart had called her friend Bonita Granville, who was a producer on the show. Lockhart was going through a divorce and needed the job. Granville replaced Baird with Lockhart.

The Last Don (1997)

Danny Aiello as Don Domenico Clericuzio (Marlon Brando)

MARLON BRANDO WAS ORIGINALLY cast as Don Domenico Clericuzio in Mario Puzo's *The Last Don*. Brando played a similar role in the film *The Godfather*, based on Puzo's novel. Marlon Brando eventually dropped out of *The Last Don* and was replaced by Danny Aiello.

Laverne & Shirley (1976-1983)

Leslie Easterbrook as Rhonda Lee (Victoria Carroll, Ilene Graff, Joanna Kerns)

THE NOVEMBER 11, 1975 episode of the hit show *Happy Days* featured Penny Marshall and Cindy Williams as Laverne DeFazio and Shirley Feeney. Two months later the characters were spun-off into the series *Laverne & Shirley*. The show followed the pair through their lives as factory workers in Milwaukee, Wisconsin in the 1950s. After four years the characters moved to California. They had a neighbor named Rhonda Lee who was an actress. Leslie Easterbrook was called in to audition for the part. Said Easterbrook, "There were more gorgeous women with cleavage than I had ever seen before. They spilled out onto the sidewalk." Easterbrook did her audition, and was told she was being called back. Casting director Bobby Hoffman advised her to wear a sundress the next time, so she would be more appropriately dressed for the character. Easterbrook excelled at her audition and made it to the final round of auditions. The other actresses up for the part were Joanna Kerns and Ilene Graff. Easterbrook won the part. At the same time she had gotten a job playing Bianca in *Kiss Me, Kate*. She was disappointed to have to bow out of the play, but was excited to sign on for the series. Before a deal could be made there was a SAG strike. Everything was postponed. A few months later Easterbrook was in San Diego when she got a call that she had to be in Los Angeles the next day to read for Cindy Williams. She flew back, and to her surprise there were new women, including Victoria Carroll, auditioning for the part she had been promised! Easterbrook said she was so intimidated playing the scene with Williams and Penny Marshall. She flew back to San Diego, and later that night got a call saying that the part was finally hers.

Leslie Easterbrook

Tracy Reiner

Photo: Ann Marie Fox

Penny Marshall's daughter Tracy Reiner appeared in the November 8, 1979 episode called "Bad Girls." Reiner was about fifteen at the time. "I was really inexperienced and shy," said Reiner. "They had to put apple boxes between me and my mom. I couldn't stop touching her. I didn't realize my character wouldn't do that." *Laverne & Shirley* was Reiner's first acting job. She continued to act, and has worked on about thirty films to date.

The Law (1975)

Judd Hirsch as Murray Stone (George Segal)

NBC HOPED TO LAND George Segal for the part of Murray Stone in the 1975 mini-series *The Law*. Judd Hirsch eventually played the part instead.

Law & Order (1990-)

Chris Noth as Mike Logan (Michael Madsen)
Richard Brooks as Paul Robinette (Eriq La Salle)

THE PILOT FOR *LAW & ORDER* was made in 1988. Barry Diller at Fox bought the show. Two days later Diller changed his mind and canceled the deal. The show was then sold to CBS. The night before they announced their schedule CBS canceled, saying the show had no breakout stars. Series creator Dick Wolf said that there weren't supposed to be any; that the star of the show was the writing. The show eventually found a home at NBC. It premiered in September of 1990.

Michael Madsen and Chris Noth competed for the part of detective Mike Logan. Although Madsen was the favorite for a time, he eventually lost the part to Noth.

Eriq La Salle and Richard Brooks auditioned to play ADA Paul Robinette. NBC liked La Salle, but series creator Dick Wolf preferred Brooks, who got the part.

Law & Order was a hit with viewers, as well as critics. The show has been nominated ten times for the Emmy for Best Drama series, winning once. The show's great success led to the subsequent series Law & Order: Special Victims' Unit, Law & Order: Crime & Punishment, Law & Order: Criminal Intent, and Law & Order: Trial by Jury. The series has been on the air for sixteen years, and is still in production to date.

Law & Order: Criminal Intent (2001-)

Vincent D'Onofrio as Robert Goren (Richard Dreyfuss, Danny Huston, Liev Schreiber)

CASTING DIRECTOR MARC HIRSCHFELD was very interested in Liev Schreiber for the starring role of the Sherlock Holmes-like Detective Robert Goren. Hirschfeld worked hard to convince Schreiber to take the part, but the actor wouldn't commit to the show. Creator Dick Wolf liked Richard Dreyfuss, but it was ultimately decided that a younger actor was better suited to the part. Danny Huston was considered, but Hirschfeld didn't think he was the right guy. Vincent D'Onofrio's name had been on the original list of actors. At first D'Onofrio wasn't interested. However, after he met with Dick Wolf, he changed his mind.

Kathryn Erbe's friend, NBC casting executive Nancy M. Perkins, mentioned that she was involved in the casting of Law & Order: Criminal Intent. She told Erbe that she was glad that D'Onofrio was cast and that they were looking for a female partner for him. Erbe didn't say anything to Perkins. Her manager later told her that NBC wanted to see her for the part. She was eventually hired. It was explained to her that her character of Alexandra Eames was the Watson to Goren's Holmes.

Leave it to Beaver (1957-1963)

Hugh Beaumont as Ward Cleaver (Casey Adams)
Tony Dow as Wally Cleaver (Paul Sullivan)

THE ORIGINAL UNAIRED PILOT for *Leave it to Beaver* starred Casey Adams and Barbara Billingsley as Ward and June Cleaver, with Jerry Mathers and Paul Sullivan as sons Beaver and Wally. When the series hit the air, Hugh Beaumont and Tony Dow replaced Adams and Sullivan. In the old version there was no Eddie Haskell. There was, however, a similar character named Frankie, played by a teenage Harry Shearer.

Lies of the Twins (1991)

Isabella Rossellini as Rachel Marks (Teri Hatcher, Lauren Holly)

TERI HATCHER AND LAUREN HOLLY both auditioned for the role of Rachel Marks in the 1991 TV movie *Lies of the Twins*. Ultimately, Isabella Rossellini expressed interest, and the part was hers.

The Life and Times of Captain Barney Miller (1974)

Abby Dalton as Elizabeth Miller (Nita Talbot)

CREATOR DANNY ARNOLD wanted Nita Talbot to play police captain Barney Miller's wife Elizabeth in the pilot movie *The Life and Times of Captain Barney Miller*. ABC insisted on Abby Dalton, who got the job. When the show was picked up as a series, the role was recast with Barbara Barrie.

Life with Bonnie (2002-2004)

Mark Derwin as Mark Molloy (Brian Kerwin)

David Alan Grier as David Bellows (John Michael Higgins)

LIFE WITH BONNIE starred Bonnie Hunt as talk show host Bonnie Molloy. Brian Kerwin was originally cast to play her husband, Dr. Mark Molloy. The decision was eventually made to replace Kerwin, because it was felt that he wasn't a good match for Hunt.

John Michael Higgins came very close to playing the role of Bonnie's producer, David Bellows. At the same time Higgins had another offer, which he took instead. Bonnie Hunt, who had known David Alan Grier for years, originally met him on the film *Jumanji*. She got clearance from the studio and the network, and called him to offer him the part.

Little Girl Lost (1988)

Tess Harper as Clara Brady (Elizabeth Montgomery)

ELIZABETH MONTGOMERY WAS CONSIDERED for the starring role of Clara Brady in the ABC movie *Little Girl Lost*. The part was later given to Tess Harper.

Little House on the Prairie (1974-1983)

Melissa Gilbert as Laura Ingalls (Alison Arngrim)

THE SERIES LITTLE HOUSE ON THE PRAIRIE was based on the autobiographical books by Laura Ingalls Wilder. Alison Arngrim originally auditioned for the lead role of Laura Ingalls. She lost the part to Melissa Gilbert. Arngrim did join the cast; she was given the part of nasty Nellie Olsen instead.

Live Through This (2000)

Matthew Carey as Travis Williams (Nicholas Gonzalez, Aaron Paul)

Tom Lock as Chase Rooney (Will Horneff)

Jane McGregor as Darby Parsons (Elisha Cuthbert, Lisa Sheridan)

Sarah Manninen as Lu Baker (Taryn Manning, Gina Phillips, Kiele Sanchez,
    Diva Zappa)

Jessica Welch as Olivia Rooney (Samaire Armstrong, Vanessa Evigan, January
    Jones, Sarah Lancaster, Kimberly Stewart)

Jennifer Dale as Annie Baker (Deborah Harry, Claire Stansfield, Shannon Tweed)

LIVE THROUGH THIS was about a reunion tour of the Jackson Decker Band, a fictional band from the 1980s. The members of the band bring along their families on the tour.

Nicholas Gonzalez and Aaron Paul were considered for the part of Travis Williams, but were beaten out by Matthew Carey.

Will Horneff and Tom Lock competed to play Chase Rooney. Horneff read on tape in New York and then later read live in Los Angeles. Although he gave a very strong audition, the role went to Lock instead.

Lisa Sheridan was one of the actresses vying for the role of Darby Parsons. Also in the running were Elisha Cuthbert and Jane McGregor, who were the final two actresses considered. There was a disagreement over whom to cast. Everyone in Canada and most of the people in Los Angeles wanted Cuthbert. She was easier to cast because she was from Montreal. The show was shooting in Canada, and in order to shoot there you had to have a certain number of Canadians in the cast. The director insisted on Jane McGregor, and McGregor eventually was cast.

Kiele Sanchez read for the part of Lu Baker, as did Taryn Manning, Gina Phillips and Diva Zappa, daughter of Frank Zappa. The role was given to Sarah Manninen instead.

Jessica Welch's competition for the part of Olivia Rooney included Samaire Armstrong, January Jones, Sarah Lancaster, Kimberly Stewart and Vanessa Evigan. Both Stewart and Evigan have famous fathers in real life. Stewart is the daughter of rock star Rod Stewart, while Evigan's father is actor Greg Evigan.

Deborah Harry of Blondie was seriously discussed for the part of Annie Baker. Some of the executives weren't into the idea and an offer was never made. Jennifer Dale won the role after Shannon Tweed and Claire Stansfield were both considered.

Living Dolls (1989)

Halle Berry as Emily Franklin (Vivica A. Fox)

THE OCTOBER 17, 1989 episode of the hit show *Who's the Boss?* was called "Living Dolls." It focused on Charlie Briscoe (played by Leah Remini), an old friend of Samantha's from Brooklyn. During the course of the episode Charlie meets Trish Carlin (played by Michael Learned) who runs a modeling agency. By the end of the episode Charlie becomes a model and goes to live with a group of Trish's other models. Vivica A. Fox played the part of model Emily Franklin. The episode served as the pilot for the new series *Living Dolls*. By the time *Living Dolls* premiered Fox was replaced by Halle Berry. "I read too mature with the hair and all the makeup," said Fox. "They wanted to go a little younger."

Lois & Clark: The New Adventures of Superman (1993-1997)

Dean Cain as Clark Kent/Superman (Gerard Christopher, John Allen Nelson, Kevin Sorbo)
Teri Hatcher as Lois Lane (Paula Marshall)

KEVIN SORBO AND JOHN ALLEN NELSON tried for the part of Superman in *Lois & Clark: The New Adventures of Superman*. Gerard Christopher

was also considered. Christopher played the role of a young Clark Kent/
Superboy on *The Adventures of Superboy* from 1989-1992. Casting director Ellie Kanner remembers Dean Cain's audition. "When we read Dean
Cain," she said, "at first they thought he was too young. Then we brought
him back again. I remember after he read it was at the time when we were
ready to take him to the network. He was a little concerned about the
whole men in tights thing." Kanner and casting director Geraldine Leder
pulled him aside and told him that he had a very strong chance of getting the part, which would be very helpful to his career. Cain realized they
were right. He gave a very good audition for ABC, and eventually won the
part. "The second we saw Dean Cain and Teri Hatcher together there was
no question," said Kanner. Hatcher did have some competition for the
part of Lois Lane, however. Said Kanner, "Paula Marshall was very close
to getting Lois. So close she was our first choice at one point. But she was
unavailable because she was doing a low-budget feature, and she couldn't
get out of the dates. We couldn't change our dates."

London Suite (1996)

Patricia Clarkson as Diana Nichols (Miranda Richardson)

MIRANDA RICHARDSON was pursued to play Diana Nichols in the 1996
TV movie *London Suite*. Patricia Clarkson auditioned for a different role
in the film. Director Jay Sandrich asked her if she could do an English accent. Clarkson had no problem with the request. She auditioned for, and
won the role of Diana. "There was a big, big problem in England that we
couldn't find an English actress," said Sandrich. "We had to go through the
motions when we got to England reading other actresses. Finally we could
say in all honesty we'd seen a lot, but they weren't as good as Patricia She
had this wonderful command. She's confident. You could just see she's
this really good actress."

The Long Hot Summer (1985)

Judith Ivey as Noel Varner (Cybill Shepherd)

WHEN CYBILL SHEPHERD was approached for the 1985 TV version of *The Long Hot Summer*, she had her eye on the part of Noel Varner. The former model was told she was too pretty for the part, and was cast as Eula Varner instead. Judith Ivey was given the part of Noel after being tested four times, and told she wasn't pretty enough.

Lou Grant (1977-1982)

Nancy Marchand as Margaret Jones Pynchon (Uta Hagen)
Rebecca Balding as Carla Mardigian (Sigourney Weaver)

THE MARY TYLER MOORE SHOW was such a big hit that it spawned three spin-offs: *Rhoda, Phyllis* and *Lou Grant*. While *Rhoda* and *Phyllis* were also sitcoms, *Lou Grant* was a drama.

Mason Adams' name was suggested for the part of managing editor Charlie Hume. Adams was primarily a New York actor, and had never been in a series before. Adams auditioned for the show very early on in the casting process. He was so good that executive producer Gene Reynolds told executive producer Allan Burns that they should give Adams the part. Burns liked Adams, but was concerned that they hadn't seen anyone else yet. Reynolds told Burns that when *My Three Sons* was being cast, the first kid they saw was Stanley Livingston. He was about six at the time. After that they auditioned about 900 kids, and then hired Livingston. "The fact that he's the first one doesn't mean that he's not the best after looking at 700," said Reynolds. "I said this guy is fresh, he's very intelligent, he's a likely newspaperman. He's got this wonderful kind of naturalness about him, his style of acting. He's such a refreshing actor with a refreshing face. You believe him. He's ideal." Burns agreed, and they never looked at anyone else for the part. Adams was offered the role before he had a chance to get home. His agent assumed that the show was a half-hour series, and therefore negotiated a very low money deal. Adams was fit to be tied. The producers made it up to him eventually.

Uta Hagen was offered the part of Margaret Jones Pynchon. Hagen was a New Yorker, and didn't want to come to California where the show was shot. Nancy Marchand came in to meet the producers for the role. She was offered the part before she could get off the lot. However, Marchand's feelings were similar to Uta Hagen's. She didn't want to live in California either. It was worked out that she would shoot two shows at a time in four days, and then she would be able to go back to New York.

The character of reporter Billie Newman was not in the original cast. Instead there was a character named Carla Mardigian, played by Rebecca Balding. Executive producer Allan Burns said that, although Balding was good, she lacked the authority necessary for the part. Executive producer James L. Brooks was off doing *Taxi*. When he came to see some early dailies, he told Burns that Balding wasn't cutting it. "I argued with him," said Burns, "but Jim said we needed great. Originally we wanted Sigourney Weaver for Carla. She turned us down. We were heartbroken. We knew she was going to be huge. We wrote Billie into the fifth or sixth script as a trial piece for auditions. Richard Crenna was directing the episode and was reading people. He was great. He said, 'I found her.' It was Linda [Kelsey]. She was just brilliant. We knew then she was what we wanted. I had the unenviable task of telling the other actress. It turned out to be a right decision."

Jack Bannon played assistant city editor Art Donovan. Bannon treasures his experience working on the series. "Anybody connected to that show was part of television history at its best," he said.

The Love Boat (1977-1986)
Bernie Kopell as Adam Bricker (Barry Van Dyke)
Fred Grandy as Gopher (Bruce Kimmel)

THE LOVE BOAT was an anthology series that took place on the cruise ship the *Pacific Princess*. Barry Van Dyke tested at least three or four times to play the ship's doctor Adam Bricker. "I met with the ABC people, did a film test," said Van Dyke. "They said, 'It looks really good. They really, really like you.' And then the ship line that they were actually using said, 'We would never have someone his age (I was maybe 26 or 27 at the time). We always use retired practitioners; people that have been around a long time. It's not realistic. We don't approve of that.' And I lost the part and Bernie Kopell got it and did it for eleven years, I think. A great guy. And then I ended up doing, I think, four *Love Boats* over the years."

Bruce Kimmel auditioned for the part of Yeoman-Purser Burl Smith, also known as Gopher. He came close to landing the part, but eventually lost out to Fred Grandy.

The Love Boat: The Next Wave (1998-1999)
Robert Urich as Jim Kennedy III (Patrick Stewart)

AN ACTOR WITH A LOT OF STATURE was needed for the part of Captain Jim Kennedy III on *The Love Boat: The Next Wave*. The show was a follow-up to the original *Love Boat* series. Although Patrick Stewart's name was brought up at the network, the role eventually went to Robert Urich instead.

Love, Inc. (2005-2006)
Busy Phillips as Denise Johnson (Shannen Doherty)

SHANNEN DOHERTY WAS ANNOUNCED for the part of Denise Johnson in the UPN series *Love, Inc.* She shot a pilot for the show, but never made

Jack Bannon

it on the air. When *Love, Inc.* premiered Busy Phillips had the role. The switch shocked some of the other cast members who were not told why Doherty was no longer with the show.

Love on a Rooftop (1966-1967)
Rich Little as Stan Parker (Dick Gautier)

DICK GAUTIER WAS OFFERED the supporting role of Stan Parker on *Love on a Rooftop*. He didn't like the part, and turned it down. Rich Little was later cast.

The Love She Sought (1990)
Angela Lansbury as Agatha McGee (Loretta Young)

Loretta Young was originally considered for the part of Agatha McGee in *The Love She Sought*. Writers Ron Cowen and Daniel Lipman wanted Angela Lansbury for the role. She was the only one they could see playing it. Lansbury was sent the script on a Friday. She read it on Saturday and said she would do it. On Monday the production office was opened. "We went to Ireland," said Daniel Lipman. "Joseph Sargent was the director, who is one of the most wonderful directors and one of the most wonderful people. We had an amazing time. He was so inclusive with us [Lipman and Cowen]. He wanted us to be there. He's just great; he's won many Emmys. He's just a great director. We were on the set. Angela was playing a schoolteacher. A very stern schoolteacher — very different from Jessica Fletcher [her *Murder, She Wrote* character]. She was doing the scene. We thought she was being a little too nice in the scene. We called Joe over and we told him what we thought. He said, 'Well, boys, I'll go over and tell her that, but I just want you to know the reason we're all here is because of that lady.' He walked over to Angela Lansbury. You could see he was telling her - she was eyeing us. He was called off to do something else; they were in between takes, and she marched over to us and I said to Ron, 'Ron, we better pack.' And she came over to us and she said, 'Joe told me what you said, and you must tell me every time you see me do that. I do not want this character to be anything like Jessica Fletcher. I want to nail this character, I want to be this character and you must tell me that.' And I was just so enamored. She's one of the most sensational actresses and people you've ever met . . . The work is what was important to her. That's always stayed with me. It was never about ego, it was never about power. It was only about the work and getting that character and doing the best film. Usually great people are great for a reason. She really, really is."

Loving (1983-1995)

Noelle Beck as Trisha Alden (Yasmine Bleeth)
Lisa Peluso as Ava (Nancy Sorel)
O'Hara Parker as Lorna Forbes (Marla Maples)
Robert Tyler as Trucker McKenzie (Trent Bushey)
Rena Sofer as Rocky McKenzie (Paige Turco)
Laura Wright as Ally Rescott (Jessica Collins)

YASMINE BLEETH AND NOELLE BECK were both up for the roles of Trisha Alden on *Loving* and Ryan Fenelli on *Ryan's Hope*. Beck won the part of Trisha, while Bleeth was cast as Ryan.

Nancy Sorel and Lisa Peluso were the final two actresses considered for the part of Ava. Peluso got the job, and stayed with the show for about seven years.

An unknown Marla Maples tested to play Lorna Forbes. Cast member John Gabriel tested with her. "She was very pleasant," said Gabriel. "She was fine. They were looking for a girlfriend for me for the show. They tested, I think, about ten girls. She was one of them. She was very good. They didn't think that she was right, but she couldn't have been more excited about the whole thing.

This is before Donald [Trump]. She was, of course, very pretty. But, you know, casting's a strange thing. You never know why they cast one person and not another." The part went not to Maples, but to O'Hara Parker.

Trent Bushey tested for the part of Trucker McKenzie. The role went to Robert Tyler instead.

Paige Turco auditioned to play Trucker's sister Rocky, but lost the part to Rena Sofer.

Jessica Collins was under consideration for the character of Ally Rescott. She was instead brought in to play the part of nanny Dinah Lee Mayberry for a couple of weeks. After her second day of work Collins learned that she was being signed to a three-year contract.

(From left) Ron Cowen and Daniel Lipman

Lucky/Chances (1990)
Grant Show as Marco (Maurice Benard)

CASTING DIRECTOR MERYL O'LOUGHLIN brought Maurice Benard in to read for the supporting part of Marco in the miniseries *Lucky/Chances*. Benard lost the job to Grant Show.

Mad About You (1992-1999)
Helen Hunt as Jamie Buchman (Teri Hatcher)

MAD ABOUT YOU starred Paul Reiser as documentary filmmaker Paul Buchman. There was a long search for an actress to play Paul's wife Jamie. The candidates were eventually narrowed down to Helen Hunt and Teri Hatcher. Something clicked between Hunt and Paul Reiser and she got the role. Throughout the run of the show, Reiser would joke with Hunt that they could still get Teri Hatcher.

Maigret (1988)
Richard Harris as Jules Maigret (Richard Burton)

RICHARD BURTON WAS OFFERED the title role of detective Jules Maigret, which he accepted. Sadly, Burton died shortly after saying yes. Richard Harris was cast in his place.

In late 1987 actress Annette Andre was in England when she received a call from an American named Arthur Weingarten. He was a friend of a friend, and wanted to arrange a meeting with Andre to discuss a role. She told him she was too busy. "He was going to America, but was coming back," she said. When he returned, he called Andre back. The two met for a drink. The next day Andre read for the part of Judith Hollenbeck in Weingarten's upcoming TV movie *Maigret*, and was cast shortly after. Andre and Weingarten married less than two years later.

Maigret (1992)

Michael Gambon as Jules Maigret (Michael Kitchen)

MICHAEL KITCHEN was the first choice to play Inspector Jules Maigret in the 1992 version of *Maigret*. Kitchen met with the producers three times, but ultimately decided to pass. The actor who played the role had to be English because of a deal with the production company, Granada Television. Executive producer Arthur Weingarten's wife, actress Annette Andre, suggested Michael Gambon, who was eventually cast. "He's got just the right quality," said Weingarten.

Make Room for Daddy (1953-1965)

Penney Parker as Terry Williams (Mary Tyler Moore)

    Pat Harrington, Jr. as Pat Hannigan (Dick Van Dyke)

DANNY THOMAS STARRED AS NIGHTCLUB entertainer Danny Williams in *Make Room for Daddy*. Jean Hagen played his wife Margaret, while Sherry Jackson and Rusty Hamer played their children Terry and Rusty. In 1956 Hagen left the show. It was explained that her character died. Marjorie Lord and Angela Cartwright joined the cast in 1957 as Danny's new wife Kathy and her daughter Linda.

In 1958 Sherry Jackson left the show. Mary Tyler Moore was called in to audition to replace her as Terry Williams. Moore read with Danny Thomas. Her audition went very well and Moore was called back a number of times. It eventually came down to a choice between Moore and Penney Parker. Danny Thomas told Moore that she lost the job to Parker because, "With a nose like yours, no one would believe you're my daughter." Thomas also felt that Moore was too mature for the part.

Dick Van Dyke was considered for the part of Terry's love interest Pat Hannigan. The role ended up going to Pat Harrington, Jr. instead.

Arthur Weingarten

Malcolm in the Middle (2000-2006)
Frankie Muniz as Malcolm (Martin Spanjers)
Justin Berfield as Reese (Vincent Berry)
Craig Lamar Traylor as Stevie Kenarban (Austin Stout)

FRANKIE MUNIZ AND MARTIN SPANJERS both tested at the network level for the title role of young genius Malcolm. Muniz got the part.

Vincent Berry auditioned to play Malcolm's brother Reese. Berry was a little too big for the character, and the role went to Justin Berfield instead.

Austin Stout read for the role of Malcolm's friend Stevie Kenarban. He lost the part to Craig Lamar Traylor.

Spanjers, Berry and Stout were all hired for the show's pilot episode. Spanjers played Malcolm's friend Richard, while Berry was cast as the bully Dave Spath. Austin Stout played a kid who Spath victimized.

The Man from Atlantis (1977-1978)
Patrick Duffy as Mark Harris (Christopher Reeve)

CHRISTOPHER REEVE WAS CONSIDERED for the title role of Mark Harris, the man from Atlantis. For unknown reasons, a deal was never made. Producer Robert H. Justman found Patrick Duffy, who had very little experience at the time. "I saw some tape on him," said Justman. "We interviewed him. He was very good, and also very slim. We knew that would be a problem. We started him out on a heavy duty physical therapy kind of a plan, just building up muscle as fast as we could put it on him. He would swim every day in the director's pool up on Mulholland Drive. [Executive producer Herbert F. Solow] got some stuff out of wardrobe at MGM and had Patrick put on this long sleeve sweater, and it was padded underneath so it made him look kind of formidable. He took Patrick out to NBC in Burbank to show him off. They grudgingly finally agreed."

The Man from U.N.C.L.E. (1964-1968)

Robert Vaughn as Napoleon Solo (Robert Culp)
Leo G. Carroll as Alexander Waverly (Kurt Katch)
Mary Ann Mobley as April Dancer (Stefanie Powers)

THE TWO MAIN CHARACTERS in *The Man from U.N.C.L.E.* were agents Napoleon Solo and Illya Kuryakin. Together, they worked to fight the international crime syndicate THRUSH. Robert Culp was made an offer for the part of Napoleon Solo, but he was unavailable. Robert Vaughn later took the role. David McCallum was cast as Vaughn's co-star, in the role of Illya Kuryakin.

A pilot was shot with Kurt Katch playing Alexander Waverly. NBC saw the pilot and told series creator Sam Rolfe that although they loved the pilot, they didn't like one of the actors. The executive stumbled over the name, but Rolfe figured out he was trying to say Kurt Katch. Rolfe asked if he meant Kurt Katch. He was told that was the name, and to replace him. Rolfe hired Leo G. Carroll in his place. After the pilot aired Rolfe got a call asking him what happened; he had been told to fire that actor. Rolfe said that he did just that, but then was told that the executive had been trying to say Kuryakin, not Kurt Katch! Katch was fired for no reason. David McCallum, on the other hand, was able to keep his job.

The producers went to Columbia to ask them to loan out Stefanie Powers for the guest role of April Dancer. Powers' contract with Columbia stipulated that she was not allowed to do television, and the studio refused. The role was given to Mary Ann Mobley. Not long after, the character got her own series. Powers replaced Mobley at that point, when MGM bought out her Columbia contract.

The Man from U.N.C.L.E. was a hit and ran for four years. David McCallum received two Emmy nominations for playing Illya Kuryakin. Leo G. Carroll was nominated three times.

Married: The First Year (1979)

Constance McCashin as Cheryl Huffman (Constance Forslund)

ACTOR SAM WEISMAN was appearing in the NBC miniseries *Studs Lonigan*, which was shooting on the Warner Bros. lot. Weisman wandered over to the Lorimar casting office. "They were tearing their hair out because they were just about to start work on a short-order series called *Married: The First Year*," he said. "They needed an upscale, 30-year-old woman who was very WASPy." Weisman suggested his fiancée Constance McCashin. There was another actress whose name was Constance Forslund. They thought that Weisman was referring to Forslund. Forslund was brought in and told that her fiancée recommended her. She didn't know what they were talking about. Weisman got a call back to clear up the situation. McCashin came in to read and won the part.

Married . . . with Children (1987-1997)

Ed O'Neill as Al Bundy (Sam Kinison, Michael Richards)
Katey Sagal as Peg Bundy (Roseanne Barr)
Christina Applegate as Kelly Bundy (Tina Caspary, Hope Davis)
David Faustino as Bud Bundy (Hunter Carson)

MARRIED . . . WITH CHILDREN was originally developed for Roseanne Barr and Sam Kinison, who eventually passed on the series. The producers no longer wanted to proceed with the show, but casting director Marc Hirschfeld urged them to go ahead and cast it anyway.

Michael Richards auditioned for the starring role of Al Bundy, as did Ed O'Neill. O'Neill read for the creator of the Fox network, Barry Diller. Diller hated his audition. He told the producers, "You can do whatever you want, but I think he's not a TV star." Meanwhile, O'Neill had second thoughts about doing the show, and decided to pass. He was finally convinced to take the part after some begging and a little more money was offered.

Katey Sagal won the part of Peg Bundy after being spotted playing a wacky photographer in the short-lived 1985 Mary Tyler Tyler Moore series *Mary*.

Married . . . with Children creators Ron Leavitt and Michael G. Moye worked with David Garrison on the 1984 series *It's Your Move*. The part of Steve Rhoades on *Married . . . with Children* was written for him. Amanda Bearse played Garrison's television wife Marcy. At the time Bearse was best known for her costarring role in the film *Fright Night*.

Christina Applegate was considered to play the Bundy's teenage daughter Kelly. The young actress was already committed to the show *Heart of the City*, and was unable to join the cast. Tina Caspary won the part of Kelly, and Hunter Carson (the son of Karen Black and Kit Carson) was cast as her younger brother Bud. After the pilot was picked up, the decision was made to recast the kids. While Caspary was very cute, the producers wanted Kelly to be sexier. Hope Davis auditioned, but failed to get the job. Christina Applegate, who was now available, was made an offer. Although her mother, actress Nancy Priddy, had concerns about the racy material, she allowed Applegate to play Kelly.

Hunter Carson played Bud as a slacker. The character was reconceived, and the producers wanted him to be more of an operator. David Faustino won the part.

Martial Law (1998-2000)
Louis Mandylor as Louis Malone (Dale Midkiff)

DALE MIDKIFF PLAYED detective Louis Malone in an unaired 20-minute demo film for the series *Martial Law*. When the series was picked up, Midkiff was replaced by Louis Mandylor.

Mary Hartman, Mary Hartman (1976-1978)
Louise Lasser as Mary Hartman (Farrah Fawcett, Louise Latham)
Debralee Scott as Cathy Shumway (Mary Kay Place)

PRODUCER AL BURTON had only one actress in mind for the title role of Mary Hartman - Louise Lasser. He had seen her in the movie *Slither*, and designed the role of Mary for her.

Due to a mix-up actress Louise Latham was heavily considered for the part! Burton thought that Latham was quite good as Mary, but didn't have the same quality as Lasser. Executive producer Norman Lear and director Joan Darling also thought that Lasser was the right choice, although they did consider Farrah Fawcett. "If Louise hadn't done it that's who we were going to go after," said Darling. "We thought about taking the absolute prettiest girl on the planet and putting her in a situation where her life just wasn't working."

Joan Darling

Mary Kay Place worked as a production assistant on the series *Maude*, which was created by Norman Lear. Lear told Place, "I've got this strange new show, and there's a part as Mary's sister, Cathy." Place preferred the role of aspiring country singer Loretta Haggers. Joan Darling didn't know if Mary Kay Place could act. She invited her to take an acting class she was teaching at the time to see if she was up to playing the part. Darling thought that Place was terrific. Place read for Darling and Lear and won the part of Loretta. "She was it the minute she walked in the door," said Darling. Debralee Scott was given the part of Cathy Shumway.

In the show's second season Philip Bruns, who played Mary's father George Shumway, wanted more money. Director Jim Drake had worked on soap operas before and was asked how they might handle the situation. "I jokingly said, 'Well, the way to get around that is to have whoever the individual is cleaning an oven or something of that ilk," said Drake. "And it blows up and they have to remake their face. The only thing they can do - they don't have a picture of the real individual so they grab a fan magazine with Tab Hunter and remake them as Tab Hunter.' And sure enough that's what they did. Tab Hunter did the show for thirteen weeks. Then Phil came around to terms again and said, 'I want to be back on the show and I'll take the lesser money.'"

The Mary Tyler Moore Show (1970-1977)

Edward Asner as Lou Grant (Shelley Berman, Gavin MacLeod)

Gavin MacLeod as Murray Slaughter (Charles Nelson Reilly)

Ted Knight as Ted Baxter (John Aniston, Jack Cassidy, Robert Dornan, Angus Duncan, Dick Gautier)

Valerie Harper as Rhoda Morgenstern (Linda Lavin)

Paul Sand as Robert C. Brand (Bob Newhart)

MARY TYLER MOORE and Dick Van Dyke played Laura and Rob Petrie on the immensely popular series *The Dick Van Dyke Show* from 1961-1966. In 1969 Van Dyke starred in a TV special called *Dick Van Dyke and the Other Woman*. He invited Moore to come on as his guest. The pair sang and danced, and scored a big hit with audiences. Afterwards, CBS made a deal with Mary Tyler Moore and her then-husband Grant Tinker to produce a show for her to star in.

Series co-creator Allan Burns wrote the first episode with partner James L. Brooks. The show had an on air deal, so a pilot episode was unnecessary. "That gave us time," said Burns. "We wrote the script in January or February. It wasn't shot until June."

Ethel Winant was CBS' vice president in charge of talent. She took on the job of casting the show herself.

Gavin MacLeod was originally brought in to audition for the part of news producer Lou Grant, even though Winant thought he would be better as news writer Murray Slaughter. MacLeod read the script, and indeed preferred the part of Murray. He read for Lou, and got a lot of laughs. MacLeod was honest, and said that he wanted to read for Murray also. His audition for Murray was great. Another possible Murray was Charles Nelson Reilly. Ethel Winant put out a feeler, but Reilly deiced against auditioning. McLeod found out he won the role the same day he auditioned.

Shelley Berman was briefly considered to play Lou Grant. Mary Tyler Moore's manager, Arthur Price, knew Berman from Vegas. He told the production team that Berman might be trouble. They took Price's advice and passed.

Ed Asner played newspaperman Frank Radcliff on the series *Slattery's People*. The star of *Slattery's People* was Richard Crenna. Crenna suggested Asner to his friend Grant Tinker. CBS was skeptical, since they only knew Asner as a dramatic actor. However, he started out as a comedian with Alan Arkin and Mike Nichols and Elaine May in Second City.

Asner auditioned. "He was just awful," said Allan Burns. "We were heartbroken. He was perfect physically, but he was pushing too hard. We told him it was an interesting reading. He left, but came right back. He said, 'You know how shitty I was. Why were you so polite? Tell me what you want.' He came back the next day and read. He was great. Mary read with him, and they had great chemistry." He finished and left the room. Burns told Moore, "There's your Lou Grant."

About a week before shooting was set to start the role of Rhoda Morgenstern was still not cast. Linda Lavin had auditioned, but failed to win the part. Ethel Winant saw Valerie Harper in a play called *An American Nightmare*. Winant called the theater the next day to find out who she was. She was told that the theater had rented out the space for the night, and no one there knew how to find her. Winant was desperate. Finally, her secretary came in with Harper's picture. According to Winant, it was a sheer miracle. She brought Harper in to audition. Harper thought that, since she and Mary Tyler Moore were somewhat similar physically, she was a bad choice for the part of Rhoda. She came in to read a scene from the first show. In the scene Rhoda was washing windows. Harper brought props to work with. According to Burns, although she was from Oregon, she had the Jewish New Yorker down perfectly. She was hired for the part.

Ted was originally conceived as tall, dark and handsome, and a potential love interest for Mary Tyler Moore's character Mary Richards. A strong contender was John Aniston, who fit the writers' image of the character. Aniston was in the running until the very end. It was eventually decided that he didn't have the comedy chops. Another possible choice was Dick Gautier. "They called me in for the pilot of *The Mary Tyler Moore Show* for the part of Ted," said Gautier. "And so I went in and I read for them. I knew Jim Brooks and I knew all the guys, and they said, 'Good job, Dick.' And I said, 'Well, thanks very much. Good luck with the show. It's a wonderful script, and I'm sure it will be great.' I turned to leave, and I tried to open the door through which I had just come, and it was jammed. And I turned around and I said, 'So good luck with the show. It's really great. I love it. Thanks very much. I'll see you later.' I turn. I still couldn't get it open. 'And I really mean it when I say good luck with the show.' And I'm trying to make a graceful exit, and I can't. So finally I jumped up on one of the guys' desks and I jumped out the window. And I landed in the bushes. We were on the first floor; I'm no idiot you know! And the guys looked at me and just laughed like hell." Gautier failed to win the part of Ted, but was later brought on to play Ed the sportscaster, who Mary had to fire.

Robert Dornan read twice for Ted. While his reading was good, he just wasn't a fit for the part. Dornan gave up acting not long after auditioning for the series. He went into politics, and became a conservative congressman.

Angus Duncan also auditioned for Ted. Duncan lost the part, but was cast as Mary's boyfriend Bill in the first episode.

Producer Dave Davis saw a production of *You Know I Can't Hear You When the Water's Running*. He recommended an actor from the play who he described as "hysterical." His name was Ted Knight.

Said Allan Burns, "We brought Ted in three times. The character was written in his 30s, and Ted was clearly in his 50s. Every time he would knock us out. The third time he wore a natty blue blazer he just bought [to look like a newscaster]. He was a bit player. We knew he was having a tough time as an actor. We were touched he bought it." He won the producers' hearts and the role was his. Dick Gautier said that Knight was brilliant as Ted. "I'm glad I didn't get it, 'cause he was much better than I ever would have been," said Gautier

John Gabriel

Ethel Winant suggested Cloris Leachman for the part of Mary's landlady Phyllis Lindstrom. Leachman was primarily known to the production team as the actress who played Timmy's mother on Lassie. They couldn't imagine her in the role of Phyllis. Winant told them to trust her. Leachman auditioned and won everyone over.

Allan Burns saw Georgia Engel play deaf actress Corinna Stroller in a production of *The House of Blue Leaves*. Her scene was one of the funniest he had ever seen. Engel was brought in for a single episode of the show playing a coworker of Rhoda's. She had about five lines. Burns went down to the stage where they were rehearsing. Moore grabbed him and told him that Engel was so funny she couldn't believe it. She told Burns to sign her for the show.

Ed. Weinberger and Stan Daniels wrote a script in which Phyllis' husband

Lars has an affair with someone from the station. The character was described in the script as a Betty White type. Mary Tyler Moore and Betty White were close friends. She suggested that they just hire Betty White. White wasn't initially approached because she seemed sweet. Once she came in and revealed a wicked sense of humor the part of Sue Ann Nivens was hers.

During the first season an episode was written called "Support Your Local Mother." In the episode Rhoda's mother, Ida Morgenstern, comes for a visit. Nancy Walker was hired for the part. Although Walker was 4'11, the legendary comedienne intimidated Burns and Brooks. Said Burns, "I went to the first run-thru. She wasn't giving us what we wanted." They cautiously approached Walker who responded by saying, "Boys, when the asses are in the seats you'll see the comedy." True to her word, the night of shooting Walker delivered an outstanding performance.

From 1973-1975 John Gabriel recurred as Mary's boyfriend Andy Rivers. "I was doing a commercial in Hollywood, and my agent said that they wanted to see me for this role of Mary's boyfriend, sportscaster Andy Rivers, during my lunch break," said Gabriel. "I zipped out to Studio City, and the producer Ed. Weinberger was taking an especially long lunch. I was in the first set up shot for the commercial. I couldn't wait. So I told the receptionist, 'I'm sorry. I've got to go. I have a commercial that I'm doing.' I walked to the parking lot. I was in my car. I was about to start it and a car pulls up alongside me. And I didn't know what Ed. Weinberger looked like. I just took a chance and I said, 'Are you Ed. Weinberger?' And he said, 'Yeah.' I explained my dilemma and he says, 'Come on, I'll read you real fast.' So he read me and I got the part. Another fifteen seconds and I would have been on the Hollywood Freeway."

In the November 28, 1970 episode entitled "1040 or Fight" Mary gets audited by the IRS. The part of auditor Robert C. Brand was written for former accountant Bob Newhart. Newhart declined the offer and Paul Sand was cast instead.

M*A*S*H (1972-1983)

Alan Alda as Hawkeye Pierce (Wayne Rogers)

Wayne Rogers as Trapper John McIntyre (Robert Foxworth)

THE FIRST ACTOR CAST in the TV series M*A*S*H was Gary Burghoff as Radar O'Reilly. Burghoff played Radar in the hit film *MASH*, on which the series was based.

Robert Foxworth was offered the part of Trapper John McIntyre. He was advised that the show would never sell and turned down producer Gene Reynolds.

Wayne Rogers was considered for both roles of Hawkeye Pierce and Trapper John. Rogers was eventually signed to play Trapper John. "Hawkeye was a difficult part because he had to be extremely articulate," said Reynolds. "He was a well-educated man, a lot of tension, a lot of indignation about the war, about the Army. He had to be the mouthpiece of the show; the editorial voice of the show. He had to be a light comedian. To find a light comic that's got that kind of intelligence and that kind of brightness and intellectual drive and so forth - you find a lot of comics, but you don't take them seriously when they begin to talk seriously. It was getting dangerous and I was going to have to compromise. An agent came to me on the stage that I knew and he knew me and he said, 'Listen, do you know Alan Alda?' I said, 'Yeah, I saw him in New York in *The Apple Tree*. He's wonderful.' He said, 'He lives in New York. He's got three daughters and he's a serious father. He doesn't want to tie up himself for seven, eight years. He's ready to do television. He realizes that if he's going to have a career he's going to have to come to the coast.' We sent him a script. He said, 'Well, I want to do it and so forth, but I really would like to talk to you guys (meaning me and Larry [Gelbart]) before we start.' He was on a movie up in Utah, a two-hour movie for television. All the guys in his cast said, 'Don't do M*A*S*H. They'll screw it up; they'll make a joke out of it.' He came down and we had a little cup of coffee in the coffee shop at the Beverly Wilshire Hotel. The coffee shop does not exist anymore. First thing out of his mouth is, 'I don't want it to be *McHale's Navy.*' I said, 'Well, we don't either.' And I said, 'We'd like to make a show that is funny and so forth, but the premise of which is the wastefulness of war.' You could just see him warm up. He said, 'Yeah, yeah! That's what I had in mind.'

"The pilot was crazy. The pilot was not very serious. It had some indignation in it, but for the most part the idea in the pilot was to touch on all the characters; kind of a curtain call for all the characters. We had a nice little problem in the pilot. We had to get a scholarship for the houseboy. We had to introduce all the characters and we had to keep it funny, God forbid it wouldn't be funny. So off we went. We never really got into the show until about the fourth or fifth episode when we had somebody die that was a dear friend of Hawkeye's. And then we kind of brought it close to home. We did that for the length of the show to try to show the wastefulness of war. And of course the big response was when we killed Henry Blake. He had insisted on getting off the show. CBS finally said, 'Okay, finish the year.' . . . One of the writers said, 'I think if he goes home he shouldn't make it.' We'd all struck it as being correct because a lot of boys didn't get home to Bloomington, Illinois who were in that war. I think we lost 26,000 men in the Korean War."

Larry Gelbart invented the character of Max Klinger. Gelbart heard that when comedian Lenny Bruce was in the Navy he went on watch dressed as a woman, and was subsequently thrown out. The character of Klinger was based on that story.

Gene Reynolds had directed an episode of the show *F-Troop*. In the episode was a character that was an Indian from the Catskill tribe who was a comic. The character was played by Jamie Farr. Reynolds remembered Farr and brought him in to play Klinger. "The first director that shot him, he read the script," said Reynolds. "I felt sure that he'd got it, but he didn't. We go to dailies and here's Jamie Farr playing the part and he's camping the whole thing. Both Larry and I were shocked. I ran down and said, 'You've got the wrong idea with Klinger.' He said, 'Why? What? What?' He didn't get the idea. We kept the masters but I just reshot all the close-ups."

Producer Burt Metcalfe brought William Christopher in to read for the part of Father Mulcahy. Christopher read badly and left. Reynolds thought that Christopher could do better. He called the gate and had him sent back. Christopher did well the second time around, and landed the part.

M*A*S*H was one of television's biggest hits. The show ran for eleven years. It was nominated ten times for the Best Comedy Series Emmy, winning once. The final episode of the series was an event. It was the most watched episode of any show ever on television up to that time.

Maude (1972-1978)
Rue McClanahan as Vivian (Doris Roberts)

BEATRICE ARTHUR ORIGINATED the character of Maude Findlay on *All in the Family* in 1971. The character was spun-off into her own series the following year.

Series creator Norman Lear wanted Doris Roberts to play opposite Arthur as Maude's friend and neighbor Vivian. Lear soon realized that Roberts was too similar to Arthur, which would not create any conflict. The part went to Rue McClanahan instead.

Medium (2005-)
Patricia Arquette as Allison Dubois (Hope Davis, Calista Flockhart, Maggie Gyllenhaal, Anne Heche, Keri Russell, Marisa Tomei)
Jake Weber as Joe Dubois (Patrick Dempsey, David Duchovny, Ron Eldard, Eric Jensen, Matthew Modine, Barry Pepper, Lou Diamond Phillips, Donnie Wahlberg, Fred Weller)
Miguel Sandoval as Manuel Devalos (Nick Searcy)

In 2001 STEVE STARK and Kelsey Grammer produced a pilot called *The Oracles*. The show featured paranormal experts, and included a young, vibrant woman named Allison DuBois. The producers of *The Oracles* felt that DuBois was credible, and flew her out to Los Angeles for a meeting. She told them about her life. When DuBois was six years old, she had an experience where she was able to communicate with her deceased great-grandfather. These types of experiences continued throughout her life, and DuBois eventually came to work with the police in solving crimes, as well as a jury consultant. DuBois met producer Glenn Gordon Caron, who was skeptical about her abilities. After a long lunch with DuBois, Caron was completely hooked. He created the show about DuBois, which was called *Medium*. DuBois' real name was used in the series, as was as her husband Joe's. In real life DuBois has three daughters, as does the fictional Allison. Caron and DuBois pitched the show to ABC. Caron thought the network would make a deal with them, but DuBois told him they wouldn't. That night they got the call that ABC said no. They tried their luck at NBC. They met with executives Kevin Reilly and Chris Conti. At the end of the meeting DuBois told Conti to drive carefully. Conti was freaked out for the rest of the day, although he had no real reason to worry. DuBois just wanted to ensure that he would continue thinking about her! Not long after, Caron and DuBois learned that NBC said yes.

Calista Flockhart, Keri Russell, Anne Heche and Hope Davis all passed up the chance to play Allison Dubois. Marisa Tomei and Maggie Gyllenhaal were considered. Glenn Gordon Caron's girlfriend, actress Tina DiJoseph, suggested Patricia Arquette. There was some concern that Arquette didn't have TV good looks, but that was exactly what series creator Glenn Gordon Caron was looking for. He wanted the audience to feel that she was a real soccer mom. Arquette's agent told her about the show, but assumed she wouldn't consider doing a television series. However, Arquette was interested and made a deal not long after.

Donnie Wahlberg's name came up during discussions regarding the casting of Allison's husband Joe. Matthew Modine was another possible, as well as Patrick Dempsey. Dempsey was working on David E. Kelley's show *The Practice*, and was unavailable. Barry Pepper was made an offer, which he turned down. David Duchovny was busy directing. Ron Eldard was already committed to the series *Blind Justice*. Lou Diamond Phillips read, but it was decided that they wanted an actor less well known. Executive producer Ronald L. Schwary suggested Jake Weber, who he had worked with on the film *Meet Joe Black*. The possible choices were finally narrowed down to Jake Weber, Fred Weller and Eric Jensen. Although casting director Marc Hirschfeld described Weller and Jensen as "wonderful actors" the role was given to Jake Weber.

The final two actors considered to play District Attorney Manuel Devalos were Miguel Sandoval and Nick Searcy. "Miguel was wonderful," said Hirschfeld. "I lobbied very heavily for him." Hirschfeld also thought it was a plus that Sandoval was a Latino, since the series takes place in Arizona. Hirschfeld's lobbying worked. The actor won the role.

Although NBC was always very supportive of *Medium*, the show was not picked up right away. NBC chose to concentrate on the new series *LAX*, *Hawaii* and *Medical Investigations* instead. None of these shows lasted, and *Medium* was a mid-season replacement. The show premiered to high ratings, and has been doing well since. In 2005 Patricia Arquette won the Best Actress Emmy for her portrayal of Allison DuBois.

Melrose Place (1992-1999)

Grant Show as Jake Hanson (Adrian Pasdar)
Andrew Shue as Billy Campbell (Stephen Fanning, Matthew Perry)
Amy Locane as Sandy Louise Harling (Pamela Anderson, Kathy Ireland)
Lisa Rinna as Taylor (Hunter Tylo)

AARON SPELLING ASKED Adrian Pasdar to audition to play Jake Hanson on *Melrose Place*. Pasdar decided against it. He felt that, although the money would have been good, the series was not for him. The part was eventually given to Grant Show.

Aaron Spelling hired Stephen Fanning for the part of writer Billy Campbell. Howard Deutch was brought in to direct the pilot. During rehearsals Deutch saw there was a problem. Spelling came on the set and told Deutch that Fanning wasn't working out. After a day of shooting, Fanning was fired. According to Fanning, he had just come out of theater school, and didn't understand the Spelling machine. Said the actor, "They didn't tell me what they wanted from me. I focused on the character being a writer, a Norman Mailer fan. I didn't understand they wanted it to be like *Baywatch*. I would have hit the gym. They said, 'Tell him it has nothing to do

Howard Deutch

with acting. It's like we bought a black car and now we want a red car.'" "He's a terrific actor," said Deutch. "It had nothing to do with his talent. He could act it. It's not fair; it's not fun. It's an awful thing. I felt terrible for him."

A replacement was needed. Aaron Spelling had a big casting session at his house. Andrew Shue flew in from Africa, where he was a math teacher. After his audition Deutch was told that Shue was really cute and that Tori [Spelling] agreed. Shue was hired for the part. Since he was so new to show business Deutch called Shue's sister, veteran actress Elisabeth Shue. She and Deutch met at the Beverly Hills deli Nate and Al's, and Shue agreed to coach her brother.

Matthew Perry had also been considered for the part of Billy.

Pamela Anderson and Kathy Ireland were considered for the role of Sandy Louise Harling. The part was given to Amy Locane. Locane left the show after just twelve episodes.

Hunter Tylo met with casting executive Pamela Shae. The actress was just finishing a run on *The Bold and the Beautiful*. Shae thought that Tylo was very right for *Melrose Place*. She sent a memo to Aaron Spelling. Tylo was eventually offered the role of Taylor, which she accepted. Soon after the actress learned she was pregnant. Shortly

Pamela Shae

after informing the show about her pregnancy she was fired. The actress sued Spelling Television claiming pregnancy discrimination, wrongful termination and breach of contract. Spelling Television argued that Tylo's contract allowed her to be fired if there was a dramatic change in her appearance. Tylo's lawyers called *Melrose Place* star Heather Locklear in to testify. On the stand Locklear said that the show worked around her pregnancy. Like Tylo, Locklear was also hired to play a vixen.

Lisa Rinna, the actress eventually hired to play Taylor, was also called to testify. At the time of the trial Rinna was pregnant. Her pregnancy was written into the show. Tylo would routinely show up to court dressed in sexy outfits. She later surprised the courtroom when she revealed on the stand that she was eight months pregnant.

After more than four days of deliberation the jury awarded Tylo $4 million for emotional distress and $894,601 for economic losses.

Miami Hustle (1996)

Kathy Ireland as Marsha Thomas (Pamela Anderson)

PAMELA ANDERSON WAS ORIGINALLY cast as con artist Marsha Thomas in *Miami Hustle*. Anderson dropped out of the film, and was sued by the production company for $5 million. They ultimately lost the case. Kathy Ireland was hired to replace Anderson in the film.

Miami Vice (1984-1989)

Don Johnson as Sonny Crockett (Graham Beckel, Gary Cole, Larry Wilcox)
Philip Michael Thomas as Ricardo Tubbs (Andy Garcia, Count Stovall)

THOMAS CARTER WAS HIRED to direct the pilot episode of *Miami Vice*. He saw many actors for the starring roles of detectives Sonny Crockett and Ricardo Tubbs.

Don Johnson, Larry Wilcox, Graham Beckel and Gary Cole all auditioned for the part of Sonny Crockett. At the time Larry Wilcox was the most well known, from his starring role of Jon Baker on the hit show *CHiPs*. Carter said that Wilcox did a very good reading, and came close to landing the part. "Don emerged because, I think just the whole package of him; his look, a kind of ease of style that he had made us decide to go with him," said Carter. "But not with wild enthusiasm from the network . . . He was not at all the guy who had embraced this sort of European cool that we put into the show. In fact, he didn't even get it in the beginning He didn't really want to wear the clothes the way we were designing them. He didn't get it. So he had to be sort of groomed into who Sonny Crockett was. And then eventually he embraced it and claimed it, but it's not what he brought to it immediately. It's what was sort of thrust upon him." *Miami Vice* made Don Johnson a star.

Carter was in Miami doing a quick local casting session. "We were close to the end of the process," he said. "I went in to the casting director's office, read a few people, and in walks this young guy who comes in and reads for Tubbs. It was one of those things where you go, 'Wow. I never heard of that guy. He was very good.' Where part of your brain's going, 'Wow, he's very good,' and part of your brain's going, 'But I never heard of him. Does he have enough experience? I mean, what's going on? Let me do this again.' So he read again and I thought he was really terrific. I thought he had an ease about him, he had a style, he had a charm, he had confidence, he felt like he could be from Miami. His name was Andy Garcia. But of course nobody had heard of Andy at that point, and so I said, 'Listen, man, you're really good. We're at the end of this process and I'm flying back tonight or in the morning. We're going to read people at NBC and I'd like to bring you to the network.' And he had some commitment or some scheduling conflict that was important for him at the time. He couldn't make it and we couldn't hold the session. We obviously had Phillip Michael Thomas on that list. As it happened, Andy actually did not go back to the network. I mean I called them back there and said, 'I found this guy who's really good and we should get him back.' But it couldn't be worked out in the time that it needed to be worked out. And he actually did not get back to NBC to audition when we took people to the network so he never got seen by them.

"Consequently, he never wound up in that role, which he would have been fantastic for, obviously. Andy Garcia would have been very special casting had it happened, in a very different way. In some ways I think it was lucky for him. You never know. He went on to do other movies, and got known. He's pursued his own path and been successful at it. But it was one of those moments where (I had very few of them) where you see a young actor early on and you go, 'Wow, there's something special there,' and you get to watch over the next ten years how this person actually does become known and respected."

Count Stovall also auditioned for the part of Ricardo Tubbs, but lost out to Philip Michael Thomas.

The Mind of the Married Man (1994-1995)

Sonya Walger as Donna Barnes (Patricia Arquette, Orla Brady, Saffron
    Burrows, Patricia Clarkson, Kim Dickens, Melissa Errico, Felicity
    Huffman, Sheila Kelley, Diane Lane, Kelly Rowan, Kate Walsh)
Ivana Milicevic as Missy (Erin Daniels, Vanessa Marcil)
Taylor Nichols as Doug Nelson (Doug Williams)
Jake Weber as Jake Berman (Frank Grillo)

THE MIND OF THE MARRIED MAN followed three male friends who meet
once a week to talk about their love lives. Series executive producer/direc-
tor/writer Mike Binder played married political columnist Mickey Barnes.

Doug Williams and Frank Grillo auditioned to play Mickey's friends
Doug Nelson and Jake Berman. The roles were given to Taylor Nichols
and Jake Weber instead.

Casting director Sharon Bialy and HBO agreed that the part of Mickey's wife Donna Barnes was not going to be the typical wife you always see
on TV shows. Saffron Burrows was considered as was Felicity Huffman,
Kelly Rowan, Kim Dickens, Patricia Clarkson, Patricia Arquette, Diane
Lane, Melissa Errico, Sheila Kelley, Orla Brady and Kate Walsh. Sonya
Walger was seen in a rough cut of a film directed by Mike Binder. The film
was called The Search for John Gissing and Walger played a nun. She was
flown out to test for the role of Donna Barnes and wound up winning the
part. Kate Walsh was given the smaller role of Carol Nelson.

Vanessa Marcil and Erin Daniels were both up for the part of Mickey's
assistant Missy, but lost out to Ivana Milicevic.

Miss All-American Beauty (1982)

Brian Kerwin as Michael Carrington (Tom Hanks)

TOM HANKS WAS UP for the supporting role of Michael Carrington in 1982
TV movie Miss All-American Beauty. The role went to Brian Kerwin instead.

Mission: Impossible (1988-1990)

Thaao Penghlis as Nicholas Black
    (Anthony LaPaglia)

Thaao Penghlis

TWO AUSTRALIAN ACTORS were considered for the part of Nicholas Black for the 1980's version of *Mission: Impossible* – Anthony LaPaglia and Thaao Penghlis. Penghlis was initially told he was too glamorous for the part, and changed his image for the audition. After his reading he got a standing ovation. He knew he had the part when the casting director winked at him. LaPaglia told Penghlis that he was in America because of him; if Penghlis could do it, so could he. Not long after losing the role in *Mission: Impossible,* LaPaglia made it big in films such as *Betsy's Wedding* and *29th Street.* He is currently the star of the CBS hit show *Without a Trace.*

Models Inc. (1994-1995)

Linda Gray as Hillary Michaels (Raquel Welch)

MODELS INC. WAS A SPIN-OFF of the hit nighttime soap *Melrose Place,* which starred Heather Locklear as Amanda Woodward. Woodward's mother was Hillary Michaels; the lead role on *Models Inc.* Executive producer Aaron Spelling was very involved in the casting process. "After the script the main thing he worried about was the casting," said executive producer Frank South. "He felt everything hinged on that."

Raquel Welch was up for the part of Hillary, which was eventually given to Linda Gray. "She had great energy," said South of Gray. "She brought a TV history with her. To be Amanda's mom, it had to be someone like that."

The producers saw many actresses for the other roles in the series. "Casting director Pam Shae did an enormous amount of work," said South. "She brought in different groups for each role. Then you get to that point when we're in a big office of Aaron's with the shag carpet and the long couch. I think for actors it must be quite a thing to see. He would have a lot of people on that couch, sometimes like fifteen people on one long couch. It started at the door all the way to his desk. He'd be sitting there with us. Someone would come in and read. He was always very sweet to them and very respectful. Afterwards he'd say, 'Well, what do you think?' He had very definite opinions and he would tell you why."

Monk (2002-)

Tony Shalhoub as Adrian Monk
    (Dave Foley, Terence Knox, Ron
    Livingston, Alfred Molina, Michael
    Richards, John Ritter, Stanley Tucci,
    Henry Winkler)
Bitty Schram as Sharona Fleming
    (Queen Latifah)

Frank South

THE IDEA FOR THE SERIES *Monk* came from David Hoberman. As a teenager he suffered from Obsessive Compulsive Disorder (OCD). Hoberman pitched the idea to ABC, who liked it and said yes. Hoberman hired Andy Breckman to develop the lead character of Adrian Monk and to write the pilot script. Michael Richards was considered to play Monk, as was Ron Livingston. Many of the actors who auditioned for the title role did a broad, physical interpretation of the character. It didn't work, and the project was stalled until ABC executive Jackie Lyons moved to the cable network USA and took the project with her. Henry Winkler, John Ritter and Dave Foley were all possible choices to star. USA executive Jeff Wachtel wanted to keep looking. He thought the best three actors for the part were Tony Shalhoub, Alfred Molina and Stanley Tucci.

Simultaneously, a project that Tony Shalhoub was working on wasn't picked up. Shalhoub, who was now available, came in and nailed the character. Incidentally, Terence Knox had the role at one point. He left shortly before the pilot was shot.

The July 7, 2006 episode was called "Mr. Monk and the Actor." A method actor named David Ruskin is cast as Monk in a film. In order to get his characterization right he follows Monk around to get to know him. He becomes so obsessed with Monk, he starts to think he really is him. The part of David Ruskin was played by Adrian Monk candidate Stanley Tucci.

Queen Latifah was originally considered for the part of Monk's assistant, nurse Sharona Fleming. The role was eventually given to Bitty Schram, who gave a great audition. After about three seasons Schram left the show. A casting process took place to find a replacement. "It's hard because it's all about the chemistry," said executive producer Randy Zisk. "The chemistry was so good between Tony and Bitty. It's tricky and risky because you don't want to ever upset that. It's been done before on *Cheers* and other shows and it worked. And I'm sure it's been done quite a few times where it hasn't worked. But we spent a long time. We read so many actresses. We narrowed it down to five, and they came to the studio and the network. Traylor [Howard] came out. It was a long process. We delayed our shooting schedule a few weeks because of it." "She's been an extraordinarily wonderful addition to the show," said producer Fern Field of Howard.

The Monkees (1966-1968)

Micky Dolenz, Davy Jones, Mike Nesmith and Peter Tork as The Monkees
(The Lovin' Spoonful, Paul Petersen, Stephen Stills, Paul Williams, Jerry
Yester)

AN OPEN CASTING CALL was held in Hollywood to find the guys to play The Monkees. The producers were looking for talented musicians with a great sense of humor. An unknown band called The Lovin' Spoonful was considered. It was later decided that it wasn't a practical idea and scrapped. Hundreds of kids auditioned, including Paul Williams. Jerry Yester and Stephen Stills were also considered. Stills told his friend Peter Tork about the audition. Tork went, and got the job. Stills found success with the bands Buffalo Springfield and Crosby, Stills, and Nash.

Randy Zisk

Paul Petersen of *The Donna Reed Show* was another potential Monkee. He auditioned, but failed to get the job. Micky Dolenz was one of the few auditioned who didn't have to go to the cattle call. He was brought in to audition for the producers right away. "I was going to school," he said. "I was going to be an architect, and I was going to fall back on show business if I didn't make it as an architect. But I had been going out and doing some guest work on shows. That year there were a few pilots being done about the music business and the young generation. I do recall the Monkee audition being quite unique. First of all, when I went in to the audition there were these two guys there in jeans and T-shirts. They were young guys, a little bit older than I was. I thought they were there for the audition, and they were the producers. It was quite unusual at that time for television producers to be in their 30s. Usually they were big guys in suits smoking cigars. These guys were young, and obviously part of that generation, so there was a different vibe about it immediately. I remember thinking, 'This was really cool. I'd like to get this one.'

A recent picture of Micky Dolenz

"The first audition was just in an office reading lines from sides that I had been given. I immediately sensed that there was an improvisational quality to the whole sensibility. I was improvising on my feet, goofing around and joking, and I think just intuitively I sensed that they were looking for personalities. They weren't necessarily looking for an actor to play the part that they already had preconfigured in their minds. Ultimately I was right; that is what they were going for.

"There were extensive screen tests. The thing that sticks out in my mind, and now looking back I realize it was cast much in the way you would cast a musical. I've recently been cast in a number of Broadway musicals, and the casting process was very similar. It was done on a sound-stage behind close doors, and not a theater stage, but you had to sing. You had to play an instrument. One of the screen tests was playing with a band. I played guitar at the time. That was my instrument of choice since I was a kid, and still is. I played 'Johnny B. Goode' on the guitar, the Chuck Berry tune. That was one of the screen tests. Another one was an improvisational interview. There was also a screen test of scripted scenes where they would match up myself and other guys. I remember in the first auditions there might have been sixteen guys hanging around. Then it got down to twelve, and then eight. I don't remember anybody else in those screen tests except Davy Jones. I remember David because we had similar backgrounds. We hit it off just because of our professional backgrounds. We clicked when we got in front of the camera.

"It was extensive. It was by far the most extensive interviews and auditions that I had been on for a series because it involved music and singing, movement and improvisation. Even then I could sense it was heavily weighted toward improvisation, which, quite honestly, I was not that comfortable with. Because of my background and my history in the film and television industry I was used to having a script, and you learn your lines, and you show up on the set and you say the lines. It took me a while to get used to the improvisational aspect of it."

Micky Dolenz, Davy Jones and Peter Tork were hired as well as Mike Nesmith. "What was great about those four guys," said director James Frawley, "was that each of them had a distinctive role that they fulfilled." Frawley had been an improvisational actor. For three months before they started shooting Frawley led the four guys in a class where they did improvisations so that each of them had a chance to find each other's sense of humor and rhythms. The Monkees was a hit with viewers, and scored very high in the ratings for its entire run.

Moonlighting (1985-1989)
Bruce Willis as David Addison (Harley Venton)

ABC APPROACHED GLENN GORDON CARON to make three pilots for
the network. The first two didn't sell. Then the network intervened. They
told Caron to create a male/ female detective show, something like *Hart
to Hart*. About halfway through writing the pilot episode Caron realized
that Cybill Shepherd would be perfect for his leading lady, former model
Maddy Hayes. He provided her with 50 pages of the unfinished script.
Shepherd liked what she read and agreed to meet Caron and producer Jay
Daniel. After the meeting Shepherd agreed to take the part.

An extensive search for the co-starring role of detective David
Addison was held. About 1,400 actors were considered, including Harley
Venton and an unknown Bruce Willis. Willis came in to audition wearing fatigues and an earring. During his reading he got up on the table.
Caron was impressed by Bruce Willis and knew he was the right actor
for the part. Willis was brought to the network about eleven times. ABC
executive Tony Thomopoulos finally said to stop bringing him. Undaunted,
Caron persisted and ABC eventually agreed to let him test. However,
Cybill Shepherd refused to test with him. She worried that she might lose
her part! Actress Mary Margaret Humes was brought in to read Maddy's
lines with Willis. Everyone liked his test except for the boss, who said he
wasn't a leading man. Caron made a deal that David and Maddy wouldn't
be romantically involved in the first season in order to be allowed to cast
Bruce Willis, since ABC didn't think Shepherd would be involved with
him. They finally agreed, and Willis won the part.

Bruce Willis was so popular as David Addison that, according to
Moonlighting's casting director Reuben Cannon, he set a new standard for
casting. The following season Willis became a prototype for the next pilot
season.

Moonlighting was a huge hit. The series ran for four years. By the end of the run David and Maddy had been romantically involved. Audiences had no problem believing the two as a couple.

In 1988 Bruce Willis starred as action hero John McClane in the blockbuster film *Die Hard*. The film made him a major movie star, which he remains to date.

Mork & Mindy (1978-1982)
Conrad Janis as Fred McConnell (Graham Jarvis)

THE CHARACTER OF MORK from Ork first appeared on the show *Happy Days*, where he was played by Robin Williams. That episode was more popular than any episode had been up to that point. ABC spun Mork off into his own series, *Mork & Mindy*. Pam Dawber was hired to play Mindy, while Graham Jarvis was cast as her father Fred McConnell. Shortly after, Jarvis left the show and was replaced by Conrad Janis.

Mr. Merlin (1981-1982)
Jonathan Prince as Leo (Michael J. Fox)

AN UNKNOWN MICHAEL J. FOX was considered for the part of Leo in a pilot called *Mr. Merlin*. "He was living in his car, eating McDonald's," said casting director Jerold Franks. "He was cuter than a button." Franks didn't read Fox for the part, and the role went to Jonathan Prince instead. Franks added that he's had guilt for 25 years about it. Fox

Jerold Franks with his
Artios award for casting

fared just fine. He was cast in the series *Family Ties* in 1982, and was the show's breakout star. *Family Ties* ran for seven years, while *Mr. Merlin* lasted just one.

The Munsters (1964-1966)
Butch Patrick as Eddie Munster (Happy Derman)

HAPPY DERMAN played Eddie Munster in the original pilot for *The Munsters.* Butch Patrick later replaced Derman as Eddie.

Murder in the Heartland (1993)
Tim Roth as Charles Starkweather (D.B. Sweeney, Steven Waddington)

BETWEEN DECEMBER 1957 and January 1958 19-year-old Charles Starkweather murdered eleven people, including the family of his 14-year-old girlfriend Caril Ann Fugate. He was caught, and eventually executed in the electric chair in 1959.

D.B. Sweeney and Steven Waddington were both up to play Charles Starkweather in the 1993 ABC movie *Murder in the Heartland.* Producer Michael G. Larkin had seen the movie *Reservoir Dogs* and was blown away by it. He was impressed with Tim Roth's portrayal of Mr. Orange/Freddy Newandyke. He recommended Roth for the part. The English Roth was cast, but refused to do an American accent prior to shooting. Even at the table read he spoke in his own accent. Larkin wasn't concerned. He knew that Roth had done a terrific American

Michael G. Larkin

accent in *Reservoir Dogs* and, although it wasn't the same dialect, knew he could pull it off.

Charles Starkweather is the subject of the Bruce Springsteen song "Nebraska."

Murder One (1995-1997)

Daniel Benzali as Theodore
    Hoffman (Stanley Tucci)
Bobbie Phillips as Julie Costello
    (Claudia Schiffer, Vendela)
John Fleck as Louis Hines (Linda
    Carlson)

John Fleck
Photo: Beth Herzhaft

SERIES CREATOR STEVEN BO-
CHCO had Daniel Benzali in mind for the starring role of defense attorney Theodore Hoffman. He also considered Stanley Tucci, who was cast as Hoffman's client, Richard Cross, instead.

Supermodels Claudia Schiffer and Vendela both auditioned to play the part of Julie Costello, the mistress of Richard Cross. Neither got the job; Bobbie Phillips was eventually hired.

The character of Louis Hines was originally written as a female secretary. Linda Carlson was among the many women who auditioned, as was actor John Fleck. The role eventually went to Fleck. Linda Carlson was cast as Judge Beth Bornstein instead.

Murder, She Wrote (1984-1996)
Angela Lansbury as Jessica Fletcher (Jean Stapleton)

HARVEY SHEPARD, the head of CBS, approached Richard Levinson and William Link about creating a show about a woman detective. They met with Jean Stapleton for lunch at the Bel Air Hotel. Stapleton was the first choice to play the lead role of Jessica Fletcher. Levinson, Link and co-creator Peter Fischer devised a story for the pilot and sent it to Stapleton. According to her son, actor/director John Putch, Stapleton read the pilot, and didn't see the potential in the show. She turned it down, despite those around her thinking it was a bad decision. Someone suggested Angela Lansbury. "We thought she was a wonderful actress," said Link. "But we really had trepidation about taking this name in to Harvey Shepard because few people in Hollywood knew her. I don't even think she had a TV Q in those days. She'd done, I think, some TV specials, maybe a couple of two-hour movies. But she was not a name out here. We thought, we're going to take this to Harvey Shepard who was the power to put this series on the air. Shaking in our boots, we went in to see Harvey. I couldn't believe it. He said, 'Angela Lansbury? Is she available?' We said, 'We haven't checked." It turns out he was the son of a butcher in Brooklyn. The parents loved musical comedy. So he had seen her in *Mame* and *Gypsy*. He was a big fan of hers. We couldn't have brought in a name that would have sparked him more. How's that for irony? I'll never forget, we talked to her agent and we said we wanted to meet with her, if she would be interested. He said, 'Well, she's got something else on her plate now, but she'll have the meeting.' We had the meeting at 5:00 in the President of Television's office in the black tower at Universal. She came, was very warm and charming, which is what she is. She told us, and our hearts sank, that she had a script that she was going to read that weekend, a sitcom for Norman Lear that my friend Charlie Durning was going to be in. We were very off put by that. We told her about this character, and she was English and she said, 'Oh, it's like Miss Marple.' She said, 'Look, it sounds interesting. Let me read both scripts this weekend. I want to do a television series. I'll definitely call you with my answer Monday morning. I'm a person who will do that. I'm not just putting you on here. I will let you know, and I'll do it personally. Not through my agent.' She called Monday morning and said, 'I'm yours.'"

Jean Stapleton was happy that the part went to an actress as good as Lansbury. Putch said that Stapleton graciously said that she could never have done the part as well as Angela Lansbury.

Ron Masak

Peter Fischer called Ron Masak to tell him that he was creating the role of Sheriff Mort Metzger. He told Masak the part was his if he wanted it, but that he was leaving for Europe and had to have an answer in 24 hours. Masak replied, "Okay." Fischer said, "So you will let me know?" Masak said, "I just did." Masak said that Angela Lansbury welcomed him to the cast graciously with open arms.

Murderers Among Us: The Simon Wiesenthal Story (1989)
Ben Kingsley as Simon Wiesenthal (F. Murray Abraham)

SIMON WIESENTHAL WAS A SURVIVOR of the Nazi concentration camps. Wiesenthal dedicated his life to documenting what went on during the

Holocaust, and to find the perpe-
trators who were still out there. He
established the Jewish Documen-
tation Center in Vienna, Austria,
and was involved in finding over
1,100 Nazi war criminals, including Adolf Eichmann, Franz Stangl,
Hermine Ryan, Franz Murer and
Erich Rajakowitsch. Wiesenthal's
memoir is called *The Murderers
Among Us*.

F. Murray Abraham
Photo: Bill Flanagan flanagan@wdn.com

F. Murray Abraham was considered for the starring role of Simon
Wiesenthal in the 1989 TV movie
*Murderers Among Us: The Simon
Wiesenthal Story*. Abraham's agent
advised him against going in for a meeting with the producer. "He insisted that
since I was a recent Academy Award winner I should not have to go in to
meet anyone," said Abraham. "It was a stupid thing to do, but I do not blame
him for my decision to accept his opinion; after all, we are finally responsible
for our lives. But, it was a role I wanted to do and I should have absolutely
insisted on doing it under any circumstances. The lesson to be learned here
is twofold: you are responsible for any decisions no matter what the advice,
so think carefully; and second, don't be so stupid as to stay with an agent out
of a misplaced sense of loyalty. Business is business." Ben Kingsley eventually took the role of Simon Wiesenthal.

Murphy Brown (1988-1998)

Candice Bergen as Murphy Brown (Heather Locklear, Marsha Mason, JoBeth Williams)

Grant Shaud as Miles Silverberg (Jason Alexander, Greg Germann, Jeffrey Marcus, Ben Stiller)

Joe Regalbuto as Frank Fontana (Jay Thomas)

THE ROLE OF MURPHY BROWN was written with JoBeth Williams in mind. Although Williams liked the script, she had just become a mother. "I just couldn't picture myself going to the studio every day," said Williams. "I had so wanted to become a mom, so I turned it down. It was a real emotional decision. I have to say that motherhood has been the most satisfying part of my life." Marsha Mason was another possibility, but she too turned it down. CBS suggested Heather Locklear. Candice Bergen was interested and lobbied for the part. At first series creator Diane English didn't think Bergen was right for it. After English spent some time with Bergen her mind was changed. English had to sell Candice Bergen to the studio and the network. CBS was not enthusiastic about the idea, and required Bergen to read for them. "The reading was done under unusual circumstances," said director Barnet Kellman. "Putting her through the reading process was one thing. To save her the process of having to sit in a room with three or four other actresses and going one by

Barnet Kellman

one, she was given a private reading with just us and the head of the network in his office instead of the usual place where they did these things. But that actually made it more awkward and embarrassing for everybody. It was a more unnatural situation. It was like half a meeting, and half a reading. It was just not comfortable for anyone. After her reading we were politely shown the door. It was very clear, particularly to Diane, but it was pretty clear that they weren't going to say yes. And Diane refused to leave. She did it in a very clever way. She didn't say, 'I will not leave this room.' She just said, 'You guys wait outside and I'll be right out. She stayed back with the head of the network who looked appalled because she had just been shown the door. She wasn't supposed to stay. And she pulled out the list [of other actresses considered for Murphy]. She said, 'I'll grant you, you couldn't necessarily see everything that we know and believe Candice is going to bring to the role. You could not see it in front of you today. I'm granting you that. But Candice can do it, and I want to place my chance of having a show on her shoulders. You show me somebody on this list that you'd be more excited if they were successful.' And ultimately she prevailed with that argument."

Many actors were seen for the part of Frank Fontana. The character was loosely based on Geraldo Rivera. Jay Thomas auditioned, but lost out to Joe Regalbuto.

The hardest part to cast was producer Miles Silverberg. Jeffrey Marcus auditioned four times. Jason Alexander was seriously considered, as was a very young Ben Stiller. Greg Germann was given the part. Diane English slept on it and, although she thought he was a terrific actor, he wasn't how she envisioned the character. Germann was let go. Grant Shaud auditioned on tape, along with many other actors. Kellman looked through the tapes and saw Shaud's reading with the sound muted. He put the sound on and showed him to English. They both fell in love with him immediately. Shaud was cast the Friday before the start of work on Monday.

The Music Man (2003)

Kristin Chenoweth as
Marian Paroo (Sarah
Jessica Parker)

PRODUCERS CRAIG ZA-
DAN and Neil Meron had
the television adaptation of
The Music Man in development. "They cast Matthew
[Broderick] before I was
involved," said director Jeff
Bleckner. "I went to meet
Matthew. Matthew had to
(kind of) cast me. He had
to approve me. So I actually
met him and got a chance
to see *The Producers*. He
had just opened in *The Producers* on Broadway when I
met him.

Jeff Bleckner
Photo: Charles "Chip" Hires

"I thought Matthew was almost the opposite of Robert Preston [who originated the role on Broadway]. His strengths were completely the opposite of Preston's. He doesn't have the big, brassy personality that Preston had. He has that quiet, wry, very ironic, understated personality. That's who he was."

Broderick's wife, actress Sarah Jessica Parker, was considered for the part of Marian Paroo. Parker wasn't available at that time.

"When we decided we wanted to go with Kristin Chenoweth as Marian, we called her and told her we were interested in having her do it," said Bleckner. "She thought we meant doing the young girl. She had no idea we were thinking of her for Marian. She's actually the perfect age for Marian. I thought she was fabulous for the part because usually someone who's considerably older plays it. In 1905 you were an old maid at 23. So I thought that was one of the nicest things about casting Kristin in that role because she is so youthful."

The Music Man was a critical hit. Jeff Bleckner was nominated for a DGA (Director's Guild of America) Award for outstanding directorial achievement in movies for television.

My Name Is Earl (2005-)

Jason Lee as Earl Hickey (Trace Adkins, Thomas Haden Church, Donal Logue, Michael Rapaport, Steve Zahn)
Ethan Suplee as Randy Hickey (Christopher Fitzgerald, Donal Logue)
Jaime Pressly as Joy (Laura Bell Bundy)

MY NAME IS EARL creator Greg Garcia was very interested in country singer Trace Adkins for the title role of Earl. Adkins read, but failed to impress the executives at NBC. Another possibility was Michael Rapaport. It was later decided that Rapaport came off as too urban. Casting director Marc Hirschfeld convinced Garcia to meet Jason Lee. Garcia liked Lee, and wanted him for the part. They negotiated a deal, but then Lee got cold feet and passed. Other front runners were Thomas Haden Church, Steve Zahn and Donal Logue. After a lot of negotiating, Jason Lee finally signed on for the show.

Donal Logue was also considered for the part of Earl's brother Randy. Logue turned down the part. Christopher Fitzgerald tested, but, according to Hirschfeld, "Ethan was the guy."

It came down to a choice between Jaime Pressly and Broadway star Laura Bell Bundy for the role of Earl's ex-wife Joy. Pressly's reading was so effortless she won the part.

My So-Called Life (1994-1995)

Claire Danes as Angela Chase (A.J. Langer, Alicia Silverstone)

ALICIA SILVERSTONE interviewed for the starring role of teenager Angela Chase in *My So-Called Life*. Silverstone was deemed too perfect looking and lost the role to Claire Danes. A.J. Langer also auditioned for Angela, but got the part of her wild friend Rayanne Graff instead.

My Sweet Charlie (1970)

Al Freeman, Jr. as Charles Roberts (Harry Belafonte, Sidney Poitier)

WRITER/PRODUCERS RICHARD LEVINSON and William Link wanted Patty Duke to star as Marlene Chambers in *My Sweet Charlie*. NBC okayed their choice, and Duke was hired. For the co-starring role of attorney-on-the-run Charles Roberts, the network suggested Sidney Poitier or Harry Belafonte. Levinson and Link had seen Al Freeman, Jr. in a movie where he played a villainous role. They thought he was really strong and fought for him to get the part. They had big clout at NBC and Freeman was cast.

The movie was shot on the Gulf Coast. During the shooting the police thought that Duke had drugs in her possession. A producer was flown down to tell her that if she did have drugs to get rid of them. Link was struck by the humanity of producer Sid Sheinberg who said that he would protect Duke even if they had to lose the picture. Sheinberg said that her life was more important than the movie. Duke had no drugs on her after all, and all was fine. She won an Emmy for Best Actress for the film, while Levinson and Link won for Best Screenplay. Universal loved the picture so much they released it as a feature film.

My World and Welcome to It (1969-1970)
Lisa Gerritsen as Lydia Monroe (Victoria Paige Meyerink)

VICTORIA PAIGE MEYERINK auditioned for the role of 10-year-old Lydia Monroe on *My World and Welcome to It*. Lisa Gerritsen eventually played the part.

Nancy Drew (2002)
Maggie Lawson as Nancy Drew (Christine Lakin)

CHRISTINE LAKIN and Maggie Lawson both auditioned for the title role in the 2002 ABC TV movie *Nancy Drew*. Lawson was chosen for the part.

The Nanny (1993-1999)
Charles Shaughnessy as Maxwell Sheffield (Wallace Shawn, Michael York)

FRAN DRESCHER GOT THE IDEA for *The Nanny* while interacting with her friend Twiggy's kids during a trip to England. On her flight home Drescher ran into CBS executive Jeff Sagansky. She pitched him the idea of a comedic version of *The Sound of Music*, with herself in the Julie Andrews role.

CBS eventually agreed to air the show. Drescher and her then-husband Peter Marc Jacobson served as writers and executive producers. Jacobson directed some of the episodes, while Drescher played the starring role of the nanny from Queens, Fran Fine.

Michael York and Wallace Shawn were finalists for the role of Fran's boss, the rich Broadway producer Maxwell Sheffield, but the part went to Charles Shaughnessy instead.

Naomi & Wynonna: Love Can Build a Bridge (1995)
Megan Ward as Ashley Judd (Cari Shayne)

CARI SHAYNE was originally brought in for the part of Ashley Judd in the NBC movie *Naomi & Wynonna: Love Can Build a Bridge*. The producers cast Megan Ward instead, while Shayne landed the larger part of the young Naomi Judd.

Ned and Stacey (1993-1999)
Thomas Haden Church as Ned Dorsey (Hank Azaria)
Debra Messing as Stacey Colbert (Jana Marie Hupp)
Nadia Dajani as Amanda Moyer (Leah Remini)

SERIES CREATOR MICHAEL J. WEITHORN offered Hank Azaria the starring role of Ned Dorsey in *Ned and Stacey*. Azaria said no. Casting directors Susan Vash and Debi Nathan suggested Thomas Haden Church for the part to Weithorn. Weithorn was only familiar with Church's work as Lowell on the series *Wings*, and didn't think he was right to play Ned. Vash and Nathan showed Weithorn the pilot episode of *Flying Blind*, in which Church played a character very different than Lowell. Weithorn then realized Church was perfect for the part. The two had a meeting. "I just knew he was Ned," said Weithorn. "I had written this thing, and I realized I had set the bar very high because this is an outrageous thing this guy does - a very high concept show. I said, 'I'd love for there to be some believability in the sense that you say, 'This person, I really believe that they're screwy enough to do something like this.' There are a lot of actors who came in. They were good, funny actors, but you didn't innately believe that they were capable of something like this. Tom is such an oddball, and yet so brilliantly funny, that it just kind of all seemed to make sense. Once I met with him we all felt he was the guy."

Weithorn wanted Jana Marie Hupp to play Stacey. The network refused to cast her. They felt she was a best friend type. "I went to New York to read some actresses there," Weithorn said. "Debra [Messing] was in New York at that time. She came in and read. Bob Harbin at Fox, the head of casting at the time, loved her and said, 'Oh, you've got to read Debra Messing.' I read her and, I don't know. She came in, her hair was weird She made some kind of acting choice that didn't feel right to me. And I guess I was also thinking, 'Oh, this is who the network wants. This ought to be rich.' I said, 'No. I don't like her.' Went back to L.A. to continue casting, and Debra came to L.A. for pilot season, and they said, 'She's back. She's in L.A. now. Can you please see her again? They begged me to see her again. And I did, and she said, 'What should I do different?' I gave her an adjustment and she was great."

Leah Remini tested for the supporting part of Amanda Moyer. Nadia Dajani got the job instead. Weithorn thought that Remini was great, and hoped that he would be able to work with her in the future. He did just that when he cast her in the co-starring role of Carrie Heffernan on *The King of Queens*.

Newhart (1982-1990)

Mary Frann as Joanna Loudon (Suzanne Pleshette, Jill St. John)
Tom Poston as George Utley (Jerry Van Dyke)

BOB NEWHART AND SUZANNE PLESHETTE played Bob and Emily Hartley, one of television's most memorable couples, on *The Bob Newhart Show* from 1972-1978. About ten years after the premiere of that show Bob Newhart was set to star as Vermont innkeeper Dick Loudon in the new series *Newhart*. Pleshette's name came up during discussions regarding the casting of Dick's wife Joanna. The idea was very quickly dropped. The producers thought that the public would perceive them as Bob and

Emily Hartley all over again. They were concerned that that might even be cause for a lawsuit. Both Jill St. John and Mary Frann auditioned to play Joanna. "Jill St. John was great, but too tall," said producer Sheldon Bull. He added, "Bob was most comfortable with Mary."

Jerry Van Dyke gave *Newhart* creator Barry Kemp his start in show business. *Newhart* was the first series Kemp created, and he wanted to pay Van Dyke back. He wrote the role of handyman George Utley for Van Dyke. The actor auditioned for CBS, but was turned down. CBS was so opposed to Van Dyke that they told Kemp that if he went ahead and cast him that there would be no series. After that meeting Tom Poston's name came up. Poston was approved by the network, and won the role. Kemp never forgot Van Dyke. About seven years later Kemp gave Van Dyke the role of Luther on *Coach*.

NewsRadio (1995-1999)

Dave Foley as Dave Nelson (Jason Bateman, Tim Conlon, Bob Odenkirk, Jeremy Piven, Justin Theroux)

Stephen Root as Jimmy James (Terry O'Quinn, J.T. Walsh, Ray Wise)

Maura Tierney as Lisa Miller (Lauren Graham, Molly Hagan, Leah Remini, Judy Reyes, Nina Siemaszko)

Joe Rogan as Joe Garelli (Jack Black, Ray Romano)

Khandi Alexander as Catherine Duke (Ella Joyce)

FROM THE BEGINNING *NewsRadio* creator Paul Simms wanted Dave Foley to play the show's central character Dave Nelson. At the time Foley was primarily known as a member of the Canadian comedy group The Kids in the Hall. NBC wasn't sure he was a leading man. Jason Bateman, Jeremy Piven, Bob Odenkirk and Justin Theroux all auditioned, but failed to win the part. Tim Conlon was also considered, but Simms eventually got his first choice when Foley was signed for the show.

Terry O'Quinn and J.T. Walsh were among the actors who auditioned for the part of station owner Jimmy James. Eventually the choice was narrowed down to two actors: Ray Wise and Stephen Root. When Root first read, it was not the way Simms envisioned the character. However, Root was impressive and eventually won the part.

The role of Lisa Miller was the last role cast. Molly Hagan, Leah Remini, Lauren Graham and Judy Reyes all auditioned. The day of the table read an actress still wasn't chosen. That day Maura Tierney and Nina Siemaszko gave final auditions. Everyone was sitting around the table waiting to start while the decision was made. The actresses were waiting in separate trailers to find out if they had the part or not. Paul Simms could not make up his mind. He took a walk for about an hour. When he came back, Tierney was given the part and immediately joined the rest of the cast for the table read.

Ray Romano was cast as Rick. Halfway through rehearsing Romano was fired. Reportedly, his rhythms were totally wrong for the character. Greg Lee was hired to play Rick in the pilot. However, the character underwent a change. The name was changed to Joe Garelli, and Joe Rogan was hired to play him. Jack Black auditioned for this role as well.

Ella Joyce was originally cast as Catherine Duke. Joyce was replaced by Khandi Alexander shortly after.

NewsRadio premiered in 1995, with Phil Hartman as Bill McNeal, a role that was created for him. On May 28, 1998, Hartman's wife, Brynn Hartman, murdered him and then committed suicide. The show dealt with Hartman's death by having his character die of a heart attack. To fill the void a new character was added, Max Lewis. Jon Lovitz, Hartman's *Saturday Night Live* costar and close friend, was cast.

Night Court (1984-1992)

Harry Anderson as Harry Stone (John Larroquette)

THE STARRING ROLE of the young Judge Harry Stone was based on a real Los Angeles judge. He slipped through the system to become a judge when an old governor trying to hurt the new governor filled every vacancy on the last day of his term.

John Larroquette initially auditioned for the part of Judge Harry Stone. As well as being a judge, Harry was an amateur magician. Comedian and magician Harry Anderson came in to audition for the part. He told series creator Reinhold Weege that he was the guy. Weege agreed. The network, however, wasn't so sure he was the right choice. They worried that he was too young. Weege went to bat for Anderson, who was eventually cast. John Larroquette got the part of Assistant D.A. Dan Fielding. Larroquette won four Emmys for his work on the show.

Weege spent time at a real New York City night court in order to do research for the show. *Time* magazine called *Night Court* the most accurate legal series on the air at the time.

When Richard Moll auditioned for the part of Bailiff Bull Shannon, his head was shaved because of another job. Weege wanted to hire him, but told Moll he wanted him bald. Moll told him he would shave his legs to get the part. He was hired, and had to shave his head for every episode.

The role of Bailiff Selma Hacker was written for Selma Diamond. Diamond's television career began in 1954, when she was a writer on *Caesar's Hour*. She continued as a writer throughout the 1950s. Diamond was reportedly the inspiration for the character of Sally Rogers on *The Dick Van Dyke Show*. Diamond had a successful acting career as well. She enjoyed a four-year run on the Ted Knight series *Too Close for Comfort*. Not long after, Diamond began work on *Night Court*. She only stayed with the show for a year. On May 13, 1985, the 64-year-old Diamond died of lung cancer.

Florence Halop was brought in to fill the void as Bailiff Florence Kleiner.

Like Diamond, Halop was also a heavy smoker. Ironically, she died of lung cancer on July 15, 1986. Marsha Warfield was brought on to play Bailiff Roz Russell in 1986 and stayed until the end of the show's run.

The character of Harry Stone was a big Mel Torme fan. The same was true of Weege and, coincidentally, Harry Anderson too. Torme heard that he was mentioned on Night Court. He agreed to appear on the show, and was made a recurring character.

The Night Rider (1979)
Anthony Herrera as Tru Sheridan (Michael Swan)

MICHAEL SWAN and Anthony Herrera were both up for the role of Tru Sheridan in *The Night Rider.* The part was given to Herrera.

Night Stalker (2005)
Cotter Smith as Tony Vincenzo (Michael Cerveris)

NIGHT STALKER was a remake of the 1970s series *Kolchak: The Night Stalker.*

Michael Cerveris was asked to fly to California for a screen test for the part of newspaper boss Tony Vincenzo. "The character didn't seem interesting enough to tie myself down for seven years and relocate to California, although I liked the series in general," said Cerveris. "The writer called and we had a great conversation. What he wanted to do was really intriguing. I said that maybe I would come out. But then they changed casting directors or something happened. I just never got called back again, and so I ended up not going out after all."

Nikki (2000-2002)

Nick van Esmarch as Dwight White (Tyler Labine)

NIKKI STARRED NIKKI COX as Nikki White, a Las Vegas showgirl married to a professional wrestler named Dwight White. An international search was conducted to find an actor to play Dwight. A tape came in from Canada of actor Tyler Labine. Everyone agreed that Labine was great, and very watchable. Labine was a strong candidate for the part.

Agent Brandy Gold had gone to college in Oregon with Nick van Esmarch. They did plays together as students. At the time she suggested him for the show, van Esmarch was working in a video store. Casting director Bonnie Zane loved him and knew he was the right actor for the part.

9 to 5 (1982-1983)

Valerie Curtin as Judy Bernly (Jane Fonda)
Jeffrey Tambor as Franklin Hart (Dabney Coleman)

9 TO 5 WAS SUCH A POPULAR FILM that ABC planned a version for television. The film starred Jane Fonda, Lily Tomlin and Dolly Parton. Fonda signed on as an executive producer for the show. She was begged to reprise the role of office worker Judy Bernly. She considered it for about a day, and then passed.

At the time when the show was having auditions a writer's strike was going on. The actors read dialogue from the film at their auditions. Valerie Curtin was brought in to read for the part of Judy. She gave an outstanding reading, and eventually won the role. Lily Tomlin's role of Violet went to Rita Moreno, while the Dolly Parton role of Doralee went to her sister Rachel Dennison.

Dabney Coleman played the sexist boss Franklin Hart in the film. He was offered the chance to do the series, but his representatives asked for too much money. The role was then given to Jeffrey Tambor.

Elizabeth Wilson played the part of Roz Kwith in the film. British actress Jean Marsh was the front runner to play the part in the series. ABC pointed out that she was foreign. Writer/producer Kim Weiskopf replied, "Yes, and that foreign language she's speaking is English." Marsh was eventually given the role.

Kim Weiskopf

1994 Baker Street: Sherlock Holmes Returns (1993)

Debrah Farentino as Amy Winslow
    (Kim Delaney)

KIM DELANEY AND DEBRAH FARENTINO vied for the part of Amy Winslow in the 1993 TV movie *1994 Baker Street: Sherlock Holmes Returns*. According to writer/director Kenneth Johnson, Delaney's audition was a little better. However, Farentino already had a deal with the network, which gave her the edge, and she was hired.

Northern Exposure (1990-1995)

Elaine Miles as Marilyn Whirlwind (Armenia Miles)

ACTING NOVICE ELAINE MILES beat out her mother, Armenia Miles, to win the part of Marilyn Whirlwind on *Northern Exposure*.

Not Like Everyone Else (2006)
Alia Shawkat as Brandi Blackbear (Jena Malone, Mae Whitman)
Illeana Douglas as Toni Blackbear (Linda Fiorentino)

JENA MALONE AND MAE WHITMAN were considered for the starring role of Native-American teenager Brandi Blackbear in the 2006 Lifetime movie *Not Like Everyone Else*. Director Tom McLoughlin tried to find a Native-American actress for the part, but was unable to find the right person. He then considered a larger pool of actresses, and finally gave the part to Alia Shawkat.

Linda Fiorentino was considered for the part of Brandi's mother, Toni Blackbear. The part was given to Illeana Douglas instead. McLoughlin was happy with Douglas. He felt that she was similar to the real-life person on whom the character was based.

NYPD Blue (1993-2005)
David Caruso as John Kelly (Jimmy
    Smits, Kevin Sorbo)
Carmine Caridi as Vince Gotelli
    (John Finn)
Sarah Buxton as Carlotta (Jenna
    Jameson)

NYPD BLUE was the subject of controversy before the show ever debuted. Many affiliates would not air the show because it pushed the limits of what was acceptable to show on television in terms of language and nudity. However, once

Carmine Caridi

the show premiered, it was both a critical and commercial hit, and the controversy abated.

Jimmy Smits was the first choice star as cop John Kelly, but decided against it.   Kevin Sorbo auditioned, but lost out to David Caruso. The previously unknown Caruso was suddenly hot from the success of the series. He made the decision to leave *NYPD Blue* after the first season, and focused on movies. Jimmy Smits was again made an offer to join the cast, this time for the new character of Bobby Simone. He accepted the role, and stayed with the show for about four years.

Bill Brochtrup
Photo: ABC Photo

Bill Brochtrup auditioned for the guest role of John Irvin. The character was only supposed to appear in two episodes. At the time Brochtrup was appearing periodically on *Days of Our Lives* as Hank. He did between 30-40 episodes of the soap, which he enjoyed. Said the actor, "When I got the call to audition for *NYPD Blue* I was scheduled to do *Days of Our Lives*. I had to turn it down. They were not very happy with me." Brochtrup added, "*Days of Our Lives* was money I needed. It was stressful." Brochtrup made a good decision. He won the role. The character stayed for the two scheduled episodes, and was eventually made a regular.

Carmine Caridi was in Las Vegas for a weekend trip when he ran into series creator Steven Bochco. Bochco told Caridi he would be calling him in to audition for a part on the show. When Caridi went for his audition Bochco and David Milch (Bochco's co-creator) weren't there. Caridi read a scene in which he had to cry. Afterwards, he went downstairs, and saw David Milch. Milch told him that they wanted him for the part. The actor later learned that it was between him and John Finn. The role went to Finn. Steven Bochco and David Milch intervened. They told the director that they wanted Caridi. Caridi played the role of Vince Gotelli for fifteen episodes. Finn later did four episodes of the show, as three different characters.

The October 14, 2003 episode was called "Porn Free," and featured a character named Carlotta who was a stripper. The choice was narrowed down to two: porn star Jenna Jameson and actress Sarah Buxton. Buxton said the audition was embarrassing; she had to wear a G-string. After two readings she won the part.

The O.C. (2003-2007)

Benjamin McKenzie as Ryan Atwood (Chad Michael Murray)
Mischa Barton as Marissa Cooper (Olivia Wilde)

THE PRODUCERS of *The O.C.* found it difficult to find an actor to play the part of street-smart teenager Ryan Atwood. Among the many actors considered was Chad Michael Murray, as well as an unknown actor named Benjamin McKenzie. McKenzie came for an audition. "McKenzie had no pedigree," said executive producer McG. "He just had an understanding of stillness, an understanding of quiet that was right for the role, and he was just very, very powerful. We always called him Baby Crowe because he reminded us of a young Russell Crowe. He just felt like the right guy when he walked in the room."

Peter Gallagher was the first and only choice to play Sandy Cohen. "He was the emotional core of that show," said McG. "We were delighted to land him."

Olivia Wilde was the final runner-up for the role of Marissa Cooper. Her competition was Mischa Barton. McG got resistance about giving the part to Barton. "No one wanted to cast Mischa," said McG. "We all did, Josh Schwartz, Stephanie Savage and I. We went out and shot a screen test with her and got it done. I took one look at her and said, 'This girl's going to be on the cover of every magazine in the world. She's going to be a star.'" Wilde was later cast in the recurring role of Alex Kelly.

The Odd Couple (1970-1975)

Jack Klugman as Oscar Madison (Mickey Rooney)
Tony Randall as Felix Unger (Martin Balsam, Dean Martin)

GARRY MARSHALL AND JERRY BELSON were set to create the television version of Neil Simon's hit Broadway play and movie *The Odd Couple* for Paramount Television. A pairing of Martin Balsam and Mickey Rooney was considered for the starring roles of Felix Unger and Oscar Madison, respectively. Paramount suggested Mickey Rooney as Oscar Madison with Dean Martin playing Felix Unger. Marshall and Belson balked at the idea, and even said they would quit if this were the final decision. Paramount relented and suggested Tony Randall for Felix. Marshall and Belson thought this was a good idea, but Randall was hesitant to sign for the show. Marshall and Belson went to see him perform *The Odd Couple* in Chicago. They brought with them an opera friend, who was introduced to Randall, an opera lover. The two talked at length. Some time after, Randall agreed to play Felix Unger.

To play Oscar, Marshall remembered Jack Klugman from the Broadway production of *Gypsy*. He thought that Klugman was right and brought his name up to Paramount, who reacted negatively. The studio told Marshall that they already had Klugman on tape and that they didn't like his moustache. Marshall couldn't understand what they were talking about, since Klugman had no moustache. Marshall watched the tape and discovered that it wasn't Klugman at all, but another actor named Jack Kruschen. ABC thought of Klugman as a dramatic actor only, and doubted whether he could be funny. Marshall and Belson refused to change their minds about Klugman. He was eventually made an offer, which he accepted.

Jack Klugman and Tony Randall both won Emmys for their work on the show.

The Odd Couple was enormously successful. Not long after ending its five-year run the show began airing in reruns. It can still be seen on TV to this day. In 1975 a cartoon version of the show was produced called *The Oddball Couple*. Paul Winchell and Frank Nelson provided the voices for the lead characters named Fleabag and Spiffy. ABC aired *The New Odd Couple* from 1982-1983. This updated version of the show starred Ron Glass as Felix Unger and Demond Wilson as Oscar Madison. In 1993 Randall and Klugman returned to the roles in the reunion movie *The Odd Couple: Together Again*. The film saw Felix temporarily move back in with Oscar during the planning of his daughter Edna's wedding. Also back from the old series was Garry Walberg as Felix and Oscar's poker buddy, Speed, and Penny Marshall, who played Oscar's secretary Myrna Turner.

The Office (2005-)

Steve Carell as Michael Scott (Dan Castallaneta, Dave Foley, Kevin Nealon, Bob Odenkirk, French Stewart)
John Krasinski as Jim Halpert (B.J. Novak)
Jenna Fischer as Pam Beesley (Angela Kinsey)

THE OFFICE ORIGINATED IN ENGLAND. The hit show was created by Stephen Merchant and Ricky Gervais (who also starred as boss David Brent). When NBC decided to make an American version Merchant and Gervais were very supportive.

Steve Carell, Kevin Nealon, Dan Castallaneta, Dave Foley, Bob Odenkirk and French Stewart all auditioned for the starring role of Michael Scott, the American version of Gervais' David Brent. The choice was narrowed down to either Carell or Odenkirk. Odenkirk's version of Michael was dark, while Carell was wacky. Odenkirk's interpretation was closer to Ricky Gervais'. It was eventually decided that, although both actors were great, Carell set the right tone for the American version.

John Krasinski auditioned for the co-starring role of Jim Halpert. Although Krasinski hit it out of the park, the producers spent three months searching anyway. Another Jim candidate was B.J. Novak. "Novak was wonderful," said casting director Marc Hirschfeld. "They didn't want to lose him; they wanted him to join the writing staff." Krasinski got the part of Jim, while the part of Ryan Howard was created for Novak. Novak joined the cast and also became a writer/producer on the show.

Angela Kinsey was cast as Angela, after first auditioning for the part of Pam, the receptionist. Pam was given to Jenna Fischer. When Fischer auditioned she was told by casting director Allison Jones to downplay her looks as much as possible. She also advised Fischer not to try to be funny; she told her to dare to bore her.

Stephen Merchant and Ricky Gervais came to an early rehearsal. They discussed the characters with the actors. Gervais liked Steve Carell's interpretation of the boss character. Gervais said that he had wanted to play it more like a buffoon.

The American version of *The Office* was a hit with viewers as well as critics. In 2006 it won the Emmy for the Best Comedy Series.

Oh, Grow Up (1999)

Stephen Dunham as Hunter Franklin (Greg Evigan)
Rena Sofer as Suzanne Vandermeer (Mia Cottet, Jessalyn Gilsig, Missi Pyle, Lisa Thornhill)
Niesha Trout as Chloe Sheffield (Vanessa Evigan)

OH, GROW UP told the story of three college friends (construction worker Hunter Franklin, artist Norris Michelsky and lawyer Ford Lowell) who are not only still in touch years after college, but are roommates. Real-life father and daughter Greg and Vanessa Evigan were considered for the parts of father and daughter Hunter and Chloe. The Evigans didn't work out, and Stephen Dunham and Niesha Trout played the roles. Jessalyn Gilsig, Rena Sofer, Missi Pyle, Mia Cottet and Lisa Thornhill were all possible choices to play Ford's ex-wife Suzanne Vandermeer. The part went to Sofer.

The O'Keefes (2003)
Judge Reinhold as Harry O'Keefe (Gary Cole)

JUDGE REINHOLD won the starring role of Harry O'Keefe in the short-lived WB series The O'Keefes, although Gary Cole was also considered.

One Day at a Time (1975-1984)
Joseph Campanella as Ed Cooper (Tom Aldredge)

JOAN DARLING DIRECTED the original pilot of One Day at a Time. "I called Norman Lear's casting person, and I said I wanted to read Pat Harrington for the part of Schneider," she said. "She called me back and said Pat's not available. About a week later Pat's agent called me and said, 'Joan, I don't know why you haven't called for Pat for this part, but we think he'd be wonderful in it.'" Darling explained what she had been told, and that Harrington was her first choice. Darling had the agent send Harrington over right away. He read for Darling and Norman Lear, and won the part. Schneider was initially supposed to be a moving man who helped the family move in to their new apartment. Harrington was so funny executive producer Norman Lear decided to make him the janitor and kept him as a regular.

This first pilot was called "Hello Ann." Tom Aldredge was cast as Ed Cooper, the ex-husband of Bonnie Franklin's character Ann. The concept didn't work out, and the character was eliminated from the pilot. When the role resurfaced Joseph Campanella played the part.

Darling's pilot never aired. In the original version Ann only had one daughter, played by Mackenzie Phillips. The new pilot episode was titled "Ann's Decision." Valerie Bertinelli was added to the cast as Ann's younger daughter Barbara. Hal Cooper was brought in to direct the revamped show. The series was a big hit, and ran for nine years.

One Life to Live (1968-)

Karen Witter as Tina
(Tonja Walker)
Erin Torpey as Jessica
Buchanan (Rachel
Miner)
Yorlin Madera as
Cristian Vega (Mark
Consuelos)

ANDREA EVANS was ex-tremely popular as Tina, a role she played on and off from 1978-1990. At one point Evans had an emergency health prob-lem and was taken to the hospital by ambulance. Casting director Mary Jo Slater called Kristen Vigard and asked her to come in immediately to play

Kristen Vigard
Photo: Leanna Conley

Tina for a couple of days, until Evans recovered. Vigard agreed. "Tina had just had a blowout with her boyfriend and was in a psychiatrist's office," said Vigard of her first day as Tina. "Andrea is stacked, I'm not. I'm wearing her dress and they're trying to pin it closed. On my second day I'm supposed to come in drunk yelling, 'Johnny, I love you' and knock over tables. It was so embarrassing. It was crazy and unnatural. But I pulled it off." Evans returned to work. Soon after, Vigard got a call to audition for a new character, Joy O'Neill. She won the role.

Andrea Evans left *One Life to Live* in 1990 and a replacement was needed. Tonja Walker and Karen Witter were both auditioned. Witter was given the role. Tonja Walker wasn't upset. Very soon after, she was cast as Alex Olanov, a role she played on and off for twelve years.

Tonja Walker

Eight-year-old Erin Torpey auditioned for the role of Jessica Buchanan. She was called back for a second audition. Her friend, Rachel Miner, was also there to read. Miner's father worked as a director on the show. Torpey's mother told her, "Erin, Ra-

Erin Torpey

chel Miner's dad works here. Now, wouldn't you want to work with your dad? Rachel's going to get this." To Torpey's surprise, she got the job instead of Miner.

Mark Consuelos tested for the part of Cristian Vega. The role went to Yorlin Madera instead. Shortly after, Consuelos landed the part of Mateo Santos on *All My Children*, where he played opposite Kelly Ripa. The two fell in love and were married about a year later.

Opposite Sex (2000)
Allison Mack as Kate Jacobs (Christine Lakin)

CHRISTINE LAKIN tested for the part of Kate Jacobs on *Opposite Sex*. The role was given to her friend Allison Mack instead. Lakin was cast in the guest role of Lisa in the pilot.

The Ordeal of Patty Hearst (1979)
Lisa Eilbacher as Patty Hearst (Karen Landry)

PATTY HEARST WAS AN HEIRESS who was kidnapped by the Symbionese Liberation Army in 1974. Hearst later joined her captors. She was famously photographed with a rifle during a bank robbery. Hearst was arrested in 1975. During her trial she claimed that she had been brainwashed by the SLA, and was forced into the robbery.

Karen Landry

Hearst was convicted, and sent to prison for seven years. After almost three years President Jimmy Carter commuted her sentence.

Actress Karen Landry was called in to audition to play Hearst for the 1979 television movie *The Ordeal of Patty Hearst*. She got very close to getting the part, but Lisa Eilbacher was cast instead. "I was hurt and angry," said Landry. "Then I got called to read for another part. I was still mad. I used it and got cast." Landry played SLA member Fahizah.

The Others (2000)
Julianne Nicholson as Marian Kitt
    (Missy Crider)

Missy Crider

DREAMWORKS TELEVISION produced *The Others*. DreamWorks partner Steven Spielberg brought Missy Crider in to audition for the lead role of Marian Kitt, although in the end Julianne Nicholson was cast instead. Crider was extremely flattered when she learned that the part of Ellen "Satori" Polaski had been changed to suit her. She loved playing the role.

Out of Practice (2005-2006)
Jennifer Tilly as Crystal (Cindy Ambuehl)

CINDY AMBUEHL was originally cast as Crystal on *Out of Practice*. The character was meant to be a recurring role. Ambuehl was let go and casting director Jeff Greenberg brought in Jennifer Tilly for the part. Tilly was so good the character became a regular.

Out There (**1995**)

Billy Bob Thornton as Jailbird (Wayne
    Knight)
Richard Speight, Jr. as Store Clerk
    (Quentin Tarantino)

Sam Irvin was set to direct the TV
movie *Out There*. Said Irvin, "I remember going over to the *Seinfeld* set
because I wanted Wayne Knight to
play a guy in a jail cell with Bill Campbell. He talks about lighting fires, all
kinds of weird stuff. He wasn't available. [*Out There* producer] Larry Estes saw Billy Bob Thornton. He knew
him from *One False Move*. Billy Bob was
starring on Hearts Afire. He took the part,
and then left very soon after to make his own film, *Sling Blade*."

Sam Irvin

Sam Irvin wanted to cast Quentin Tarantino in the small role of the
video store clerk. Before hitting it big as a writer and a director, Tarantino
actually did work in a video store. "He was into the idea," said Irvin, "but a
whole bunch of conflicts came up. He was going to be out of the country
promoting a movie." Richard Speight, Jr. played the clerk.

The Outsiders (**1990**)

Jay R. Ferguson as Ponyboy Curtis (Leonardo DiCaprio)

THE OUTSIDERS was written by S.E. Hinton, and published in 1967. In
1983 director Francis Ford Coppola's film, based on the book, was released. Seven years later a television version premiered. The TV series

was a follow up to the film, and was produced by Coppola. Leonardo Di-Caprio auditioned to play Ponyboy Curtis. Ponyboy was the novel's central character. DiCaprio, who was about 16 at the time, was deemed too young for the part. Jay R. Ferguson was cast instead. Ferguson is less than six months older than DiCaprio.

Paper Dolls (1984)
Nicollette Sheridan as Taryn Blake (Daryl Hannah)
Terry Farrell as Laurie Caswell (Alexandra Paul)

DARYL HANNAH and Alexandra Paul starred as teenage models Taryn Blake and Laurie Caswell in the 1982 TV movie *Paper Dolls*. In 1984 *Paper Dolls* became a series. Neither Hannah nor Paul were available for the show and turned it down. Nicollette Sheridan and Terry Farrell were their replacements.

Passions (1999-2007)
Dalton James as Hank Bennett (James Hyde)

WHEN JAMES HYDE auditioned for *Passions*, he was up for the part of Hank Bennett. Hyde was hired by the show, as Hank's older brother Sam instead, while Dalton James was cast as Hank.

Perfect Strangers (1986-1993)
Mark Linn-Baker as Larry Appleton (Louie Anderson)

PERFECT STRANGERS was created with Bronson Pinchot in mind, due to his standout performance in the film *Beverly Hills Cop*. Louie Anderson was cast opposite Pinchot as his cousin Larry Appleton. "Louie did the pilot," said producer William Bickley. "It's one of those things that happen quite a lot. The network looked at the pilot. They said, 'We loved the pilot, now recast.' They were just not thrilled with Louie. I think because Louie had that sort of biting, sharp sarcastic edge to his comedy, which is very funny. They wanted us to replace Louie. They wanted us to go on the air within a month or less. We had to cast very quickly. We brought in four actors to screen test and Mark Linn-Baker, who was very high on our list because he had done *My Favorite Year*. He was just brilliant. Mark came in. There was something in the beginning of the scene that I realized very quickly was impossible to do, where Larry Appleton comes into the room. He's very excited about something and he jumps onto what he thinks is the couch, and it turns out to be an armchair because Balki has rearranged the furniture. Well, immediately, I realized that's impossible to do unless the character's blind. The other four actors dealt with it as best they could; it wasn't believable. It didn't work. We didn't hold it against them. Mark Linn-Baker walked into the scene and made me believe that he didn't notice the difference between an armchair and a couch. I thought if an actor can do that, he can do anything. As soon as he walked in front of the cameras in the screen test, we never wanted anybody else."

Petticoat Junction (1963-1970)
Jeannine Riley as Billie Jo Bradley (Sharon Tate)

SHARON TATE landed the part of Billie Jo Bradley in *Petticoat Junction*. She was later dropped from the show and replaced with Jeannine Riley.

Picket Fences (1992-1996)

Kathy Baker as Jill Brock (Bess Armstrong, Wendy Crewson, Lindsay Crouse,
    Tess Harper, Isabella Hoffman, Lucinda Jenney)
Tom Skerritt as Jimmy Brock (James Brolin, Peter Fonda, David Morse)
Lauren Holly as Maxine Stewart (Sarah Buxton)

BESS ARMSTRONG, TESS HARPER, Lindsay Crouse, Isabella Hoffman, Wendy Crewson and Lucinda Jenney all auditioned for the part of Dr. Jill Brock on *Picket Fences*. Kathy Baker was another possibility. Initially, CBS thought she wasn't sexy enough for the part. However, they eventually realized that she was real, and right for the role, and finally gave their approval. However, Baker's agent, Tracey Jacobs, didn't want her to do the show. Casting directors Sharon Bialy and Richard Pagano took turns calling Jacobs every day until Baker signed on.

Peter Fonda, James Brolin and David Morse all read for the part of Sheriff Jimmy Brock for series creator David E. Kelley. Also under consideration was Tom Skerritt, whom CBS made the decision to hire.

Sarah Buxton came very close to getting the role of cop Maxine Stewart. She was eventually told she was too young and Lauren Holly was cast instead.

David E. Kelley loved Fyvush Finkel, and offered him the role of lawyer Douglas Wambaugh, which he accepted. Finkel won an Emmy for his performance in the series.

Ray Walston was initially hired for a guest spot as Judge Henry Bone. Walston appeared in the pilot and was then brought back for Season 2, when he became a regular cast member.

Pink Lightning (1991)

Sarah Buxton as Tookie (Martha Byrne)

MARTHA BYRNE and Sarah Buxton competed for the starring role of Tookie in the 1991 TV movie *Pink Lightning*. Buxton won the part. Byrne was also cast in the movie, as the sexy Jill.

Planet of the Apes (1974)

Ron Harper as Alan Virdon (Bruce Jenner)
James Naughton as Pete Burke (Marc Singer)

RON HARPER beat out Olympian Bruce Jenner for the role of astronaut Alan Virdon in the television version of the 1968 hit film *Planet of the Apes*.

    Marc Singer tested to play fellow astronaut Pete Burke. He didn't get the part, but was hired as a guest star for the series' second episode.

Police Woman (1974-1978)

Earl Holliman as Bill Crowley (Henry Darrow)

EARL HOLLIMAN beat out Henry Darrow to win the part of Lieutenant Bill Crowley in *Police Woman*.

Popular (1999-2001)

Leslie Bibb as Brooke McQueen (Carly Pope)
Carly Pope as Sam McPherson (Tamara Mello)
Sara Rue as Carmen Ferrara (Marissa Jaret Winokur)
Bryce Johnson as Josh Ford (Kip Pardue)
Tammy Lynn Michaels as Nicole Julian (Leslie Grossman)

POPULAR WAS DEVELOPED at a time when there were many teenage pilots being made. This one was one of the few shows that actually got on the air.

Leslie Bibb and Carly Pope both auditioned for the part of the very popular Brooke McQueen. Bibb won the part, and runner-up Pope was given the co-starring role of unpopular teen Sam McPherson.

Tamara Mello originally auditioned to play Sam, but was cast as Lily Esposito instead.

Sara Rue and Marissa Jaret Winokur made it down to the final round of auditions for the part of Carmen Ferrara. Although both actresses were great, Rue's reading was more dramatic, which got her the job. Winokur came to fame a few years later when she starred as Tracy Turnblad in the Broadway musical *Hairspray*. Winokur won the Tony for her performance in the show.

Kip Pardue was originally cast as football player Josh Ford. He was replaced in the role by Bryce Johnson.

Tammy Lynn Michaels and Leslie Grossman competed to play Nicole Julian. The role went to Michaels. Writer Ryan Murphy liked Grossman so much that he created the character of Mary Cherry for her.

The Powers of Matthew Starr (1982-1983)

Amy Steel as Pam Elliott (Heather Locklear, Tonja Walker)

AMY STEEL beat out both Heather Locklear and Tonja Walker for the costarring role of Pam Elliott on *The Powers of Matthew Starr*.

The Practice (1997-2004)

Dylan McDermott as Bobby Donnell (Oliver Platt)
Marla Sokoloff as Lucy Hatcher (Hilary Swank)

OLIVER PLATT turned down the starring role of lawyer Bobby Donnell on *The Practice*. Dylan McDermott was eventually cast. The two actors worked together on the 1999 film *Three to Tango*.

Hilary Swank auditioned to play secretary Lucy Hatcher. The future Oscar winner lost the part to Marla Sokoloff.

Pride and Prejudice (1995)
Julia Sawalha as Lydia Bennet (Lucy Davis)

LUCY DAVIS AUDITIONED for the part of Lydia Bennet in the 1995 mini-series *Pride and Prejudice*. Her audition was impressive enough that she was asked back for a screen test. At the time Davis didn't even know what a screen test was! The producers ultimately decided that since she had little acting experience, she was not ready to tackle a part as big as Lydia. They instead gave her the smaller role of Maria Lucas. Julia Sawalha was given the part of Lydia Bennet, without even having to test.

Prison Break (2005-)
Wentworth Miller as Michael Scofield (James Badge Dale, Matthew Davis)
Dominic Purcell as Lincoln Burrows (Eric Dane, Brian Van Holt)
Sarah Wayne Callies as Sara Tancredi (Sarah Clarke, Lola Glaudini)
Wade Williams Brad Bellick (Jude Ciccolella, Christian Stolte)
Peter Stormare as John Abruzzi (William Forsythe, Chris Penn)

MATTHEW DAVIS and James Badge Dale tried for the starring role of Michael Scofield in *Prison Break*. Executive producer Brett Ratner had been scheduled to direct the film *Superman Returns* at one point. He remembered Wentworth Miller, who had auditioned for the film. He brought Miller in to audition to play Scofield. Miller nailed his audition and got the part.

Eric Dane and Brian Van Holt were up for the part of Michael's brother, death row inmate Lincoln Burrows. The role went to Dominic Purcell, who already had a deal with Fox.

Sarah Clarke, Lola Glaudini and Sarah Wayne Callies all made it to the final round of auditions for the part of Dr. Sara Tancredi. Callies' audition went over big with the network. "She left the room and they loved her," said casting director Wendy O'Brien. "It was pretty much hers."

Jude Ciccolella and Christian Stolte were considered for the role of prison guard Brad Bellick. The part went to Wade Williams. Stolte was given another role; he played Corrections Officer Keith Stolte.

Chris Penn and William Forsythe auditioned on tape for the part of John Abruzzi. The role was later given to Peter Stormare.

Providence (1999-2002)

Mike Farrell as James Hansen (Lawrence Pressman)
Concetta Tomei as Lynda Hansen (Holland Taylor)

MELINA KANAKAREDES headed the cast of *Providence* as plastic surgeon Sydney Hansen. Sydney moves back to her hometown of Providence, RI from Beverly Hills after the sudden death of her mother Lynda.

The final two actors up for part of Sydney's father, Dr. James Hansen, were Mike Farrell and Lawrence Pressman. The part was eventually given to Farrell.

Holland Taylor was sought to play Lynda Hansen. Negotiations fell through. Concetta Tomei was hired after shooting had already started.

Punky Brewster (1984-1988)

Soleil Moon Frye as Punky Brewster (Ami Foster)
George Gaynes as Henry Warnimont (Fred Gwynne)

NBC EXECUTIVE BRANDON TARTIKOFF went to school with a girl named Punky Brewster. He liked the name. He told writer David W. Duclon to see if he could find anything to go with it. Duclon liked the name as well and created the series *Punky Brewster*.

Open auditions were held to find a newcomer for the title role of Punky in Chicago, New York, Miami, Los Angeles and San Francisco. Soleil Moon Frye was not a newcomer. Someone who had seen her in a play suggested her. The producers decided to give her a chance anyway. The six-year-old gave a fantastic audition and got the job.

Fred Gwynne was interested in starring as Punky's guardian Henry Warnimont. Frye was to read with Gwynne at his audition. She saw Gwynne and asked him if he was Herman Munster, a role he played from 1964-1966 on *The Munsters*. Gwynne was upset by the remark since he had gone to some effort to change his image. Tartikoff said that Gwynne's reading was not his best. The role went to George Gaynes instead. Gaynes was proud that he had been chosen to play the protector of a young child.

Ami Foster originally auditioned for the title role of Punky Brewster. She wasn't right for that part. In the fifth episode of the series the character of Punky's friend Margeaux Kramer appeared. Foster was right for that part, and was cast in the guest-starring role. Foster was initially hired just for the one episode, but soon became a recurring character.

On the show Punky had a dog named Brandon. The dog was named after Brandon Tartikoff.

Pursuit of Happiness (1987-1988)
Paul Provenza as David Hanley (Chris Noth, Bradley Whitford)

CHRIS NOTH AND BRADLEY WHITFORD were considered for the role of Assistant Professor David Hanley in *Pursuit of Happiness*. The role was given to Paul Provenza instead.

Push (1998)
Eddie Mills as Scott Trysfan (David Lipper)

DAVID LIPPER was brought in to audition for *Push*. Director Ken Olin liked him, but thought Lipper was reading for the wrong role. He asked him to take a look at the part of Scott Trysfan instead. Lipper had 5-10 minutes to prepare. The role went to Eddie Mills instead. *Push* was cancelled after only three episodes aired.

Queer as Folk (2000-2005)
Scott Lowell as Ted Schmidt (Peter Paige)
Peter Paige as Emmett Honeycutt (Billy Porter, Wayne Wilderson)

QUEER AS FOLK aired on the cable network Showtime. The series followed the lives of a group of gay friends living in Pittsburgh, PA. Peter Paige was asked to audition for the part of the straight-laced Ted Schmidt. "Quite honestly, I gave a kickass audition," said Paige. "The casting director said, 'That was beautiful. I'm going to give you a callback.' So I said, 'You know what? Let me read for Emmett.' She said, 'Did you not hear me? I said I was giving you a callback.' I said, 'I know, but let me read for Emmett for you.' She said, 'Fine.' So I read for Emmett and I finished and she said, 'I don't think I've ever said this before, but which part would you like to come back for?' I was very flattered and I said. 'You know what? You brought me in for Ted, so why don't I come back for Ted.' When I went for my producer session, I walked in and started reading for Ted and within about three seconds the executive producers were whispering to each other. And finally they said, 'That was lovely. We don't really think you're a Ted. We think maybe you're an Emmett. So would you come back in and read Emmett for us?' I just looked at the casting director and smiled and said, 'I think that sounds like a great idea.'" Paige was the first person to read for Emmett. At the final audition for the part of Emmett, Paige tested against Billy Porter and Wayne Wilderson. Paige won the role.

Scott Lowell was the first actor to read for Ted. "I loved the script," said Lowell, "and I was scared to death of it." He liked and understood the character. He thought Ted was a universal character; one that could reach out to the straight world. "When I went in to audition, I felt like I was not physically right. I was freed by thinking I wouldn't get it." Lowell was called back to read for executive producers Daniel Lipman, Ron Cowen and Tony Jonas. After his callback Lowell left town to

Peter Paige.
Photo: Kevyn Major Howard

Scott Lowell.
Photo: Kevyn Major Howard

visit his mother in Connecticut. While he was there, he found out that he had to come back early to test for the network. He was the only actor testing for Ted. He found out later that day that he got the job.

The Friday before the network test on Monday morning, there was no one to bring in for the pivotal role of Brian Kinney. That afternoon at 4:00 p.m. Cowen and Lipman received a call from casting director Linda Lowy saying, 'He's here. Come to my office.' They raced to the office and Lowy introduced them to Gale Harold. "We said to him, 'Can you be at the test at 8:00 on Monday morning?' said Lipman. "He lit up a cigarette in a very Brianesque way and he said, 'Nah. I don't think so.' I said, 'What do you mean?' He said, 'I'm with this theatre company and we're striking a show on Sunday night and I'll be doing that all night, and I can't come.' I said to Gale, 'You've got to come.' He was the only person we gave the tape and the script of the British version 'cause we wanted him to know that his role demanded a lot more than the other roles. Saturday morning Ron and I were sitting here writing. At noon the phone rings. I said, 'Hello?' And he said, 'Hello, this is Brian Kinney calling.' And that's how Gale got in ... The entire rhythm of the show; the whole tone of the show was based on the sexuality of that character. So we had to have somebody who was very sexy, could translate that. And we're very lucky to have found Gale. Even after all this time I cannot think of anyone who could have done it. He somehow clicked into that role and was able to project that. I was very grateful to him."

Debbie Novotny was the last role to be cast. Someone had given Sharon Gless a copy of the script. She decided she had to do the series, and paid for her own flight from Chicago for a meeting. "We never saw another person," said Cowen. "She walked in the room and she was wonderful, and she was Debbie, and that was it. She never read and we never saw another actress for the role. We didn't need to. She was it."

"Sharon Gless came in to see us for *Queer as Folk* because she wanted to talk to us," said Lipman. "But she didn't have to do that. We could have just made an offer to her. She is charming, she's warm. Audiences love her. She would walk down a street - she looks a little different in life, she doesn't have the red wig, she has her blonde hair. She has so many stories about gay men who would come up to her and start to weep, just weep and say, 'My parents rejected me. I watch the show and I wish that I had a mother like you. Someone who gave me unconditional love.' I think it had a great impact on her as well as the audience. She was just super."

Rachel Gunn, R.N. (1992)
Christine Ebersole as Rachel Gunn (K.T. Oslin)

RACHEL GUNN, R.N. told the story of a ballsy nurse in a hospital in Oklahoma. CBS thought the right actress to play the title role was K.T. Oslin, who was from Arkansas. Christine Ebersole was eventually cast instead. "She was so good," said writer/producer Kim Weiskopf. "The best comedy actress. She's the greatest. She gets things you don't even see." The show ran for two half seasons.

Raid on Entebbe (1977)
Peter Finch as Yitzhak Rabin (Richard Burton)

RICHARD BURTON was considered for the starring role of Yitzhak Rabin in the 1977 NBC movie Raid on Entebbe. The film was shot on location. Burton turned it down saying, "I'm not getting malaria for this."

Rear Window (1998)

Daryl Hannah as Claudia Henderson (Sherry Stringfield)

CHRISTOPHER REEVE rose to fame when he won the starring role in the 1978 film *Superman*. In May of 1995 Reeve suffered an accident while horseback riding, which left him paralyzed.

Reeve decided to star in a television adaptation of the classic movie *Rear Window*. He played the lead role of wheelchair-bound Jason Kemp. Jeff Bleckner was offered the chance to direct. "At first I thought it was insane to remake a movie that Alfred Hitchcock had directed," said Bleckner. "Then I started thinking about it and I thought, 'This is a perfect vehicle for Chris, and the perfect story for him.' When I met with him and Steven Haft, who was the executive producer, I realized what was going to be involved in working with him; how difficult it was going to be to make the movie. I just had to do it for him. It became an incredibly inspirational experience for almost everybody who worked on it. Just his ability to come to work every day, and what he had to go through in order to come to work every day was extraordinary. He was incredibly inspirational to all of us.

"He had a certain limited amount of time he could work in any given day, and a certain amount of exercise he had to do, and then he had a certain regimen that he had to go through every day. At that time he could speak in certain rhythmic patterns depending upon his breathing pattern at the time, and how much he was on the respirator and then off the respirator. There were so many things that I didn't know about. You got sort of into the education curve of what his life was like, which is why he was so inspiring. When we were trying to figure out how to schedule the film his doctor said he could only work a certain amount of hours per day. We had to try to figure out how to schedule the film so we could work with him a certain number of hours, and then have a body double so that we could shoot behind him, and send him home. A great amount of the film took place in the daytime and then a lot of the film would take place at night.

When we worked on the film, we found these two warehouses that were opposite each other in Yonkers. Most of the actors lived in New York. Chris lived up in Westchester. It was in between. He would come down from Westchester, and everybody else would come up from Manhattan every day. We built an apartment into one warehouse. Then we built the set of apartments that are across the way across an alley in the other warehouse on the other side. You could see one from the other. We really had to deal with day and night because it was a real alley.

   "When we were originally scheduling the film, we had asked Chris if we could work all day for two of the weeks, and then work all night for two of the weeks, and schedule it that way. Chris said that that would be fine. Two days before we were about to start to shoot, we got a call from Chris' doctor who said that we couldn't possibly do that, even though Chris said he could. He just could not work all night. It would be impossible for him to turn his schedule around. His biorhythms were set. If we flipped that around it could be disastrous for him. It was something Chris never thought of. When his doctor heard about it, he was apoplectic. It forced us to work Chris more hours than we wanted to each day. It was an amazing experience working with him. How extraordinary he was just to work with; what he had to do just to show up every day and get through every day. He was an incredible human being. Almost everybody who was on that show was there for him."

   Sherry Stringfield was originally cast opposite Reeve as Claudia Henderson. Stringfield was unable to continue with the project and left. Daryl Hannah was hired to replace her at almost the very last minute.

Red Water (2003)

Kristy Swanson as Kelli Raymond (Teri Hatcher)

LOU DIAMOND PHILLIPS was cast as John Sanders in the made-for-TV movie Red Water. The biggest problem the producers faced in casting was finding an actress to play opposite him. A major contender was

Teri Hatcher. "We really wanted her," said executive producer Michael G. Larkin, "but the part was so physically demanding that we were worried about Teri's safety." Kristy Swanson ultimately won the part.

Relativity (1996-1997)
Kimberly Williams as Isabel Lukens (Cari Shayne)

KIMBERLY WILLIAMS' competition for the lead role of Isabel Lukens in *Relativity* included Cari Shayne. Although Shayne had several meetings with producer Edward Zwick, the role was given to Williams.

Rescue from Gilligan's Island (1978)
Judith Baldwin as Ginger Grant (Tina Louise)

GILLIGAN'S ISLAND creator Sherwood Schwartz invited all the cast members from the series to reprise their roles for this reunion movie. Tina Louise had a hard time making up her mind about whether or not to return to the role of actress Ginger Grant. "She was on it and off it about four times in the place of a month," said Schwartz. "It finally came so close to shooting that I said, 'I can't deal with this anymore.' She wanted as much money as all the other castaways put together. Certainly more than Bob Denver, and he was the star of the show... Her demands were so outrageous that I tried every way that I could, promising her this and that. Then she said she'd do it and then, two weeks later I get a call from her agent; she's decided not to do it. And it was like a game for a couple of weeks. And then I said, 'Shooting is coming up and I just can't get through to her.' I mean, she can't erase the past. She didn't want to be identified as that bombshell on *Gilligan's Island*. She wanted to do other more dramatic work and she said it was a stumbling block. Well, it made her a star. That happens." The role of Ginger was recast with Judith Baldwin.

Rescue Me (2004–)
Jack McGee as Jerry Reilly (Lenny Clarke)

DENIS LEARY AND PETER TOLAN discussed doing a show about fire-fighters after the terrorist attacks of September 11, 2001. At the time the pair was already producing the show *The Job*. When *The Job* was canceled, they went forward with show, which would be called *Rescue Me*.

Leary's cousin Jeremiah Lucey was a firefighter in Worcester, MA. On December 3, 1999 there was a fire in a vacant building. Over 75 firefighters went into the burning building. Sadly, six men were killed: Paul A. Broth-erton, Timothy P. Jackson, James F. "Jay" Lyons III, Joseph T. McGuirk, Thomas E. Spencer and Lucey. In response, Denis Leary founded the Leary Firefighter's Foundation, which provides fire departments with funding and resources for up-to-date equipment and training.

Leary starred in *Rescue Me* as firefighter Tommy Gavin. The part of Chief Jerry Reilly was written for Lenny Clarke. Clarke was unavailable and had to turn the part down. Actor Jack McGee is a former NYC fire-fighter. He heard about the show, and tried to contact Peter Tolan, who was an old friend of his family's. McGee reached executive producer Jim Serpico. He told Serpico that he would be making a big mistake if he didn't see him for the part of Reilly. McGee continued saying that he was on his way to the airport to go to a wedding in Hawaii. He told Serpico that he would go to see him instead, with no obligations. Serpico gave Peter Tolan the message. At first Tolan didn't remember who McGee was. Then he realized that McGee was a friend of his ex-wife's family. McGee was asked to send a tape. Three days later Tolan called McGee, who was in Hawaii by then. McGee was awarded the role. Lenny Clarke later joined the cast as Tommy Gavin's Uncle Teddy.

Rhoda (1974-1978)
David Groh as Joe Gerard (William Devane)

VALERIE HARPER played the supporting role of Rhoda Morgenstern on *The Mary Tyler Moore Show*. The character was so popular the spin-off Rhoda was created.

Nancy Walker and Harold Gould played Rhoda's parents Ida and Martin Morgenstern on *The Mary Tyler Moore Show*. Both actors were on board for *Rhoda*. The September 29, 1973 episode of *The Mary Tyler Moore Show* was called "Rhoda's Sister Gets Married." In the episode Rhoda's sister was named Debbie, and was played by Liberty Williams. For this new series the character was completely changed. "She was good, but we didn't think she was strong enough," said series co-creator Allan Burns. "She was too pretty. We really needed somebody schlumpier, which wouldn't have worked for Liberty." The character's name was changed to Brenda, who was not married. *Rhoda* writer/producer David Davis saw Julie Kavner in a play in a small theater in West Los Angeles called *Where Has Tommy Flowers Gone*. He sent Burns co-creator James L. Brooks to see it. Said Burns, "She was just hysterical. We knew we had her. She had such a voice and such an approach to the character. I am attracted to voices. Distinctive voices really help in a series. Dave not only found her, he lived with her for 15 years, and married her."

William Devane was sought for the part of Rhoda's husband Joe Gerard. Fred Silverman, the head of CBS, thought Devane was a bad choice. Devane knew how Silverman felt, and refused to test. He knew he wouldn't be cast anyway. After a long search the part was given to David Groh.

Producer (and series developer) Lorenzo Music wanted to be the voice of Carlton the doorman. He was turned down. A lot of actors read. Because they were not seen, they tended to push it over the top. The other producers finally decided that Music's voice was so unique that he was the best choice for the part.

Richie Brockelman, Private Eye (1978)
Dennis Dugan as Richie Brockelman (Bruce Kimmel)

BRUCE KIMMEL auditioned for the title role of Richie Brockelman. He was called back a number of times, but the part went to Dennis Dugan instead.

Rituals (1984-1985)
Marc Poppel as Brady Chapin (Jon Lindstrom)

JON LINDSTROM read for the pilot of *Rituals*. He was considered for the part of the rich, spoiled Brady Chapin. "I didn't get past the casting director," said Lindstrom. "I really did not do well. So I went back to waiting tables." The part went to Marc Poppel. "About three months later I got a call to come back and read for the same part," Lindstrom continued. They were considering replacing Poppel. "I read for it and I said, 'That's great that you remembered to bring me back considering how bad I was last time. But I'm leaving for Europe tomorrow. I'm going to backpack through Europe.' I was still in my 20s then. Then the casting director of course got really mad at me. I said, 'I told that to my agent and he was supposed to

Jon Lindstrom
Photo: Myra Vides

tell you that. I'm sorry. If you need me in three months, I'd be happy to come back for you again.' I left and went to Europe. About a month or two after I came back from Europe I got another call. They had switched casting directors. Now they actually were looking to replace that role, and the third time turned out to be a charm for me. I went in. It turns out the casting director was someone I knew. She took me straight to the producers and the network executives, and I did my song and dance for them. They said, 'Okay, what's the problem? Hire him.' I had the job by the time I got home. But I had to bartend that night and tell them I was quitting, 'cause I was starting the next day."

The Road Raiders (1989)
Susan Diol as Lt. Johanson (Amy Yasbeck)

SUSAN DIOL was flown from New York to L.A. to test for *The Road Raiders*. Amy Yasbeck also auditioned, but the role went to Diol.

Rodney (2004-2005)
Nick Searcy as Barry (Bill Smitrovich)

STAND-UP COMEDIAN RODNEY CARRINGTON starred as Rodney Hamilton in the ABC comedy *Rodney*. Bill Smitrovich was considered for the part of Rodney's best friend, Barry. The role eventually went to Nick Searcy instead.

Room 222 (1969-1974)
Lloyd Haynes as Pete Dixon (Billy Dee Williams)

THE CHARACTER OF ALICE JOHNSON was a young student teacher. "It was very, very hard," said executive producer Gene Reynolds. "I just didn't find a girl who got the humor. It's very hard to get a twenty-one-year-old comedienne who isn't just a goofy comic ... I went through a lot of girls. Finally I called a friend of mine, Bill Brademan, who was a casting director and a producer by the time I called him. I said, 'I'm looking for an ingénue. I'm looking for a girl who's got some comedy.' He said, 'There's a really cute girl. I saw her on Miss Teenage America. She mimed records. Karen Valentine.' Well, Karen came in. She read one page and I stopped her. I said, 'Okay. You've got it.' She had the humor. She just had the naiveté; very sweet and eager and funny as hell. It was just natural. It flowed from her. Beautiful. So I said, 'When you drive home do not get hit by a truck.'"

Reynolds went to New York where he found a wonderful actor for the show who was very experienced and attractive. He flew the actor, named Billy Dee Williams, to California for a screen test. Reynolds showed the screen test to the network. One of the ABC executives said that he wasn't funny. Reynolds explained that it wasn't that kind of a show. While the actor needed to play light comedy, it wasn't necessary for him to be a comic. Reynolds added that the people around him should be funny. The executive, who hadn't read the whole script, walked out of the meeting. "He was a big enough shot that the other guys said, 'Yeah, he's right,'" said Reynolds. "So then I went around and I looked at some more people and I came up with Lloyd Haynes."

Rosetti and Ryan (1977)

Tony Roberts as Joseph Rosetti (Al Pacino)

AL PACINO was considered for the part of lawyer Joseph Rosetti on the NBC drama *Rosetti and Ryan*. Pacino didn't want to do the part, and Tony Roberts was eventually cast.

Roswell (1999-2002)

Shiri Appleby as Liz Parker (Majandra Delfino)
Katherine Heigl as Isabel Evans (Shiri Appleby, Majandra Delfino)
Majandra Delfino as Maria DeLuca (Shiri Appleby)

THE SCIENCE-FICTION SERIES *Roswell* was based on the series of *Roswell High* books. 20th Century-Fox went to writer Jason Katims with the book. Katims loved it, and thought it had the possibility of succeeding as a series.

About 200 actors were seen for the starring role of Max Evans. Katims and the pilot's director David Nutter heard a lot about actor Jason Behr. When Behr was available to come in to read, he was so sick that he was unable to drive himself to the audition. Although Behr had trouble speaking, his reading was wonderful. He was brought back to test, and wound up with the part.

A young Calista Flockhart was the type sought to play Max's love interest Liz Parker. Shiri Appleby came in to audition. She read for all three of the female leads, as did Majandra Delfino. Appleby got the part of Liz, while Delfino was cast as Maria DeLuca. Katherine Heigl was hired to play Isabel.

Colin Hanks had less than ten auditions in his career when he came to audition for *Roswell*. Although he was an inexperienced actor, he gave an outstanding audition and won the role of Alex Whitman.

Ryan's Hope (1975-1989)

John Gabriel as Seneca Beaulac (Ron Harper)
Yasmine Bleeth as Ryan Fenelli (Noelle Beck)

RON HARPER was offered the role of Dr. Seneca Beaulac on *Ryan's Hope*. The night before, John Gabriel and his wife Sandy were at Harper's house for dinner. Harper wasn't interested in the job, and suggested Gabriel.

John Gabriel played Seneca from 1975-1989.

Kelli Maroney

Noelle Beck auditioned for the part of Ryan. At the same time Beck was also up for the part of Trisha Alden on *Loving*. Beck lost the part on *Ryan's Hope* to Yasmine Bleeth, but won the part on *Loving* (which Bleeth had also read for).

In 1979 the character of Kimberly Harris was added. Finding an actress to play the role proved difficult. Searches in New York and Los Angeles had been unsuccessful. Around the same time a teenage Kelli Maroney had just moved from Minnesota to New York. "I was going to conservatory school, and I wanted very much to take the fall program," said Maroney. "To do that I had to move to New York City, and I was just a kid. My mother said I could go. I went there to register and try to find a place to live all by myself, $500 to my name, trying to get an apartment." In looking for a roommate Maroney ran into someone who told her, 'You know my friend is an agent and they've been looking for a long time for this sex kitten on a soap opera. Do you have a picture of yourself?" "I did, from Minnesota," said Maroney. "I was helping the photographer do his book. I looked much older in the picture because I was all made up and everything. They must have been shocked when they saw me coming through the door. So I went in and then they put me on tape. I was scared to death. I'm this little hick from Minnesota, but yet I still felt that this is how it's supposed to happen. I mean I knew what I saw in the movies. I was so scared. I was so out of my element. I saw this guy - John Gabriel - and I could see that he was tired. He probably was because he was auditioning all these girls all day long. And so I gave him a pat on the face on camera. And they saw that. And they went, 'There's more to this kid than just your average teenager.' That's what they told me. It was because I patted him on the face like, 'That's okay.' I was scared to pieces and it read all over the place, but I took time to pat him on the face. And I got the part. I called my mother. I was there maybe two weeks. I said, 'Mom, I'm on TV.' I didn't have an agent, didn't have any credentials, didn't have a place to live, didn't have anything! To this day I know that anything can happen. Apparently they had been looking all over the place for a Midwestern girl. I guess the whole point was they didn't want a professional with a whole lot of pizzazz. They wanted someone who didn't know what the hell they were doing. And I fit the bill!

"It was so Dorothy in *The Wizard of Oz* that I focused on one thing – Don't screw this up! The first thing they did was cut all of my hair off because they didn't want to tip their hat. They wanted me to be a kid and then as my hair grew out I was going to become more and more evil. So here I was with like an inch of hair on my head and they're shooting, and [costar] Louise Shaffer was so nice to me. She said, 'See that red light?' She went and looked out at me on the monitor. She said, 'The camera loves you. You look beautiful. Your only friend in the world some days is going to be that red light going on. That's the only thing you have to worry about. Don't be afraid of it. Let that be your friend.' She was fantastic. I'm still friends with her to this day.

"They were stunned that I couldn't do things like cry on cue. I had to learn how to do that. If I couldn't do it, they would just get somebody else. I was expected to have all the chops that anybody else would have going in there. I had to learn fast."

Maroney was enormously popular on the show, although most of the show's fans didn't like her character! "It was hard for me as a kid. Here I was, all of a sudden famous. Part of an actor is you want everyone to like you. Everyone hated me! That was where Louise came in. She kept talking me off the ceiling going, 'You can't worry about that. You're going to have to develop a thick skin. If they hate your character it means you're doing a good job.'"

In 1981 Maroney left *Ryan's Hope*. She went out to California and landed her first feature film, *Fast Times at Ridgemont High*. Shortly after, she heard that *Ryan's Hope* was bringing her character back. Said Maroney, "I couldn't stand the thought of somebody else playing my part. So I said I would come back. I called my agent and I said, 'They're going to bring my character back. Call them up and see what's going on. Tell them I'll come back.' When he called, they said, 'Yes, we are bringing the character back, but that's not the direction we're going to go at this time.' So I called up the producer and I said, 'I'll come back.' She said, 'You will?' They doubled my money. I was supposed to be out in Hollywood, because now was the time, and they said they would move heaven and earth to make sure I got to do other things. Well that was a total lie. They did not lift a finger to see that I got to do anything. They called me back to do some more things on *Fast Times at Ridgemont High*, and the show said, 'Sorry.'

"They wrote me out again in what we like to call the *St. Valentine's Day Massacre*. They brought the Kirkland family in and wrote us all out in like two weeks. This memo came out asking everyone to forego their vacations because they had an important storyline to get out. I went to the producer Ellen Barrett and I said, 'They're writing me out again.' She said, 'No, they're not. They wouldn't do that. You're just being ridiculous, but because I know you're upset by this I will call them and I will find out.' I said, 'I'm not giving up my vacation so that they can write me out again.' She calls up and hangs up the phone and said, 'Have fun on your vacation. I can't believe it.'

"I had a blast doing *Ryan's Hope*. I learned how to think on my feet. It put me so far ahead of the game as far as any other actor breaking in to film because that's how I was taught. You get ready to do it and you do it.

You have to do something really big for them to stop tape, like swear or something. Otherwise, they just keep going. You'd better be on your toes. So that really served me, because no one could believe I could get something in a take."

In 1981 Christopher Reeve made a guest appearance on the show. "He started on daytime," said Maroney. "He was always so wonderful. We had this storyline, Delia's Crystal Palace. It was supposed to be Tavern on the Green. The thing was all the celebrities in New York were there. He came on and played himself. He couldn't be a lovelier guy. He said, 'Well, these are my old stomping grounds.' I was like, 'It's SUPERMAN!' He just came in and was just a soap opera actor that day. That knocked my socks off.

"I just really learned everything there. You can go to school until your eyeballs fall out and not learn as much as you're going to learn in one day on a soap opera set."

Sable (1987-1988)

Lewis Van Bergen as Jon Sable/Nicholas Fleming (Gene Simmons)
Holly Fulger as Mike Blackman (Yvonne Suhor)

SABLE FOLLOWED CHILDREN'S BOOK AUTHOR Nicholas Fleming who, at night, transformed into superhero Jon Sable. Rock star Gene Simmons (from the band KISS) was under consideration to play the title role. Co-executive producer Gary Sherman was crazy about him; however his fellow executive producer Richard P. Rosetti didn't think Simmons had the right look. Simmons refused to test, but was eventually signed for the role anyway. He didn't last long. Simmons told the press that he wanted to concentrate on his music and was leaving the show. Rosetti felt that this was a good move, since he thought that Simmons was having trouble with his lines. Lewis Van Bergen was brought in to replace him.

Former model (and acting newcomer) Rene Russo played the supporting role of Fleming's agent, Eden Kendell. Holly Fulger and Yvonne Suhor competed to play illustrator Mike Blackman. "We were extremely different," said Fulger. "I was tall and blonde and she was dark and short." Fulger was cast. Suhor was brought on as a guest star in the fifth episode.

Although the series only ran for two months, it was a positive experience for Fulger. "Rene Russo was my idol," said Fulger. "She was so beautiful. I loved that show. Boy, was it fun!"

Santa Barbara (1984-1993)
Page Mosely as Dylan Hartley (Jon Lindstrom)

JON LINDSTROM INITIALLY READ for the role of Dylan Hartley on *Santa Barbara*. "What I was told was that they liked my audition enough; they actually invented a role that I ended up working a year on," said Lindstrom. "That worked out very well for me." The role Lindstrom played was Mark McCormick.

Saturday Night Live (1975-)
Eddie Murphy as Cast Member (Robert Townsend)
Pamela Stephenson as Cast Member (Geena Davis, Andrea Martin)
Julia Sweeney as Cast Member (Lisa Kudrow)

LORNE MICHAELS CREATED *Saturday Night Live* in 1975. The late-night sketch comedy show featured a cast of unknowns, including John Belushi, Dan Aykroyd, Chevy Chase, Gilda Radner, Jane Curtin, Garrett Morris and Laraine Newman. The show was an enormous hit with audiences, and is still on the air to date. Every week a different celebrity came on as a guest host. There were different musical guests weekly as well. In 1980 *SNL* creator Lorne Michaels left the show. By that time all of the original cast members had left as well. Jean Doumanian was hired as executive producer. Doumanian hired Robert Townsend for the show. Soon after, a teenage Eddie Murphy called talent coordinator Neil Levy to ask for an audition. Levy told Murphy that they were no longer hiring, but that didn't stop Murphy from calling. After about a week of calls Levy brought Murphy in for an audition, thinking he could use him as an extra. He was overwhelmed by Murphy's audition. He took him to audition for Doumanian. She thought that Murphy was good, but she preferred Townsend. Levy was so irate that he threatened to quit. He was sure that, although both Townsend and Murphy were talented, Murphy was the better fit for the show. Levy pressured Doumaninan until she relented. Since Townsend hadn't yet signed a contract, he was out and Murphy was in. However, Doumanian only hired Murphy as a featured player and not a regular cast member. Eddie Murphy was one of the show's most popular performers. He was eventually made a regular cast member.

Geena Davis, Andrea Martin and Pamela Stephenson competed to be a cast member for the 1984-1985 season. Davis was eliminated, and the choice was between Martin and Stephenson. Cast member Martin Short was friends with Andrea Martin, and wanted her to get the job. However, Stephenson's audition tapes were impressive enough to get her hired.

Lisa Kudrow and Julia Sweeney vied for a spot on the show in 1990. Sweeney got the job. A few years later Kudrow was cast as Phoebe Buffay on the show *Friends*, which was a huge success, and made her a star.

Saved By the Bell (1989-1993)

Tiffani Thiessen as Kelly Kapowski (Elizabeth Berkley, Jennie Garth)

TIFFANI THIESSEN, Elizabeth Berkley and Jennie Garth were all up for the part of cheerleader Kelly Kapowski on the Saturday morning show *Saved By the Bell*. Thiessen eventually won the part. The producers were so impressed with Berkley that they created the role of Jessie Spano just for her.

Scooby-Doo, Where Are You! (1969-1972)

Casey Kasem as Norville "Shaggy"
Rogers (Frank Welker)

TELEVISION EXECUTIVE Fred Silverman wanted a cartoon series which
would be a comedy mystery. The detectives in the show were a group of kids
similar to the Archies. Creators Joe
Ruby and Ken Spears had the idea to
put a dog in the show. It was originally
going to be a Great Dane, but Ruby
worried about it being too much like
Marmaduke. They decided to make it
a shaggy dog named Too Much. Silverman didn't like Too Much, and Ruby
and Spears decided to change him back
to a Great Dane. The dog's personality
was modeled after Bob Hope's early
film persona of a cowardly guy who
went forward in the face of fear. Silverman was on a plane listening to Frank
Sinatra music. When he heard the lyric
"Scooby Dooby Doo" he got the idea
to call the dog Scooby-Doo. The focus
of the show changed from the kids to
the dog. Ruby and Spears wrote a pilot,
as well as the series. Silverman loved it,
and sent them a telegram congratulat-
ing them.

Joe Ruby

Ken Spears

Frank Welker auditioned to play Shaggy, but the part went to Casey Kasem. Welker was instead cast as Fred.

Scrubs (2001-)

Zach Braff as J.D. (James Franco,
  Jason Lee, Michael Rosenbaum,
  Paul Rudd, Eric Szmanda, Craig
  Zimmerman)

Marc Hirschfeld

THE CENTRAL CHARACTER of *Scrubs* was intern Dr. John "J.D." Dorian. *Scrubs* originally came to us with Craig Zimmerman as J.D.," said casting director Marc Hirschfeld. "We rejected that choice; we didn't feel he was the guy." Jason Lee and Paul Rudd were both offered the part, but neither wanted to commit to a series at the time. James Franco and Michael Rosenbaum both auditioned, as did Zach Braff and Eric Szmanda. "Zach came out of New York. He was wonderful," said Hirschfeld. "Everyone wondered if he was enough of a leading man. Sometimes you've got to go with funny."

Second Chance (1987-1988)

Kiel Martin as Charles Russell (John Bennett Perry)

SECOND CHANCE was about a man (Charles Russell) who died and came back to try to influence his younger self to stay out of trouble. This was his second chance. A teenage Matthew Perry was cast as the younger version, Chazz. The Fox network wanted Perry's real-life father to play Charles, the older version of the character. The older Perry didn't have much experience doing comedy. Director Jim Drake spent a week working with him. "He kept trying to do it broader and broader," said Drake. "I said, 'This is real. You're really involved with this person.' He said, 'Yes, yes. We got it.' I walked into the room and said, 'Okay, he's really got it. This is terrific.' He came in and thinking better of it he went broad. He lost the job."

Seinfeld (1990-1998)

Julia Louis-Dreyfus as Elaine Benes (Susan Diol, Susie Essman, Patricia Heaton, Gina Hecht, Helen Hunt, Wendie Malick, Megan Mullally, Rosie O'Donnell, Heidi Swedberg)

Michael Richards as Kramer (Larry Hankin, Kenny Kramer, Tony Shalhoub, Steve Vinovich)

Jason Alexander as George Costanza (Steve Buscemi, Larry David, Kevin Dunn, Anthony Edwards, David Alan Grier, Brad Hall, Nathan Lane, Larry Miller, Robert Schimmel)

Wayne Knight as Newman (Dan Schneider, Tony Shalhoub, Armin Shimerman)

Philip Bruns as Morty Seinfeld (Philip Sterling)

Liz Sheridan as Helen Seinfeld (Barbara Barrie, Doris Roberts)

Bradford English as Cop (Rick Rockwell)

Ivory Ocean as Officer Morgan (Daniel Benzali)

Carlos Jacott as Ramon (Danny Hoch)

SEINFELD'S ORIGINAL CAST of characters consisted of Jerry, George, Kramer and Claire. Claire was a waitress, played by Lee Garlington, who gave advice to Jerry and his friends. After the pilot the character was dropped. A new female character was introduced named Elaine. Elaine was Jerry's former girlfriend with whom he remained friends. Helen Hunt was asked to audition for the part, but she decided against it. Rosie O'Donnell did a hilarious audition. However, she had the wrong energy for the show, and was passed over. Patricia Heaton, Susie Essman, Heidi Swedberg, Gina Hecht, Wendie Malick and Susan Diol all auditioned but failed to win the role. "Jerry was there for all the preliminary auditions with actors," said Diol. "He read with every actor that came in."

Megan Mullally was a front runner for the part. However, the producers were interested in Julia Louis-Dreyfus. At the time Louis-Drey-

Susan Diol

fus was already committed to the series *Day By Day*, and was unavailable. Her option expired on June 15. Casting director Marc Hirschfeld called her manager constantly. He called again on June 15, when she became available, and Louis-Dreyfus came in on the 16th. She didn't have to read; she got the part. Swedberg, Mullally, Diol and Malick were later given parts on the show. Mullally appeared on the February 25, 1993 episode, titled "The Implant." Malick was on the show just about two years later, in the episode "The Kiss Hello." She played Wendy, a friend of Elaine's whose hairdo was in need of an update. Diol was cast as Audrey, George's girlfriend with a very big nose. "That was a lot of fun," said Diol. "The interesting thing was how people treated me differently. The day we shot it I had to wear the prosthetic nose the whole day. People ignored me; they didn't know who I was."

Nevertheless, Diol had a very positive experience with *Seinfeld*. "That was the greatest show to work on," she said. "I was a little nervous. It was a hit show. We're sitting on the set and Jerry was trying to figure out a joke, and said, 'Well, what do you think, Susan? Do you think that was funny? Let's do it again, you tell us what you think.' Each person who came out as a guest star (I had a friend who was on the same episode as I was); it's like a total collaboration. The guest actors were not treated any differently from the regular actors. It was so nice, and Jerry Seinfeld was wonderful. So was Larry David. They were just great to work with, really creative thinkers and lots of fun on the set."

Of all the potential Elaines, Heidi Swedberg fared the best. She was cast in the recurring role of Susan, George's ill-fated fiancée.

Gina Hecht was brought in numerous times to read for many different roles. Said the actress, "I auditioned so many friggin' times for *Seinfeld*. Jason [Alexander] would have cast parties and I would see Jerry. One year I was in about five times to audition. I saw Jerry at Jason's party and said, 'I can't wait to see how many times I see you in the upcoming year.' Jerry said, 'I'm so embarrassed. I'm not calling you in anymore.' I told him, 'I'm fine with it.'" Hecht was finally cast in the role of George's therapist Dana Foley.

Jerry's parents were introduced in the series' second episode, called 'The Stakeout.' Philip Sterling was cast as Jerry's father but was replaced by Phil Bruns by the time shooting started. Doris Roberts and Barbara Barrie were considered to play Jerry's mother, but the role was eventually given to Liz Sheridan. The characters reappeared in season 2, at which point Philip Bruns was gone, and replaced by Barney Martin. Martin and Sheridan were made recurring characters, and were with the show until the end of the series.

In episode 3, called 'The Robbery,' Jerry's apartment is robbed. Rick Rockwell auditioned to play a cop who takes Jerry's statement. The role was given to Bradford English instead. About ten years later Rockwell came to fame when he starred in the Fox special *Who Wants to Marry a Multi-Millionaire?* This reality special had Rockwell, the multi-millionaire, and a group of 50 women he had never met, all vying for the chance to marry Rockwell live on television at the end of the show. Rockwell chose Darva Conger. A few days later Conger and Rockwell decided to have their marriage annulled.

Seinfeld co-creator Larry David's neighbor was Kenny Kramer. The character of Kramer on the series was based on Kenny Kramer. Kramer auditioned to play the part, but it was felt he wasn't a strong enough actor.

Tony Shalhoub and Larry Hankin were among the actors considered for Kramer. The choice finally came down to Michael Richards and Steve Vinovich. Said Marc Hirschfeld, "Steve was more right for the role as written. He was written as a shut in, laconic. Steve played it to a tee. Michael Richards exploded into the room. He was dynamic, a wild card. It was so clear they had to go with him. He was an original. He took the role to another level." There was some concern as to whether or not Richards was going to play Kramer too broad or too crazy. "I felt the crazier you were going to go the better," said Art Wolff, who directed the pilot episode. "The thing that so attracted me to the series to begin with was not only, of course how funny I thought Jerry was, but how original it was. To do a pilot that had, really, no story line . . . Every day we heard, 'Have you made the story stronger? Isn't there more plot?' Larry and Jerry would not change. There would be no hugging. That was big in terms of the actors that were chosen . . . Michael Richards was

Art Wolff

also so physical. Any trepidation about whether Michael was going to be too far out was really put to rest by Brandon Tartikoff, who was head of programming at NBC at the time. He said, 'Who was the funniest person? Who made you laugh most?' Everyone said Michael. He said, 'Well then, it's got to be Michael. Don't worry about anything else.'"

Larry Hankin appeared on the show in the episode called "The Pilot." He played Tom Pepper, the actor who was cast to play Kramer in Jerry and George's television pilot, Jerry.

"One of the things Jerry had to learn when we worked on the pilot was how to separate Jerry Seinfeld the character from Jerry Seinfeld the person, because every time Michael would do something, which would always be funny, Jerry would laugh," said Wolff. "There were many instances in the script when, of course, Jerry would not laugh (Jerry the character).

"The pilot came out of the relationship between Larry [David] and Jerry. Larry was George. Jerry kept saying, 'Why don't we just have me and Larry?' Nobody knew at that particular point how wonderful Larry was as an actor. He's great, of course, on his HBO series [Curb Your Enthusiasm]. Everybody said, 'Two stand-up comics? We don't want to do that.'"

The competition for the part of George included Anthony Edwards, Steve Buscemi, Jason Alexander, David Alan Grier, Nathan Lane, Larry Miller, Kevin Dunn, Brad Hall and Robert Schimmel. Schimmel was brought in for an audition, and said that he didn't think much of the script. The final choice was between Larry Miller and Jason Alexander. Miller was one of Jerry Seinfeld's best friends. Seinfeld and co-creator Larry David were very conflicted. Seinfeld wanted Miller, while David thought that Jason Alexander was the right choice. The role ultimately went to Alexander.

Tony Shalhoub was considered to play Newman, but wasn't available to audition. Other possibilities were Armin Shimerman and Dan Schneider. The role was later given to Wayne Knight.

Daniel Benzali was originally going to play Officer Morgan in the episode entitled "The Scofflaw." The role was recast with Ivory Ocean.

Danny Hoch was hired for the part of Ramon the pool guy in the November 16, 1995 episode titled "The Pool Guy." He was eventually let go and replaced by Carlos Jacott.

Senior Trip (1981)
Jeffrey Marcus as Jon Lipton (Kevin Bacon, Keith Gordon)

JEFFREY MARCUS' competition for the part of Jon Lipton in the 1981 TV movie *Senior Trip* included Kevin Bacon and Keith Gordon. "I went in and felt like something special was happening," said Marcus. "I told writer/director Kenneth Johnson that I had gone to Carnegie-Mellon, where he also went. He threw the script up in the air and said, 'Cast him.'"

Jeffrey Marcus

Sesame Street (1969-)
Roscoe Orman as Gordon Robinson (David Downing, Robert Guillaume)

MATT ROBINSON played the part of Gordon when the educational children's program *Sesame Street* premiered in 1969. Robinson left the show in 1972, and Hal Miller was cast as Gordon. In 1974 Miller left the show, and a third actor was sought for the part. After auditioning possible Gordons the finalists were narrowed down to three: Robert Guillaume, Roscoe Orman and David Downing. The finalists all had screen tests, which consisted of two parts. In the first part they had to perform a scripted scene with the Muppet character Oscar the Grouch. The second part consisted of a semi-improvisational scene with a child. All three men were experienced and talented actors, but the part was given to Roscoe Orman. Orman joined the cast in 1974 and is still playing Gordon to date.

Seven Brides for Seven Brothers (1982-1983)

Richard Dean Anderson as Adam
   McFadden (Grainger Hines)

Grainger Hines competed with Richard Dean Anderson for the role of Adam McFadden in the television version of the classic film *Seven Brides for Seven Brothers*. Anderson won the part, and Hines was later cast in the recurring role of Sheriff Lewis.

Grainger Hines.
Photo: Aloma Ichinose

Seventh Heaven (1996-2007)

Stephen Collins as Eric Camden (Tim Matheson, Tom Selleck)

EXECUTIVE PRODUCER Aaron Spelling told casting executive Pamela Shae that he wanted a big name to play the part of Reverend Eric Camden on *Seventh Heaven*. Tom Selleck was one of the many stars that were considered. Tim Matheson was another possibility, and came very close to playing the part. Three days before shooting the Matheson deal fell through. Spelling, who loved the show, was upset. He asked director Sam Weisman who he thought might be able to do the part. Weisman suggested Stephen Collins. Collins had already been contacted about the part, but wasn't interested. Weisman offered to call him. "I called Steve Collins, who I'd known for years," said Weisman. "I hadn't seen him in a long time, but I'd known him dating back to the early '70s. He was literally walking out the door to take his wife away on an anniversary weekend. They were going from L.A. to Ojai, which is about 100 miles away. They had reservations at this place called the Ojai Valley Inn. It was all planned. I said, 'I'm doing this pilot for Aaron Spelling. I think you'd be great for this part.' He said, 'Because it's you I'll take a look at it. We're walking out the door right now.' I said, 'Stephen, this starts in two days.' He said, 'Well, I can't possibly do it. I've got this four-day weekend.' I said, 'Why don't you just look at it?' And this is in the days before you would e-mail scripts. He said, 'I can't wait for the script. I'm just going to have to go. You'll have to try to get it to us in Ojai.' They literally got a teamster; a driver working at one of their other shows to drive the script to Ojai. And he read it that day and agreed to do it. The next day he came down for wardrobe fittings. Aaron Spelling said, 'I'll pay for a new weekend.'"

Sex and the City (1998-2004)

Sarah Jessica Parker as Carrie Bradshaw (Lysette Anthony, Rosanna Arquette, Brenda Bakke, Anita Barone, Andrea Bendewald, Caprice Benedetti, Corinne Bohrer, Katy Boyer, Lara Flynn Boyle, Yancy Butler, Julia Campbell, Finn Carter, Marcia Christie, Kari Coleman, Alicia Coppola, Carrie-Anne Moss, Cynthia Nixon, Lori Singer)

Kim Cattrall as Samantha Jones (Denise Crosby, Allison Janney, Lou Thornton

Cynthia Nixon as Miranda Hobbes (Sandra Bernhard, Jessica Hecht)

Andrea Boccaletti as Derek, The Bone (Michael Bergin)

WHEN CYNTHIA NIXON auditioned to be a cast member of *Sex and the City*, the part she was up for was the main role of Carrie Bradshaw. Nixon didn't think she was right for the part. She called her agent and told her that she was still interested in being on the show. Nixon got what she wanted. She won the role of attorney Miranda Hobbes.

The first choice to play Carrie was always Sarah Jessica Parker. Parker wasn't sure if she wanted to commit to the show. Offers went out to Lara Flynn Boyle and Rosanna Arquette, who both said no. Many other actresses were considered, including Carrie-Anne Moss, Lori Singer, Lysette Anthony, Anita Barone, Corinne Bohrer, Yancy Butler, Julia Campbell, Finn Carter, Andrea Bendewald, Caprice Benedetti, Brenda Bakke, Kari Coleman, Katy Boyer, Marcia Christie and Alicia Coppola. Coppola's audition was very funny. She came very close to getting the part, but Parker eventually decided she wanted to do the show, and the role was hers.

Kim Cattrall was the first choice for the part of Samantha Jones. Cattrall turned it down, not wanting to do a series or relocate to New York. Denise Crosby and Allison Janney both auditioned for the part. The role was given to Lou Thornton, who was 29 at the time. Right away concerns about Thornton's age were voiced. She was younger than the rest of the cast, which posed a problem. Series creator Darren Star's partner, director Dennis Erdman, called Kim Cattrall and told her he thought the part of Samantha was right for her. She eventually came around, and agreed to play the part. Thornton got a call saying they decided to go older with the part.

Sandra Bernhard was considered to play Miranda. The final two contenders for the part were Cynthia Nixon and Jessica Hecht.

Candace Bushnell interviewed model Michael Bergin when she was writing the book *Sex and the City*. When the character of the male model appeared on the series, Bergin was called in for an audition. Although the character was based on him (to some degree), he lost out to Andrea Boccalletti.

Shattered Innocence (1988)

Jonna Lee as Pauleen Anderson (Patricia Arquette)

SHATTERED INNOCENCE was a fictional account of the story of adult film star Shauna Grant. Grant, who was born Colleen Applegate, broke into the adult film industry when she was about 18. Not long after, she developed a cocaine habit. At the age of 20 Grant committed suicide by a self-inflicted gunshot.

Patricia Arquette was up for the Grant-esque part of Pauleen Anderson in *Shattered Innocence*. She eventually took herself out of the running and the role went to Jonna Lee instead.

She Said, He Said (2006)

Lindsay Sloane as Beckie Gethers (Lacey Chabert)

IN 2006 TWO TELEVISION networks, UPN and The WB, merged to form The CW. Lori Openden was named senior vice president of talent and casting for the new network. According to Openden the network was very committed to racial diversity. "The CW is going to be a real competitive force," she said.

One of the first pilots that were made was called *She Said, He Said*. The show looked at the battle of the sexes from both the male and female point of view. Nick Lachey was hired to star as Kurtwood Weymouth. Lacey Chabert and Lindsay Sloane both read for the part of Beckie Gethers, the female lead. Chabert was too young for the role, and it was given to Sloane. Chabert was then cast as Beckie's younger sister.

She Spies (2002-2004)

Kristen Miller as D.D. Cummings (Julie Benz, Rachel Blanchard)
Natashia Williams as Shane Phillips (Sybil Azur, Stacey Dash)

NATASHA HENSTRIDGE made her film debut in the starring role of Sil in *Species*. The film was a hit, and Henstridge quickly became a star. Although she was primarily known for making movies, she agreed to head the cast of the series *She Spies* as Cassie McBain.

Rachel Blanchard, Julie Benz and Kristen Miller were the final three candidates for the part of D.D. Cummings. The role went to Miller.

Casting director Zora De-Horter-Majomi brought Natashia Williams in to audition for the part of Shane. She thought that Williams was really right for the part and was rooting for her to get it. Williams' most serious competition was Stacey Dash and Sybil Azur, who tested against her in front of the executives from UPN. Williams got the job.

Zora De Horter-Majomi

Sheena, Queen of the Jungle (1955)
Irish McCalla as Sheena (Anita Ekberg)

BOTH ANITA EKBERG and Irish McCalla tested for the title role of Sheena. Ekberg got the part. However, Ekberg failed to show up to shoot the pilot. McCalla was contacted and offered the role, which she accepted.

She's Too Young (2004)

Alexis Dziena as Hannah Vogul (Elizabeth Rice)

ELIZABETH RICE AUDITIONED for the starring role of Hannah Vogul in the 2004 TV movie, *She's Too Young*. Director Tom McLoughlin was impressed by her reading, but felt she wasn't quite right for the part. The role went to Alexis Dziena instead. About a year later McLoughlin was casting the Lifetime movie *Odd Girl Out*. He remembered Rice, and brought her in to audition for the film. She won the supporting role of Nikki.

The Shining (1997)

Steven Weber as Jack Torrance (Tim Daly)

TIM DALY was offered the chance to star as Jack Torrance in the 1997 miniseries *The Shining*. Daly wasn't interested, but he told his *Wings* costar Steven Weber about the project. Weber wanted the job, and was eventually cast.

Shogun (1980)

Richard Chamberlain as John Blackthorne (Sean Connery, Albert Finney, Roger Moore)

SEAN CONNERY was the first choice for the starring role of John Blackthorne in *Shogun*. James Clavell, the author of *Shogun*, suggested Roger Moore. Albert Finney was considered as well. NBC liked Richard Chamberlain, and he was eventually hired.

Silk Stalkings (1991-1999)
Mitzi Kapture as Rita Lee Lance (Crystal Carson)

CRYSTAL CARSON auditioned for the part of Sgt. Rita Lee Lance on *Silk Stalkings*. She was called back to read for the producers, but eventually lost the role to Mitzi Kapture. Said Carson, "Mitzi was so great. I was glad she got it. At least you lose out to somebody great. We had distinctly different looks."

Simon & Simon (1981-1988)
Jameson Parker as A.J. Simon (Larry Manetti)

A.J. AND RICK SIMON were brothers, as well as partners in a detective agency. Larry Manetti auditioned to play the A.J., the conservative brother. He lost the part to Jameson Parker.

The Simple Life (2003-)
Nicole Richie as Herself (Nicky Hilton)

SISTERS PARIS AND NICKY HILTON were approached to appear in the reality series *The Simple Life*. Paris signed on; Nicky did not. Paris Hilton's friend Nicole Richie (daughter of singer Lionel Richie) was cast instead.

The Simpsons (1989-)
James Woods as Himself (Michael Caine)

JAMES WOODS played himself on the February 10, 1994 episode of *The Simpsons* called "Homer and Apu." Writer Greg Daniels initially wanted Michael Caine for the part. The joke was that Caine had a reputation for taking any job offered to him. Ironically, Caine turned down the part.

The Single Guy (1995-1997)

Jessica Hecht as Janeane Percy-Parker (Kim Dickens)
Joey Slotnick as Sam Sloan (Donal Logue)
Ming-Na as Trudy Sloan (Audra McDonald)

THE SINGLE GUY starred Jonathan Silverman as struggling writer Jonathan Eliot. One of Jonathan's best friends was Janeane Percy-Parker. Kim Dickens was considered to play Janeane, but the role went to Jessica Hecht instead.

Donal Logue tested for Joey Slotnick's role of Sam Sloan.

Audra McDonald was considered to play Sam's wife Trudy Sloan. The role went to Ming-Na instead.

Sister Mary Explains It All (2001)

Diane Keaton as Sister Mary Ignatius (Lily Tomlin)

VICTORIA TENNANT AND KIRK STAMBLER worked with Christopher Durang to make a television movie out of his play, *Sister Mary Ignatius Explains It All for You*. They brought in Marshall Brickman to direct. Brickman, who is also an acclaimed writer (he won an Academy Award for writing *Annie Hall* with Woody Allen), helped with the screenplay. He met with Lily Tomlin to see if she would be interested in playing Sister Mary. Tomlin had the idea to take the production to a local theater in Los Angeles. Brickman knew that her idea

Marshall Brickman

was too elaborate for his movie and called his old friend Diane Keaton. Keaton said she would do it. With Keaton attached, Showtime agreed to air the film.

Sisters (1991-1996)
Sela Ward as Teddy Reed (Patricia Kalember)

SISTERS FOLLOWED THE LIVES of the four Reed sisters: Teddy, Alex, Georgie and Frankie.

Patricia Kalember originally auditioned for the part of the free-spirited Teddy Reed. Although her audition was very good, she didn't seem quite right for that part. *Sisters* creators Ron Cowen and Daniel Lipman thought she would be better for the part of Georgie Reed Whitsig instead. After her audition, Lipman ran after her to ask her if she would come back to read Georgie the following day. "It took a little convincing, because she wanted to be Teddy," said Cowen. "Sometimes you have to be a little diplomatic and help an actor to change the way they're seeing themselves."

Cowen and Lipman knew the role of Teddy was pivotal to the show's success. Four days before the first day of work they still had nobody to play Teddy. Sela Ward came in to audition. The pair was familiar with Ward from her other work. They remembered her as very glamorous with long hair. Ward came in with a short haircut, wearing jeans and a tank top. "She blew us away," said Lipman. "This was not the Sela Ward that anyone had ever seen or ever known. She had an acting coach. Even after she won her Emmy her coach was on the set. I've never seen anyone work so hard to accomplish this character. She certainly deserved the Emmy. We finally had our Teddy."

Cowen and Lipman got a message that Swoosie Kurtz wanted to come in and audition for the part of Alex. The character was originally the smallest part of the four sisters. Kurtz and Cowen and Lipman all sat on a curb and shared a tuna sandwich off of the lunch truck on the Sony lot together while they discussed the show. Once Kurtz was in place the role was built up into a starring part.

An unknown Ashley Judd auditioned to play Alex's daughter Reed Halsey. Lipman and Cowen were won over by Judd's charm, wit and voice. "She's very pretty, but everybody's pretty here," said Cowen. "It's meaningless. If one pretty person isn't available there are 2000 more standing outside the door. But she was so charming and she had a quality, a smokiness . . . " "A confidence," added Lipman. "You really listened when she spoke," said Cowen. "She had a way of enunciating words that was captivating. I think as writers we responded to that voice and the way she spoke. Of course she comes from a family of people who have done very well vocally!" "She was really a lovely person, too," said Lipman. "Her mother, Naomi, was on the show too at one point. Naomi was very charming. I remember after we cast Ashley, Ron and I were working on a Saturday morning and the UPS truck pulled up. These two huge boxes arrived, one for Ron and one for me. We opened them up and there were all these gifts from Naomi Judd. The card was, 'Thank you two angels for taking care of my angel.' There were these books of days which she had written, two of them, every single day she had written quotes and her favorite poetry personally, handwriting to us. I remember writing her or calling her saying, 'I don't know how to thank you for this.'" "She was remarkable," said Cowen.

Julianne Phillips rounded out the cast as the youngest Reed daughter Frankie.

George Clooney had a deal with Warner Bros. Les Moonves called Ron Cowen and Daniel Lipman to suggest Clooney for the recurring role of Detective James Falconer. Moonves said that Clooney wouldn't read, so they should meet him, which they did. They thought that Clooney was wonderful, but they still had meetings that were already set up with other actors. After half of the first day of casting they decided to let everyone go. They felt no one else could do the role as well as George Clooney. NBC was unsure about Clooney, and wanted him to read with Sela Ward. Cowen and Lipman called Moonves and NBC's Warren Littlefield and asked them to work it out. "Ultimately Leslie won and George got the role," said Cowen. "That was in July of that year. By pilot season that same year NBC was so impressed with George and Sela together (we wanted to spin them off actually, that didn't work out) they sent George two pilots. One was something called *Golden Gate*, where he'd play a detective. The other was *ER*. He chose *ER*." "And the rest is history," added Cowen.

Heather McAdam played the part of Kat. "We had to have a little kitten come in," said Lipman. "We set up this casting call for a little girl. She probably had to be around seven or eight years old. So it would be maybe, someone ten years old playing the role. The parade of children start coming in. It's so cliché, some are these professional children who just sort of smile at you, there's nothing there, other children who didn't even want to read. I remember saying to quite a few of them, 'Do you enjoy this?' and they would look around like they didn't know what to answer. I said, 'No, you can be honest, you can be truthful.' They said, 'No, not really. My mother wants me to do this.' It was very discouraging until this one little girl, ten years old, walks into the office and reads. Had absolutely no credits, nothing, blew me away. And I said, 'We have been seeing children for two days, and this is the first actress. This was not a child; this was an actress. So we signed Kirsten Dunst to do this role. She did two or three episodes. Three months later she got into Interview with the Vampire and I was not surprised. I said this is an actress, and obviously I was correct. One day coming back from Toronto where we shot Queer as Folk, Kirsten Dunst was on the plane sitting across from me with her mother and her little dog. I was thinking to myself, 'Should I say something? Why not.' So I went over to her mother who was sitting across the aisle. I said, 'You probably don't remember me. But I was the executive producer of *Sisters* and we cast Kirsten in the role.' She looked at me and she said, 'Oh my God, do I remember you? That gig on *Sisters* kept us going. Are you kidding? We came out to California; we got on *Sisters* and, wow! That kept us going.' Her mother was very sweet. That was really interesting when you discover someone like that. That was very gratifying."

Six Feet Under (2001-2005)

Michael C. Hall as David Fisher (Peter Krause)
Lauren Ambrose as Claire Fisher (Anna Faris)
Rachel Griffiths as Brenda Chenowith (Dina Spybey)

SIX FEET UNDER told the story of the Fisher family, owners of a funeral home. Peter Krause was considered for the part of the younger brother David Fisher. However, there was no leading candidate for the part of David's brother Nate. Krause was suggested for that part as well. Series creator Alan Ball realized that Krause was right for Nate, and the part was his.

Michael C. Hall was playing the Master of Ceremonies in *Cabaret* when he auditioned for the part of David Fisher. Ball knew Hall was a great choice for the role as soon as Hall came in to audition. Hall's reading only confirmed to Ball his intuition was correct.

Anna Faris read for the part of Claire Fisher. Faris auditioned reading a serious scene. Creator Alan Ball thought that Faris was very funny. The actress lost the part to Lauren Ambrose, who gave an outstanding audition.

Dina Spybey auditioned for the part of Brenda Chenowith. Alan Ball thought she was better for the guest role of Tracy Montrose Blair in the pilot episode. Spybey did such a good job in the pilot that Ball brought her character back throughout the first season.

Film star Rachel Griffiths expressed interest in the part of Brenda. Ball's only reservation was if the Australian Griffiths could master an American accent. She came in for a meeting and put his fears to rest.

In 1999 Alan Ball created the series *Oh, Grow Up*. One of the cast members was Freddy Rodriguez. Ball thought Rodriguez was terrific, and wrote the part of Federico Diaz on *Six Feet Under* with him in mind.

The Six Million Dollar Man (1973-1978)

Lee Majors as Steve Austin (Monte Markham)

THE SIX MILLION DOLLAR MAN was based on the novel *Cyborg* by Martin Caidin. Caidin wanted Monte Markham to play the starring role of Steve Austin in the series. ABC wanted to give Lee Majors a show, and cast him instead. Markham later showed up in two episodes as an evil bionic cyborg who was a rival to Steve Austin.

Sliders (1995-2000)

Kari Wuhrer as Maggie Beckett (Pamela Anderson, Mili Avital, Maria Bello, Lara Flynn Boyle, Yancy Butler, Melinda Clarke, Jennifer Connelly, Alicia Coppola, Missy Crider, Karen Duffy, Erika Eleniak, Angie Everhart, Angela Featherstone, Farrah Forke, Claire Forlani, Gina Gershon, Cynthia Gibb, Heather Graham, A.J. Langer, Paula Marshall, Samantha Mathis, Cheryl Pollak, Gabrielle Reece, Perrey Reeves, Kelly Rowan, Jeri Ryan, Talisa Soto, Kylie Travis, Nancy Travis, Christy Turlington, Julie Warner, Peta Wilson)

Zoe McLellan as Logan St. Claire (Perrey Reeves)

Roger Daltrey as Angus Rickman (Gregg Allman, Eric Bogosian, Powers Boothe, David Bowie, Peter Coyote, Tim Curry, Victor Garber, Corey Glover, Rutger Hauer, Michael Hutchence, Ice-T, Billy Idol, David Johansson, David Patrick Kelly, Ted Levine, Christopher Lloyd, Lyle Lovett, Michael Madsen, David Morse, Ving Rhames, Eric Roberts, Henry Rollins, Chris Sarandon, Tom Sizemore, Richard Tyson, Tom Waits, Peter Weller, Montel Williams, Michael Wincott)

Ryan Alosio as Morgan (Adam Ant, Ian Astbury, Billy Corgan, Evan Dando, John Doe, Flea, John Frusciante, Billy Idol, Chris Isaak, Martin Kemp, Anthony Kiedis, Tommy Lee, Donovan Leitch, Duff McKagan, Frank Military, Trent Reznor, Axl Rose, Gene Simmons, Slash, Chad Smith, Steven Tyler, Michael Wincott, Dweezil Zappa)

Tommy Chong as Van Elsinger (David Garrison, Austin Pendleton)
Duff McKagan as Harker (Ryan Alosio)

SLIDERS FOLLOWED A GROUP OF FRIENDS and their adventures traveling through parallel worlds.

The character of Captain Maggie Beckett was added to the cast of *Sliders* in Season 3. Many actresses, including Pamela Anderson, Maria Bello,
Lara Flynn Boyle, Jennifer Connelly, Gina Gershon, Heather Graham,
and Peta Wilson, were considered for the part. The producers wanted
someone of note for the role. Cheryl Pollak was asked to audition, but
didn't. Casting director Dino Ladki thought that Kari Wuhrer would be a
great addition to the cast. He worried that if she auditioned the producers might tear her apart and she wouldn't be hired. He told her agents at
William Morris that all she had to do was come in and meet. Then he told
the producers that her agency didn't want her to audition, but she would
come in for a meeting. "She charmed them like I knew she would, and she
was hired," said Ladki.

Wuhrer's first episode was called "The Exodus." It was a two-part
show. There was a character called Col. Angus Rickman. Many actors as
well as musicians were considered for the part, including Ice-T, Montel
Williams, Tim Curry, David Bowie, Christopher Lloyd, Billy Idol and
Tom Waits. Ladki spoke to Roger Daltrey, of the band The Who, about
the possibility of him playing the part. He pointed out that the title of the
episode was a lyric in The Who song "Baba O'Reilly." Daltrey eventually
agreed to take the part.

Perrey Reeves and Zoe McLellan both auditioned for the guest role of
Logan St. Claire. McLellan won the part. Soon after, Reeves was brought
in to play another guest role, Taryn Miller. She got the part without having to audition.

Series star Jerry O'Connell directed the May 9, 1997 show entitled
"Stoker." "Stoker" was a rock star vampire episode with characters based

on characters from the classic *Dracula*. Many musicians were considered for the part of Morgan, including Duff McKagan of the band Guns N' Roses. McKagan had no agent, but Dino Ladki was best friends with one of his roadies. "Through three degrees of separation I got to Duff," said Ladki. McKagan was a little nervous about auditioning. Ladki went to his house to coach him. They worked for hours. His audition went very well. Although he failed to win, the part of Morgan, he was cast as Harker. A gracious McKagan gave Ladki credit for helping him.

Ryan Alosio, of the band Black Radio, originally auditioned for the part of Harker. His audition went very well. While he was there, he told a story about being on Marilyn Manson's tour bus. Based on how he told the story, he got the lead role of Morgan.

David Garrison and Austin Pendleton were considered for the part of Van Elsing. Tommy Chong eventually played the role.

Small Wonder (1985-1989)
Tiffany Brissette as Vicki (Candace Cameron)

SMALL WONDER centered on the Lawson family. The family consisted of father Ted, mother Joan, son Jamie and robot daughter Vicki. Candace Cameron auditioned to play Vicki, but lost out to Tiffany Brissette. About two years later Cameron landed the part of D.J. on the hit series *Full House*.

Soap (1977-1981)
Jennifer Salt as Eunice (Diana Canova)
Robert Urich as Peter Campbell (John Bennett Perry)

THE PRIME-TIME SERIES *Soap* was a satire of soap operas. The show focused on the lives of two families: the Tates and the Campbells. Susan

Harris created the series. She would flesh out the characters with her producing partners, Paul Junger Witt and Tony Thomas, and then go and write the pilot script on her own. Harris, Witt and Thomas felt they had something special with *Soap*, but didn't know how the show would play to audiences.

Diana Canova was brought in for the part of the uptight Tate daughter Eunice. It was later decided that the character of Corinne (Eunice's sister) had to be cast with a very likeable actress, and

Susan Harris

switched Canova to that role. Jennifer Salt was given the part of Eunice.

John Bennett Perry was originally cast as tennis pro Peter Campbell. Perry shot the pilot, but was later replaced by Robert Urich.

The character of butler Benson DuBois was based on a man who worked for executive producer Tony Thomas' family. Thomas knew the man all his life and loved him. Many actors were read for the part. Robert Guillaume was put on tape. The network wasn't especially interested in his audition. Two days before an audience run thru the part was still vacant. Guillaume was brought in just for the day. Guillaume went over so well with the audience he was signed for the series. His performance in the show was so outstanding that after two years he was spun-off into his own series, *Benson*, which ran for seven years.

Soap was a critical and commercial hit. The show ran for four seasons, and amassed an impressive amount of Emmy nominations.

Something Wilder (1994-1995)

Gene Wilder as Gene Bergman (Judd Hirsch)

Hillary Bailey Smith as Annie Bergman (Jennifer Grey)

Gregory Itzin as Jack Travis (Cliff Gorman, Tony Roberts)

SOMETHING WILDER was written with Judd Hirsch in mind. Hirsch wasn't interested and turned it down. The producers flew to Connecticut to make an offer to Gene Wilder. When Wilder accepted, the show was rewritten to suit him.

Jennifer Grey was originally cast as Annie Bergman, the wife of Gene Wilder's character Gene. Grey, who is almost 27 years younger than Wilder, just looked too young to play opposite him and had to be replaced. Executive producer Barnet Kellman knew Hillary Bailey Smith, and knew she would be right for the part.

Tony Roberts was one of the leading candidates for the part of Jack Travis. Roberts read for the network, as did Cliff Gorman and Gregory Itzin. Kellman never expected Itzin to win the role. However, Kellman said it was Greg's day, and the part was his.

Sons & Daughters (2006)

Amanda Walsh as Jenna Halbert (Christine Lakin)

FRED GOSS AND NICK HOLLY created *Sons and Daughters*. Goss also acted in the show, playing the central role of Cameron Walker.

Christine Lakin tested for the part of Cameron's half-sister, waitress Jenna Halbert. The show was improv based. Lakin had an extremely positive experience with the audition process. "I never had an audition like this," said Lakin. "My whole studio, network test was me sitting in a room with Fred Goss, the creator and the star. They put me on tape and he and I bantered and just improved for about 20 minutes. Then they edited my audition down to five. They did that with everybody, and those were the tapes they sent to the network. I didn't end up getting it, but Fred was very sweet and supportive. He and Nick Holly called me. It was very nice. They called to say what a great job I did, and they would love to figure out something for me to do on the show. Sure enough, about four episodes in, they called me in to be a guest star. Being that it's a totally improvised show, I made up an entire character, what I did for a living. I became the sort of slutty older woman on the show. I was dating one of the younger boys. Just ridiculous. But it was just too much fun, and then they brought me back for another episode so I ended up doing a recurring role on the show. Which goes to show you, you never know who's watching you and you never know who's in the room. You've always just got to do good work. You never know where it could lead. That was a great experience."

The Sopranos (1999-2007)

James Gandolfini as Tony Soprano
(Anthony LaPaglia, David Proval)
Edie Falco as Carmela Soprano (Lorraine
Bracco)
Lillo Brancato as Matt Bevilacqua (Max
Casella)
Jason Cerbone as Jackie Aprile, Jr. (Max
Casella)
Burt Young as Bobby "Bacala" Baccalieri,
Sr. (Carmine Caridi)

Max Casella

DAVID PROVAL AUDITIONED to play the lead role of New Jersey mob boss Tony Soprano. He failed to win the part, but was later brought on the show as Richie Aprile. Anthony LaPaglia was another consideration for Tony, but the role went to James Gandolfini. LaPaglia said that Gandolfini was the right person for the part.

Lorraine Bracco was originally considered for the part of Tony Soprano's wife, Carmela. Bracco already played a similar character in the film *GoodFellas*, for which she was nominated for an Academy Award. Bracco felt that she wouldn't be able to top that performance, and took the part of Tony's therapist Jennifer Melfi instead. HBO suggested Edie Falco to play Carmela. Falco appeared on the network's prison series *Oz*, as Officer Diane Whittlesey. Falco read once, and the part of Carmela Soprano was hers.

Max Casella auditioned for The Sopranos twice before joining the cast as Benny Fazio. He first auditioned for the part of Matt Bevilacqua, later played by Lillo Brancato. The second role he went up for was Jackie Aprile, Jr., which ultimately went to Jason Cerbone. "It's good, because those guys are dead anyway," joked Casella. "I'm still here five years later. It's better to be there for the long haul because you're more in the consciousness of the people who watch the show, than if you had a bigger splash but it was short lived and was a couple of years ago. It's been good to be on the show."

Carmine Caridi auditioned to play Bobby "Bacala" Baccalieri, Sr. The part went to Burt Young instead, who Caridi said did a wonderful job.

South Central (1994)
Tina Lifford as Joan Mosely (Sheryl Lee Ralph)

SHERYL LEE RALPH was considered for Tina Lifford's role of single mother Joan Mosely on *South Central.*

Jennifer Lopez was cast in the small role of a cashier in the pilot. Executive producer Michael J. Weithorn noticed that CBS executive Jeff Sagansky took an interest in Lopez. Weithorn called the head of 20th Century-Fox, Peter Roth, and said that they should make Lopez a regular. Weithorn suspected Sagansky wouldn't buy the series. He also thought that he would try to snatch Lopez away. Roth replied, "Jennifer Lopez is not going anywhere." Weithorn's suspicions were on the money. CBS passed on the show, which then went to Fox. CBS did, however, make a holding deal with Lopez.

Southern Comfort (2006)
Eric Roberts as Ray (Chris Mulkey)

CHRIS MULKEY was considered for the part of Ray *in Southern Comfort,* eventually played by Eric Roberts.

Space: 1999 (1975-1977)

Martin Landau as John Koenig (Robert Culp)
Barbara Bain as Helena Russell (Katharine Ross)

SERIES CREATOR SYLVIA ANDERSON was interested in Robert Culp and Katharine Ross for the leads in *Space: 1999*. However, the people financing the show were intent on the parts going to the husband-and-wife team of Martin Landau and Barbara Bain instead.

Spies (1987)

George Hamilton as Ian Stone (Tony
    Curtis)
Gary Kroeger as Ben Smythe (Timothy
    Busfield)

Gary Kroeger

SPIES CENTERED ON the characters Ian Stone and Ben Smythe. Tony Curtis was the first actor cast to play spy Ian Stone. Gary Kroeger and Timothy Busfield both auditioned to play Stone's sidekick Ben Smythe. Kroeger got the part. A pilot was shot, which was later recast. George Hamilton came in as the new Ian Stone. Kroeger had to audition for his part all over again. His competition, once again, was Timothy Busfield. "I went to network both times against Timothy," said Kroeger. "When we were waiting to hear who got it, we were both nervous and wanted the role. I remember him saying to me, 'What ever happens is fate. If one of us doesn't get it, it's because something better is coming along.' I got it and thirtysomething came along for him. Of course ... *Spies* didn't go anywhere ... "

Sports Night (1998-2000)

Josh Charles as Dan Rydell (Joshua Malina)

Peter Krause as Casey McCall (Bill Campbell, James Denton, Noah Emmerich, Andrew Lowery, John C. McGinley)

Felicity Huffman as Dana Whittaker (Leila Kenzle, Kirsten Nelson)

Sabrina Lloyd as Natalie Hurley (Mary Lynn Rajskub)

PETER KRAUSE was doing a play when he auditioned for the Aaron Sorkin series *Sports Night*. For the play Krause had long hair, as well as facial hair. He was disregarded as a candidate because he looked very different than the character of the clean-cut sportscaster Casey McCall. James Denton, Andrew Lowery, Noah Emmerich, John C. McGinley and Bill Campbell all tested. Casting director Bonnie Zane remembered that McGinley's cell phone went off while he was auditioning.

Zane called her favorite choices for Casey and told them what creator Aaron Sorkin was looking for. When she called Krause (whose play had finished its run) she told him to cut his hair and shave. She told him, "I think this is your part." Krause nailed his audition and won the role.

Felicity Huffman tested against Leila Kenzle and Kirsten Nelson for the part of producer Dana Whitaker. Aaron Sorkin wanted Huffman from the start, and the role was hers.

Joshua Malina originally auditioned for Josh Charles' role of sportscaster Dan Rydell. He was instead cast as associate producer Jeremy Goodwin. The role of Jeremy was reconceived for Malina to play.

Mary Lynn Rajskub and Sabrina Lloyd both tested for the part of Natalie Hurley. Lloyd had on her lucky socks, which were her neighbor's. The neighbor turned out to be an old boyfriend of Bonnie Zane's! The socks worked, as Lloyd was hired for the show.

Robert Guillaume came for a meeting to discuss the role of Isaac Jaffe. While he was there, he offered to read for the part. Guillaume was offered the job, which he accepted.

St. Elsewhere (1982-1988)

Ed Flanders as Donald Westphall (Josef Sommer)
Howie Mandel as Wayne Fiscus (Richard Lewis, David Paymer)
Cynthia Sikes as Annie Cavanero (Ellen Bry, Caitlin Clarke, Barrie
    Youngfellow)

THE ORIGINAL PILOT of *St. Elsewhere* saw Josef Sommer cast as Dr. Donald Westphall and David Paymer as Dr. Wayne Fiscus. The director was Lou Antonio. After about three days the production was shut down. The tone of the show was wrong. Antonio was fired, and Sommer and Paymer were also let go. Thomas Carter was hired as the new director, and had to cast the now vacant roles of Drs. Westphall and Fiscus.

Ed Flanders was hired to replace Sommer as Dr. Donald Westphall. Two candidates for the part of Dr. Wayne Fiscus were comedians Richard Lewis and Howie Mandel. Carter wanted someone who would bring an

Ellen Bry
Photo: Bader Howar

offbeat sensibility to the role. Lewis came very close to getting the part, but it went to Mandel instead.

The final candidates for the part of Dr. Annie Cavanero were Cynthia Sikes, Ellen Bry, Barrie Youngfellow and Caitlin Clarke. The first choice was Youngfellow, but her agent and the producers were unable to negotiate a deal. Sikes got the part instead. "I still really wanted to be a part of the show," said Ellen Bry. She looked at the small role of nurse Shirley Daniels. "It was one scene, but it was a good scene, a funny scene. Because she's a nurse in the hospital, she had a chance of recurring." Bry was right. "I became a series regular in the first season, partly because I started testing to do parts on other shows. [Producer] Bruce Paltrow didn't want to lose me." NBC executive Brandon Tartikoff also didn't want to lose Bry. He made the decision to put her under contract and have the writers develop a storyline for Shirley Daniels.

Bry was with the show for four years. She was in one of the show's most memorable scenes in which her character shoots suspected rapist Dr. Peter White.

James Coco was offered the guest role of Arnie on the Season 1 episode called "Cora and Arnie." After reading the script he called his dear friend Doris Roberts and told her she had to play Cora. Roberts called Bruce Paltrow, and was cast. Coco and Roberts both won Emmys for playing the homeless couple.

Stacked (2005-2007)

Elon Gold as Gavin P. Miller (Tom Everett Scott)
Marissa Jaret Winokur as Katrina (Pamela Adlon)

TOM EVERETT SCOTT was hired to play bookstore owner Gavin P. Miller in the Pamela Anderson series Stacked. Scott shot the pilot, but was quickly replaced by Elon Gold.

Pamela Adlon auditioned for the part of bookstore employee Katrina. At the same time Adlon was also auditioning for the female lead in the HBO series *Lucky Louie*. When Louis C.K., the star and creator of *Lucky Louie*, found out that Adlon had gone to studio for *Stacked*, he became worried. Said Adlon, "He ended up calling me from Peoria, Illinois from a comedy club at the end of that week saying, 'You can't do that Pamela Anderson show. You have to do my show. You have to marry me on television.' And I said, 'Nobody's offering me either show!' They wanted me to go to network on Stacked, and they were waiting because HBO does things slower. [HBO Chairman and CEO] Chris Albrecht wasn't in town yet. I had to walk away from network on *Stacked* in order to gamble; to see if I was going to get *Lucky Louie*." Adlon got the job on *Lucky Louie*, while the role of Katrina on *Stacked* went to Broadway star Marissa Jaret Winokur. "She is lovely and I adore her," said Adlon of Winokur.

Star Trek (1966-1969)

Leonard Nimoy as Mr. Spock (Michael Dunn, DeForest Kelley, Martin
    Landau)
Jeffrey Hunter as Christopher Pike (Lloyd Bridges, James Coburn)
John Hoyt as Phillip Boyce (DeForest Kelley)
Susan Oliver as Vina (Elizabeth Ashley, Joan Blackman, Dyan Cannon, Yvonne
    Craig, Barbara Eden, Jane Fonda, Anne Francis, Anne Helm, Piper Laurie,
    Carol Lawrence, Diana Millay, Yvette Mimieux, Maggie Pierce, Suzanne
    Pleshette, Janice Rule, Jean Seberg, Stella Stevens)
Michael Ansara as Kang (Joseph Campanella)
James Daly as Flint (Carroll O'Connor)

STAR TREK'S pilot episode featured Captain Christopher Pike, not Captain James T. Kirk. Creator Gene Roddenberry asked Lloyd Bridges if he would be interested in playing Pike. Bridges didn't want to do science fiction and turned the show down. James Coburn's name was mentioned, but he was dismissed as not sexy enough. Jeffrey Hunter, who costarred with John Wayne in *The Searchers*, was given the part. Hunter's contract was only for the pilot. After it was shot, executive Herbert F. Solow and Roddenberry ran the pilot for Hunter's wife in a projection room. Hunter was supposed to have been there, but didn't show. After the screening she said that Hunter was a movie star, not a television star and would not be coming back for the series. There was a scramble to find a new captain. William Shatner was hired to play the new character, Captain James T. Kirk.

The doctor in the original pilot was named Phillip Boyce. DeForest Kelley was considered, but the part was given to John Hoyt.

Gene Roddenberry mentioned the part of Vulcan Mr. Spock to DeForest Kelley. Kelley wasn't interested in that role, but was eventually cast as Dr. McCoy instead. Martin Landau told writer Lee Goldberg that he was offered the part of Mr. Spock, but turned it down. Gene Roddenberry considered Michael Dunn to play Spock, but eventually decided the right choice was Leonard Nimoy.

Stella Stevens

Another character in the original pilot was Vina. The role was somewhat difficult to cast because it required dance skills. Gene Roddenberry suggested several actresses, including Janice Rule, Anne Francis, Barbara Eden, Diana Millay, Piper Laurie, Maggie Pierce, Anne Helm, Yvette Mimieux, Dyan Cannon, Yvonne Craig, Suzanne Pleshette, Jean Seberg and Joan Blackman. Elizabeth Ashley and Stella Stevens were other possible choices, but were already committed to films. Jane Fonda was mentioned, but wasn't interested in doing television at that time. Carol Lawrence was pregnant and therefore unavailable. Roddenberry finally decided that the right actress was Susan Oliver, who was an excellent dancer.

The November 1, 1968 episode was called "Day of the Dove." The script featured the already established character of Kor. John Colicos, who played Kor, was already committed to a movie, and was unavailable for the episode. The character was rewritten as the new character of Kang. Joseph Campanella was considered to play Kang, but Michael Ansara was eventually cast.

Carroll O'Connor was writer Jerome Bixby's first choice to play Flint in the February 14, 1969 episode called "Requiem for Methuselah." O'Connor turned the part down, and James Daly was cast instead.

Star Trek: Deep Space Nine (1993-1999)
Avery Brooks as Sisko (Gary Graham)
Rene Auberjonois as Odo (Eric Menyuk)
Armin Shimerman as Quark (Max Grodenchik)

GARY GRAHAM WAS CONSIDERED to play Captain Sisko on *Star Trek: Deep Space Nine*. Graham made it down to the final three, but lost the part to Avery Brooks. Eric Menyuk auditioned to play Odo. The part was eventually given to Rene Auberjonois, who Menyuk describes as a phenomenal actor.

Armin Shimerman and Max Grodenchik were the final two actors considered for the part of Quark. Shimerman go the job, while Grodenchik also joined the cast in the role of Rom.

Star Trek: The Next Generation (1987-1994)

Patrick Stewart as Jean-Luc Picard (Stephen Macht)
LeVar Burton as Geordi La Forge (Tim Russ)
Jonathan Frakes as William T. Riker (Bill Campbell)
Denise Crosby as Tasha Yar (Marina Sirtis)
Michael Dorn as Worf (Count Stovall)
Marina Sirtis as Deanna Troi (Denise Crosby)
Brent Spiner as Data (Eric Menyuk)
Matt Frewer as Berlingoff Rasmussen (Robin Williams)
Saul Rubinek as Kivas Fajo (David Rappaport)

STEPHEN MACHT was one of many actors considered for the role of Captain Jean-Luc Picard in *Star Trek: The Next Generation*. Very early in the production, producer Robert H. Justman and his wife were auditing a course at UCLA regarding humor in the arts. "The professor who was running the show got up and said a few words," said Justman. "He introduced the two actors who would do some cold readings of Shakespeare comedies and Noel Coward plays. There was a man and a woman. I didn't know either by name. I still don't know who the woman was because everything blew out of my head when I saw Patrick [Stewart] walk out on stage and sit down. I wasn't so sure, but when he began to talk and read his lines I just knew it. You know how those perfect moments come, when something really, really clicks. I was just stunned. I heard the first few lines from Patrick and I turned to my wife Jackie and I said, 'I think I found our new captain.'" Justman got in touch with Stewart, who was waiting to go back to London. He arranged a meeting at *Star Trek* creator Gene Roddenberry's house. "We had a wonderful conversation with him," said Justman. "Patrick said he had to go because he had to drop his car off and catch a plane for London. We walked him to the door and he drove off. We watched him go, and then Gene closed the door and turned to me and he said, 'I won't have him.' I said, 'Why not?' He refused to answer that question. It was that way for the next few months until we reached a point where we were only a few short weeks to shooting. Casting was going fine in all the other departments, all the other roles. On this one we weren't having any success. I finally decided to use a little psychology. I wasn't the only one who wanted Patrick. When my co-partner on producing, Rick Berman, joined up with us he was very excited about Patrick also, as was our casting director. The only one who didn't want him was Gene. Eventually I purposely threw a tantrum in front of everyone. 'That's it! I'm out of here! I don't want to hear Patrick's name. We've got to find our captain because we're going to start shooting in a few

Robert H. Justman on the set

weeks, so forget it!' I was using reverse psychology. Unbeknownst to me Rick was doing very much the same kind of a thing, only he wasn't throwing fits. Gene and I were so close from our years of working together that someone like my co-partner would be more effective in convincing him. We were up to our last possible candidate. He had done a reading for us. We thanked him and he left the room and closed the door behind him. It was utter silence in the room. In the room were Gene and Rick Berman and a casting director and her assistant and myself. That was all. There was silence in the room. We were stuck with a very difficult and very expensive, pardon the expression, enterprise. What were we going to do? Gene finally heaved this enormous sigh, and he turned to us. He looked at Rick and myself and he said, 'All right, I'll go with Patrick.' You'd never seen anything like this before. We all flew out of the room in every direction to get the wheels turning. I got Patrick to send for his hair piece from London, which he put on in my office. We said, 'Oh no, it's awful. Take it off!' He had to go up to get approved by the people who ran the television department at Paramount. They were thrilled. Everything just clicked right into place."

Denise Crosby originally read for the role of Deanna Troi. The character was described as tall, svelte and European. Marina Sirtis was under consideration to play Tasha Yar. Both actresses made it to the final round of auditions for Gene Roddenberry. Roddenberry loved both of them, but felt that Sirtis was better suited to the role of Deanna Troi. He cast Sirtis as Troi and Crosby as Tasha Yar.

Eric Menyuk lost the part of Data to Brent Spiner. Menyuk was cast as the Traveler in the episode called "Where No One Has Gone Before."

Count Stovall lost out to Michael Dorn for the part of Worf.

Gene Roddenberry's first choice for the part of Riker was Bill Campbell. Jonathan Frakes was another possibility for the part. Frakes auditioned seven times in a six-week period before finally landing the role.

Tim Russ read for the part of Georgi La Forge, which went to LeVar Burton instead. Russ later became a cast member on *Star Trek: Voyager*, in which he played Tuvok.

The guest role of Berlingoff Rasmussen was developed for Robin Williams. Williams was interested in doing the show, but unavailable to work when the episode was being filmed. Matt Frewer was later given the part.

David Rappaport was cast to play Kivas Fajo in the episode called "The Most Toys." Rappaport filmed for two days. He then had to be hospitalized due to an attempted suicide. Rappaport died after a second attempt not long after. The role was recast with Saul Rubinek.

Star Trek: Voyager (1995-2001)

Kate Mulgrew as Kathryn Janeway (Genevieve Bujold, Gary Graham, Nigel
Havers, Eric Pierpoint)

GARY GRAHAM AND ERIC PIERPOINT were among the actors who were
considered for the starring role of Captain Janeway on *Star Trek: Voyager*.
Although Kate Mulgrew and Nigel Havers were both strong contenders,
the part went to Genevieve Bujold instead. Bujold left after one taping.
She disliked the fast pace of television, and felt it was compromising her
as an actress. Kate Mulgrew, who had always been the runner-up, was contacted. She was thrilled, since she needed the job. A deal was made and
Mulgrew was on board as Janeway.

Stargate: Atlantis (2004-)

Torri Higginson as Elizabeth Weir
(Thea Gill)

THEA GILL AUDITIONED for
about five or six different roles on
Stargate: Atlantis, most notably for
the part of Dr. Elizabeth Weir. The
role was eventually played by Torri
Higginson.

Thea Gill

Stark Raving Mad (1999-2000)

Tony Shalhoub as Ian Stark (Alan Cumming)
Heather Paige Kent as Maddie Keller (Jessica Cauffiel)
Dorie Barton as Tess (Christine Taylor)

ALAN CUMMING was originally slated for the lead role of author Ian Stark. After many meetings and discussions Cumming finally passed. The producers had worked with Tony Shalhoub on *Wings*, and hired him to play Stark. After the pilot was shot the network heard that Alan Cumming might be interested once again. They wanted to replace Shalhoub with Cumming, but series creator Steve Levitan stuck by Shalhoub.

Jessica Cauffiel was selected to play the part of Maddie Keller. During the first week of production Cauffiel was replaced by Heather Paige Kent.

Christine Taylor and Dorie Barton tested for the part of Tess. Barton got the job.

Step by Step (1991-1998)

Staci Keanan as Dana Foster (Angela Watson)
Christine Lakin as Al Lambert (Alisan Porter)
Sasha Mitchell as Cody (David Lipper)

PATRICK DUFFY'S NAME was brought up as a possible choice for the starring role of construction worker Frank Lambert in the sitcom *Step by Step*. Series creators William Bickley and Michael Warren weren't enthusiastic about Duffy, who was just coming off a long run in the drama *Dallas*. They were looking for an actor who was very funny. Then they watched the gag reel from *Dallas*. Duffy made them laugh so hard that they didn't consider anyone else after that.

Staci Keanan and Angela Watson were both considered for the part of Dana Foster. Bickley and Warren thought that Watson was very pretty, but wanted to cast Keanan. Executive producers Thomas Miller and Robert Boyett thought Watson was the better choice. They compromised by giving the part of Dana to Keanan, and added the role of Karen Foster for Watson.

Christine Lakin.
Photo: Inda Reid

Christine Lakin's mother brought her from Atlanta to Los Angeles during a break from school, with the intention of going on some auditions, as well as just having fun. Lakin lived in Atlanta, but her agent, Barbara Cameron, was in L.A. They planned on staying for a week at the Hilton at Universal City. "While I was here, they decided to make a demo tape of me," said Lakin. "That way they had something to show. I had this monologue and I had been practicing. It's the monologue Drew Barrymore says on the stand in *Irreconcilable Differences*. Barbara pulled some strings to get somebody to film it for us so it looked really nice. So she actually brought us to the set of *Full House* [Cameron's daughter, Candace Cameron, was one of the show's stars]. They were having a rehearsal that day. So I get on the set of *Full House* and like, I'm eleven. I'm thinking to myself, 'Oh my God, I'm on the set of *Full House*!' I was so excited. I'm sitting there and the camera's there. They blocked off this little area. I start my monologue. At eleven, for some reason, I had the ability to cry on cue, and I've always been like that. I'm crying and carrying on and doing this 2-3-minute monologue. They cut and we do it another time, and that was it. At the same time (this I didn't know until much later), Bob Boyett, who produced *Step by Step* and

Full House, was upstairs at the monitor walking around and he sees this little girl on TV, on the monitor, crying, and asks someone, 'What is wrong with this little girl?' And they're like, 'Oh, it's one of Barbara's new clients. We're doing this as a favor.' And he said, 'Oh, okay, fine. No problem.' I went home, didn't think a thing of it. About a month later they had cast a girl in my role on *Step by Step* - Alisan Porter. Something wasn't going to work out with her deal. I guess they eventually parted ways. [According to Porter, at the time she needed a temporary break from show business.] This was a Wednesday. They were going to start to film the following Monday. Apparently, Bob Boyett somehow remembered, 'Who was that little girl onscreen crying?' Somebody called Barbara Cameron and they sent my tape over, and they watched my tape. So I was at home one Wednesday afternoon and my mom and dad sat me down when I got home from school and they said, 'Okay, look. Remember that tape you made? Well some producers saw it and they really want to see you for this series, and they really, really like you. Your audition's tomorrow but it's in Los Angeles.' I remember saying to my dad, 'Dad, this is ridiculous. I'm never going to book it. This is stupid! Why are we going to spend all this money to fly out to L.A.?' And my dad said, 'You don't have to do it if you don't want to. If you're not interested in it, we'll say no.' I said, 'I want to do it, but I feel horrible.' And my dad said, 'Don't worry. I've got the frequent flyer miles.' They didn't fly us out for the audition or anything. I think my parents knew more than they were telling me. They knew I was pretty close already. So my mom and I hop on a flight that night. We get to L.A. the next morning. Barbara picks us up. We go back to the hotel, shower, change, the whole thing. I remember going over to ABC Castle City, which is no longer there, which was on Avenue of the Stars. I went up to this little room. I had my sides, and I had read them over with Barbara a couple of times. I mean I got all the material that night on the airplane. And as a kid I was just so fearless. I think kids are, and I think that's what makes them great actors sometimes. I thought, 'I don't care. I'm probably not going to get it anyway.' And I went into this room with Ted Hann, who was the casting director, Bob Boyett and [executive producer] Tom Miller. I remember sitting down with them. They were the nicest men. I read the scene. They laughed a whole lot. I got up and left. They said, 'Okay, can you just wait in the lobby?' I waited in the lobby and then they called me in again, and they had me read it again. They laughed the same way. So then I went back in the lobby. Barbara said, 'If you want to see her do anything else, because they're from Atlanta, they're going to get back on a plane, just let us know now.' They said, 'No, that's great. Thank you very much.' We went back to the hotel. We didn't hear anything that night. We figured I didn't get it. No big deal. So the next morning I'm getting up, getting ready to go and the phone rings and it was my agent. She'd been trying to call us all night; the phone was off the hook. And she told me I got the pilot. This is Friday morning and we start work on Monday. They moved us from the Hilton over to the Century Plaza Hotel. It just became this whirlwind of Monday morning we're at Magic Mountain and the whole park is closed for us, and we're filming the main titles of our show at Magic Mountain. It was amazing for a twelve-year-old. Magic Mountain and roller coasters and a suite and the Century Plaza. It was crazy. I was so wide eyed and just enjoying every minute of it. I suddenly had five brothers and sisters. I had all these kids to run around with. So we spent two weeks out here. We had clothes for, maybe, three days. I remember we went to Nordstrom's and it was such a big deal 'cause my mom let me buy a pair of Guess? jeans, so I was really excited. We didn't have any clothes. We were out here for two weeks, and we filmed the pilot. I ended up having this really big part in the pilot. We didn't know what we were getting ourselves into. My mom was reading every single book she could. She was doing research. She just wanted to figure out the ins and outs of everything. Staci Keanan's mom was like, 'Staci's done pilots. They haven't gone. Don't get your hopes up.' My mom braced me for the fact that this is a great experience, but there was no guarantee. So I went home and finished sixth grade. We got a call in June that it had gotten picked up for thirteen episodes. We then had to figure out how the heck we were going to work this out. My parents just worked overtime and made it all happen for me."

About two weeks after moving to California, newcomer David Lipper got an audition for the part of Cody on *Step by Step*. "People give you an opening when you're brand new," said Lipper. He was told that his audition was great. He was brought to audition for the producers. The candidates for the part were narrowed down to just he and Sasha Mitchell. Said William Bickley, "When Sasha came in, however far out we had written the character, he took it to another galaxy, just because that was who he really was. He was one of the few people that was actually pretty much like the character on the screen. He comes in. I think he's wearing farmer's denim coveralls with no shirt. Maybe no shoes; I could be wrong about that. He's got tattoos down one shoulder. He's very charming, but you have no idea what's going to come out of his mouth. He was a hoot in the office. But he scared a couple of the producers half to death. Michael and I were very high on Sasha. We cast him because it was unpredictable." David Lipper was brought on the show in a small role in the first season. In 1996 Sasha Mitchell left *Step by Step* following his arrest for alleged domestic abuse. Lipper was then told by one of the producers, "God, we wish we'd gone with you."

In January of 2002 Sasha Mitchell appeared on the entertainment news program *Entertainment Tonight*. He said that the charges stemmed from his trying to protect his children, who he has full custody of to date.

David Lipper

Still Standing (2002-2006)

Jami Gertz as Judy Miller (Kirstie Alley, Anita Barone, Justine Bateman, Lisa
    Darr, Amy Farrington, Kathy Griffin, Jennifer Irwin, Kirsten Nelson, Ally
    Walker)

CASTING DIRECTOR DEBORAH BARYLSKI worked for four months casting the pilot of *Still Standing*. CBS wanted a name for the starring role of Bill Miller. Mark Addy, star of the film *The Full Monty*, was given the part.

CBS was very interested in Kirstie Alley to play Bill's wife Judy. Kathy Griffin auditioned, as did Ally Walker and Jennifer Irwin. Irwin failed to win the part, but was cast in the regular role of Judy's sister Linda Michaels instead. Justine Bateman, Anita Barone, Lisa Darr, Kirsten Nelson and Amy Farrington all tested for Judy, but lost the part to Jami Gertz.

Strong Medicine (2000-2006)

Rosa Blasi as Luisa Delgado (Jessica
    Alba, Roselyn Sanchez)

ROSA BLASI WAS ASKED TO READ for the costarring role of Dr. Luisa Delgado on *Strong Medicine*. The actress turned down the audition. She thought that, at 27, no one would buy her as a doctor with a 13-year-old son. She eventually changed her mind and went in for the part. Blasi got the job despite strong competition from actresses such as Jessica Alba and Roselyn Sanchez.

Rosa Blasi

Studio 60 on the Sunset Strip (2006-2007)

Matthew Perry as Matt Albie (Richard Coyle, Jeremy Northam)

JEREMY NORTHAM and Richard Coyle both tested to play writer Matt Albie on *Studio 60 on the Sunset Strip*. Neither won the part; it went to Matthew Perry instead.

Suddenly Susan (1996-2000)

Nestor Carbonell as Luis Rivera (Craig Ferguson)

THE SCOTTISH-BORN CRAIG FERGUSON auditioned to play photographer Luis Rivera on *Suddenly Susan*. Ferguson was told he didn't seem Hispanic, but was recommended for another job – Nigel Wick on *The Drew Carey Show*. Ferguson got the part of Mr. Wick, and stayed with *The Drew Carey Show* for seven years.

Summer Dreams: The Story of the Beach Boys (1990)

Michael Reid MacKay as Charles Manson (Joe d'Angerio)

JOE D'ANGERIO was offered the chance to audition for the part of Charles Manson in the 1990 TV movie *Summer Dreams: The Story of the Beach Boys*. D'Angerio ultimately decided

Joe d'Angerio.
Photo: Andrew Cooper

against auditioning, as he just didn't want to play the part. The role later went to Michael Reid MacKay.

Sunset Beach (1997-1999)

Ashley Hamilton as Cole Deschanel
(Eddie Cibrian)

Sarah Buxton

EDDIE CIBRIAN AUDITIONED for the original cast of the daytime drama *Sunset Beach*. He lost out to Ashley Hamilton. When Hamilton left the show Cibrian was called back and cast in the part.

Sarah Buxton was shooting the film *The Climb* in New Zealand when she was asked to audition for *Sunset Beach*. At the time Buxton wasn't interested in doing a soap opera. She was told that since Aaron Spelling was producing the show, it was a big deal and she should go. She went for the interview wearing a shapeless dress and flats. She was told she needed to be sexier. When she came back to meet Spelling, she wore a tight skirt, a man's shirt and carried a Chanel bag. Spelling told her, "I love what you're wearing." "I wore it for you," Buxton replied. Everyone in the room laughed. Spelling was so impressed by Buxton she was cast as Annie without having to test.

Sunset Beat (1990)

Erik King as Tucson Smith (Ving Rhames)

VING RHAMES AND ERIK KING competed for the part of undercover cop Tucson Smith. Director Sam Weisman liked Rhames, who the network rejected in favor of King.

Superboy (1988-1992)

Michael DesBarres as Adam Verrell (Miguel Ferrer)

MIGUEL FERRER was hired for the guest role of Adam Verrell on *Superboy*. Ferrer was working on another show, which went over schedule and made him unavailable to work on *Superboy*. Michael DesBarres stepped in as a replacement.

The Survivor's Club (2004)

James Remar as Roan Griffin (Dean Cain)

ROMA DOWNEY was hired to star in the 2004 TV movie *The Survivor's Club*. Downey played Jillian Hayes. Jacqueline Bisset played the supporting role of Carol Rosen. Jillian and Carol had both been raped by a serial killer. They join forces to bring down their attacker.

Dean Cain was suggested for the role of detective Roan Griffin. He turned out to be too expensive for the production. Director/producer Christopher Leitch explained the casting process for the film. "When you have someone like a Roma Downey, she's your hot ticket star. The network then was more willing to go for breakage on the Jackie Bisset character, because they really wanted Jackie. It was kind of one week in the scheduling, where as the James Remar character would have been the entire run of the show. That's where the negotiations came down to; if we get Jackie Bisset we can't go after Dean Cain."

Sybil (1976)

Sally Field as Sybil Dorsett (Audrey Hepburn, Lily Tomlin, Natalie Wood)

THE 1976 TV MOVIE *Sybil* was based on a real young woman named Shirley Ardell Mason, who developed 13 different personalities.

Natalie Wood met with writer Stewart Stern and Mason's real-life psychiatrist, Cornelia Wilbur, to discuss the possibility of her playing the title role. Stern didn't want a star for the part and turned Wood down. The actress was offended, and she and Stern didn't speak for two years. Wood's husband Robert Wagner eventually brought them back together.

The studio said that if the part was not going to be played by Natalie Wood, Audrey Hepburn had to play it. They even threatened to cancel the film without Hepburn. Hepburn was in Europe and wasn't going to agree to take the part. The studio decided that, without a star, the film was too big a risk for them to make.

Stern went to his friend Joanne Woodward's house and told her his dilemma. Woodward asked if she might be a big enough star for them. Stern asked her to play Cornelia Wilbur. Woodward told Stern that she would do anything for him and said yes. She called Lee Rich, the production supervisor, right then. With Woodward attached, the film was back on.

Lily Tomlin was considered for the part of Sybil. Sally Field's agent, Susan Smith, called every day to get Field an audition for the part. Field was fighting her image as *The Flying Nun,* a role she played on TV from 1967-1970. Field surprised everyone with her outstanding audition, and eventually won the part.

Sybil was a hit with audiences as well as with critics. The film won four Emmy Awards, including Best Special and Best Actress in a Special (Sally Field).

Tabitha (1977)

Lisa Hartman as Tabitha Stephens (Pam
   Dawber, Susan Dey, Season Hubley,
   Liberty Williams)
David Ankrum as Adam Stephens
   (Bruce Kimmel)

Bruce Kimmel

SUSAN DEY, SEASON HUBLEY and
Liberty Williams were among the
actresses vying to play the grown-up
version of witch Tabitha Stephens in
this spin-off of the 1964 sitcom *Bewitched*. Williams won the part, and
Bruce Kimmel was cast as her brother
Adam. According to Kimmel, "Williams just was not Tabitha. She was more
like Valerie Harper." He thought that Dey
and especially Hubley were much more right for the part. The pilot was
scrapped and reshot. When they approached Kimmel to work on the new
pilot he was unavailable. David Ankrum was brought in to replace him.

The two finalists for the title role of Tabitha were Pam Dawber and Lisa
Hartman. Hartman had a budding music career. ABC thought that might add
something to the show, and gave her the part.

Coincidentally, the night the pilot aired, one of the first commercials
shown was one that starred Pam Dawber.

Take Me Home Again (1994)

Craig T. Nelson as Larry (Michael Douglas)

KIRK DOUGLAS WANTED to make *Take Me Home Again* with his son,
actor Michael Douglas. The two had wanted to do a father and son

piece for many years. By the time the movie was finally ready to go into production Michael was already signed for a feature film. Kirk still wanted to do the part. He chose Craig T. Nelson to play his son. Kirk and Michael Douglas finally made their film together with the 2003 feature, *It Runs in the Family.* Also in the cast was Michael's son Cameron Douglas and mother Diana Douglas.

Tales from the Crypt (1989-1996)

David Hemmings as Mr. Stronham (Jack Palance)

THE JUNE 15, 1991 episode of the HBO anthology series *Tales from the Crypt* was called "Loved to Death." In the episode a man (played by Andrew McCarthy) gets a love potion from his landlord in order to win over his neighbor (Mariel Hemingway).

Writer/director Tom Mankiewicz wanted Jack Palance to play Mr. Stronham, the landlord. Palance's agent had a hard time finding him. When he was finally tracked down, Palance was told of the offer. He turned it down when he learned that he would have to work for scale. David Hemmings was cast instead.

Taxi (1978-1983)

Judd Hirsch as Alex Rieger (Carmine Caridi, Cliff Gorman)
Jeff Conaway as Bobby Wheeler (Cleavon Little)
Marilu Henner as Elaine Nardo (Shelley Long)
Tony Danza as Tony Banta (Charles Haid)
Randall Carver as John Burns (Jeff Conaway)
Richard Foronjy as Nick (Andy Kaufman [as Tony Clifton])
Amanda McBroom as Olivia (Michele Conaway)

THE PRODUCERS' FIRST CHOICE for the starring role of cabbie Alex Rieger was Judd Hirsch. Actor Carmine Caridi wanted the part. He called series co-creator James L. Brooks to ask for an audition, which he was granted. Caridi was told that if Hirsch turned them down, he had a good chance at the part.

Unlike the producers, ABC didn't want Judd Hirsch. They viewed him as too ethnic, and made an offer to Cliff Gorman. Gorman wasn't interested and turned it down. ABC eventually gave in and cast Judd Hirsch.

Jeff Conaway was initially brought in to audition for the part of John Burns. After Conaway read the entire script he decided the part he wanted was actor/cabbie Bobby Wheeler, then called Bobby Taylor. The producers agreed to let him try for the role. Not long after his reading Conaway was told that he was the only white actor being considered for the part. However, the producers were now interested in seeing black actors. One of the actors to audition was Cleavon Little. Conaway went back to read with Judd Hirsch. He did well, and ended up with the job.

Marilu Henner beat out Shelley Long to win the role of Elaine Nardo.

The role of cabbie/boxer Tony Banta was originally written as Irish. Charles Haid auditioned, as did Tony Danza. When Danza was cast the character was made Italian to suit him.

The December 12, 1978 episode was titled "A Full House for Christmas." In the episode taxi dispatcher Louie DePalma's brother, Nick, comes to visit. The producers gave the part to Tony Clifton. However, Tony Clifton did not really exist. He was a character of cast member Andy Kaufman's. The cast was rounded up and told that Kaufman was not going to appear in the episode, but Tony Clifton would. They were also told that, although Clifton may look like Kaufman, he was a different person. Clifton was late for work, and obnoxious on the set. People became irritated. Clifton was fired and caused a scene. According to the head of Paramount Television, Gary Nardino, Kaufman and producer Ed. Weinberger agreed that Clifton was too disruptive, and had to go. Kaufman arranged for Clifton to be fired in front of a rehearsal audience. The role was recast with Richard Foronjy, a real person.

Jeff Conaway's sister, Michele Conaway, auditioned for the part of Olivia in the February 15, 1979 show, "Bobby's Big Break." She lost the part to Amanda McBroom because the character of Olivia had to kiss Bobby Wheeler, the role her brother played. Michele Conaway got another role that week instead. She played an actress on a soap opera Bobby was working on.

Temporarily Yours (1997)
Joanna Gleason as Joan Silver (Caroline Aaron, Suzanne Pleshette)

CAROLINE AARON auditioned for the part of Joan Silver on the Debi Mazar sitcom *Temporarily Yours*. Before Aaron was even out of the room, she heard someone ask if Suzanne Pleshette was available. Aaron lost the part, not to Pleshette but to Joanna Gleason. Gleason called Aaron, who completely understood. "It's always better if someone who takes your job is talented," said Aaron.

The Temptations (1998)
Bianca Lawson as Diana Ross (Rhonda Ross Kendrick)

THE ROLE OF DIANA ROSS in the 1998 NBC movie *The Temptations* was offered to Rhonda Ross Kendrick. Ross Kendrick is Ross' daughter. She turned the role down, and Bianca Lawson was cast instead.

Texas (1980-1982)
Terri Garber as Allison Linden (Alice Barrett)

ALICE BARRETT TESTED for the part of Allison Linden in *Texas*. The role went to Terri Garber instead.

That Certain Summer (1972)

Hal Holbrook as Doug Salter (Cliff Robertson)

WRITER/PRODUCERS RICHARD LEVINSON and William Link had seen Martin Sheen in *The Subject Was Roses* on Broadway. They were impressed by his performance and cast him as Gary McClain in the ABC movie *That Certain Summer.*

The role that proved difficult to cast was the part of gay divorced father Doug Salter. A script was sent to Cliff Robertson's agent. According to Link, Robertson hated it and turned it down. Hal Holbrook was also high on their list. They sent him the script, which he thought was terrific. His wife and son also read it and encouraged him to sign on. Holbrook was nominated for an Emmy for his performance in the film.

That Girl (1966-1971)

Lew Parker as Lou Marie (Harold Gould, Groucho Marx)
Rosemary DeCamp as Helen Marie (Penny Santon)

SAM DENOFF AND BILL PERSKY worked as producers on *The Dick Van Dyke Show.* During the last few months of the show producer Danny Thomas asked them to create a show for his daughter, Marlo.

The original cast of *That Girl* included Marlo Thomas as actress Ann Marie, Ted Bessell as Donald Blue Sky, her boyfriend/agent, with Harold Gould and Penny Santon as her parents Lou and Helen Marie. ABC liked the show, but had problems with the cast. They wanted to fire Ted Bessell. There was a big discussion as to whether or not Bessell was good looking enough. "We had worked with Teddy," said producer Ronald Jacobs. "We knew him; we loved him. You talk about a likeable guy on the screen, also off the screen. We thought he would be wonderful. There were people who thought he wasn't good looking enough. You put the two together and, boy, they had great chemistry." The producers fought very hard to keep him, and were eventually successful in convincing ABC that the problem was the character, not the actor. Bessell kept his job as Donald, but the character's name was changed to Donald Hollinger. Ann's agent was now George Lester, and was played by George Carlin.

Harold Gould and Penny Santon were being replaced as Ann's parents. Word was that ABC felt that they were too ethnic. "We call it too cosmopolitan, too Mediterranean," said Jacobs. "We gave them rhythmic comedy lines, and so they were a little old country. But they were wonderful." Groucho Marx was discussed for the role, of Lou Marie, but Lew Parker was hired instead. Rosemary DeCamp was cast as Helen.

That '70s Show (1998-2006)

Laura Prepon as Donna Pinciotti (Jessica Alba, Selma Blair, Linda Cardellini, Erika Christensen, Kelly Monaco, Piper Perabo, Ellen Pompeo)
Ashton Kutcher as Michael Kelso (Jason Biggs)
Danny Masterson as Steven Hyde (James Franco, Ryan Gosling)
Kurtwood Smith as Red Forman (Micky Dolenz)

EXECUTIVE PRODUCERS BONNIE and Terry Turner found the star of *That '70s Show* at their daughter's school play. Topher Grace was a classmate of their daughter's, and was starring in the school musical. Although he had no professional acting experience, they chose him for the starring role of Eric Forman.

Laura Prepon beat out Jessica Alba, Ellen Pompeo, Kelly Monaco, Selma Blair, Erika Christensen, Linda Cardellini and Piper Perabo for the role of Eric's girlfriend, and next door neighbor, Donna Pinciotti.

Jason Biggs was considered for the role of Michael Kelso. Ashton Kutcher was another choice. Although Kutcher had very little experience when he auditioned, everyone fell in love with him. The problem was that he was already wanted for another pilot. Fox made him a straight offer, so as not to lose him.

James Franco and Ryan Gosling were both considered for the role of Steven Hyde. Danny Masterson was hired instead.

Micky Dolenz was up for the part of Eric's father Red Forman. The role was eventually given to Kurtwood Smith.

That's My Mama (1974-1975)
Ted Lange as Junior (Count Stovall)

COUNT STOVALL lost out to Ted Lange for the part of Junior on the 1974 ABC show *That's My Mama*

That's So Raven (2002-)
T'Keyah Crystal Keymah as Tonya Baxter (Charnele Brown, Jennifer Holliday)

T'KEYAH CRYSTAL KEYMAH'S competition for the role of Tonya Baxter included Jennifer Holliday and Charnele Brown.

These Old Broads (2001)
Joan Collins as Addie Holden (Lauren Bacall)

DEBBIE REYNOLDS, ELIZABETH TAYLOR and Shirley MacLaine all agreed to star in the 2001 TV movie *These Old Broads*. Reynolds' daughter, Carrie Fisher, wrote the film. Fisher's parents, Reynolds and Eddie Fisher, were divorced in May of 1959. Later that month Eddie Fisher married Elizabeth Taylor. Shirley MacLaine played a fictional version of Debbie Reynolds in the 1990 film, *Postcards from the Edge*, also written by Carrie Fisher.

Lauren Bacall's name came up as a possibility for the part of actress Addie Holden, but the role eventually went to Joan Collins instead.

3rd Rock from the Sun (1996-2001)

John Lithgow as Dick Solomon (Christopher Lloyd)

Jane Curtin as Mary Albright (Christine Baranski)

French Stewart as Harry (Lewis Black, Cedric the Entertainer, Anthony Clark, Andy Dick, Chris Elliott, Jon Favreau, Paul Giamatti, Bobcat Goldthwait, Bill Irwin, Kevin James, Tom Kenny, Carlos Mencia, Bob Odenkirk, Jeremy Piven, Rob Schneider)

Kristen Johnston as Sally (Jennifer Coolidge, Roma Downey, Jami Gertz, Mariska Hargitay, Felicity Huffman, Mary McCormack, Nicollette Sheridan, Sarah Silverman)

CHRISTOPHER LLOYD was considered for the lead role of alien Dick Solomon in 3rd Rock from the Sun. The part was later given to John Lithgow.

The original concept for the part of Harry was a Chris Farley type. Just about every overweight comedian in the country (among other types) came in to read. Andy Dick, Jeremy Piven, Kevin James, Cedric the Entertainer, Rob Schneider, Jon Favreau, Chris Elliott, Anthony Clark, Carlos Mencia, Lewis Black, Paul Giamatti, Bobcat Goldthwait, Bob Odenkirk, Bill Irwin and Tom Kenny all auditioned. Casting director Marc Hirschfeld brought French Stewart in, even though he was the wrong physical type. His reading was so good he landed the job.

Felicity Huffman, Nicollette Sheridan, Mariska Hargitay, Jami Gertz, Roma Downey, Sarah Silverman, Jennifer Coolidge and Mary McCormack all tried for the part of Sally. Kristen Johnston was flown from New York to Los Angeles three times to test for the part. She finally decided she didn't want to test anymore. Hirschfeld told her to just get on the plane one more time. She did, and was awarded the part.

Christine Baranski was a possible choice to play Mary Albright. Jane Curtin was a friend of the creators of the show, Bonnie and Terry Turner. One night Bonnie Turner called her to see if she would be interested in playing Mary. Although Curtin knew very little about the show, she said yes right away. She was happy with her decision, and has said that working on *3rd Rock from the Sun* was more fun than she could have imagined.

Third Watch (1999-2005)

Molly Price as Faith Yokas (Mariska Hargitay)
Skipp Sudduth as Sully (Miguel Ferrer)
Jason Wiles as Bosco (Eddie Cibrian)

MARISKA HARGITAY auditioned to play Officer Faith Yokas on *Third Watch*. Although Peter Roth, the president of Warner Bros. Television Production, wanted her for the part, series co-creator and executive producer John Wells didn't want such a glamorous Hollywood beauty and turned Hargitay down. Soon after, Hargitay was cast as a police officer on another show, *Law & Order: Special Victims Unit*.

Finding an actor to play Carlos Nieto proved difficult. Finally, Anthony Ruivivar came in and read. Casting director John Levey was so impressed by Ruivivar he fell out of his chair and did a Kirk Gibson home run gesture. Ruivivar was signed for the part.

Miguel Ferrer was considered for the part of John Sullivan, "Sully." Ferrer was too much of a conventional TV leading man for John Wells, who gave the part to Skipp Sudduth instead.

Eddie Cibrian tested for the role of Officer Maurice "Bosco" Boscorelli. He lost the part to Jason Wiles, but was given the role of Jimmy Doherty.

30 Rock (2006-)

Jane Krakowski as Jenna Maroney (Rachel Dratch)

Tina Fey came to fame from her job as an anchor on *Saturday Night Live's* "Weekend Update" segment. She was also the show's head writer. She later wrote the screenplay for the movie *Mean Girls*, which was produced by *Saturday Night Live's* creator Lorne Michaels. The film came out in

2004, and was a smash hit. Fey then created the TV series *30 Rock*, in which she also starred as Liz Lemon. Lemon was the head writer of a sketch comedy show not unlike *Saturday Night Live*. Her *SNL* castmate Rachel Dratch was signed for the supporting role of Jenna Maroney. Dratch even appeared in the show's promos. A decision was later made to replace Dratch with Jane Krakowski. Rachel Dratch stayed with the show, playing a different character in every episode.

thirtysomething (1987-1991)
Melanie Mayron as Melissa Steadman (Polly Draper, Rita Wilson)

THIRTYSOMETHING centered around the lives of a group of friends, all in their 30s. Melanie Mayron auditioned for the part of photographer Melissa Steadman. Series creators Edward Zwick and Marshall Herskovitz knew Mayron's

Melanie Mayron

work from the film *Girlfriends*, which had gotten her a lot of attention. She and Polly Draper were the only two actresses flying out from New York to test. They met on the plane. "They checked us in at the Century Plaza Hotel, and then the next day we went across the street to ABC," said Mayron. "In that room we were waiting and I met the other actors. Polly and I were the only ones who had other people reading for our parts. All the other parts, it was just them. The other girl that was going in for the network with me was Rita Wilson. Polly and I auditioned. I had a scene with Peter Horton. He jumped half a page of dialogue; I was sweating bullets. Then we flew back to New York. I got a call that they wanted me. Apparently they had asked Polly to play my part. They were going to give somebody else her part. She said, 'No, I really want to play this part. You should hire Melanie for that part. I knew it was a really great script. I thought, 'It won't get picked up, which is good because my friend Catlin [Adams] and I had just raised $3.5 million to do this independent film that we wrote, that we produced, that I was going to be one of the stars in and Catlin was going to direct called *Sticky Fingers*. I needed $30,000 to pay for the distribution deal for the feature, and the pilot was going to pay me exactly that. So I could just take the money and hand it to the lawyer to get the dream project off the ground. That was going to be it."

Despite what Mayron initially thought, the series was picked up. The show was a big hit. In 1989 Mayron won an Emmy for her portrayal of Melissa.

The Thorn Birds (1983)

Rachel Ward as Meggie Cleary (Kim Basinger, Olivia Newton-John, Michelle Pfeiffer, Jane Seymour)

THE ROLE OF MEGGIE in *The Thorn Birds* was so coveted that actresses such as Olivia Newton-John, Kim Basinger and Michelle Pfeiffer were willing to read. The choice was finally narrowed down to two actresses - Jane Seymour and Rachel Ward. Both actresses made screen tests. Seymour had recently had a baby. During her test, she was lying on top of Richard Chamberlain, when all of a sudden her breast milk seeped out onto his bare chest. Seymour was mortified. She lost the part to Rachel Ward, who was more able to portray the character's vulnerability.

Thou Shalt Not Kill
(1982)
Robert Englund as Bobby Collins
   (Gary Graham)

Gary Graham

GARY GRAHAM WAS CALLED in to audition for the NBC TV movie *Thou Shalt Not Kill*. At the time, Graham was trying to get a foothold in the business. He had a shot at the part of Bobby Collins, which would require four days of shooting. Graham showed up at the audition and read. He was asked to wait outside. He was later called back in to read again, and asked to wait outside again. He was called back in a third time. Graham was reading for executive producer Edgar Scherick, who Graham described as " . . . funny, unpredictable, a little intimidating and quirky." Scherick was putting during Graham's audition. Afterwards, Scherick asked him if he would mind learning other scenes. Scherick told Graham he wanted him to read for the lead role of Ray Masters. Graham read the other scenes for about an hour. He came back in the room. Scherick was still putting. Graham read. He was asked a few questions about himself, and the audition was over. Graham worried that he lost the lead role as well as the four-day role. Later that afternoon he got the news that he won the lead role. Robert Englund was cast as Bobby Collins.

Three On a Date (1978)

Forbesy Russell as Stephanie Barrington (Pam Dawber)

LESS THAN A WEEK before shooting the ABC movie *Three On a Date* the role of the flighty Stephanie Barrington was still not cast. Executive producer Ronald Jacobs and director Bill Bixby found two actresses who were under contract to the network. The network flew them out to California from New York. "We read both of them," said Jacobs. "One was marvelous. I told her manager right afterwards she was going to be a star. There was no question in my mind. But she was too much in control; the other girl was better for that role. So we got that girl." Jacobs was right about the actress he didn't hire. Later that year she won the co-starring role of Mindy McConnell on *Mork & Mindy*. The show was a smash hit, and made a star out of Pam Dawber.

Three's Company (1977-1984)

John Ritter as Jack Tripper (Billy Crystal, Barry Van Dyke)
Joyce DeWitt as Janet Wood (Valerie Curtin, Joanna Kerns)
Suzanne Somers as Chrissy Snow (Loni Anderson, Joyce DeWitt, Denise
    Galik, Joanna Kerns, Susan Lanier, Suzanne Zenor)
Audra Lindley as Helen Roper (Carolyn Jones)
Jenilee Harrison as Cindy Snow (Priscilla Barnes, Tonja Walker)

THREE'S COMPANY was based on the British show, *Man About the House*. The series ran from 1973-1976. It followed the lives of roommates Robin Tripp, Jo and Chrissy, as well as their landlords, George and Mildred Roper.

Larry Gelbart and Gary Markowitz wrote the pilot for *Three's Company*. They changed the name of Robin Tripp to Jack Bell. His roommates were the brunette Jenny and the blonde Samantha.

John Ritter auditioned to play Jack, as did Barry Van Dyke and Billy Crystal. Van Dyke remembers there was a lot of improv at his audition.

"They were checking to see if I could do Dick Van Dyke," he said. (Barry Van Dyke is Dick Van Dyke's son.) The role eventually went to John Ritter.

Joyce DeWitt and Valerie Curtin were among the actresses who auditioned for the part of Jenny. However, DeWitt thought she was better suited to the part of Samantha. She was allowed to read, but was ultimately rejected for both parts because, although she was the right age for either role, Gelbart thought she looked too young. Valerie Curtin won the part of Jenny, while Suzanne Zenor rounded out the cast as the third roommate Samantha.

The pilot was shown to ABC. It wasn't picked up for the fall 1976 season. ABC executive Fred Silverman felt that the female roommates were not working. He wanted to get new actresses for the parts. Joanna Kerns auditioned for both parts, but didn't get either one. Loni Anderson read for Chrissy (formerly Samantha). Joyce DeWitt came under consideration once again. DeWitt was under contract to the network at the time, and was given the part of Janet (Jenny). Denise Galik was cast as Chrissy. John Ritter's character was now called Jack Tripper. The actors started work on the second pilot. Things still weren't working out, and after a few days of rehearsal Galik was let go. Susan Lanier tested to replace Galik. "I was in the grocery store," said Lanier. "My agent called and said, 'Put down your groceries and get over to ABC. You're going to test for this pilot. They've fired this other actress.'" Lanier got the part. "They were already four days into rehearsal," she said. "I had to cram lines, and I had a huge part in the pilot. I had to cram and shoot in about three days. I had never had to have that kind of pressure on myself before, but I was pretty confident at the time. In retrospect, I would have been more pleased with my own performance had I had the normal week turnaround time, and not had to cram so fast. I think Suzanne Somers did a great job on her character. I only chose to look at it recently. I was disappointed in my own work. For a long time I regretted the result of that. In retrospect, as I've gotten older and wiser, I feel like everything happens for a reason, and it's just fine the way it worked out."

"What saved the show was Fred Silverman," said producer George Sunga. "Fred still had a lot of faith in the idea of *Three's Company*. He was exposed to that idea when he was at another network. Then he went over to ABC, remembered the project and just wouldn't let it die. Even though we shot the pilot with a different blonde [Lanier], it just didn't have that special chemistry necessary. It was Fred Silverman who said, 'I've got a lady I think you'd better look at,' and that was Suzanne." Silverman had seen Suzanne Somers on *The Tonight Show*, and was impressed by her. "The pilot was basically dead," said Sunga. "We had taken our shot and were not picked up until Fred Silverman said, 'Let's take another look at this.' We were quite lucky because it was now November. Executive producers Don Nicholl, Michael Ross and Bernard West said, 'If they think enough of her [Somers] then we should also do the same.' Mickey Ross is a wonderful director. He's mostly a theatrical director. He took her and he worked so well with talent that he was able to get Suzanne to understand her character and to be able to think like Chrissy. That takes great talent. We only had a couple of days to do that. In the meantime, John Ritter and Joyce met Suzanne, fell in love with her and they couldn't do enough to help her. I thought that was terrific. Finally the time came, which was only a couple of days later, that Fred Silverman said, 'Okay, bring her in. We're not going to shoot anything. Bring her in the office.' The three of the talent went in there having rehearsed the scene with Nicholl, Ross and West, and possibly even [ABC executive] Ted Bergmann. They did a live audition in Fred Silverman's office. Fred just got knocked out and said, 'We're on.'"

Three's Company premiered on March 15, 1977. The show was a huge hit, and ran for seven years.

Carolyn Jones auditioned to play Mrs. Roper, but failed to win the role. The part was eventually given to Audra Lindley. Norman Fell was hired to play her husband Stanley Roper.

In 1981 Suzanne Somers left *Three's Company* after a dispute with ABC over money. Her character was eventually written out of the show. A new character was introduced in 1980. She was Chrissy's cousin Cindy. Cindy moved in with Jack and Janet after Chrissy moved out. Priscilla Barnes auditioned for the part, but was rejected. A younger actress was sought. Tonja Walker auditioned, and came very close to getting the part. Rams cheerleader Jenilee Harrison came in to audition. She stumbled, which actually helped her get the job. The producers decided to make the character a klutz. The character of Cindy didn't work out, and a new roommate was needed. Priscilla Barnes was signed to play nurse Terri Alden. She premiered on the show in 1981 and stayed until the end of the series.

In 1979 the Ropers were spun off into their own series. A character was needed as a replacement landlord. A Don Knotts type was sought. After seeing many actors someone finally asked if anyone had called Don Knotts. Knotts was interested and took the job.

Three's Company was an audience favorite. The show survived numerous cast changes throughout the years, and remained a solid hit. It was so successful that when it finally ended, the character of Jack Tripper got his own show called *Three's a Crowd*.

Thunder Alley (1994-1995)
Diane Venora as Bobbi Turner (Felicity Huffman)

ED ASNER STARRED in *Thunder Alley* as retired stock car driver Gil Jones. Felicity Huffman was cast as Gil's daughter Bobbi Turner in the pilot. ABC didn't think she was the right choice and recast the role with Diane Venora. She shot seven episodes of the show. Everyone felt that the ideal Bobbi had not been found, so it was back to the drawing board. Robin Riker was cast and played the role until the series was canceled.

A 4 ½-year-old Haley Joel Osment auditioned for the series. Casting director Deborah Barylski described his audition as brilliant. "He was just amazing," said director Barnet Kellman. "He just amazed us from day one. You just started wanting to do bits with him. He was magic. You couldn't take your eyes off him. And as sweet as can be. I still get paternal palpitations when I see him. He was just lovely. He was pure magic. That was a gift from God. Haley Joel Osment was great at age four. He was alive and in the moment. He was listening. That's the biggest thing in acting. He was really there, he was really in the moment, he was really listening, he was really reacting. He wasn't chanting words. He wasn't singing songs. He wasn't remembering lines or doing things by rote. Sometimes, especially when you're dealing with children, the best you wind up getting is somebody who approximates the reality of a spontaneous child. But somebody who can actually perform, a real person, that's hard. And Haley had that."

Titans (2000-2001)

Victoria Principal as Gwen Williams (Jaclyn Smith)
Perry King as Richard Williams (James Brolin, Tom Selleck)
Lourdes Benedicto as Samantha Sanchez (Priscilla Garita)

JACLYN SMITH was considered for Victoria Principal's role of Gwen Williams on the prime-time soap *Titans*.

James Brolin's name was at the top of the list to play Richard Williams. Tom Selleck was also considered, but the role went to Perry King instead.

Priscilla Garita played Richard Williams' assistant Samantha Sanchez in the show's original pilot. Lourdes Benedicto later replaced her.

Titus (2000-2002)

Stacy Keach as Ken Titus (Lee Majors)
David Shatraw as Tommy Shafter (Steve Carell)

TITUS WAS BASED ON comedian Christopher Titus' real life. He played himself in the show, while Cynthia Watros was cast as his wife Erin. Lee Majors was considered for the role of Titus' father Ken Titus. The role was later given to Stacy Keach.

David Shatraw and Steve Carell were the final two actors considered for the part of Tommy Shafter. According to Fox casting executive Marcia Shulman, Shatraw gave the better reading and won the part.

Too Cool for Christmas (2004)

George Hamilton as Santa Claus (Ned Beatty, Rick Moranis, George Segal)

TOO COOL FOR CHRISTMAS tells the story of a sixteen-year-old girl who gives Santa Claus a makeover. Director Sam Irvin offered the part of Santa Claus to George Segal, but the actor didn't want to don the Santa beard. Irvin considered Ned Beatty, as well as Rick Moranis. Said Irvin, "I talked to Moranis. He's all but retired. He likes being with his family." The film was to be shown on the gay network Here TV. Paul Colishman, the head of Here TV, thought of George Hamilton. "Everybody liked the idea," said Irvin. "It seemed to take the film to a whole other level." There was even a scene in the movie where the girl takes Santa to a tanning booth!

A straight version of the film was also shot at the same time. The only difference between the two films is that in one version the girl has two fathers (Barclay Hope and Adam Harrington); while in the other she has a father and a mother (Barclay Hope and Ingrid Torrance). The straight version was called *A Very Cool Christmas*, and aired on the Lifetime network.

A Touch of Grace (1973)

Marian Mercer as Myra Bradley (K Callan)

K Callan
Photo: Don Williams

K CALLAN WAS LIVING IN NEW YORK when her agent sent her to audition for a pilot called *A Touch of Grace*. She met with the producers, but did not have to audition. She later won the part and shot the pilot. Said Callan, "I was perfectly happy for it not to go. My agent called and said the show was picked up, but I was replaced." Callan was devastated when the show hit the air and she saw the part was recast with Marian Mercer. "I called my agent and said, 'She's the same type as me!' He said, 'I guess they didn't like you very much.'" *A Touch of Grace* ended after just 13 episodes.

Touched by an Angel (1994-2003)

Roma Downey as Monica (Liza Minnelli, Tracey Ullman)

CBS' HEAD OF PROGRAMMING Jeff Sagansky suggested Liza Minnelli or Tracey Ullman for the role of angel Monica on *Touched by an Angel*. John Masius, the creator of the series, knew Roma Downey. She came in for an audition. Downey read the part with an American accent. Afterwards, he asked her to read in her native Irish accent. She was more confident that way, and her reading benefited. Not long after Downey was awarded the part. Della Reese, another of Sagansky's suggestions, was cast opposite her as fellow angel Tess.

The Tracey Ullman Show (1987-1990)

Yeardley Smith as Lisa Simpson (Nancy Cartwright)

THE TRACEY ULLMAN SHOW was a sketch comedy show. In between sketches and commercials were animated shorts featuring the Simpson family. Nancy Cartwright was called in to audition to be the voice of Lisa Simpson. She met with animator Matt Groening who created the Simpsons. Cartwright told him that although she was there to read for Lisa, she was more interested in the part of her 10-year-old brother Bart Simpson. Groening had no problem with the switch and allowed her to try. After her reading Groening offered her part on the spot.

The Simpson family was so popular that they received their own show, appropriately titled *The Simpsons*. The show debuted in 1989, and still remains in production to date. In July of 2007 the feature film *The Simpsons Movie* was released.

Trauma Center (1983)

Wendie Malick as Brigitte Blaine (Ellen Bry)

WENDIE MALICK'S COMPETITION for the part of Dr. Brigitte Blaine on *Trauma Center* included Ellen Bry. Bry lost the role, but got a job on another show set in a hospital, *St. Elsewhere*.

Trinity (1998-1999)

Jill Clayburgh as Eileen McCallister (Anne Meara)
John Spencer as Simon McCallister (Philip Bosco)

ANNE MEARA AND PHILIP BOSCO were originally cast as Eileen and Simon McCallister in the short-lived drama *Trinity*. The McCallisters were the parents of five grown children. A decision was made to replace Meara and Bosco in an effort to make the parents younger. Jill Clayburgh and John Spencer were given the parts.

TV 101 (1988-1989)

Sam Robards as Kevin Keegan (Jim Carrey, Michael O'Keefe)

MICHAEL O'KEEFE was sought for the part of teacher Kevin Keegan on *TV 101*. O'Keefe was on a trip in the Grand Canyon, but agreed to look at the script. A copy of it was air lifted to him in the Grand Canyon. Jim Carrey was also considered for the part. He auditioned, but lost out to Sam Robards.

24 (2001-)

Kiefer Sutherland as Jack Bauer (Carlos Bernard, Richard Burgi)
Elisha Cuthbert as Kimberly Bauer (Vanessa Evigan)

JOEL SURNOW came up with the idea to do a show in real time. He paired up with Robert Cochran, and together they tried to find a premise for the show. They originally came up with the idea of doing a romantic comedy, which would take place the day before a wedding. They soon realized that doing a show in real time would work much better if there were a race against time, and the stakes were high. They needed to find a reason why someone would be awake for a twenty-four-hour period. They developed the main character of federal agent Jack Bauer. Bauer had to save a presidential candidate as well as his kidnapped daughter.

Richard Burgi and Carlos Bernard auditioned to play Jack Bauer. Bernard was also asked to read for the part of Andrew Gellar. He did well and got the part, which was renamed Tony Almeida to better suit him.

Kiefer Sutherland rose to fame when he was in his 20s, appearing in films such as *The Lost Boys*, *Flatliners* and *Young Guns*. Sutherland was suggested for the part of Jack. Surnow and Cochran still thought of Sutherland as very young, and didn't think anyone would believe him as the father of a teenage daughter. They reconsidered when they were told that Kiefer Sutherland actually had a teenage daughter.

Sutherland wasn't sure if he wanted to commit to the series. A friend mentioned to him that there was a good possibility the show wouldn't get picked up, so why not do the pilot. Sutherland agreed.

24 did get picked up, and was a big hit. The show has been nominated for an Emmy for best drama series every season it's been on the air. Sutherland has been nominated for best actor every season as well. In 2006 both Sutherland and the show won the award.

Vanessa Evigan was brought in to audition for the part of Jack Bauer's daughter Kimberly. The role was later given to Elisha Cuthbert.

The Twilight Zone (1959-1964)
Rod Serling as the Narrator (Westbrook Van Voorhies, Orson Welles)

WESTBROOK VAN VOORHIES was hired to narrate *The Twilight Zone*. CBS heard his voice and decided it sounded too haughty. A search for a new narrator was on. Orson Welles was sought, but his asking price was too high. Finally, Rod Serling, the creator of the series, decided to narrate the show himself.

The Twilight Zone (1985-1987)
Kerry Noonan as Charity Payne (Justine Bateman)

THE TWILIGHT ZONE was resurrected in 1985. Justine Bateman was hired to star as Charity Payne in the November 1, 1985 episode called "A Message from Charity." The producers allegedly had a problem with her in the part. Bateman was fired and Kerry Noonan was brought in as her replacement.

Twin Peaks (1990-1991)

Walter Olkewicz as Jacques Renault
   (Chris Mulkey)

Chris Mulkey

TWIN PEAKS CO-CREATOR Mark Frost went to the University of Minnesota with actor Chris Mulkey. When *Twin Peaks* was being cast, Mulkey was asked to read for two roles: Jacques Renault and Hank Jennings. "I read the sides and didn't understand the goofy dialogue," said Mulkey. He didn't know if the show would go or not. His agent persuaded him to audition. Mulkey saw Walter Olkewicz waiting to audition. He told him, "I'm only going to read for Hank. They're going to hire you for Jacques." Mulkey was right. Olkewicz was cast as Renault, and he was hired to play Hank.

Casting director Johanna Ray liked actor James Marshall. She brought his headshot to executive producer David Lynch with the James Dean-like character of James Hurley in mind. According to Marshall, it was a bad picture. "They were about to cast somebody else," he said. "Johanna insisted - they almost had a fight." Marshall read, and eventually won the part.

Marshall stayed with *Twin Peaks* for the run of the series. After the show ended he was in demand. Unfortunately, he became very ill with colitis. He spent almost five months in the hospital. During that time he missed out on some very important auditions, including one to play a young Darth Vader in the *Star Wars* series. Marshall lost a lot of weight, and didn't look the same as people remembered. He was told he looked like a drug addict at an audition. Marshall's health has improved since then, and he is still working as an actor.

Two of Us (2000)

Jared Harris as John Lennon (Robert Carlyle, Aidan Quinn, David Thewlis)

TWO OF US IS THE FICTIONAL STORY of Paul McCartney paying a visit to John Lennon in 1976. The film's director, Michael Lindsay-Hogg, has a history with the Beatles. He directed some of their videos, as well as their last movie, *Let It Be*.

VH1 wanted actors with brand recognition to play the roles of Lennon and McCartney. Aidan Quinn was discussed early on for the role of Paul McCartney. Quinn was more interested in playing John Lennon, but was hesitant to sign for the film. He admired the Beatles very much, and didn't want to get it wrong. Robert Carlyle was approached to play Lennon, but was too busy shooting the James Bond movie *The World Is Not Enough*. David Thewlis passed on the role as well. Lindsay-Hogg saw Jared Harris in a movie in which he played a Russian cab driver. Lindsay-Hogg was convinced that the director of the film had gotten a real Russian cab driver for the part. He was very impressed when he found out it was Harris, who he was already familiar with. He signed him for the part of John Lennon. Lindsay-Hogg went back to Aidan Quinn, who finally agreed to play Paul.

After shooting was completed Aidan Quinn was on vacation with his family. As he checked in to his hotel, he looked over and saw that Paul McCartney was there as well. Soon after Quinn approached McCartney and told him that he just played him in the film. The two became friends. McCartney later saw the movie and liked it very much.

The Two of Us (1981-1982)
Mimi Kennedy as Nan Gallagher (Dixie Carter)

Dixie Carter starred as talk show host Nan Gallagher in the original pilot of *The Two of Us*. That version of the pilot never made it to television. It was redone with Mimi Kennedy replacing Carter.

The Unit (2006-)
Dennis Haysbert as Jonas Blane (James Frain, Eriq La Salle, Patrick Swayze, Mykelti Williamson) Scott Foley as Bob Brown (Kenneth Mitchell)

Audrey Marie Anderson as Kim Brown (Amy Acker, Gillian Jacobs, Charlotte Salt)

Demore Barnes as Keenan William (Gabriel Casseus, Chris Duncan)

Abby Brammell as Tiffy Gerhardt (Sarah Avery, Alexa Fischer, Sienna Guillory, Bellamy Young)

Robert Patrick as Tom Ryan (Keith Carradine, Tate Donovan, David Keith, D.B. Sweeney)

Regina Taylor as Molly Blane (Angela Bassett, Vanessa Bell Calloway, Audra McDonald, Elizabeth Pena, Gloria Reuben, Anna Deveare Smith, Lynn Whitfield, Alfre Woodard, Charlayne Woodard)

PLAYWRIGHT DAVID MAMET created the television series *The Unit*. The show followed the daily lives of a group of elite U.S. Army Special Forces officers.

Many actors were considered for the role of Sergeant Major Jonas Blane, including Patrick Swayze, Mykelti Williamson, James Frain, Eriq La Salle and Dennis Haysbert. According to casting director Sharon Bialy, Dennis Haysbert had a lot of presence, and was the best person for the part.

Kenneth Mitchell was a possibility for the part of Staff Sergeant Bob Brown. However, Scott Foley was also interested in playing the character.

Foley already had a deal with the network. He really wanted this part and came in at least twice to meet with the producers. Foley was subsequently given the job. Kenneth Mitchell was brought in to play Keith Soto in the May 9, 2006 episode called "Exposure."

Amy Acker was originally cast as Bob's wife Kim. Said Bialy, "Acker was a lovely actress; they just wanted to change the direction of the role." Charlotte Salt and Jillian Jacobs were other possible choices, but the actress who finally played the part was Audrey Marie Anderson.

Demore Barnes won the part of Keenan William despite Chris Duncan and Gabriel Casseus also being in the running.

Sienna Guillory, Bellamy Young, Alexa Fischer and Sarah Avery all lost out to Abby Brammell for the part of Tiffy Gerhardt. Mamet and executive producer Shawn Ryan liked Alexa Fischer so much that they cast her as Sophie in the episode called "Security," broadcast April 11, 2006.

Keith Carradine, David Keith, Tate Donovan and D.B. Sweeney all read for the part of Colonel Tom Ryan. However, Robert Patrick came in and gave the best reading, and won the role.

Lynn Whitfield and Regina Taylor auditioned to play Jonas' wife, Molly Blane. Also considered were Alfre Woodard, Angela Bassett, Anna Deveare Smith, Gloria Reuben, Audra McDonald, Charlayne Woodard, Vanessa Bell Calloway and Elizabeth Pena. Regina Taylor won the role.

The Untouchables (1993-1994)
David James Elliott as Paul Robbins (Tom Amandes)

CASTING DIRECTOR JANE ALDERMAN brought Tom Amandes in to read for the supporting role of Agent Paul Robbins in the 1993 version of The Untouchables. Amandes gave a very good audition. After he left the room the director and producer asked Alderman if she knew Amandes long. She said that she did. She went on to tell them that Amandes had been a student at DePaul University, and that he could do anything—Shakespeare, broad comedy, etc. They all agreed that he was also sexy. Amandes was brought back in and asked if he would come back in a day to read for the starring role of Eliot Ness. Executives from Paramount came to see Amandes audition as Ness. The producer, the director and Alderman really fought for the unknown Amandes to land the role. They were quite surprised when Paramount agreed. David James Elliott was later cast as Paul Robbins.

Jane Alderman.
Photo: Brian McConkey

Upstairs, Downstairs (1971-1975)

Lesley-Anne Down as Georgina Worsley (Jane Seymour)

UPSTAIRS, DOWNSTAIRS followed the lives of the wealthy Bellamy family, as well as their servants.

Jane Seymour and Lesley-Anne Down were the final two candidates for the part of Georgina Worsley. Producer John Hawkesworth eventually chose Down.

V (1983)

Jane Badler as Diana (Barbara Parkins)
Marc Singer as Mike Donovan (Michael Swan)
Blair Tefkin as Robin Maxwell (Dominique Dunne)

V TOLD THE STORY of aliens who came to Earth. The aliens pretended to be friendly, but eventually took control of the planet.

Barbara Parkins read for the starring role of the aliens' leader Diana. According to V creator Kenneth Johnson, Parkins' reading was too theatrical. He gave the part to Jane Badler instead.

Michael Swan read for the part of TV anchorman Mike Donovan. Although he gave a good audition, the role went to Marc Singer.

Dominique Dunne was cast as Robin Maxwell, the mother of a half alien baby. Dunne had been romantically involved with chef John Thomas Sweeney. Their relationship was abusive, so much so that when Dunne was hired to play an abused woman on *Hill Street Blues* she already had real bruises on her body. Four weeks into production on *V*, Sweeney strangled Dunne. She was brain dead, and was removed from life support days later. A shocked and sad Johnson brought Blair Tefkin in to play Robin Maxwell. Sweeney was sentenced to six years in prison for the murder of Dominique Dunne, but was released after serving two and a half years.

Vampire Bats (2005)

Tony Plana as Sheriff Herbst (Paul
    Wensley)
Brandon Rodriguez as Aaron (Bobby
    Camposecco)

PAUL WENSLEY AUDITIONED on tape to play Sheriff Herbst in the made-for-TV movie *Vampire Bats*. CBS didn't think he was right for the part, and director Eric Bross gave the part to Tony Plana instead. Wensley was also cast in the film, as Dil, an airboat operator.

Bobby Camposecco auditioned for the part of Aaron. Eric Bross felt

Paul Wensley

that Camposecco wasn't "charactery" enough to work with the other actors he cast in the film, but he liked him and wanted to find a part for him. He offered Camposecco the smaller role of Don, which the actor took. Brandon Rodriguez was given the part of Aaron.

Vega$ (1978-1981)
Robert Urich as Dan Tanna (Tom Selleck)

TOM SELLECK AUDITIONED for the starring role of Dan Tanna, as did Robert Urich. "Urich blew everyone away," said casting director Mike Fenton. "He was the guy."

Veronica Mars (2004-2007)
Kristen Bell as Veronica Mars (Amanda Seyfried, Alona Tal)
Teddy Dunn as Duncan Kane (Jason Dohring)
Charisma Carpenter as Kendall Casablancas (Heather Graham)
Alyson Hannigan as Trina Echolls (Tara Reid, Denise Richards)

KRISTEN BELL, AMANDA SEYFRIED and Alona Tal all auditioned for the title role of Veronica Mars. Seyfried was cast as Veronica's murdered friend Lily Kane instead. Kristen Bell was chosen to play Veronica. Tal, who was the runner-up for Veronica, was given the role of Meg Manning.

Jason Dohring auditioned to play Duncan. The role went not to him, but to Teddy Dunn. Dohring did join the cast. He was given the part of Logan Echolls.

Heather Graham was the second choice for Kendall Casablancas. The first choice was Charisma Carpenter, who played the part.

Denise Richards and Tara Reid were both considered for Alyson Hannigan's role of Trina Echolls.

Veronica's Closet (1997-2000)
Christopher McDonald as Bryce Anderson (Tim Matheson)

TIM MATHESON AUDITIONED to play Veronica's husband, Bryce Anderson, on *Veronica's Closet*. Christopher McDonald was chosen instead.

A Very Brady Christmas (1988)
Jennifer Runyon as Cindy Brady (Susan Olsen)

SUSAN OLSEN WAS THE ONLY cast member of *The Brady Bunch* who didn't appear in the 1988 television movie *A Very Brady Christmas*. Olsen was approached, but was unable to come to terms with the producers. Olsen was also getting married and had already made her honeymoon travel plans, which interfered with the shooting schedule. Jennifer Runyon replaced her.

The View (1997-)
Lisa Ling as Co-Host (Lindsay Brien, Rachel Campos, Monica Lewinsky, Tammy Faye Messner, Anne Marie Powell, Lauren Sanchez)

WHEN *THE VIEW* PREMIERED in 1997, the five co-hosts were Barbara Walters, Meredith Vieira, Star Jones, Joy Behar and Debbie Matenopoulos. After about two years on the show Matenopoulos was fired. She was told that audiences didn't like her. On the show one morning Barbara Walters invited Monica Lewinsky to audition for the now vacant job. Colin Powell's daughter Anne Marie Powell was interested, as was Tammy Faye Messner. Former *Real World* housemate Lindsay Brien tried out, but failed to make the cut. After months of searching the finalists were narrowed down to three: Lisa Ling, Rachel Campos (another *Real World* alum) and Lauren Sanchez. Ling was eventually chosen. She stayed with the show for about three years, and then decided to leave. Elisabeth Hasselbeck was brought in as Ling's replacement.

Both Meredith Vieira and Star Jones exited the show in 2006. Vieira left to replace Katie Couric on *The Today Show*. Rosie O'Donnell was brought in to fill the void on *The View*. O'Donnell was enormously popular on the show, but decided to leave after a year because she and the producers could not come to terms on her contract. It was announced that O'Donnell would leave the show on June 21, 2007. However, on May 23, 2007, O'Donnell and Elisabeth Hasselbeck had a heated argument on the air about comments O'Donnell made about the U.S. action in Iraq. The following day O'Donnell announced she would not return to the show.

The Waltons (1972-1981)
Michael Learned as Olivia Walton (Abby Dalton, Pat Priest)

EARL HAMNER, JR. created *The Waltons*. The show was based on his memories of growing up with his family. Hamner also served as the show's narrator.

Richard Thomas was cast as the Hamner-like character of John Boy Walton. Ralph Waite played his father John. Michael Learned beat out Abby Dalton and Pat Priest for the part of John Boy's mother, Olivia Walton.

The Waverly Wonders (1978)
Joe Namath as Joe Casey (Judd Hirsch)

"JOE NAMATH IS ONE OF the nicest people I've ever met in my life," said Bill Bickley, who created *The Waverly Wonders*. "At the time we were casting *The Waverly Wonders*, Michael Warren (my producing and writing partner at the time) and I had written the main character specifically for Judd Hirsch. Once we finished the script and NBC had had given us the go ahead to make the pilot, Judd was doing *Chapter Two* in New York. He wasn't interested in ever doing television, not knowing that *Taxi* would come along. But Judd was out. So we began a casting search. I swear we must have met every man in his thirties in town. Sitting around the office one day, it was myself, my partner Michael Warren, an executive producer named Marc Merson and a network executive. We're sitting around not having been able to find anybody to play the lead in this series that NBC's dying to put on the air, and I made a joke. Joe Namath at that point in time was sitting on the bench for the Rams, very clearly basically sitting out his last year in professional football. The joke went something like this, 'How about Joe Namath? He'll need a job next year.' Everybody in the room laughed. Great athlete, but not an actor. So we laughed and all went home. Well, the network executive didn't go straight home. He went straight to the network and pitched the idea. They loved the idea. We went from looking at experienced actors, to the network and studio getting very excited about the idea of casting Joe Namath in the role. Lorimar and NBC made a blind deal with Joe because his representation said they wouldn't even tell him about the offer until it was a firm deal because they didn't want him to experience disappointment. The deal was made. It was an enormous deal for movies and money guarantees and stuff like that. I'm very happy for Joe that he got such a great deal. And that's how Joe Namath came to play the lead in that series. And I will hand it to him. He'd never acted, and I have never seen anybody work so hard to try to learn on the job as Joe did."

Welcome Back Kotter (1978)
Marcia Strassman as Julie Kotter (Farrah Fawcett, Susan Lanier)
Ellen Travolta as Mrs. Horshack-O'Hara (Doris Roberts)

WELCOME BACK KOTTER starred Gabe Kaplan as high school teacher Gabe Kotter. Farrah Fawcett and Susan Lanier were both considered for the part of Kotter's wife Julie. Fawcett tested, but the role was given to

Marcia Strassman instead. Lanier was brought on the show as a guest star. She played Bambi, a new student who pretended to be a California surfer girl, on two episodes.

John Travolta starred on *Welcome Back Kotter* as Vinnie Barbarino. Two of the producers of the show had worked as actors in the Broadway production of *Gypsy* with Travolta's sister Ellen Travolta. They asked John if Ellen was available to audition for the show, for the part of Arnold Horshack's mother. Travolta tested for the part four times. ABC wasn't familiar with her, and wanted to hire Doris Roberts instead. Producer James Komack went to bat for Travolta, and she got the part. She later bought Komack a little gold bat to say thank you.

The West Wing (1999-2006)

Rob Lowe as Sam Seaborn (Bradley Whitford)
Allison Janney as C.J. Cregg (Janel Moloney, CCH Pounder)
Richard Schiff as Toby Ziegler (Eugene Levy)
Bradley Whitford as Josh Lyman (Timothy Busfield)
Martin Sheen as Josiah Bartlett (Alan Alda, John Cullum, Bob Gunton, Dakin
    Matthews, Sidney Poitier, Jason Robards)

WRITER AARON SORKIN was scheduled for a meeting with producer John Wells. Sorkin thought it was just a general meeting, but soon realized that Wells expected to hear a pitch for a series. Off the cuff Sorkin said he had an idea to do a show about senior staffers at the White House. Sorkin was offered a deal almost immediately.

According to producer Llewellyn Wells, the role of President Josiah Bartlett was originally intended to be a secondary character. The show was to be about the White House staff. The first offer to play the president went to Jason Robards, who passed. "I think I was one of the first people to read for the president on *The West Wing*," said Dakin Matthews. "I knew

I wasn't going to get it. I read very well and the casting director came out and said, 'No one's going to read better than that,' but you could tell from the role that it's a star turn. So I knew I was not going to get it. I went in determined to give the best possible performance I could, knowing full well that it didn't make a damn bit of difference. At least I did my best."

Casting director John Levey showed Aaron Sorkin and pilot director Thomas Schlamme actors John Cullum and Bob Gunton. Both men were tested for Bartlett, but neither fit the part quite right. Alan Alda and Sidney Poitier were also considered. Once the producers learned Martin Sheen was available and interested a decision was made to turn the part of Josiah Bartlett into a lead role.

Film star Rob Lowe was up for the part of Sam Seaborn. Between Lowe's audition and his getting the job, there was a period of time where it seemed like he wasn't going to do the show. Bradley Whitford was considered to play Sam, although he was also considered for the part of Josh Lyman. If Whitford was cast as Sam, then Timothy Busfield was a strong contender for the part of Josh. Lowe eventually was cast as Sam, and Whitford as Josh. Busfield got the recurring role of Danny Concannon, and was with the show on and off for the entire run.

Eugene Levy auditioned for the part of Toby Ziegler. "He gave the best audition I've ever seen that didn't get the job," said Levey. "His audition was extraordinary. He was brilliant. He was funny beyond the scope of the show." In the end the decision was made to go with Richard Schiff instead. Schiff had worked for executive producer John Wells when he did a guest role on Wells' show *ER*.

Janel Moloney read for the part of C.J. She was cast as Donna Moss instead. The final two candidates for the part of C.J. were Allison Janney and CCH Pounder. The role was given to Janney. Pounder was brought in as a guest star during the series' first season.

Where Are My Children? (1994)

Marg Helgenberger as Vanessa Meyer Vernon Scott (Farrah Fawcett)

WHERE ARE MY CHILDREN? told the true story of a single mother who was separated from her children for 25 years after being arrested by the FBI. Farrah Fawcett was considered for the starring role of the mother (Vanessa Meyer Vernon Scott), but the part eventually went to Marg Helgenberger.

Who Do You Trust? (1956-1963)

Johnny Carson as Host (Dick Van Dyke)

EDGAR BERGEN WAS THE HOST of the CBS nighttime game show *Do You Trust Your Wife?* According to producer Don Fedderson, the quiz show scandals forced all the audience participation shows off the air. The show was then moved to ABC, and aired in the daytime under the new title *Who Do You Trust?* Fedderson needed a new emcee. Dick Van Dyke and Johnny Carson were both considered. Carson was chosen for the job. The show's announcer was none other than Ed McMahon. After leaving *Who Do You Trust?* in 1962, Carson and McMahon worked together on *The Tonight Show*, where they stayed for thirty years.

Who's the Boss? (1984-1992)

Tony Danza as Tony Micelli (Mark Arnold, Hart Bochner, Roscoe Born, Jeff
Conaway, Richard Cox, Bobby Di Cicco, Robert Dubac, Jeff Goldblum,
Jerry Houser, Cooper Huckabee, John Kapelos, Paul Land, Terrence
Mann, Ben Masters, Cyril O'Reilly, Judge Reinhold, Charlie Rocket, Barry
Van Dyke, Todd Waring)

Judith Light as Angela Bower (Kirstie Alley, Adrienne Barbeau, Ellen Barkin,
Belinda Bauer, Christine Ebersole, Alexa Hamilton, Catherine Hicks,
Dee Hoty, Andrea Howard, Gail Matthius, Cindy Morgan, Randi Oakes,
Catherine O'Hara, Cristina Raines, Ellen Regan, Mimi Rogers, Elizabeth
Savage, Jane Seymour, Kathleen Turner, Sean Young)

Katherine Helmond as Mona Robinson (Leslie Easterbrook)

Danny Pintauro as Jonathan Bower (David Faustino)

ABC WAS INTERESTED IN TONY DANZA to star in their upcoming sitcom,
Who's the Boss? In October of 1983 Danza's representatives and ABC started
negotiations. A deal was just about finalized when Danza's manager, Jerry
Weintraub, called casting executive Eve Brandstein. He told her that Danza
would not be doing the series. Brandstein knew Danza personally, and called
him at home. The actor was hesitant to commit to the show. ABC decided
to look for other candidates to play the former baseball player-turned-house-
keeper, Tony Micelli. The list of possible choices included Danza's former *Taxi*
costar Jeff Conaway, as well as Jeff Goldblum, Judge Reinhold, Charlie Rocket,
Hart Bochner, Jerry Houser, Terrence Mann, Barry Van Dyke, Roscoe Born,
Bobby Di Cicco, John Kapelos, Todd Waring, Mark Arnold, Robert Dubac,
Ben Masters, Cooper Huckabee, Paul Land, Richard Cox and Cyril O'Reilly.
Series creators Martin Cohan and Blake Hunter only wanted Danza, who fi-
nally came around and agreed to play Tony.

Many actresses were considered for Tony's boss Angela Bower, including Jane Seymour, Kirstie Alley, Ellen Barkin, Mimi Rogers, Sean Young
and Adrienne Barbeau. Judith Light auditioned, as did Randi Oakes,

Cristina Raines, Gail Matthius, Dee Hoty, Alexa Hamilton, Ellen Regan, Andrea Howard and Elizabeth Savage. The candidates were narrowed down to four: Light, Raines, Regan and Hamilton, all of whom had screen tests with Tony Danza on October 20, 1983. The clear choice was Judith Light. However, Light had already committed to two other pilots for ABC. She had to put one show in first position, which means that if the show in first position were picked up she would no longer be available for the other two series. She had no idea which to choose, and wound

A grown-up Jonathan Halyalkar.

up putting a show called *Staff of Life* first. After her screen test she knew she made a mistake. When she learned that *Staff of Life* was not picked up she was extremely happy to be able to join the cast of *Who's the Boss?*

The character of Mona was originally conceived as Angela's sister. Many actresses auditioned, including Leslie Easterbrook. Katherine Helmond was pitched for the role. Eve Brandstein came up with the idea of making Mona Angela's mother. Cohan and Blake thought it was a good idea, and Helmond came on board.

Danny Pintauro's competition for the part of Angela's son Jonathan included David Faustino. Faustino later came to fame playing Bud Bundy in *Married...With Children*.

A five-year-old Jonathan Halyalkar joined the cast in 1990 as Billy Napoli. According to Halyalkar there was a lot of competition for the part. Halyalkar had worked with the director, Tony Singletary, before on *The Cosby Show*. Halyalkar was advised to be natural. He did well, and got the job. Halyalkar said working on *Who's the Boss?* was a very positive experience.

Will & Grace (1998-2006)

Eric McCormack as Will Truman (Bill Brochtrup, Sean Hayes)

Debra Messing as Grace Adler (Pamela Adlon, Kristin Dattilo, Marin Hinkle, Nicollette Sheridan)

Sean Hayes as Jack McFarland (Peter Paige)

Megan Mullally as Karen Walker (Leigh Allyn Baker, Judy Gold)

Wendie Jo Sperber as April (Cyndi Lauper)

BILL BROCHTRUP AUDITIONED to play the lead role of lawyer Will Truman. The part eventually went to Eric McCormack. Brochtrup wondered whom they would find to play the supporting part of Will's outrageous friend Jack McFarland. Brochtrup felt that he wouldn't have known what to do with the role.

Sean Hayes starred as Billy, a gay photographer, in the film *Billy's Hollywood Screen Kiss*. The movie was seen by the production team of *Will & Grace*. They wanted Hayes to read for the show. Hayes was initially interested in playing Will, but was eventually convinced that the role he was right for was Jack. Hayes' audition was impressive, and he was awarded the part.

Peter Paige also auditioned to play Jack. Said Paige, "The week I went in for my first audition they were taking Sean to network. And when I went in they said, 'We love you, and we will take you to network if the guy that we're taking doesn't fly. So there we go. The rest is history." Paige made a guest appearance on the show in the second season.

Nicollette Sheridan, Pamela Adlon, Marin Hinkle and Kristin Dattilo auditioned for the part of Grace Adler. The role was given to Debra Messing.

Judy Gold and Leigh Allyn Baker auditioned to play Grace's secretary Karen Walker. The part was offered to Megan Mullally, who passed. She changed her mind after a lot of convincing. Leigh Allyn Baker was cast in the recurring role of Will & Grace's friend Ellen.

The February 2, 1999 episode was entitled "My Fair Maid-y." Cyndi Lauper was hired for the part of April, Will and Grace's cleaning lady. There were problems with the story and the script had to be rewritten. Lauper's role was made smaller. She was let go and replaced by Wendie Jo Sperber.

Wings (1990-1997)

Tim Daly as Joe Hackett (Nick Cassavetes, Bryan Cranston, Boyd Gaines, Daniel Stern)

Steven Weber as Brian Hackett (Hank Azaria, George Clooney, David Duchovny, Greg Germann, Fisher Stevens)

Crystal Bernard as Helen Chapel (Marcia Cross, Lisa Darr, Gina Gershon, Peri Gilpin, Marcia Gay Harden, Mariska Hargitay, Catherine Keener, Julia Louis-Dreyfus, Julianne Moore, Megan Mullally, Rita Wilson)

BRANDON TARTIKOFF, THE HEAD of NBC, thought that *Wings* had great potential. The series focused on brothers Joe and Brian Hackett. The brothers were pilots who ran a one-plane commuter airline called *Sandpiper Air*. Tartikoff knew that it would be difficult finding two great leading men for the show.

Bryan Cranston, Daniel Stern, Nick Cassavetes and Boyd Gaines auditioned to play older brother Joe. Gaines tested, but the producers were unable to make a deal with him. The part was later given to Tim Daly.

Fisher Stevens, Hank Azaria, George Clooney, David Duchovny and Greg Germann read for the part of Brian, which was given to Steven Weber instead.

The part of mechanic Lowell Mather was written for Thomas Haden Church. Church had done a guest spot on the producers' other show, *Cheers*, as a deadpan friend of Carla's husband Eddie (played by Jay Thomas). "He blew everyone away so much - I think it was his first job - that they created this role for him," said casting director Jeff Greenberg.

The part of Helen Chapel was originally written as a Greek immigrant's daughter. Peri Gilpin auditioned. She dressed down for her reading, which she thought was right for the character. After her audition Jeff Greenberg told Gilpin that she had to look better. She was brought back, and this time she looked the part. Gilpin auditioned for the show eight times in six weeks. According to Greenberg, although the producers liked Gilpin very much, NBC rejected her saying, "She's not a cover of *TV Guide*."

Other actresses, such as Lisa Darr, Catherine Keener, Gina Gershon, Julia Louis-Dreyfus, Mariska Hargitay, Marcia Cross, Megan Mullally, Rita Wilson, Julianne Moore and Marcia Gay Harden, also read for the part.

"We had our whole cast and we couldn't find the girl," Greenberg said. "We turned down Peri. We brought other ladies to the network. They wouldn't approve anyone. The sets were built, the actors were hired and we had to wait. We couldn't shoot the pilot. We really had to keep looking until we were out of actors. And then they said, 'We have to reconceive the role. We're not finding a Greek actress.' We kept looking and looking. We saw actors who we weren't sure if they were available. We finally saw Crystal Bernard, who had done two other pilots already. When you test people that have done other things that they have a hold on, you take them in second position or third position. It's very dangerous because if those shows get picked up you're screwed. You can't use the actress. We lucked out and she wasn't picked up for those other two shows. She worked out great. She was really fantastic."

The Winner (2006)

Linda Hart as Irene (Julie Hagerty)

ROB CORDDRY STARRED as Glen Abbott in *The Winner*. Julie Hagerty was originally cast as Glen's mother Irene. After Fox saw the pilot they wanted to take the character in another direction, and recast the role with Linda Hart.

Wiseguy (1987-1990)

Ken Wahl as Vinnie Terranova (John Travolta)
Kevin Spacey as Mel Profitt (Gary Cole)
Paul Winfield as Isaac Twine (Frank Sinatra)
Mick Fleetwood as James Elliot (Bob Dylan)

WISEGUY ORIGINATED as a two-hour TV movie directed by Rod Holcomb. Co-executive producer Les Sheldon thought of John Travolta for the starring role of undercover agent Vinnie Terranova. "We were both staying in the same hotel," said Sheldon. "We were standing in the lobby and I went over and introduced myself. He's just the nicest, sweetest guy I've ever met in my life, and a wonderful actor. This was before *Pulp Fiction*. It didn't go over well with the network. They didn't want him. They figured, 'He's doing *Look Who's Talking*, he was in *Welcome Back Kotter*, he was kind of a

Les Sheldon

teen idol with *Grease*, he's not a star, he doesn't have the edge.' I said, 'I tell you, this guy is a wonderful, wonderful actor.' It went on and on. I was kind of told, 'There's no reason to bring him up anymore. We think he's really good for certain things, but he's going a different route now and he's not the type.' I don't know whether John would have done it or not. I never asked him, but I knew he was going to be available, and I just loved him and I really believe that he was this wonderful actor. We talked about it a little bit because he asked me what I was doing and I told him. He said, 'That's fascinating.' Ultimately, a year later, Quentin Tarantino grabbed him. That's all history."

Ken Wahl came in to meet for the part. "We were sitting in Steve Cannell's office," said Sheldon. "There was this big, hulky guy sitting there with his head down, kind of mumbling. I thought it was an act. I liked Ken, but I didn't know anything about whether or not he could pull of this character or not. The network was a little hesitant because they couldn't quite figure him out. There were a couple of other people that were up for it, but Ken ended up getting the nod. He had this kind of mysterious charisma." CBS loved the dailies, and decided to make *Wiseguy* a regular series.

Kevin Spacey and Joan Severence were brought in as brother and sister Mel and Susan Profitt. Gary Cole was originally scheduled to play Mel. He fell ill, and had to be replaced by Spacey.

Frank Sinatra loved *Wiseguy*. "He was real interested in coming in," said Les Sheldon, "but the schedule was tough for him. He was going to go on tour. It was the closest I ever came to working with Frank Sinatra. He loved the show, and watched it every week. He was a big fan. So when I heard that I took advantage of it and made a phone call. But we couldn't work it out." The role was later given to Paul Winfield.

Mick Fleetwood was cast as James Elliot. "Those were the days, although we didn't know, Mick didn't really talk," said Sheldon. "It was supposed to be Bob Dylan. Dylan bailed out at the last minute, so we went to Mick Fleetwood. I didn't know he wasn't talking. So we rewrote the part for this silent weird guy. He was wonderful!"

Without a Trace (2002-)

Marianne Jean-Baptiste as Vivian Johnson
  (Kimberly Scott)

Tony-nominated actress Kimberly Scott auditioned to play FBI investigator Vivian Johnson. The role eventually went to Marianne Jean-Baptiste. Scott had no problem with the decision, and referred to Jean-Baptiste as a great actress.

Kimberly Scott
Photo: Elizabeth Tobias

WKRP in Cincinnati (1978-1982)

Gary Sandy as Andy Travis (Ross
　Bickell)
Howard Hesseman as Johnny Fever
　(Dick Libertini)
Gordon Jump as Arthur Carlson
　(Roddy McDowall)
Loni Anderson as Jennifer Marlowe
　(Susan Lanier)
Frank Bonner as Herb Tarlek (Howard
　Hesseman, Rod McCary)

Frank Bonner

WKRP IN CINCINNATI was a work-
place comedy that took place at a radio station. Roddy McDowall was considered for the part of general manager
Arthur Carlson. McDowall didn't sign for the show, and Gordon Jump
played the part instead.

Dick Libertini was cast as DJ Johnny Fever. Libertini got a movie and
dropped out of the show.

Susan Lanier was approached to test for the part of receptionist Jennifer Marlowe. She had to turn the audition down, because she'd already accepted the role of Sandi Chandler on the Ned Beatty series *Szysznyk*. Loni
Anderson won the part of Jennifer.

WKRP in Cincinnati was actor Frank Bonner's big break, although he
had been working steadily as an actor for nine years already. "The original
concept of [ad sales manager] Herb was not what ultimately wound up on
the television screen," said Bonner. "He was really a good-looking, 6', chis-
eled featured kind of lady killer who came on too strong, etc. When I walked
in to my first audition and I saw this whole room full of Marlboro looking

guys, I thought, 'Hmm. Either I'm at the wrong audition or maybe I've got a chance at this because I'm the only character actor in here. In the first phase it came down between myself and a good friend of mine, Rod McCary. He had a pretty good background. A good-looking guy; that leading man type. But interestingly enough, it came down between he and I. In the meantime, Rod got another pilot, one across town at MGM, *Mother, Jugs and Speed*, from the film. He got that as well. They decided to go with Rod on *WKRP* 'cause he had a track record and I was coming off commercials here and there and one-day jobs on different series. He was a little more high profile than I was, and so they went with him. He went across, like I said, and got the other job as well. He essentially went, 'Hmm, *WKRP* or *Mother, Jugs and Speed*. What do I want to do?' After a little discussion with himself he figured that *WKRP* was not going to go, and that *Mother, Jugs and Speed* would. He opted for the other and I came in, and there I was. But what I think is even more interesting about the role of Herb is that originally, before they went the other route with regard to the leading man type, Howard Hesseman (who played Dr. Johnny Fever) was initially approached to do Herb. He and Hugh Wilson, who created the show, knew each other because they'd worked together on *The Bob Newhart Show*. Hugh had said to Howard, 'Hey, I'm doing a pilot. Look at the role of Herb. I think you'd be good for it.' He read it and said, 'You know I don't particularly care for this role of Herb, but I do like Johnny Fever.' And Hugh said, 'We've already got a Johnny Fever.' Howard passed. The guy opted for a movie of the week. So then Hugh called Howard and said, 'Come in and read this and let me see what it sounds like.' Howard ended up with the Johnny Fever role and I came in, essentially, if you will, in third place in the casting!"

Ross Bickell was called back three times for the part of program director Andy Travis. Gary Sandy was one of six actors who tested for the role. Wilson and Grant Tinker were debating about two of the other actors when Tinker's then-wife, Mary Tyler Moore, came in. She asked to see the tests of all six men. Her choice was Gary Sandy, who got the job.

Working Girl (1990)
Sandra Bullock as Tess McGill (Nancy McKeon)

MIKE NICHOLS DIRECTED the 1988 film *Working Girl,* which starred Melanie Griffith as wronged secretary Tess McGill. Harrison Ford played her love interest, businessman Jack Trainer, while Sigourney Weaver was cast as her evil boss Catherine Parker. The film was a smash hit and was nominated for six Academy Awards.

NBC decided to develop the film for television. Nancy McKeon was originally cast in the starring role of Tess McGill. She left the show and was replaced by an unknown Sandra Bullock. Producer/director Matthew Diamond thought that Bullock's audition was fantastic. In fact, he said that he had never before or since seen a better network audition. Despite Bullock's talent, the series was not a hit. It lasted just twelve episodes. Bullock became a big star a few years later with her breakthrough role in the film *Speed.*

The X-Files (1993-2002)
David Duchovny as Fox Mulder
     (Christopher Cass, Kevin
     Sorbo)
Gillian Anderson as Dana Scully
     (Jill Hennessy, Cynthia
     Nixon)
Robert Patrick as John Doggett
     (Clive Owen)

PRODUCER CHRIS CARTER wanted to make a scary show. The result was *The X-Files.* He

Christopher Cass

pitched the series twice before the Fox network bought it. The two lead characters were Fox Mulder and Dana Scully. Mulder was Carter's mother's maiden name, while Fox was the name of someone he grew up with. The name Scully came from L.A. Dodgers announcer Vin Scully, who Carter listened to growing up. Mulder and Scully were FBI agents. Carter was adamant that they should not be romantically involved.

Kevin Sorbo auditioned to play Fox Mulder, as did Christopher Cass. Cass read the script and thought it was great. He even thought that it was too good for network television. Cass was called back, but eventually lost the part to David Duchovny.

Gillian Anderson's competition for the part of Dana Scully included Cynthia Nixon and Jill Hennessy. However, Anderson's reading had the seriousness and intensity Carter was looking for. He told the network that the only actress he would make the series with was Anderson. Carter was persuasive, and Anderson was hired.

A new character named John Doggett was introduced when David Duchovny left the series. Casting executive Marcia Shulman had seen the movie *Croupier*. She sent the film's star, Clive Owen, to see Chris Carter, saying he was the guy for the part. "Chris just didn't see Clive in the role," she said. The part was eventually given to Robert Patrick.

A Year in the Life (1986-1988)

Wendy Phillips as Anne Gardner Maxwell (Karen Landry)

Karen Landry auditioned to play Anne Gardner Maxwell in *A Year in the Life*. Landry got the smaller part of Roseanne instead, while Wendy Phillips was cast as Anne.

The Yellow Rose (1983-1984)

Cybill Shepherd as Colleen Champion (Priscilla Presley)

CYBILL SHEPHERD beat out Priscilla Presley for the part of 29-year-old widow Colleen Champion in *The Yellow Rose*.

Yes, Dear (2000-2006)

Liza Snyder as Christine Hughes (Judy Gold)
Mike O'Malley as Jimmy Hughes (Brian Haley)

JUDY GOLD WAS CONSIDERED for the part of Christine Hughes on *Yes, Dear*. The role was eventually given to Liza Snyder instead.

Brian Haley was asked to audition for the part of Christine's husband Jimmy. Haley didn't think the show was right for him and said no. The role was later given to Mike O'Malley.

The Young and the Restless (1973-)

Peter Bergman as Jack Abbott (Jeff Trachta)
Jay Bontatibus as Tony Viscardi (Ricky Paull Goldin)

TERRY LESTER ORIGINATED the role of Jack Abbott in 1980. Lester stayed with *The Young and the Restless* through 1989. When he left, Jeff Trachta auditioned to replace him as Jack Abbott. The producers thought that Trachta would be better suited to the role of Thorne Forrester on their other show *The Bold and the Beautiful*. He was cast as Thorne, while the part of Jack went to Peter Bergman.

Vivica A. Fox played the part of Stephanie Simmons in 1995. The wife of a producer of the upcoming film *Independence Day* saw Fox on the show. She suggested her for the role of stripper Jasmine Dubrow in the movie. Fox read for the film six times, and finally got the job.

Nick Scotti originated the character of Tony Viscardi in 1996. Jay Bontatibus auditioned when the show was recasting the role. "I auditioned in New York. They put me on tape," he said. "They sent the tape to L.A. [Casting directors] Marnie Saitta and Meryl O'Loughlin went to watch the tape, and the machine ate it! They sent the machine with the tape in it out to be fixed." In the meantime, O'Loughlin and Saitta put together a group of actors to be tested for the part. They finally got the machine back and watched the tape. Bontatibus got a two day notice for the screen test. "Marnie couldn't have been more helpful," said Bontatibus of Saitta. "She was really on my side. She tries to get the best out of everybody." Six actors were tested, including established daytime star Ricky Paull Goldin. Jay Bontatibus won the part.

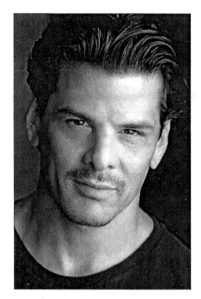

Jay Bontatibus.
Photo: theoandjuliet.com

Zorro (1957-1959)

Jolene Brand as Anna Maria Verdugo (Shirley Knight)

SHIRLEY KNIGHT lost out to Jolene Brand for the part of Zorro's love interest Anna Maria Verdugo.

Zorro (1990-1993)

James Victor as Jaime Mendoza (Rene Enriquez)

Efrem Zimbalist, Jr. as Don Alejandro de la Vega (Henry Darrow)

JAMES VICTOR WON THE PART of Sergeant Jaime Mendoza in the 1990 series *Zorro* over Rene Enriquez. Enriquez is best known for his work on Hill Street Blues.

Henry Darrow was offered the role of Zorro's father, Don Alejandro de la Vega. At the time Darrow was working on the soap opera Santa Barbara. He considered taking the job on Zorro, but ultimately decided against relocating to Spain (where the show was shot) from California. Efrem Zimbalist, Jr. was later cast. When Zimbalist left the show, Darrow was approached again. His contract with the soap was up and they wouldn't tell him definitively whether or not they were going to pick up his option. This time around Darrow chose Zorro.

Random Quotes

"On TV women can't have a best friend with the same color hair as her." - Caroline Aaron, actor

"The job usually goes to whoever's job it's supposed to be."-Peter Paige, actor

"You never know. You do your best. How people relate to an individual is intangible."- Salvatore Lanucci, CBS

"You're going to get the part you're supposed to get. I don't care if you're in a hole someplace, they're going to find you and you're going to get the part. And if you're not supposed to get the part all you're going to do is make an idiot of yourself trying to get the part because you're not going to get it." -Kelli Maroney, actor

"The difference between one actor and another is less than you'd think."-David Black, producer

"TV shows become hits generally because an actor emerges."-Kim Weiskopf, writer

"Usually one actor gives the role a life no actor has given it."-William Bickley, producer

"Final decisions are about who mixes with who."-Missy Crider, actor

"It usually becomes clear who the actor should be."-Casey Childs, director

Robert Ginty

"It's like dating; it's easy to rule people out, harder to rule people in."-Ellen Bry, actor

"So many actors come in the room and try to be clever, and I was as guilty of that as the next one. Trying to be clever or trying to punch up the material or comment on the material, trying to make it either funnier or not doing the words as written. The writers, who are generally the producers in television, are the guys who wrote those words and they want to hear the words that they wrote in the room at 2:00 in the morning. They don't want to hear your paraphrased version of it. It's a big no-no to come in and try to paraphrase or embellish the material. You can embellish it with business or moments that's great. But don't embellish it with your own words."-Wil Shriner, director

"Actors rarely score on a taped audition."-Tony Thomas, producer

"If somebody won't read, it sets off all kinds of bells and whistles."-Linda Laundra, director

"The last thing you want to do is go in and look desperate. That does not sit well."-Micky Dolenz, actor

"If someone goes off the script, they've lost the part." -Kim Weiskopf, writer

"It's more a matter of luck; timing and circumstance. Actors shouldn't

Robert Joy
Photo: Lorenzo Hodges

over prepare. Be as confident as you can under difficult circumstances." Robert Ginty, director

"What you're trying to do is go in there and assure these guys they don't have to worry about this part anymore."-Robert Joy, actor

"You have to have the ability to morph."-Billy Parrott, actor

"Come in with some definite choices and commitment to what you're going to do, and then stay with it. If we want to see less it's better to say, 'Hey, could you just take it down a notch,' as opposed to trying to say, 'Hey, could you bring it up two notches?' Generally it doesn't go up, but it does come down."-Wil Shriner, director

"My goal is to do well in the room and not feel like an asshole." -Pamela Adlon, actor

"They have in their mind's eye what they're looking for. It's very important to be personable. People will remember that. Very often you won't book that gig, but they will remember you and bring you back."-Micky Dolenz, actor

"I remember bringing in favorites like Jack Nicholson. It almost got me fired. They didn't like his style of acting."-Fred Roos, casting director/producer

"No matter how big you are, you almost always have to audition."-Conrad Janis, actor

"I always tried to find the best actor that I could. I didn't care whether he was important or not."-Paul Bogart, director

"I was watching The Tonight Show one night and Bob Saget was on. I liked him a lot. I called the network and said, 'I would like to use Bob Saget.' Oddly enough, one of the people at the network said, 'Who's Bob Saget?' He was already on *Full House* for a year! These things happen."-Vin DiBona, producer (on choosing a host for *America's Funniest Home Videos*)

"A lot of times the best actors don't get the roles. It's who's hot at the time."-Judith A. Strow, casting director

"I've always believed in the importance of casting. There's nothing more important than an actor who gets what you've written, and some give you more."-Kim Weiskopf, writer

"After casting the lead, the rest of casting is easy."-Frederick Muller, producer

"99% of all shows are cast at the last minute."-Arthur Weingarten, producer

"Casting has very little to do with talent. Choices are made because the director or producer feels intuitively or subjectively that one actor is better for the role."-Ed Sherin, producer

Andrew Prowse

"Casting's not a precise science. You think you know what you're looking for and you spread the casting net with some image in mind of what you want. You may even have a specific actor in mind, and then you see someone who blows you away and the fact that they're so interesting often makes you rethink the character. That's both one of the frustrations and joys about the process - it *often surprises you. Sometimes you see a bunch of actors for a role, and among them you find someone who's completely wrong for the part you're casting, but who has such presence that you start thinking about what kind of role you can tailor for them."*-Andrew Prowse, director

"Having been an actor you always saw the room as me against them, and it's really not. Having been on both sides of the camera. In the room all we want to do is find somebody who's going to be great in that role so we can move on and get to the next meeting, job, shot; whatever we're doing next."-Wil Shriner, director

"The hardest part of casting for a producer is finding somebody the producers and network can agree on."-Frederick Muller, producer

"On television the director is not the boss, like in movies. It's a lot of group discussions and decisions."-Charles Shyer, director

"It's less about who's the perfect person than who's perfect that we can get to."-Bobby Moresco, producer

"There are so many people that have to say yes, it's almost impossible to get anyone cast. There are so many ways and so many reasons for someone to say no. It's so easy to say no that it's almost impossible to get anybody in."-Jeff Bleckner, director

"Networks have a big influence on casting."-Al Schwartz, producer

"Casting is one of the key ingredients, more so with TV than movies."-Sherwood Schwartz, producer

"Any actress reading for a role that requires nudity has to disrobe in a casting

session. It's just the casting director and the director. You have to make sure you see the body. You do it in the most respectful way. You reduce the number of people in the room, and make sure you have a female in the room."-Ron Wolotzky, producer (on casting the HBO adult comedy *Dream On*)

"As an actor you deal with almost daily rejection. An actor that books one in thirty auditions would rightly consider that a good average."-Jud Tylor, actor

"There are about 400 actors who do all the work out of thousands of actors in SAG. 1-2%. The odds are so against it."-Conrad Janis, actor

"You should treat everyone you're casting as though they're a star."-David Black, producer

"It's hard when your child's rejected."-Suzanne Schachter, manager and mother of actresses Felice, Simone and Janine Schachter

"We just want the next person who walks through the door to be that part, just nail it, do something different, make some interesting choices."-Wil Shriner, director

"Straighten your hair, make it blonde and don't look so Jewish"-Judy Gold, actor (on what she has been told)

"Most people who are persistent and can survive hang in there."-Steve Spiker, casting director

"You don't know until you see it. In TV particularly it's a very intimate experience. It's a close-up of someone's face. If you like them you're in."-Leonard Goldberg, producer

"80% is already done by the time you walk in the door."-John Posey, actor

"You cannot take it personally. God knows what they're thinking."-Judy Gold, actor

"Henry Winkler and I are fraternity brothers. He very graciously asked me to be the line producer on the first year of MacGyver. We had had lunch, and at that time the Paramount commissary was across from a casting office. Henry and I came out of lunch and there was this young guy. He might have been around 18 or 19. He was waiting to go into the casting office, and he was very nervous. As an actor Henry saw it. Henry walked over to the kid and said, 'Hi, how are you doing?' Well, he almost crapped his pants. But then Henry started to talk to him and said, 'You're going in for an audition?' He said, 'Yeah, I'm really, really nervous.' And Henry said, 'You think you're nervous? You've got to realize those people in there haven't found the actor for your part yet. They're nervous they're not going to get him. So you've got one up on them. Just go in there and do your thing and be great, and you'll be fine.' This kid inhaled air and his chest popped out about two inches. It was a great story from one actor to another."-Vin DiBona, producer

"If it isn't me, then I hope it goes to my friend."-Jay Bontatibus, actor

"I always sympathized. I realized what a terrible job it is to audition most of the time."-Allen Baron, director

"I've lost roles to friends, acquaintances and girls I've worked with in the past. I've even lost a role to a friend, only to beat her out for another project later. The longer you're in this

Jud Tylor

industry the smaller it seems to get, and you definitely see the same faces over and over. If it's really a friend I'm losing a job to I'm happy for her."-Jud Tylor, actor

"I've become good friends with the women I see at auditions. You have a short-hand with each other; you know what each other's lives are like." -Kimberly Scott, actor

"It's very stressful. I've tried to find a way to enjoy it and the way is the camaraderie. We're all in this together. I've enjoyed that kind of camaraderie."-Bill Brochtrup, actor

"You're not competing with other actors; you're brothers in arms."-Leo Burmester, actor

"I hate the audition process. I've never understood it."-Thea Gill, actor

"The only thing I didn't like about readings is how uncomfortable it is for the actor."-Paul Bogart, director

"We found in many cases the actors are so good it's just a flip of the coin."-William Link, writer

"Writing is everything until you get to casting."-Matthew Diamond, director

"An audition is a horrible experience."-Michael York, actor

"Casting is about the most inhumane thing you can do to an actor."-Kim Weiskopf, writer

"I hate casting because I hate seeing people suffer."-David Black, producer

Bibliography

Much of the information in this book came from interviews with the following people:

A

Caroline Aaron
F. Murray Abraham
Pamela Adlon
Jane Alderman
Annette Andre
Candice Azzara

B

Jack Bannon
Allen Baron
Deborah Barylski
Fran Bascom
Robert Berlinger
Sharon Bialy
William Bickley

John Billingsley
Bruce Bilson
David Black
Rosa Blasi
Jeff Bleckner
Paul Bogart
Gregory J. Bonann
Frank Bonner
Jay Bontatibus
David Braff
Marshall Brickman
Bill Brochtrup
Corbin Bronson
Eric Bross
Ellen Bry
Sheldon Bull

Michael J. Burg
Leo Burmester
Allan Burns
Al Burton
Sarah Buxton

C

Andy Cadiff
K Callan
Carmine Caridi
Robert Carradine
Crystal Carson
Thomas Carter
Max Casella
Christopher Cass
Michael Cerveris
Casey Childs
Gary Collins
Richard Compton
James L. Conway
Ron Cowen
Missy Crider
Roark Critchlow
Emily Cutler

D

Joe d'Angerio
Joan Darling
Kristin Dattilo
Matt Dearborn

Rob Decina
Zora DeHorter-Majomi
Cristian de la Fuente
Doug Denoff
Sam Denoff
Howard Deutch
Matthew Diamond
Vin DiBona
Susan Diol
Micky Dolenz
Jim Drake
Keir Dullea
James Patrick Dunne

E

Leslie Easterbrook
Vanessa Evigan

F

Stephen Fanning
Mike Fenton
Fern Field
John Fleck
Vivica A. Fox
Jerold Franks
James Frawley
Holly Fulger

G

John Gabriel

David Garfield
Dick Gautier
George Gaynes
Thea Gill
Robert Ginty
Judy Gold
Lee Goldberg
Leonard Goldberg
Philip Goldfarb
David Graham
Gary Graham
Brian Lane Green
Bruce Seth Green
Jeff Greenberg

H

Charles Haid
Brian Haley
Jonathan Halyalkar
Susan Harris
Gina Hecht
Grainger Hines
Marc Hirschfeld
Celeste Holm
Tim Hunter

I

Salvatore Ianucci
Sam Irvin
Ivy Isenberg

J

David Jacobs
Ronald Jacobs
Conrad Janis
Kenneth Johnson
Gemma Jones
Robert Joy
Robert H. Justman

K

Steve Kanaly
Sean Kanan
Ellie Kanner
Marshall Karp
Barnet Kellman
Larry Kennar
T'Keyah Crystal Keymah
Bruce Kimmel
Sally Kirkland
Jack Klugman
Gary Kroeger
Paul Kurta

L

Dino Ladki
Christine Lakin
Karen Landry
Susan Lanier
Michael G. Larkin
Jack Larson

Linda Laundra
Christopher Leitch
John Levey
Jerry Levine
Michael Lindsay-Hogg
Jon Lindstrom
William Link
Daniel Lipman
David Lipper
Jerry London
Scott Lowell

M

Tom Mankiewicz
Jeffrey Marcus
Kelli Maroney
James Marshall
Ron Masak
John Masius
Dakin Matthews
Melanie Mayron
McG
Tom McLoughlin
Daniel McVicar
Eric Menyuk
Burt Metcalfe
Victoria Paige Meyerink
Larry Mintz
Bobby Moresco
Chris Mulkey
Frederick Muller

O

Wendy O'Brien
Lori Openden
Ion Overman

P

Peter Paige
Betsy Palmer
Frank Parker
Billy Parrott
John Pasquin
Michael Pavone
Thaao Penghlis
John Philbin
Herbie J. Pilato
Alisan Porter
John Posey
Stefanie Powers
Robert Prosky
Andrew Prowse
John Putch

R

Betsy Randle
Tracy Reiner
Gene Reynolds
John Rich
Fred Roos
Richard P. Rosetti
Joe Ruby

S

Jay Sandrich
Suzanne Schachter
Linda Schuyler
Al Schwartz
Sherwood Schwartz
Kimberly Scott
Pamela Shae
Alys Shanti
Cari Shayne
Les Sheldon
Ed Sherin
Wil Shriner
Marcia Shulman
Charles Shyer
James Sikking
Tucker Smallwood
Marilyn Sokol
Frank South
Ken Spears
Steve Spiker
Sandor Stern
Stella Stevens
George Sunga
Michael Swan

T

Tony Thomas
Berlinda Tolbert

Erin Torpey
Ellen Travolta
Jud Tylor

V

Barry Van Dyke
Kristen Vigard

W

Tonja Walker
Arthur Weingarten
Kim Weiskopf
Sam Weisman
Michael J. Weithorn
Llewellyn Wells
Paul Wensley
Dan Wilcox
Kathleen Wilhoite
JoBeth Williams
Art Wolff
Ron Wolotzky

Y

Michael York
Roger Young

Z

Bonnie Zane
Randy Zisk

Books

A

Alexander, David, *Star Trek Creator* (New York: ROC, 1994), 211-212.

Alley, Kirstie, *How to Lose Your Ass and Regain Your Life: Reluctant Confessions of a Big-Butted Star* (Rodale Books, 2005), 10.'

Alley, Robert S., Irby B. Brown, *Love Is All Around: The Making of the Mary Tyler Moore Show* (New York: Delta, 1989), 16-18.

Anderson, Loni with Larkin Warren, *My Life in High Heels* (New York: William Morrow and Company, Inc., 1995), 100.

Asherman, Allan, *The Star Trek Interview Book* (New York: Pocket Books, 1988), 8, 9, 43, 98, 147.

B

Bianculli, David, *Teleliteracy* (New York: Touchstone, 1992), 82.

Birtwistle, Sue and Susie Conklin, *The Making of Pride and Prejudice* (London: Penguin Books, 1995), 17-19.

C

Condon, Jack and David Hofstede, *Charlie's Angels Casebook* (Beverly Hills: Pomegranate Press Ltd., 2000), 145.

Corkery, Paul, *Carson: The Unauthorized Biography* (New York: Randt & Company, 1987), 76.

Courrier, Kevin, Susan Green, *Law & Order: The Unofficial Companion* (Los Angeles: Renaissance Books, 1998), 25, 26, 122.

Cox, Stephen, *The Beverly Hillbillies* (Chicago: Contemporary Books, 1988), 79.

Cox, Stephen, *The Hooterville Handbook: A Viewer's Guide to Green Acres* (New York: St. Martin's Press, 1993), 6.

Cox, Steve with Howard Frank, *Dreaming of Jeannie: TV's Prime Time in a Bottle* (New York: St. Martin's Griffin, 2000), 211.

D

Desperate Housewives (New York: Hyperion, 2005), 20, 36, 110.

Dolenz, Micky and Mark Bego, *I'm a Believer* (New York: Hyperion, 1993), 64.

E

Eisner, Joel, *The Official Batman Batbook* (Chicago: Contemporary Books, Inc., 1986), 8.

Ellis, Kathryn, *Degrassi Generations* (New York: Pocket Books, 2005), 78, 84.

Erdmann, Terry J. and Paula M. Block, *Monk: The Official Episode Guide* (New York: St. Martin's Griffin, 2006), 5, 8.

Etheridge, Melissa, *The Truth Is . . . : My Life in Love and Music* (New York: Random House, 2001, 2001), 73.

G

Gitlin, Todd, *Inside Prime Time* (New York: Pantheon Books, 1983), 100-102.

Graham, David, *Casting About* (Lincoln: iUniverse.com, Inc., 2001), 251.

Graham, Jefferson, *Frasier* (New York: Pocket Books, 1996), 108.

Gross, Edward and Mark A. Altman, *Captains' Logs* (Little, Brown & Co, 1995), 11, 151, 234, 336, 345, 350.

H

Heitland, Jon, *The Man from U.N.C.L.E. Book* (New York: St. Martin's Press, 1987), 21, 24.

Hirshenson, Janet and Jane Jenkins with Rachel Kranz, *A Star Is Found* (Orlando: Harcourt, Inc., 2006), 227.

J

Johnson, Russell with Steve Cox, *Here On Gilligan's Isle* (New York: HarperPerennial, 1993), 26.

K

Kendt, Rob, *How They Cast It: An Insider's Look at Film and Television Casting* (Los Angeles: Lone Eagle Publishing Company, 2005), 14-19, 108, 135.

L

Lance, Steven, *Written Out of Television: A TV Lover's Guide to Cast Changes 1945-1994* (Lanham: Madison Books, 1996), 49-50, 152-155, 170-171, 300, 368, 448, 451, 455.

Lovece, Frank with Jules Franco, Hailing *Taxi: The Official Book of the Show* (New York: Prentice Hall Press, 1988), 7. 63.

M

Manetti, Larry with Chip Silverman, *Aloha Magnum: Larry Manetti's Magnum, P.I. Memories* (Los Angeles: Renaissance Books, 1999), 216.

Mann, Chris, *Come and Knock On Our Door: A Hers and Hers and His Guide to Three's Company* (New York: St. Martin's Griffin, 1998, 7-10, 14-19, 192.

Marshall, Garry with Lori Marshall, *Wake Me When It's Funny* (Holbrook: Adams Publishing, 1995), 153-155.

N

Nemecek, Larry, *The Star Trek The Next Generation Companion* (New York: Pocket Books, 1992, 1995), 125-126.

O

O'Flaherty, Terrence, *Masterpiece Theatre* (San Francisco: KQED Books, 1996), 57, 58, 208.

Orman, Roscoe, *Sesame Street Dad* (Portland: Inkwater Press, 2006), 86-87.

P

Phillips, Mark and Frank Garcia, *Science Fiction Television Series* (Jefferson: McFarland & Company, Inc, 1996), 362, 445, 489.

Poll, Julie, *As the World Turns: The Complete Family Scrapbook* (Los Angeles: General Publishing Group, 1996), 269.

R

Rich, John, *Warm Up the Snake* (Ann Arbor: The University of Michigan Press, 2006), 118-120, 148.

Roberts, Doris with Danelle Morton, *Are You Hungry, Dear?: Life, Laughs, and Lasagna* (New York: St. Martin's Press, 2003), 104, 106

Russo, Joe, Larry Landsman Edward Gross, *Charlton Heston, Planet of the Apes Revisited* (New York: Thomas Dunne Books, 2001), 243.

S

Sackett, Susan, *Prime Time Hits* (New York: Billboard Books, 1993), 281.

Sandoval, Andrew, *The Monkees* (San Diego: Thunder Bay Press, 2005), 23, 26.

Shales, Tom, James Andrew Miller, Live From New York: An Uncensored History of Saturday Night Live (Boston, New York, London: Little, Brown and Company, 2002), 199-200, 261-262, 366.

Shepherd, Cybill with Aimee Lee Ball, Cybill Disobedience (New York: HarperCollinsPublishers, 2000), 190, 212-213, 245.

Spelling, Aaron with Jefferson Graham, Aaron Spelling: A Prime-Time Life (New York: St. Martin's Press, 1996), 123.

T

Tartikoff, Brandon and Charles Leerhsen, The Last Great Ride (New York: Turtle Bay Books, 1992), 83-84, 85-86.

W

Waldron, Vince, Classic Sitcoms (Los Angeles: Silman-James Press, 1987, 1997), 183-184.

Warner, Gary, All My Children: The Complete Family Scrapbook (Los Angeles: General Publishing Group, 1994), 230.

Warner, Gary, General Hospital: The Complete Scrapbook (Los Angeles: General Publishing Group, 1995), 276, 277.

Weisbrot, Robert, Xena Warrior Princess: The Official Guide to the Xenaverse (New York: Doubleday, 1998), 7-8, 10.

West, Adam with Jeff Rovin, Back to the Batcave (New York: Berkley Books, 1994), 133, 176.

Wild, David, The Showrunners (New York: HarperCollinsPublishers, 1999), 98.

Z

Zenka, Lorraine, Days of Our Lives: The Complete Family Album (New York: ReganBooks, 1995), 220, 240.

Zicree, Marc Scott, The Twilight Zone Companion (New York: Bantam Books, 1982, 1989), 24-25.

Newspapers

New York Daily News (New York), 19 December 1997.
19 March 1999.
7 May 1999.
2 July 1999.
11 January 2000.
10 February 2000.
20 August 2001.
26 September 2001.
15 January 2004.

Periodicals

"Audition Scenes" *Soap Opera Digest*, 13 May 1997, 101, 102, 104, 105. 106. "Roundup" *Soap Opera Digest*, 4 September 1990, 18, 19, 20.

Bednarz, Stella, "Days's Hot New Storylines" *Soap Opera Digest*, 16 April 1991, 9.

Caploe, Roberta, "True Love" *Soap Opera Digest*, 31 March 1992, 9.

Caploe, Roberta, "Was Wheeler Wheedled Out of Role?" *Soap Opera Digest*, 15 October 1991, 62.

Carter, Alan, "Julia Roberts, Soap Washout" *Entertainment Weekly*, 30 July 1993, 48.

DeCaro, Frank, "The Mob Squad" *TV Guide*, 8 January 2000, 24.

Flaherty, Mike, "Case Closed" *Entertainment Weekly*, 17 May 2002, 38.

Fretts, Bruce, "Everything's Relative" *Entertainment Weekly*, 28 November 1997, 47.

Fretts, Bruce, "The Tony Rewards" *Entertainment Weekly*, 6 December 2002, 82.

Henderson, Kathy, "Rocking the Cradle" *Soap Opera Digest*, 23 June 1992, 126.

Hoke Kahwaty, Donna, "Movie Maniac" *Soap Opera Digest*, 16 April 1991, 125.

Hollywood Kids, "Q&A: Mary Wilson" *Movieline*, June 1997, 34.

Howard, Ellen, "Whatever Happened To…Lynn Benesch" *Soap Opera Digest*, 12 February 1985, 107.

Jacobs, A.J., "'Profit' Motives" *Entertainment Weekly*, 12 April 1996, 54.

Jensen, Jeff, "Life As We Knew It" *Entertainment Weekly*, 10 September 2004, 129.

Johnson, Ted, "Western Reserve" *TV Guide*, 8 January 2000, 32.

Kelley, Adam, "Mauceri On Top" *Soap Opera Digest*, 13 May 1997, 58-59.

Kirschling, Gregory, "A Season of Hope" *Entertainment Weekly*, 23 December 2005, 47.

Logan, Michael, "From Harlem to Hollywood" *Soap Opera Digest*, 11 July 1989, 107-108.

Logan, Michael, "The Greatest Story, Retold" *TV Guide*, 6 May 2000, 20.

Logan, Michael, "Poster Boy" *TV Guide*, 4 May 2002, 80.

Logan, Michael, "She Gave In to Temptations" *TV Guide*, 3 October 1998, 36.

Malcom, Shawna, "Casting Off" *TV Guide*, 10 May 2003, 41.

Rebello, Stephen, "Girl We Love" *Movieline*, April 1998, 94.

Robins, J. Max, "The Robins Report: A Happy Ending for a Musical Tale" *TV Guide*, 18 October 1997, 53-54.

Schneider, Wolf, "Strong Stuff" *Movieline*, August 1997, 63.

Schwartz, Missy, "Who's Afraid of Anna Faris?" *Entertainment Weekly*, 31 October 2003, 43.

Schwed, Mark, "Hollywood Grapevine" *TV Guide*, 19 August 2000, 8.

Schwed, Mark, "The Shining: It Lives Again" *TV Guide*, 26 April 1997, 20-21.

Shaw, Jessica, "Paper Mate" *Entertainment Weekly*, 20 October 2006, 42.

Snierson, Dan, "The Last of the Red Hot Mamas" *Entertainment Weekly*,

13 June 2003, 35.

Vered, Annabel, "Behind the Lines On 'The Simpsons'" *TV Guide*, 3-9 January 1998, 21.

Williams, Stephanie, "Young, Sexy… and Spoken For" *TV Guide*, 14 February 1998, 28.

Index

Printed in the United States
115302LV00003B/8/P